Themes in Modern European History, 1890–1945

Themes in Modern European History, 1890–1945 brings together an international team of scholars to address an eclectic range of developments and issues in European history in the period between 1890 and the end of World War Two. This lively collection of essays adopts a thematic approach in order to explore comprehensively a period of great change and upheaval in Europe.

Concentrating on the main powers in Europe, from Germany, Italy and Russia to the UK and France, the book links developments in society, the economy, politics and culture, and establishes them in their political framework. Commissioned chapters discuss key issues including:

- popular culture
- the relationship between East and West
- intellectual and cultural trends
- the origins and impact of two world wars
- communism, dictatorship and liberal democracy
- the relationship of Europe with the wider world.

Including a chronology and maps, as well as suggestions for further reading, this comprehensive volume is an invaluable and authoritative resource for students of modern European history.

Nicholas Atkin is Professor of Modern European history at the University of Reading. He has published extensively on twentieth-century France and has recently edited *The Daily Lives of Civilians in Wartime Twentieth-Century Europe*. He is currently writing a history of British tourism to France since the 1850s.

Michael Biddiss is Emeritus Professor of History at the University of Reading, and General Editor of the Routledge 'Themes' series. His previous publications include *Disease and History* (co-author, 2000) and *The Humanities in the New Millennium* (co-editor, 2000).

Themes in Modern European History

General editor: Michael Biddiss, University of Reading

Already published

Themes in Modern European History, 1890–1945

Edited by
Nicholas Atkin and Michael Biddiss

Routledge
Taylor & Francis Group

LONDON AND NEW YORK

First published 2009
by Routledge
2 Park Square, Milton Park, Abingdon, Oxon OX14 4RN

Simultaneously published in the USA and Canada
by Routledge
270 Madison Ave, New York, NY 10016

Routledge is an imprint of the Taylor & Francis Group, an informa business

Typeset in Times New Roman by Taylor & Francis Books
Printed and bound in Great Britain by CPI Antony Rowe,
Chippenham, Wiltshire.

British Library Cataloguing in Publication Data
A catalogue record for this book is available from the British Library

Library of Congress Cataloging-in-Publication Data
Themes in modern European history, 1890-1945 / edited by Nicholas Atkin and
Michael Biddiss.
     p. cm. – (Themes in modern European history)
   1. Europe–History–1871-1918. 2. Europe–History–1918-1945. I. Atkin,
Nicholas. II. Biddiss, Michael Denis.
   D395.T54 2008
   940.5–dc22
                          2008023452

ISBN10: 0-415-39145-8 (hbk)
ISBN10: 0-415-39184-9 (pbk)
ISBN10: 0-203-88689-5 (ebk)

ISBN13: 978-0-415-39145-0 (hbk)
ISBN13: 978-0-415-39184-9 (pbk)
ISBN13: 978-0-203-88689-2 (ebk)

Contents

List of contributors

Nicholas Atkin is Professor of Modern European History at the University of Reading. He has published *Church and Schools in Vichy France, 1940–1944* (1991), *Pétain* (1997), *The French at War, 1934–1944* (2001), *The Forgotten French. Exiles in the British Isles, 1940–1944* (2003) and the *Fifth French Republic* (2005). With Frank Tallett, he wrote *Priests, Prelates and People. A History of European Catholicism since 1750* (2003). Together they edited *Religion, Society and Politics in France since 1789* (1991), *Catholicism in Britain and France since 1789* (1996) and *The Right in France from Revolution to Le Pen* (2003, 2nd edn). He has recently edited *The Daily Lives of Civilians in Wartime. Europe's Twentieth-Century Experience* (2008), and is currently writing a history of British tourism to France since the 1850s.

Michael Biddiss is Emeritus Professor of History at the University of Reading, and General Editor of the Routledge 'Themes' series. He previously taught at Cambridge University (as a Fellow of Downing College) and the University of Leicester (as Reader in History), and has also held visiting professorships in Canada, South Africa, Australia and China. He was President of the Historical Association from 1991 to 1994, and is also a former Vice-President of the Royal Historical Society. He is the author of numerous articles on modern European political thought, historiography, and intellectual developments in general. Books include *Father of Racist Ideology* (1970); *Gobineau: Selected Political Writings* (editor, 1970); *The Age of the Masses: Ideas and Society in Europe since 1870* (1977); *Images of Race* (editor, 1979); *Thatcherism* (co-editor, 1987); *The Nuremberg Trial and the Third Reich* (1992); *The Uses and Abuses of Antiquity* (co-editor, 1999); *Disease and History* (co-author, 2000); and *The Humanities in the New Millennium* (co-editor, 2000).

António Costa Pinto is Professor of Modern European History and Politics at the University of Lisbon's Institute of Social Science. He holds a PhD from the European University Institute, Florence (1992). He has been a Visiting Professor at Stanford University (1993) and Georgetown (2004), and was a Senior Visiting Fellow at Princeton University (1996) and at the University of California, Berkeley (2000). From 1999 to 2003, he has been a Visiting Professor at the Institut d'Études Politiques, Paris. His research interests include fascism and authoritarianism, democratization, the European Union and the comparative study of political change in Southern Europe. He is the author of *The Blue Shirts: Portuguese Fascism in Inter-war Europe* (2000), and co-edited *Southern Europe and the Making of the European Union* (2002), *Who Governs Southern Europe? Regime Change and Ministerial Recruitment* (2003), and *Charisma and Fascism in Interwar Europe* (2007).

Detmar Klein is Lecturer in Modern European History at University College Cork, Ireland. Publications include: contributions to Gregory Claeys (editor), *Encyclopedia of Nineteenth-Century Thought* (Routledge, 2005); 'The Virgin with the Sword: Marian Apparitions, Religion and National Identity in Alsace in the 1870s', *French History*, 21 (2007), 411–30; 'Becoming Alsatian: Anti-German and Pro-French Cultural Propaganda in Alsace, 1898–1914', in Barbara Kelly (ed.), *French Music, Culture and National Identity, 1870–1939* (2008), 215–33. Currently he is preparing a monograph on the relationship between Imperial Germany and German-annexed Alsace, exploring processes of nation-building and the formation of collective identities.

Giacomo Lichtner is Lecturer in History and Film at Victoria University of Wellington, New Zealand. His research interests focus broadly on the cultural history of modern Europe, especially France and Italy. He has contributed to several international symposia and edited collections on the subject of Holocaust representation, and is the author of *Film and the Shoah in France and Italy* (2008). His current interests are exploring film and postcolonial identity in India, Australia and New Zealand.

Gordon Martel is Professor of History at the University of Northern British Columbia. He has been a visiting professor/research fellow at St Antony's College, Oxford, the University of Ulster, the University of Western Australia and Nuffield College, Oxford. He was a founding editor of *The International History Review* and is the author of *Imperial Diplomacy* (1986), *The Origins of the First World War* (2003, 3rd edn), and, with James Joll, *The Origins of the First World War* (2006, 3rd edn). Among his edited works are: *A Companion to International History, 1900–2001* (2007) and *A Companion to Europe, 1900–1945* (2006); *The World War Two Reader* (2004); *The Times and Appeasement: The Journals of A. L. Kennedy* (2000); *The Origins of the Second World War Reconsidered: A.J.P. Taylor and the Historians* (1999, 2nd edn) and *Modern Germany Reconsidered* (1992). He is Editor-in-Chief of the five-volume *Encyclopaedia of War* to be published by Blackwell in 2011, and is engaged in the writing of *After Armageddon: The Impact of the First World War.*

Steve Morewood is Senior Lecturer in international history at the University of Birmingham. He is the author of *The British Defence of Egypt 1935–1940* (2005) and numerous chapters and articles centred on British diplomatic and military involvement in the eastern Mediterranean from 1919 to 1941. With G. Bruce Strang he is co-editing a volume on the international dimensions of the Abyssinian Crisis, and is researching a book on Britain and the Abyssinian Crisis, 1934–36.

Pamela Pilbeam is Emeritus Professor of French History, Royal Holloway, University of London, and a Leverhulme Emeritus Fellow 2007–09. She has published extensively on nineteenth-century European history. Her recent books include *Madame Tussaud and the History of Waxwork* (2006, 2nd edn) and *French Socialists before Marx. Workers, Women and the Social Question in France* (2000). Her other books include *The Constitutional Monarchy in France, 1814–48* (1999); *Republicanism in Nineteenth-Century France* (1995); *The 1830 Revolution in France* (1991); and *The Middle Classes in Europe, 1789–1914* (1990). She has edited *Themes in Modern European History, 1780–1830* (1995) and is currently writing *From Free Love to Algeria. The Saint-Simonians in Nineteenth-Century France.*

Frank Tallett is senior lecturer in History at the University of Reading. Alongside the many things he has edited with Nicholas Atkin, he is the author of *War and Society in Early Modern Europe, 1485–1715* (1997, 2nd edn). He has additionally written several articles on military and religious history. With David Trim, he has recently edited *European Warfare, 1350–1750.*

Matthew Worley is Reader in History at the University of Reading. He has written widely on British political and international communist history. His books include *Class Against Class: A History of the Communist Party of Great Britain between the Wars* (2002); *In Search of Revolution: International Communist Parties in the Third Period* (editor) (2004); and *Labour Inside the Gate: A History of the British Labour Party between the Wars* (2005). He has recently co-edited, with Kevin Morgan and Norry Laporte, a collection of essays on Stalinization, and is currently researching the New Party formed by Sir Oswald Mosley in 1931.

List of Abbreviations

AEG	Allgemeine Elektrizitäts-Gesellschaft
BDM	Bund Deutscher Mädel
CCP	Chinese Communist Party
CGT	Confédération Générale du Travail
CGTU	Confédération Générale du Travail Unitaire
CGPF	Confédération Générale de la Production Française
Cheka	All-Russian Extraordinary Commission for Combating Counter-Revolution and Sabotage
CPGB	Communist Party of Great Britain
DAF	Deutsche Arbeitsfront
DAP	Deutsche Arbeiterpartei
DNSAP	Danmarks Nationalsocialistiske Arbejderparti
DORA	Defence of the Realm Act
FET	Falange Española Tradicionalista
FNC	Fédération Nationale Catholique
HG	Hlinkova Garda
HJ	Hitler Jugend
HSLS-SSNJ	Hlinkova Slovenská L'Udová Strana-Strana Slovenskej Národnej Jednoty
ILP	Independent Labour Party
KPD	Kommunistische Partei Deutschlands
LP	Legião Portuguesa
MNS	Movimento Nacional Sindicalista
MP	Mocidade Portuguesa
NEP	New Economic Policy
NKVD	People's Commissariat of Internal Affairs
NS	Nasjonal Samling
NSB	Nationaal-Socialistische Beweging
NSDAP	Nationalsozialistische Deutsche Arbeiterpartei

NUWCM	National Unemployed Workers' Committee Movement
OND	Opera Nazionale Dopolavoro
ONR	Obóz Narodowo Radykalny
PCF	Parti Communiste Français
PNF	Partito Nazionale Fascista
PPF	Parti Populaire Français
PSF	Parti Social Français
PSI	Partito Socialista Italiano
PVDE	Polícia de Vigilâcia e de Defesa do Estado
RAF	Royal Air Force
RCP	Russian Communist Party
RSDLP	Russian Social Democratic Labour Party
SA	Sturm abteilung
SFIO	Section Française de l'Internationale Ouvrière
SLS	Slovenská L'Udová Strana
SPD	Social Democratic Party
SRs	Socialist Revolutionaries
SS	Schutzstaffel
SSAU	Sailors' Soldiers' and Airmen's Union
TUC	Trades Union Congress
UN	União Nacional
VNV	Vlaams Nationaal Verbond
VF	Vaterländische Front

Acknowledgements

The present collection of essays supersedes one that Routledge published under the same title in 1992, three years before the death of its editor, Paul Hayes. Having ourselves been contributors to that book, we are sad not to have had the opportunity to work with him again. Even while bringing together this entirely new set of essays, and doing so with the benefit of nearly twenty years of further scholarship on the 1890–1945 period, we have remained much indebted to the wisdom and enthusiasm that Paul himself brought to the preparation of that earlier venture. Our thanks also extend to all the contributors to the present volume and to the production team at Routledge. We would like to dedicate our co-editorial work on the overall preparation of this book to Charlotte and Benjamin Atkin; Cameron and Alasdair Leask; Tom and Henry Hollinrake; and Lara Coleman.

Nicholas Atkin and Michael Biddiss
June 2008

Map 1 Europe in 1890

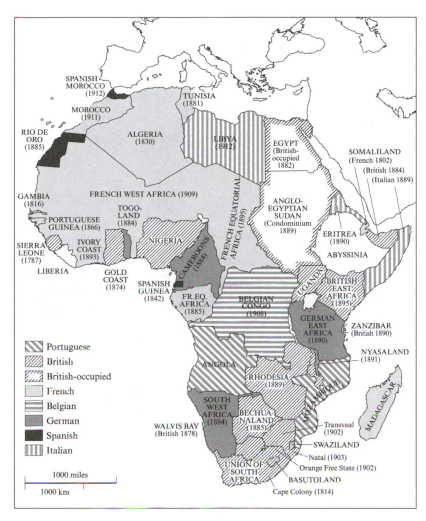

Map 2 European expansion into Africa by 1914

Legend:
- Portuguese
- British
- British-occupied
- French
- Belgian
- German
- Spanish
- Italian

1000 miles

1000 km

Map labels:

SPANISH MOROCCO (1912)

MOROCCO (1911)

RIO DE ORO (1885)

TUNISIA (1881)

ALGERIA (1830)

LIBYA (1912)

EGYPT (British-occupied 1882)

SOMALILAND (French 1802) (British 1884) (Italian 1889)

GAMBIA (1816)

FRENCH WEST AFRICA (1909)

TOGO-LAND (1884)

PORTUGUESE GUINEA (1866)

SIERRA LEONE (1787)

IVORY COAST (1893)

NIGERIA

CAMEROONS (1884)

FRENCH EQUATORIAL AFRICA (1895)

ANGLO-EGYPTIAN SUDAN (Condominium 1889)

ERITREA (1890)

ABYSSINIA

LIBERIA

GOLD COAST (1874)

SPANISH GUINEA (1842)

FR. EQ. AFRICA (1885)

BELGIAN CONGO (1908)

UGANDA

BRITISH EAST AFRICA (1895)

GERMAN EAST AFRICA (1890)

ZANZIBAR (British 1890)

NYASALAND (1891)

ANGOLA

RHODESIA (1889)

MOZAMBIQUE

MADAGASCAR

SOUTH WEST AFRICA (1884)

WALVIS BAY (British 1878)

BECHUA-NALAND (1885)

Transvaal (1902)

SWAZILAND

Natal (1903)

UNION OF SOUTH AFRICA

Orange Free State (1902)

BASUTOLAND

Cape Colony (1814)

Map 3 Europe after World War I

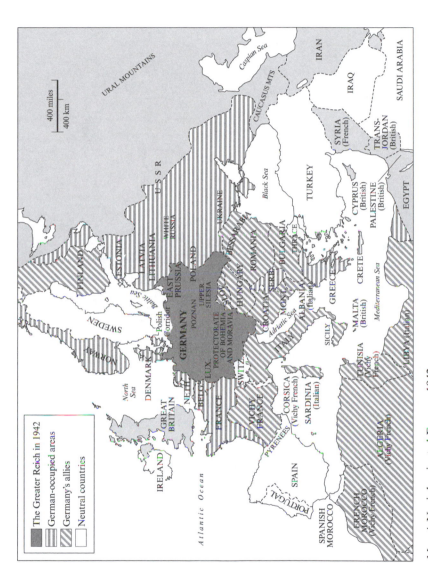

Map 4 Nazi-dominated Europe, 1942

Map 5 Europe and the Cold War

Introduction

Nicholas Atkin

In 1890, Europe enjoyed an influence, self-confidence and affluence unparalleled in its history. In its political institutions, in its forms of economic organization, in its culture and in its technological progress, Europe appeared to have put behind it the upheavals of the eighteenth and nineteenth centuries, which had resulted in war, revolution and ideological conflict – forces that had come together in spectacularly destructive fashion during the French Revolution. By 1890 the leading European powers had also managed to establish a hegemony over much of the rest of the world through the enlargement of empire, the extension of military influence and the creation of new markets. Small wonder that many Europeans began to regard their civilization as blessed and destined for a great future. In the words of Gordon Martel, the world had become 'European', and the continent's inhabitants had every expectation that the ensuing century would be theirs.[1] Admittedly, there were dissenting voices. Notable was the Swiss historian and philosopher Jacob Burckhardt, who was deeply sceptical about notions of historical progress and who presciently feared that the twentieth century would belong to demagogues.[2] It should additionally be remembered that a majority of Europe's citizens, especially those in central and eastern states, were governed by autocratic or semi-autocratic governments, and did not share in the material wealth conspicuously enjoyed by the bourgeoisie of northern countries. As Richard Vinen observes, 'it is easy to forget that the mass of Europe's population spent the summer of 1914 in back-breaking labour, preparing to get the harvest in.'[3] Yet this does not detract from the general point: in 1890, Europe was at the peak of its powers and the height of its self-belief.

In 1945, the picture was very different. The photographs and films taken at the end of World War Two reveal a ravaged continent of broken buildings, bomb craters, human corpses, dead animals, food queues, orphaned children, displaced persons and concentration camp victims.

Evoking and reflecting on such images, Tony Judt writes, 'everyone and everything – with the notable exception of the well-fed Allied occupation forces – seems worn out, without resources, exhausted.'[4] Shortly after liberation from Nazism, Europe suffered further indignity as it was overcome by a Cold War in which the two superpowers, the USA and USSR, asserted their primacy. It is frequently said that the erection of the Berlin Wall in 1961 was a physical and painful reminder of how far Europe's influence had declined since the late nineteenth century.[5] Its construction seemed to bear out Churchill's gloomy prediction in 1946 that the peoples of Europe would forever scan 'the dark horizons for the approach of some new peril, tyranny or terror'.[6]

In view of this fundamental shift, it is compelling to ask what went wrong. How did the affluent, self-assured Europe of 1890 become the physical wreck of 1945? A large part of the answer is to be found in the experience of war. In his memoirs and political writing, the British intellectual and early Labour Party supporter Leonard Woolf found a direct link between the Marne and Mauthausen.[7] That war was fundamental in shaping Europe's fortunes is unquestionable, yet it is naïve to believe that before 1914 Europeans had discovered the path to progress and that somewhere along the way they took a wrong turn, resulting in calamity. The journey was far more complicated, and it must be remembered that alongside change there is always continuity and the intervention of the unexpected. As Tim Blanning writes, 'A history which presents only changes is a history which tells only half the story: for every value or institution which is modified or disappears altogether there is another which remains the same.'[8] With that caveat firmly in mind, this volume seeks to identify the key themes of the period. Focusing on the main powers in Europe, from Germany, Italy and Russia, to the UK and France, the book links together social, economic, and cultural developments, and establishes them in a wider political framework.

One obvious theme can be readily identified – that is Europe's changing geopolitical shape, a point established by Paul Hayes in an earlier collection that he edited under this same title.[9] As Eric Hobsbawm observes, during the early modern period Europe's frontiers were constantly moving, yet in their basic contours they were not so dissimilar to what they had been in the Middle Ages. He suggests that, although some states were beginning to take on their modern 'characteristics', much of the continent still featured a peculiar mix of territories whose form had been conditioned by convention and historical accident, the most glaring example being the Holy Roman Empire.[10] In the course of the French revolutionary and Napoleonic wars, all this was to change. Frontiers were redrawn several times over and were redesigned once again at the Congress of Vienna in 1814–15. Boundary changes continued throughout the nineteenth century, whether because of revolution, ideology, war, great power ambition, or even happenstance. Those alterations carried on into the period 1890–1945. As before, war was chiefly responsible; but more evolutionary processes were sometimes at work, as in 1905 when the Swedish government finally conceded independence to the Norwegians, acting on its understanding that their claims to independence could not be resisted forever. Regrettably, such a grasp of reality was delayed longer in the case of the UK's handling of nationalism in Ireland, where partition and the formation of the so-called 'Free State' were held back until 1921.

The most dramatic overhaul of boundaries had come two years earlier when the peacemakers had the difficult task of redrawing the map of Europe in the aftermath of World War One.[11] In the course of that conflict, the four empires of Germany, Austria-Hungary, Russia and Turkey fell apart, though the latter had been in the process of disintegration for some time. At the peace conferences of 1919–20, there emerged a collection of smaller, frail and often competing polities. As Frank Tallett observes in Chapter 5, 'these included Poland (back on the map for the first time since 1795), Lithuania, Latvia, Estonia, Finland, Czechoslovakia and Yugoslavia (initially as the Kingdom of the Serbs, Croats and Slovenes) together with a truncated Austria, a fully independent Hungary, and an enlarged Romania.' The shift was thus away from multinational empires towards the formation of nation-states. Even though fewer Europeans would now be living under foreign rule, most of these new constructs were still not ethnically homogeneous. Peacemaking in 1919–20 was a muddled and messy affair, conducted in a pressurized environment in which national self-determination was only one of several variables that informed the wider business. The result was that many ethnic groups continued to live under foreign governments. It is a familiar list: Albanians and Macedonians in Yugoslavia; Ruthenes and Poles in Czechoslovakia; Macedonians in Greece; Hungarians in Austria and Czechoslovakia; Germans in Denmark, Belgium, France, Hungary, Romania, Czechoslovakia, Poland and the Baltic states; and Jews more or less everywhere, though notably in Poland and the USSR. Nor had the days of multinational empires come to a close, even if one such regime was now being overseen by the Bolsheviks rather than the Romanovs, while another would soon be the product of Nazi rather than earlier Hohenzollern ambitions. Russia begrudgingly gave up territory in 1918, but was quick to reclaim this in 1939–41, taking advantage of the Nazi–Soviet Pact to seize the

Baltic states of Lithuania, Latvia, Estonia and parts of Finland, together with the former Romanian territories of Bessarabia and northern Bukovina. Russian victory in 1945 was another opportunity for territorial aggrandisement, as it would have been in 1918 had the Bolsheviks been on the winning side. As to Germany, in the course of World War Two Hitler established a greater Reich, a development described as 'power without plan or purpose'.[12] At the hub of this ever-shifting entity, writes Henri Michel, lay Germany as designated by the 1919 settlement, to which were attached Austria, the Sudetenland, Memelland, Alsace-Lorraine, Luxembourg, Eupen and Malmédy, Poznan, Silesia, the Polish corridor and Danzig so as to form the so-called *Grossraum* (Greater Germanic Estate).[13] Had Hitler not been stopped, the map of Europe would have been a strange and disorienting place in which whole countries, such as France, would have disappeared altogether. Instead, the victorious Allies of Britain, the USA and the USSR agreed in 1944–45 that the continent would be rebuilt in such a way that the Americans dominated the west and the Russians the east, a principle that was more or less accepted save for the disputes over Berlin in 1948–49.[14]

Beyond Europe, the global map was also in a state of flux. This was largely due to the 'new imperialism' that (after the French established an important foothold in Algeria in 1830) got under way in the 1860s, and is described thus to distinguish it from the early modern imperialism practised chiefly by the Dutch, Portuguese, Spanish and British. The geographical foci of this fresh phase of expansion were Africa and the Far East. By 1914, the African continent represented a crazy mosaic in which the British, French, Germans, Italians, Portuguese, Belgians and Dutch had established a series of zones of influence. It was, however, Britain that had acquired the 'lion's share', taking control over Egypt, so-called Anglo–Egyptian Sudan, British Somaliland, British East Africa, Uganda, Northern Rhodesia, Southern Rhodesia, Bechuanaland, Nigeria, Gold Coast, Sierra Leone and Gambia, and remaining hugely influential in what was known after 1910 as the Union of South Africa.[15] In the Far East, it was the French who pressed into Indo-China, while the Russians were seeking to control Manchuria, provoking tensions with the Japanese who had their eyes on Korea. More generally still, even where the European powers did not formally establish colonies, they created patterns of imperial influence, 'informal empire', usually comprising commercial links, such as those which Britain extended into Latin America.[16]

Paradoxically, it was not until the European powers were well advanced in this quest for territory that the first explanations of empire began to appear. In 1902, the British liberal thinker and journalist J. A. Hobson published his groundbreaking study on imperialism, which influenced Lenin among others, and which identified economic factors as the key drivers. In the enormous historiography that has subsequently grown up around the origins of empire, historians have reflected on several other factors, and have seen the chief impetus coming either from within Europe itself, so-called 'metropolitan' explanations, or from without, 'peripheral' explanations which are located in Africa and the Far East.[17] If there is any agreement, it is that no single causal factor can explain empire: in practice, it was often acquired in a random fashion by explorers, pirates, traders, adventurers, settlers, missionaries and others. An unexpected result was that its acquisition frequently became an end in itself, although the European powers were fully aware of the international prestige that it conferred upon them. Governments might also have been conscious of the ways in which empire played to the public at home, a means of consolidating existing social and economic hierarchies, and thus resisting forces of modernization.[18] Niall Ferguson has recently urged the provocative argument that empire, or rather that belonging to Britain, was beneficial for the wider world by establishing the foundations of liberal capitalism and by providing an institutional template for developing nations to follow, although he is quick to acknowledge that British rule was not without its sins.[19] Whatever the case, Europe's contact with the wider world had a profound impact on cultural life, and advanced an understanding of anthropology, languages, religions and science.

The relationship between Europe and its possessions was complicated by challenges from various forces. Among these was the USA, a country that had thrown off colonial rule and had become peopled largely with migrants of European stock: by the 1890s it was an emerging world power that now wanted its own share of imperial influence, whatever its rhetoric might otherwise have suggested. Japan was another rising power, modernizing its economic and governmental structures, confident of its own cultural superiority, and itching to challenge western hegemony. Increasingly, too, European authority would be challenged by the nationalism developing among the colonized peoples of Africa and Asia. In 1919, however, the victorious European powers were in no hurry to relinquish control. They appropriated Germany's former possessions, and partitioned those that had once belonged to Turkey in the Middle East and Asia Minor. Even so, by 1932 Britain had effectively yielded independence to Iraq. Through the 1931 Statute of Westminster, the UK had also granted full legislative sovereignty to its self-governing Dominions, as due reward for the contribution they had made towards what had essentially been a European war. The impact of World War Two was not so dissimilar to that of World War One in that, during the conflict itself, the European powers again vied for additional territory. Yet in the aftermath of 1945 there would be no going back on decolonization. This proved an extremely uneven and eventful journey, undertaken begrudgingly by Europeans. Crucially, however, their invincibility, already in question in the interwar years, had been broken, giving heart to the many nationalist movements that now successfully broadened their appeal to take in the support of the masses, and not just of largely western-educated elites.

In this education, many nationalist leaders were influenced more by Marxism than liberal democracy, although the progress of the latter ideology had earlier seemed unstoppable. As Detmar Klein writes in Chapter 1, by 1914 western Europe was viewed as 'the cradle of economic progress and of liberal political ideologies, as epitomized by the parliamentary monarchies of Britain, the Netherlands, Belgium, Denmark, Sweden and Norway (since 1905, no longer in personal union with Sweden), and by the parliamentary republics of France and Switzerland.' True, none of these states had yet embraced universal suffrage: except in Norway (from 1913) and Sweden (from 1862 for local elections), women remained entirely unenfranchised, while male voting rights were completely unrestricted only in Switzerland, France, Denmark and Norway. It is none-the-less significant that, within the countries cited by Klein, the executive had become answerable to a representative body which alone had the right to initiate legislation. Within the Russian, German and Austro-Hungarian empires, parliaments existed, belatedly in the case of Russia (1905), yet their powers were severely restricted, as was the franchise, always remembering that the Cisleithanian half of the Austro-Hungarian empire conceded male suffrage from January 1907 onwards. In short, these were reactionary, semi-absolutist and autocratic states, fearful of extending any meaningful say to the popular classes and the many ethnic minorities which lived in their lands.

In this situation, it was inevitable that Britain, France and Italy should have presented World War One as a struggle for freedom, although they were aware that their own liberal democratic credentials were not without fault and that their ally, autocratic Russia, spoiled the message.[20] From a propagandist viewpoint at least, the new Bolshevik regime's decision to withdraw from the conflict early in 1918 was, therefore, welcome. It certainly eased President Wilson's task of justifying the USA's involvement to a sceptical home front. He also hoped that liberal democracy and national self-determination would guide the peace-making process and form the basis of those states that emerged from the old Austro-Hungarian, German and Russian empires. This aspiration was realized only imperfectly in these new countries, particularly where ethnic rivalries were not so much resolved as merely placed within a different framework. It is also questionable whether, within these same regions, the creation of parliamentary government and the foundation of a mass electorate did much to curb the influence of vested interests such as the Church, army, judiciary, big business and upper bourgeoisie, even if these elites felt threatened, especially by the spread of Bolshevism.[21] Depressingly, by the 1930s this earlier vogue for progressive government appeared to have passed with the formation of fascist or semi-fascist states in much of central and eastern Europe. As stated in Chapter 8, 'only in Britain, France, the Irish Free State, Belgium, Luxembourg, Holland, Switzerland, Czechoslovakia and the Nordic countries did liberal democracy subsist, and even in these nations there were challenges from the extremes.'

Although it was insufficiently appreciated at the time, the epoch of the 1920s and 1930s did not provide an especially healthy environment for the growth of liberal democracy. Much of the blame must be attached directly or indirectly to World War One for creating a series of instabilities, many of which have already been touched upon. The peacemakers of 1919–20 could not truly adjudicate between competing nationalisms with the result that many minorities were left under foreign rule and felt discriminated against. Also within Europe's central and eastern lands, the lack of confidence on the part of the vested interests meant that they were reluctant to rally wholeheartedly behind the new democracies that had been imposed upon them. At the other end of the social spectrum, returning soldiers were promised a land fit for heroes; yet in the event they were often forgotten and taken for granted by governments. It did not help that the war seemed to have legitimized violence so that ensuing social and economic protest was extremely confrontational in nature. Most seriously of all, the conclusion of the war and the resulting peace settlements produced severe economic dislocation, again felt most acutely in central and eastern Europe. Although much of this was resolved by the mid-1920s, the situation quickly worsened once again amid the Great Depression of the early 1930s. In this swirl of ethnic, social and economic unrest, it is not surprising that many people looked to new political parties, new forms of political action and new value systems as a solution to their problems. Even previously good liberals and intellectuals began to start doubting their own ideological commitments.[22]

Most obviously, the answers came in the shape of fascism and communism. In addition to the examples of Italy and Germany, where fascism took firmest hold, by the middle of the 1930s nearly every other European country could boast its own far-right movement. The British Union of Fascists in the UK; the Croix de Feu and other paramilitary leagues in France; the Rexists in Belgium; the Nationaal-Socialistische Beweging in the Netherlands; Nationalsocialistiske Arbejderparti in Denmark; the Nasjonal Samling in Norway; the Falange in Spain; the Iron Guard in Romania; the Arrow Cross in Hungary – the list is almost endless.[23] A small number of these movements would achieve power in the 1930s, often in collaboration with conservative elites; others would remain on the fringes; and some would attain office in wartime collaboration with Hitler, even though he was unwilling to cede to them any real power lest they became the vehicle for a revanchiste nationalism directed at Germany.[24] Making sense of the ideology of these disparate groups is no easy matter. While there is general agreement that fascism's roots may be traced back to the 1890s and 1900s, there is disagreement as to which traditions it borrowed from. It has been provocatively argued that the crucial intellectual synthesis occurred in pre-1914 France, and that fascism featured a curious intermeshing of ideals drawn from left and right alike.[25] Unsurprisingly, no consensus exists, although historians have endeavoured to identify a 'generic' type of fascism.[26] Given the evolutionary nature of this most elusive of ideologies, its ability to change its spots at a moment's notice, its willingness to play to the gallery and its capacity to indulge in outlandish boasts, this has been no easy task. As António Costa Pinto reflects in Chapter 7, writers have been puzzled when searching for answers to the most basic set of questions. Who supported the fascists, and why? Why did some movements thrive and come to power, and others disappear? Why, for instance, did the National Socialist German Workers' Party become the most influential of grouping in Weimar Germany when there were several other similar far-right organizations. In these discussions, national context has been identified as key. Certain factors were undeniably common in the rise of the various fascist movements, yet it is striking that so many countries were capable of withstanding their challenge, at least before Hitler's conquests in 1939–41.

Communism was the other ideology that seemed to offer a cure to Europe's ills in the 1920s. Up to 1917, the left had been gaining ground across Europe. In Germany, by 1912 the Social Democratic Party had become the largest single party in the Reichstag, even if that parliament had little other than budgetary power. Meanwhile, in 1905 Jean Jaurès had pulled off the amazing feat of bringing together the many disparate and fractious strands of French socialism into a united party.

Yet, as Matthew Worley explains in Chapter 6, such unity was largely superficial. With the partial exception of Britain, where a much more moderate strain of socialism eventually found expression in the Labour Party, European socialists and trade unionists were divided broadly between reformists, those who believed in an evolutionary route to power via the ballot box; and revolutionaries, who preferred to take direct action, notably through strikes, and who rejected any participation in bourgeois politics. In 1903 such debates had split the Russian Social Democratic Labour party between Mensheviks and Bolsheviks, and it was the coming to power of the latter in 1917 that fostered similar divisions across Europe, as Communist parties broke away from the socialist fold and assembled under the protective fold of the Moscow-inspired Comintern, committed to engendering international revolution. In hindsight, it is not hard to see why Communist Russia then enjoyed such popularity. Unlike other governments in Europe, the Bolsheviks bore no responsibility for World War One. Although they would soon have plenty of blood on their hands, the appalling violence they meted out against their enemies, real and imagined, was not well publicized at the time – a fact that enabled many on the left to hail the Soviet Union as a model to be emulated, rather than to view it as one whose brutality would eventually be matched only by that of Nazi Germany. There was thus a real worry on the part of ruling elites about the spread of revolution, yet with the failure of the 1919 revolts in Berlin, Munich and Budapest, and with the failure of the extreme left to exploit social unrest in postwar Britain and France, the impetus was lost. Within Soviet Russia itself, the appetite for fomenting revolution overseas was also fading, especially after the death of Lenin in 1924. Although Trotsky advocated a theory of 'permanent revolution', Stalin believed that the USSR should concentrate on its own destiny, 'socialism in one country'; and it was the latter who won this particular ideological battle, exiling his rival in 1929 and embarking on a massive programme of economic renewal in the Five Year Plans. Although in the 1930s the USSR still paid lip-service to world revolution, in practice it was not very forthcoming in its support and it kept a tight hold on all the foreign fellow-travellers within the Comintern. The Spanish Civil War was an illustration of the extent, and more crucially the limits, of Stalin's readiness actively to support socialism outside Russia.

The legacy of Stalinism and Hitlerism has tended to obscure more rewarding intellectual and cultural developments, especially around the turn of the century. This was truly an epoch 'of extraordinary artistic, cultural, philosophical, and scientific endeavour,' a revolution in ideas at least as profound in its consequences as the Enlightenment.[27] One of its salient features was a challenge to the uncritical positivism that had developed due to ideas articulated most notably in the mid-nineteenth century by the French philosopher Auguste Comte. As Michael Biddiss writes in Chapter 3, for positivism 'science ... provided the supreme model for all reliable knowledge. It followed that the insights claimed by other disciplines were valuable only to the extent that they incorporated or imitated scientific habits of enquiry, observation, testing, and commitment to rational causality.' Before long, positivism had influenced a wide range of writers operating in different intellectual spheres, among them Emile Zola, Herbert Spencer, Emile Durkheim and Max Weber. Between 1890 and 1914 there was, however, a growing awareness that the Comtean version of positivism had been unduly simplistic. The reconsideration was driven most crucially by a revolution in physics that encompassed, for example, Konrad Röntgen's discovery of X-rays, Max Planck's exploration of the energy quantum, and Albert Einstein's development of the special and general theories of relativity. Here were advances that presented a world of scientific processes, and of scientific laws, that were in many ways far less predictable and vastly more mysterious than anything captured by Comte's imagining.

From the end of the nineteenth century onward, other realms of cultural and intellectual activity – art, literature, and music, together with newer domains such as sociology, economics, anthropology and psychoanalysis – also seemed to be in a process of particularly rapid transformation, questioning received wisdoms and hitherto accepted patterns of aesthetic discourse or social custom. What made this upheaval all the more unsettling, and exciting, was that these ideas were widely disseminated, and were not restricted to the salon, academy and university lecture hall. Higher rates of literacy (always accepting that huge pockets of illiteracy persisted), improved transportation, new forms of communication (the cinema, radio, newspaper and phonograph), developing educational systems and processes of economic growth meant that the spread of new ideas acquired a speed and a breadth of audience hitherto unimaginable. This was something noted by contemporaries, including the sociologist Gustave Le Bon and the criminologist Gabriel Tarde, who feared that, in this new world, the masses would be malleable in the hands of the elites. Some widely influential figures, such as the philosopher Friedrich Nietzsche (whose work attained international renown during the quarter-century after he actually ceased to write in 1889) were fearful of the future, their pessimism seemingly borne out by World War One. Amid this uncertainty, it is perhaps no wonder that many people clung on to what they knew.

This was especially evident in the area of religion. Late nineteenth- and early twentieth-century Europe was undoubtedly characterized by a process of secularization, hastened through the growing separation between church and state, as well as through the spread of urbanization and industrialization. Yet it is too easily forgotten that in many parts of Europe – whether Catholic, Orthodox or Protestant – popular practice and belief remained vibrant, especially when religion addressed the needs of ordinary people in coping with a period of rapid social and economic disruption.

That upheaval was driven partially by Europe's burgeoning population. This continued to grow, sustained by advances in medicine, better sanitary conditions and improved food supplies, although rates of increase were very uneven from country to country (and indeed were notably absent in the case of France, the population of which remained steady at around 40 million for much of this period). World War One inevitably acted as a check, yet that conflict did not interrupt longer-term trends. In 1914, with the notable exceptions of Britain and Germany, a majority of people still lived in rural communities; by 1939, except in the most backward of countries, most Europeans resided in towns and cities. There was also movement of peoples between countries, including the substantial numbers who continued to seek emigration to the USA in their search for a better quality of life. Standards of living depended hugely on where one lived. Urban centres were squalid, intimidating places, yet governments at last appeared to be taking a responsibility for improving living conditions, and took pride in the regeneration of their capitals. Within cities themselves, there was further movement as the middle classes settled in leafier suburbs. As to the countryside, life on the land remained tough and unforgiving, subject to the vagaries of the seasons, variations in landholding patterns, and the wider fluctuations of the international economy. Methods of production were changing yet, as Pamela Pilbeam observes in Chapter 2, it would take the experience of World War Two to convince governments that agricultural efficiency depended on larger farms, greater mechanization and a smaller rural workforce.

War also had an impact on the production of coal, iron, steel and textiles – the great staples upon which the industrial revolution had been founded – and gave them an important boost at a time when they were competing with so-called 'new' industries such as electricals, chemicals and car manufacturing. Whatever the particular sector, labour–capital relationships remained fractious. Even if trade union membership remained low, strikes were numerous both immediately before and after World War One. It did not help the social peace that governments were reluctant to provide social welfare, although in some countries, notably Britain, just enough was done to stave off massive upheaval. Within the workforce itself, there was concern at the growing presence of women. No longer restricted to domestic service and rural labour, they were increasingly occupying low-paid posts in teaching, light industry or clerical and shop work. In the course of World War One, they also took on men's jobs. Yet women found it difficult to sustain that pattern in peacetime, or indeed to break into middle-class professions. Rather than operating as doctors, lawyers and captains of industry, they were still more likely to be found working as sales assistants in large department stores. There the vast array of wares illustrated the pace of consumerism – a growth of material choice for those with the surplus resources to exercise it within societies that were still marked by major disparities of wealth.

Quite why Europe should have imperilled the spread of its prosperity by embarking on two disastrous world wars is a vexing question. When the first of these broke out in August 1914, it was anticipated that the conflict would be brief – much like the Wars of Italian and German Unification, and thus likely to be over by Christmas. Generals were fully alive to the capabilities of new weaponry, particularly machine guns and artillery. They thus knew that war was going to be hell. But they had not properly gauged either the need or the capacity of their soldiers to withstand that hell over a sustained period. World War One was indeed a conflict unprecedented in scale: in the extent of the fighting fronts; in the mobilization of home fronts; in the scale of the slaughter; and in the encroachment of the state into every aspect of civilian life. Contemporaries were astounded, and it is no surprise that the first explanations for war appeared immediately. As Gordon Martel remarks in Chapter 4, 'People began asking themselves what caused war to break out from the moment that the first shots were fired in August 1914, and historians have continued to ask questions about it ever since.' A similar debate has surrounded the origins of World War Two. At the time, the Allies were quick to attribute all the blame to Hitler. Yet, as Steve Morewood suggests in Chapter 9, other factors must also be taken into account. These include the power vacuum within central and eastern Europe created by World War One; the failure in the 1920s of collective security; and the conflicting messages sent out by the policy of appeasement pursued by Britain and France. Whatever its causes, World War Two was a conflict even more momentous than World War One, truly a 'total war'.[28] As the present author has written elsewhere, 'Populations were uprooted to a frightening degree, creating millions of refugees in the process; because of advances in military technology, there was not a sole fighting front, in a traditional sense, but several, with the result that civilians were frequently caught up in the violence, especially that perpetrated from the skies; the extent of Nazi hegemony meant that populations confronted a series of uncomfortable dilemmas about their responses to the occupier; material shortages, notably of food, clothes, and fuel, were felt through all levels of society; in order to remain in the fight, states routinely interfered in the lives of their citizens and had little hesitation in telling people what to do, something as true of the liberal democracies as it was the authoritarian regimes; and the inhumanity that was Nazism and Stalinism brought terror, deportation, and genocide.'[29]

A war on this scale could not help but leave an indelible imprint on Europe. As Giacomo Lichtner and Michael Biddiss both suggest in the final essays in this volume, the conflict effectively ended Europe's global influence, and ushered in a new world order dominated by the superpowers, the USA and USSR, who were armed with nuclear weapons. World War Two also brought to a close Germany's ambition to rule over the Continent, an ambition that increasingly took hold after the unification undertaken by Bismarck in 1870–71. As Morewood indicates, the division of Germany (and the emergence of the Federal Republic in particular) paved the way for reconciliation with France and moves towards European integration. Yet the conflict left a terrible legacy. In his ambition to build a Greater Reich, Hitler had systematically murdered millions – Slavs, Gypsies, homosexuals, Soviet prisoners of war, common criminals, religious minorities and, of course, Jews. It is arguable that his campaign of antisemitic genocide, even though incompletely implemented, was not only the most terrible, but also the most successful, of the Führer's ventures. The fact that it could not have been pursued without the active complicity of others, including many non-Germans, has served to ensure that responsibility for the Holocaust remains a particularly contested and sensitive area of ongoing historical debate. What does seem indisputable, however, is the extent to which this genocidal endeavour contributed towards making the Europe of 1945 a 'dark continent' in a sense that would have been barely imaginable back in the era around 1890.[30]

Notes

1 Gordon Martel, 'Introduction: Europe in Agony', in Gordon Martel (ed.), *A Companion to Europe, 1900–1945* (New York: Blackwell, 2006), p. xxi.
2 Donald Sassoon, *The Culture of the Europeans from 1800 to the Present* (London: Harper Press, 2006), especially chapter 10.

3 Richard Vinen, *A History in Fragments. Europe in the Twentieth Century* (London: Abacus, 2000), pp. 14–15.
4 Tony Judt, *Postwar. A History of Europe since 1945* (London: Pimlico, 2007), p. 13.
5 See Patrick Major, *Behind the Wall. East Germany and the Frontiers of Power* (Oxford: Oxford University Press, 2008).
6 Churchill, quoted by Asa Briggs and Patricia Clavin, *Modern Europe: 1789–1945* (London: Longman, 1997), p. 377.
7 See Victoria Glendinning, *Leonard Woolf. A Life* (London: Pocket Books, 2007 edn).
8 T. C. W. Blanning (ed.), *The Oxford Illustrated History of Modern Europe* (Oxford: Oxford University Press, 1996), p. 2.
9 Paul Hayes, 'Introduction', in Paul Hayes (ed.), *Themes in Modern European History, 1890–1945* (London: Routledge, 1945), pp. 2–5. The following two paragraphs draw heavily on the examples and ideas in this essay.
10 See E. Hobsbawm, *The Age of Revolution, 1978–1848* (London: Abacus, 1977 edn), p. 113.
11 See Margaret Macmillan, *Peacemakers. The Paris Conference of 1919 and its attempts to End War* (London: John Murray, 2001).
12 Werner Rings, *Life With the Enemy: Collaboration and Resistance in Hitler's Europe, 1939–1945* (London: Weidenfeld & Nicolson, 1982), p. 21.
13 Michael Burleigh, *The Third Reich: A New History* (London: Pan, 2000), p. 410; and Henri Michel, *Shadow War: Resistance in Europe, 1939–1945* (London: Deutsch, 1972), pp. 21–22.
14 See Steven Morewood, 'Divided Europe. The Long Postwar, 1945–89', in Rosemary Wakeman (ed.), *Themes in Modern European History since 1945* (London: Routledge, 2003).
15 See Bernard Porter, *The Lion's Share* (London: Longman, 2004, 4th edn) and Andrew Porter (ed.), *The Oxford History of the British Empire: The Nineteenth Century* (Oxford: Oxford University Press, 2001).
16 Matthew Brown, *Informal Empire in Latin America. Culture, Commerce and Capital* (Oxford: Blackwell, 2008).
17 A good introduction to these debates is to be found in Andrew Porter, *European Imperialism, 1860–1914* (London: Macmillan, 1996).
18 Such is the thesis of Hans-Ulrich Wehler, *Bismarck und der Imperialismus* (Cologne: Knieppenheuer und Witsch, 1969).
19 Niall Ferguson, *Empire: How Britain Made the Modern World* (London: Allen Lane, 2003).
20 See Gary Sheffield, *Forgotten Victory. The First World War. Myths and Realities* (London: Headline, 2002).
21 Good overviews are to be found in Martin Blinkhorn (ed.), *Fascism and the Right in Europe, 1919–1945* (London: Longman/Pearson, 2000) and Stanley Payne, *A History of Fascism, 1914–1945* (London: UCL Press, 1995).
22 See Alistair Hamilton, *The Appeal of Fascism. A Study of Intellectuals and Fascism, 1919–1945* (London: Anthony Blond, 1971).
23 See R. O. Paxton, *The Anatomy of Fascism* (London: Penguin, 2005).
24 H. R. Kedward, *Occupied France. Resistance and Collaboration, 1940–1944* (Oxford: Basil Blackwell, 1985).

25 See especially Zeev Sternhell, *The Birth of Fascist Ideology* (Princeton, NJ: Princeton University Press, 1995) and his *Neither Right nor Left: Fascist Ideology in France* (Princeton, NJ: Princeton University Press, 1995).

26 See Roger Griffin, *The Nature of Fascism* (London: Routledge, 1993, 2nd edn).

27 Nicholas Atkin and Frank Tallett, *Priests, Prelates and People. A History of European Catholicism since 1750* (London/New York: Tauris/Oxford University Press, 2003), p. 168.

28 See also Roger Chickering and Stig Förster, 'Are We There Yet? World War Two and the Theory of Total War', in Roger Chickering, Stig Förster and Bernd Greiner (eds), *A World at Total War: Global Conflict and the Politics of Destruction, 1937–1945* (Cambridge: Cambridge University Press, 2005), pp. 1–18.

29 Nicholas Atkin, 'The Daily Lives of Civilians in Wartime: Europe's Twentieth-Century Experience', in Nicholas Atkin (ed.), *The Daily Lives of Civilians in Wartime Twentieth-Century Europe* (Westport, CT: Greenwood, 2008).

30 See Mark Mazower, *Dark Continent: Europe's Twentieth Century* (London: Penguin, 1999), especially chapter 5.

1 West, East and Centre: patterns of governance in pre-1914 Europe

Detmar Klein

In 1914 the Central powers of Germany and Austria-Hungary embarked on a brutal war with the Western powers of Britain and France and the Eastern power of Russia. All five states proclaimed that they were fighting for the sake of civilization, and thought their cause just. At the beginning of the 1890s, when the autocratic and backward Tsarist Empire seemed separated from parliamentary Britain and republican France by a set of opposing values and interests, few would have predicted such a scenario. Yet, in the summer of 1914, 'East' and 'West' united to align themselves against the 'Centre'.

By then, these three terms, which give shape to the present chapter concerning the governance of Europe's leading regimes, were the principal coordinates used in discourse about its political geography. They continued to be applied until the mid-twentieth century, when a bipolar system emerged out of the catastrophe of World War Two. Historically, it was the West that had initiated the process of modernization and industrialization, thus serving as model for the whole continent. This was also where the idea of the nation-state was born and put into practice, linking nationality to state territory with the goal of promoting national integration. The idea of the nation-state was diametrically opposed to the geopolitical realities of the Centre and the East, where there existed the multinational Habsburg and Romanov empires. The West was also the cradle of economic progress and of liberal political ideologies, as epitomized by the parliamentary monarchies of Britain, the Netherlands, Belgium, Denmark, Sweden and Norway (since 1905 no longer in personal union with Sweden), and by the parliamentary republics of France and Switzerland. In these states, the executive was answerable to an elected body, which alone made the laws. In the Centre and East, there was a more complex picture. Although Germany, Austria-Hungary and eventually Russia possessed parliaments, these states essentially exhibited authoritarian, semi-absolutist, or even autocratic forms of governance.

Nowhere did parliamentary government equate with democracy in the sense that we understand it today. Most states had a restricted franchise, favouring the upper and middle classes. France, Switzerland, Denmark and Norway were the most democratic in so far as they had universal male suffrage; in 1913, Norway even introduced the vote for women. While there was also universal male suffrage for the election of the German national parliament, its powers were severely restricted. In 1907, the Austrian part of the Habsburg dual monarchy also introduced universal suffrage but, as in the case of Germany, parliamentary influence remained limited. Even Britain, although known as the 'mother of parliaments', had only half its adult male population enfranchised by 1914. A similar lack of democratic representation was true for the parliamentary monarchy of Belgium. Still, in terms of power, the decisive factor in the political life of parliamentary regimes was their claim to be representing 'the people'.

The West: Britain and France

Britain was one of the two major model states of the West. Its proper name was the United Kingdom of Great Britain and Ireland. The Irish, however, were striving for Home Rule, which (with the Ulster question still far from settled) was finally granted in 1914, but immediately suspended because of the war. Britain headed an empire on which 'the sun never set'. It ruled directly over India and had many colonies, particularly in Africa; however, the empire was changing, as former self-governing colonies were upgraded in status to so-called dominions, such as Canada (1867), Australia (1901) and New Zealand (1907). Britain had a distinctive political framework, within which its constitutionalism depended not on a single written document, but on a combination of customary law and parliamentary statutes that had been evolving over centuries.

The British Parliament consisted of the Lords and the Commons, forming respectively the upper and lower legislative chambers. The Commons were elected representatives of their constituencies. The monarch, in turn, appointed as prime minister that politician whose administration could muster the majority most crucially needed in the Commons. The House of Lords was – aside from the senior Anglican clergy – a hereditary chamber, representing the interests of the nobility and the upper class at large. It was also the highest judicial power, acting as the supreme court of appeal for most cases. The power of the Lords, which had been losing influence from 1832 onwards, was severely curtailed by the Parliament Act of 1911. It stipulated that the chamber was empowered only to delay, but not to veto, the lower house's legislation. This almost revolutionary act was the endpoint of a process that had started in 1906 with the landslide victory of the Liberals over the Conservatives, who until then had ruled for a decade. The two elections of 1910 kept the Liberals in power with the aid of the Irish nationalists and the emergent Labour Party, a reformist (rather than revolutionary) grouping. Liberals now embraced a progressive programme, which advocated that the state should intervene for the benefit of the weak. Outside of Parliament, the trade unions were growing stronger, and their 'pressure tool' of strikes was getting sharper, particularly after the 1906 Trade Disputes Act, which considerably strengthened their legal and financial standing. Due to the impact of the growing workers' movement and Labour's electoral success, the Liberals felt compelled to enact social welfare reforms. Much of the cost of these and of the accelerating arms race with Germany was to be borne by the big landowners, a policy to which the Lords objected; the ensuing fight with the Commons led to the peers' defeat in 1911 and to further waning of their power. While the bourgeoisie had gained ground, it also felt threatened by the rising working class. Industrial unrest endangered the middle-class triumph. However, Britain was still in 1914 the industrial and trading powerhouse of Europe, and its decision to enter the war was not determined primarily by domestic factors. Rather, this stemmed from the need to counter an aggressive and economically expanding Germany that was threatening the balance of power.

The other model parliamentary state was the republic of France, born out of defeat by the nascent German Reich in 1870–71. The bicameral National Assembly was the decisive legislative power: its upper house (Senate) was chosen by electoral colleges in the departments, and its lower house (Chamber of Deputies) was elected nationally through universal male suffrage. The President of the Republic, selected by the Assembly, was the head of the executive; his power lay in directing foreign policy and in deciding who should form the cabinet. It was the prime minister (President of the Council of Ministers) who governed the country, so long as he retained the confidence of the Chamber of Deputies.

The survival of the new republic was in doubt well into the 1880s, as monarchists, Bonapartists and other critics of parliamentarianism questioned the system. However, the Right proved incapable of mustering enough support to overthrow it, and the army ultimately remained loyal. Therefore the republic survived even the Dreyfus Affair, which shook France for a decade from the mid-1890s onwards. In political terms, the regime became dominated by the bourgeoisie: the number of nobles in the Chamber of Deputies declined from 34 per cent in 1871 to only 9 per cent in 1914.[1] Although the nobility no longer had much political clout, their influence in the socio-economic realm remained considerable. Nobles participated in business, and they sought links with the rich bourgeoisie by means of marriage; on the eve of World War One, the moneyed bourgeoisie and the landed aristocracy had to a large extent amalgamated into a single plutocracy.[2]

From the turn of the century onwards, the Radicals – representing the republican, liberal and secularist Centre-Left – were the major force in French political life. Within the general context of mass politicization, in 1901 they created a genuine party: the *Parti républicain, radical et radical-socialiste*. The various socialist groups also decided to concentrate their forces into a unified *Section Française de l'Internationale Ouvrière* (SFIO: French Section of the Workers' International). Collaboration between the Radicals and socialists tentatively started in 1899 when the former led the creation of a *gouvernement de défense républicaine*, which included the independent socialist Alexandre Millerand. This collaboration was intended to counteract the far-right threat to the republic and was the precursor of the *Bloc des Gauches* of 1902. French socialists were, in principle, Marxists, whose ultimate goal was the classless utopia of communism; but they were divided on one issue, namely, whether to participate in bourgeois governments. This question reflected their debate over the nature of Marxism and the path towards socialism – ones that also took place among left-wingers in countries such as Germany or Russia. The Guesdistes (followers of Jules Guesde) were classical Marxists and were opposed to any participation in bourgeois government; the followers of Jean Jaurès, however, propagated a more reformist, evolutionary line, and initially did not object to entering a coalition with the middle-class parties. The Bloc existed for only a few years until 1904, when the socialist ministers withdrew. It conducted strongly anticlerical policies and targeted the religious orders, resulting in the closure of over 2000 Catholic schools; ultimately this fight led to the 1905 laws separating church and state.

In the early twentieth century, such extra-parliamentary movements as the *Ligue des Patriotes*, the *Ligue de la Patrie Française* and *Action Française* extolled a 'new' nationalism of the Right, which was ethnic, racist and antisemitic, and which differed from the 'old' nationalism of the Left. Standard-bearers of this radical Right were Charles Maurras and the French novelist, journalist and politician Maurice Barrès. It influenced the Centre-Left by making the latter's nationalism more focused on ethnicity and more aggressive towards Germany; in view of the domestic background and the worsening international situation, prominent liberal politicians such as Poincaré and Clemenceau also adopted an increasingly anti-German and anti-pacifist stance. Yet, despite the domestic troubles at the end of the nineteenth and beginning of the twentieth century, this period is referred to as the *Belle Epoque*, signifying important achievements in the realm of science, culture and the arts. The main beneficiaries were the bourgeoisie. Mass politicization and the rise and threat of socialism after the turn of the century also brought improvements for the lower classes, notably in the realm of social welfare, albeit on a lesser scale than in Germany.

By 1914, the regime looked much more secure than ever before. France had managed to surmount various crises and the bourgeois republic seemed to cope well with domestic problems. Furthermore, it had achieved much in its foreign policy. It possessed a substantial colonial empire, and, in diplomacy, had managed to woo autocratic Russia. Since Germany had not renewed its alliance (the Reinsurance Treaty) with the tsarist regime in 1890, France had seen the possibility of breaking out of its international isolation (imposed earlier by Bismarck) and of initiating a *rapprochement* with Russia through the alliance of 1892 (finalized in January 1894). Additionally, the Republic soothed its colonial differences with Britain, securing the establishment of the Entente Cordiale in 1904. Although the latter was only a loose arrangement (Britain never liked to commit itself fully to automatic obligations), it still amounted to a form of coalition – one that was complemented by the Anglo–Russian Entente of 1907. This Triple Entente provided France with the security needed against Germany, its powerful 'arch enemy', and enabled the nation to stand up to the Reich when the moment came in 1914.

The East: the Russian empire

Whereas Britain and France were the leading forces in the West, Russia was the predominant power in the East. The tsar ruled over a huge, multinational empire with some 150 million or more inhabitants before 1914, which included Finland, Poland, Ukraine, Estonia, Latvia, Lithuania, the Caucasus and regions of Central Asia. Fewer than half of these peoples were ethnic Russians; if Ukrainians and Byelorussians are added into the mix, the ethnic tapestry looks even more complex.[3] The peoples of the Western areas of the empire – in Poland, Finland and the Baltic provinces – did not consider themselves 'Easterners', not least because none of them shared in the Orthodox religious faith of the Russians. As for the ethnic Poles, who had suffered a threefold partition of their territory in the late eighteenth century, many of them were now under German or Austrian rule. 'Congress-Poland' had been given to Russia as a separate kingdom at the Congress of Vienna, with the tsar as its king; after an uprising its constitution had been abolished in 1832. Following a further insurgency in 1863–64, any remaining autonomous Polish institutions had been dismantled. From the 1880s onwards, the process of Russification affected the Poles also in the cultural realm: Russian became the only official language in administration and education, and the activities of the Roman Catholic Church were hindered. There was a short-lived reversal of this process due to the Russian Revolution of 1905, but after 1907 a policy of forceful Russification was taken up again with renewed vigour.

Finland fared only slightly better. It had been seized from Sweden in the Napoleonic era and, since then, the tsars were also its grand dukes. In the search for greater efficiency, Alexander II had granted Finland some autonomy, but in the early 1890s the first era of Russification started. The tsarist February Manifesto of 1899 decreed that Finland was under direct rule from St Petersburg, without involving the country's Diet (an estates-based legislative assembly) or its Senate (the highest administrative body, consisting of Finns appointed by the tsar). There followed a purge of civil servants opposed to Russification, as well as decrees concerning tight censorship, mandatory service in the tsarist army, and dictatorial powers for the Russian governor-general. Although there was widespread resistance among all classes of Finnish society, real relief came only with the 1905 revolution in Russia, which led to the repeal of the February Manifesto and the suspension of the conscription law and other dictatorial measures. A parliament based on universal (male and female) suffrage was created; it had formal legislative rights, but no effective parliamentary regime developed and the tsar retained extensive powers. After 1908, with the Russian government having regained its strength, Finland was once again in the throes of Russification and lost most of its recently gained autonomy.

The short-lived reversal of Russification enjoyed by Poland and Finland was due to the 1905 revolution. This event was a major watershed in pre-1914 Russian history, even if the tsarist regime soon reverted to type. Until 1905, this was a fully fledged autocracy, backed by the nobility and by the Russian Orthodox Church with the tsar at its head. It was a police state, ruled with an iron fist by Nicholas II from 1894 to 1917. Until the turn of the century, the bourgeoisie and the working class were relatively limited in number, due to relatively low levels of urbanization and industrialization, although that situation was about to change. Peasants constituted the mass of the population. The tsar had full autocratic powers in the executive and legislative realms, administering the country through provincial governors; he was also entitled to overrule the judiciary. He appointed ministers who were all individually answerable to him; as there was no collective responsibility, they constantly intrigued against each other. On the one hand, this situation increased the autocratic power of the tsar; on the other, it caused problems for the effective government of the empire.

The problems were also reflected at the bureaucratic level. The administration of the huge empire, with the enormous distances to travel, would have been difficult even at the best of times. The major difficulty was the lack of an efficient, well structured and well staffed bureaucracy, working within a framework of strict legal and political accountability. The country was divided into provinces, each headed by a governor. Limited local self-government existed in Russia in three forms: *duma*, *zemstvo* and *mir*. Each city had a municipal council (*duma*), which was elected on the grounds of a restricted franchise based on property and wealth. The *zemstvo* system administered tasks such as health, education and poor relief in each province. It consisted of self-governing institutions, all of which had an executive board and an elected assembly comprising the three estates of nobility, town citizenry and peasantry; the franchise for the *zemstvo* assembly was limited, the provincial governor having the right to select the peasant representatives, which meant that the dominance of the noble gentry was guaranteed. Each district *zemstvo* sent delegates to a provincial one. Village communities had some administrative powers through the so-called *mir*. This acted as intermediary between the individual peasant and the state authorities, and it was also responsible for allocating land. At irregular intervals the village plots were redistributed among the major local families, according to the number of their male members. This system encouraged population growth, and caused hardship and even famine for many rural communities. In order to survive, peasants had to rent additional land from the nobility. Former serfs were also paying back the redemption fees demanded by the landowners and the state from the time of abolition (1861). Often peasants had to work for their former masters once again, in order to meet these payments. *Duma*, *zemstvo* and *mir* decisions were, in turn, all subject to the intervention of the provincial governor. *Zemstvo* executives did not have any power over the governor's officials, and this caused tensions and disaffection at local level. This situation had been made worse in 1889 with the introduction of so-called land captains, who wielded administrative, judicial and police powers over the rural communes in their given canton: they could ignore the *zemstvo* and overturn actions of the *mir*, and they acted as a watchdog against politically 'unreliable elements' who could be removed from any position they had in the administrative system. No wonder that such a regime was seen by everybody as arbitrary.[4]

Western ideas of liberalism had found their way into Russia in the course of the nineteenth century. However, many of those who harboured them were convinced that the way forward was not evolution, as had been the case in Britain, but rather revolution. There was dispute between Westernizers, proponents of the Western European model of parliamentarianism and modernization, and Slavophiles, advocates of a Russian special path. The latter, while not necessarily liking the tsar's autocracy, thought that the Orthodox church and the institution of the *mir* formed a better framework for achieving a more egalitarian and 'spiritual' society than the ideals of Western parliamentarianism and materialism seemed to offer.

On the eve of the 1905 Revolution, there were three major revolutionary groupings. These were the Socialist-Revolutionary Party, together with the mutually hostile Menshevik and Bolshevik factions of the Social Democratic Labour Party. The Social Revolutionaries played an important role in encouraging the 'masses' to revolt in the lead up to the 1905 Revolution. This party assembled the *Narodniki* (populists, or 'Friends of the People') who had departed from their earlier views of the peasantry being the only revolutionary class, and thus targeted industrial workers as well. Several decades earlier the *Narodniki*, young urban upper-class romantics idealizing the peasant, had gone in their thousands into the countryside to initiate a revolution based on the ideas of collectivism as embodied in the *mir*. Opposed not just to capitalism, but also to the version of Marxism found in the West, the Social Revolutionaries aimed for a distinctively Russian style of socialism, which often included anarchist elements. The Social Democratic Party was a revolutionary party based on the Marxist model of achieving a classless society after a proletarian revolution. It had been founded in 1898, but split into two factions in 1903: the Mensheviks (the 'minority') and the Bolsheviks (the 'majority'). The latter were, despite their name, numerically the smaller party, as Lenin, their leader, insisted on a restricted circle of committed revolutionaries eager to act as the vanguard of the proletariat (most of whom he believed to lack sufficient class consciousness), and thus to initiate a workers' revolution without waiting first for a bourgeois one. This stance distanced the Bolsheviks from the classical Marxist interpretation of historical development still favoured by the Mensheviks. The latter were willing to ally themselves with liberals to exact concessions from the state. The Mensheviks were right in so far as the proletariat was still not numerous, despite the recent explosive growth of industry; the bourgeoisie, however, was also weak in numbers and the prospect of a middle-class revolution (as the first stage in the revolutionary process) was not very realistic. In fact, it was mostly the state – which held the greatest accumulation of capital in its hands – that acted as an industrial entrepreneur, setting up factories and mines. The state had initiated, and was conducting, a wide-scale industrialization programme, with the help of foreign, mainly French, capital. The prospect of achieving concerted strike action was enhanced by the fact that most workers were concentrated in large-scale companies, and by the consideration that the majority of such enterprises were geographically clustered in the major cities.

The 1905 Revolution had two midwives: defeats in the Russo-Japanese war of 1904–5, which weakened the empire, and the 'Bloody Sunday' massacre of January 1905, which shattered the myth of the tsar as the benevolent father of the nation. 'Bloody Sunday' was sparked off by a strike in St Petersburg. Such withdrawal of labour was illegal, as workers' interests were allowed to be pursued only in the context of welfare associations that were controlled by the government. The participation in this strike, however, was massive, involving over 100,000 workers. When many of the demonstrators marched to the tsar's palace, demanding reforms and justice, troops opened fire; several hundred died, many more were injured, and among the casualties were women and children. Afterwards strikes swept the country and spread to the borderlands of Poland, Finland and the Baltic provinces. Revolutionary councils (soviets) sprang up throughout the country under the leadership of the radical parties, and claimed to be organs of popular direct democracy. Finally, a general strike in October crippled the country, and, with most army troops still being at the Eastern front, the weakened tsar felt compelled to issue the so-called October Manifesto. This established a freely elected national assembly (the State Duma), promised civil liberties such as free speech and a free press, abolished redemption fees, and looked to the promotion of linguistic and religious rights for ethnic minorities.

The outburst of political freedom was short-lived; counterrevolution set in by the end of the year. Many of those who had been active in the revolution were arrested. Antirevolutionary radical nationalists (known as the Black Hundreds), who were in favour of unrestricted tsarist rule, unleashed a wave of terror. Although the so-called Fundamental Laws of April 1906 nominally provided a constitution, the tsar's autocratic powers were not seriously curtailed. He remained Commander-in-Chief of the army and navy, as well as deciding on peace and war and initiating foreign policy. Although the constitution proclaimed the supremacy of the law, the enactments of the State Council (as the upper house) and the State Duma (as the lower house) needed the tsar's endorsement. Initially, he appointed half the State Council's members, with the remainder being elected by several sections of society such as the clergy, noble corporations, universities or *zemstva*. However, after 1910 it was once again the tsar who appointed all its members. Not surprisingly, the State Council proved a powerful obstacle to any meaningful reform programme. Ministers were appointed by Nicholas II and were responsible only to him. He could still issue decrees when the Duma was not in session, and he reserved the right to dissolve it at his pleasure. Thus the autocracy remained intact, and there was only a mock constitutionalism. Still, the Duma had the right to approve the state budget, even if it could not rule on military expenditure.

The elections to the First Duma took place in March 1906. The franchise was fairly broad, but indirect and unequal. Electoral colleges (*curiae*), based on social classes, chose the deputies in several stages; the votes of peasants and workers counted far less than those of the bourgeoisie and landed gentry. In the event, the principal political parties in that first assembly were the so-called Octobrists and Kadets. The former, with a predominantly bourgeois or liberal noble background, backed Nicholas II's October Manifesto and stood for constitutional monarchy with a strong parliament. The latter, known alternatively as Constitutional Democrats, formed at the height of the 1905 Revolution a distinctly liberal-democratic party consisting of professionals such as lawyers or university professors, some industrialists and members of local *zemstva*. They eventually became the strongest grouping in the First Duma. That first assembly was relatively radical in Russian terms, even though revolutionary parties such as the Bolsheviks were not represented. Together with the *Trudoviki*, a rural-based, moderate socialist-democratic party, the Kadets formed a leftist-liberal majority, strongly opposing the government. They debated land reform – obviously anathema to the tsar and the vast majority of nobles – and they demanded a genuine parliament to which ministers were responsible, and one that could not be neutralized by either the crown or the State Council. As the First Duma was not to the tsar's liking, it was quickly dissolved by the prime minister, Stolypin; the Second Duma suffered the same fate. The manufacturing of 'tsar-friendly' electoral regulations in 1907, which ran counter to the spirit of the 1906

Fundamental Laws and came close to a 'coup from above', favoured wealthy landowners and reduced even further the electoral weight of the lower classes and of non-Russian nationalities, thus finally creating an assembly with which the tsar could live. The Octobrists became the strongest faction in the Third Duma (1907–12) and in the Fourth (which then survived formally until 1917), but they were still outnumbered by nationalists and supporters of tsarist autocracy on the extreme Right. On the eve of the war, even the once-loyal Octobrists opposed the government.

Stolypin, an aristocratic landowner, initiated some land reforms which were designed to form a class of well-to-do peasants (the so-called *kulaks*) by means of enclosing common lands and transferring them into private peasant ownership. Still, the system of the *mir* survived; only a quarter of peasants withdrew from their commune.[5] The reforms did not solve the difficulties associated with antiquated cultivation methods. The persistence of rural poverty was a major problem, as agriculture remained by far the most important economic sector. Nor did the abolition of redemption fees improve matters. As for landowners, many became impoverished due to the agricultural crisis, and they opposed Petersburg's attempts towards centralizing rural bureaucracy.[6]

At the same time, industrialization was gathering speed, which resulted in dire living conditions for the urban poor; in the last few years before the outbreak of war, strikes were commonplace. Although the industrial proletariat was very small when compared with the peasantry, it still presented a powerful force because most workers were employed in huge factories and were concentrated in key urban centres; in addition, many of them were now literate and thus more exposed to revolutionary propaganda. As they generally maintained close ties with their families in the countryside, the workers developed discontents that increasingly fused with those of the peasants.[7] As for the bourgeoisie and intelligentsia, they were unhappy because they were still excluded from political power.

By now, Russian society was in a state of discontent, and indeed of crisis; it was definitely no longer unified enough to be ruled autocratically. This was a change that had been brought about by the state itself, as the latter had been imposing and promoting industrialization from above in order to catch up with the other European powers. When compared with Britain or Germany, industrialization was not so impressive, but in relative terms the percentage growth of industrial output was remarkable. In the period between 1907 and 1913, there was an average annual increase in industrial production of 9 per cent;

as for steel production on the eve of war, Russia even surpassed France.[8] Stolypin did not, and could not, heal the ills of Russia, given the fact that the autocracy was hardly touched by the mock constitutionalism and was unwilling to pursue genuine modernization. Even before his assassination in 1911, it was clear that his ideas of reform, which were by no means radical, were stillborn. However, the events of the year 1905 and its aftermath contradict any notion of irretrievable Russian 'backwardness'; the prospect of revolutionary change was increasingly present.

Although the ruling elites thought in terms of state and dynasty, rather than 'people', they still used the ideology of nationalism to gain support and possibly avoid reforms; non-Russian nationalities suffered greatly from that policy.[9] Particularly after the Habsburg annexation of Bosnia in 1908, there was a strengthening of Russian Pan-Slavism. Its proclaimed aim was to support and potentially to unify all Slavic peoples, preferably under direct Russian leadership. This was an ideology that was not entirely unrelated to the Slavophilia that concentrated on the Russian heartland and emphasized the non-Western essence of its character. Many who belonged to other Slavic peoples viewed Russian Pan-Slavism as synonymous with tsarist imperialism; the Poles, in particular, saw that concept as a mere guise for Russification. Rival versions of the Pan-Slav ideal could be found elsewhere, notably in the Czech lands, in Slovakia, and across much of the Balkans. In the latter region, the emphasis fell on unifying the Southern Slavs. This might be achieved through the Habsburg Empire's acceptance of the chance to forestall imperial dissolution by yielding to its Slav subjects the degree of autonomy already conceded in 1867 to its Magyar population. Alternatively, it might come through the leadership of Serbia, and thus involve instead a major Slav secession from Austrian rule. In that context especially, the South Slav movement was looking for Russian support, which St Petersburg was only too glad to give in order to expand its own imperial sphere of interest. Pan-Slavism and Russian nationalism, in general, were gaining in strength. Concerns about Russia's great power status compared with Austria-Hungary, and especially the fear of Germany, were likewise growing, not only among the ruling elites but also among the educated classes in general. The economic and military threat coming from Germany, the existence of a Pan-German movement which was denigrating Slavs and looking for *Lebensraum* in the East, and nagging self-doubts regarding the economic and cultural clout of Russia *vis-à-vis* a rapidly modernizing Germany, all contributed to a pro-Slav and anti-German belligerence.[10] Coupled with a growing nationalism was the increasing social instability of Russia and its empire, which was marked by multiple antagonisms: the landowning aristocracy versus the mass of poor peasants; the new industrial bourgeoisie versus the emerging proletariat; the intelligentsia versus a state that tried to silence their criticisms; liberal aspirations pitted against an autocratic state keen on obstructing the development of a genuine civil society; and recalcitrant peoples on the Western fringe versus an oppressor keen on Russification. In 1913, the 300th anniversary of Romanov dynastic rule was celebrated with opulent seventeenth-century pageantry – as if to symbolize the tsar's unwillingness to modernize along Western lines, and his determination to maintain an archaic autocracy.[11] During the first six months of 1914, however, there were more than one million Russian workers on strike, clamouring for progressive changes.[12]

This situation provides the domestic context for resort to war in 1914. Can this decision be seen as a means of diverting the attention of workers and peasants from their misery, a 'social imperialist' strategy of glossing over the deepening frictions in the Tsarist Empire and of thus unifying the country? This is certainly one way of looking at Russia's actions in the summer of 1914, as is discussed in Chapter 4 by Gordon Martel. There is also the further question as to whether revolution had become inevitable by 1914. Some historians argue that the fall of the monarchy was by no means a foregone conclusion, and that tsarism could have evolved peacefully into a capitalist democracy; others argue that the forces of reform were too weak to avert a cataclysm, and that revolution was definitely waiting in the wings. In either case, Russia's entry into the war appears as a pivotal event, whether in tipping the scales decisively towards such an upheaval, or simply in accelerating the pace of its unavoidable arrival.[13]

The Centre: (i) the Austro-Hungarian empire

Between the autocratic East and the liberal-parliamentarian West, there were the two major powers of the Centre: the German Empire, and the multinational Habsburg Empire of Austria-Hungary. Both were theoretically constitutional monarchies, but it will be recalled that, with weak parliaments, these regimes might best be regarded as embodying semi-autocratic forms of governance. Even within these territories, it is possible to notice a gradient running eastward towards increasingly authoritarian and almost semifeudal social structures. This gradient was very noticeable in Austria-Hungary, especially in economic terms. The Habsburg Empire occupied a middle position between West and East with respect to economic development. By virtue of its extraordinary rate of growth, Germany seemed to be tilting towards the West, whereas the experience of the Habsburg territories, not least due to their multinational character, appeared closer to that of the tsarist regime. Tensions within the Austro-Hungarian empire were also the trigger for the outbreak of World War One, although hostilities would not have broken out if its ally Germany had not embarked on a policy of brinkmanship, preparing for a preventive war against East and West alike.

Some historians argue that the Habsburg Empire was on the brink of collapse in 1914, and that it would have fallen even without the war; others disagree, stressing that victory would have ensured survival.[14] The nationality issue was unquestionably at the heart of the matter. On the eve of World War One, the empire included the territories of present-day Austria, Hungary, the Czech Republic, Slovakia, Croatia, Slovenia and Bosnia-Herzegovina, as well as parts of today's Poland, Ukraine, Romania, Serbia, Montenegro and Italy. Habsburg defeat in the German War of 1866 had spelled the end of the German Confederation and had signalled Austria's exclusion from the unified Reich that would shortly be proclaimed under Prussian leadership. It also encouraged the disaffected Hungarians to bid for autonomy from Vienna, and thus for recognition within the empire as a 'state people' equal in status to the Austro-Germans themselves. This situation led to the Compromise (*Ausgleich*) of 1867, which created the dual monarchy of Austria-Hungary – the '*k und k*' (*kaiserlich und königlich*) regime that linked, through the person of a single ruler, the 'imperial' crown of the former country with the 'royal' one of the latter. Austria and Hungary formed a currency and customs union, and shared only three ministries: those of war and foreign affairs, together with that of finance (but only regarding expenditure on military and external policy). Each partner in the *Ausgleich* had its own government, headed by a prime minister who was appointed by the emperor/king and could not be directly toppled by parliamentary vote. As there were two separate parliaments and no provision for joint sessions, any legislation concerning the three common ministries had to be dealt with in parliamentary committees, called delegations. Customs and currency affairs were legislated upon by each parliament separately, albeit along common guidelines.

The monarch also held the ancient crown of Bohemia (in his capacity as Austrian emperor) and that of Croatia (in his capacity as Hungarian king), but neither of these territories became equal partners with Austria and Hungary. The Austrian element in the dual monarchy consisted of 17 so-called crown lands, comprising the German-speaking

Austrian heartland, the Croat-inhabited Dalmatian coast, Slovenia, the Czech lands of Bohemia and Moravia (both with sizeable German minorities), Austrian Silesia with its substantial Polish minority, Galicia (inhabited mainly by Poles, but with a Ruthenian minority), and Bukovina with its strong Ukrainian and Romanian populations. In 1910 these regions (often known collectively as Cisleithania, as distinct from Hungarian-controlled Transleithania) totalled some 28 million inhabitants. Even as the biggest single nationality, the Germans formed only 35.6 per cent of the population, followed by the Czechs, who constituted 23 per cent. The issue of majority/minority nationalities was exacerbated by the fact that several Austrian crown lands had mixed populations. The most embittered conflict took place between Germans and Czechs: in Bohemia, two-fifths of the inhabitants were German, while in Moravia there was also a strong German minority numbering more than a quarter of that province's population.[15]

The other half of the empire was just as multinational as the Austrian one. The Hungarian-speaking Magyars, who were politically and socially dominant, totalled 10.1 million in 1910, just under half of Transleithania's overall population.[16] The state itself comprised two parts: the kingdom of Hungary proper (over 18 million inhabitants) and Croatia-Slavonia (2.6 million inhabitants). Despite the Hungarian-Croatian Compromise of 1868, the Budapest government refused to implement the promised autonomy of Croatia-Slavonia and to respect its Slavic languages and cultures. Even worse discrimination against non-Magyar nationalities took place within the Hungarian kingdom itself, affecting the Romanians of Transylvania and the Slavs of Slovakia. Furthermore, there were sizeable German minorites scattered throughout the Hungarian state. The diversity of such ethnic groupings across the Habsburg Empire as a whole, and the fact that in many areas majorities and minorities lived very closely side-by-side, made the nationality issue the most burning and most explosive problem on the eve of the war.

Monarchical government in the Cisleithanian half of the empire operated according to the so-called December Constitution of 1867. A bicameral assembly, the Austrian Reichsrat, had the right to approve the budget and legislate on all matters that were deemed to be common to all the crown lands. The emperor, however, had an absolute right of legislative veto. The Reichsrat's upper house (Herrenhaus) represented the interests of the upper clergy and nobility, but it also ranked among its members 169 citizens who had been nominated by the emperor as a reward for their contributions to the state, church, science or the arts. Until 1896, the lower house, the Chamber of

Deputies, was elected by means of an indirect franchise based on the four electoral colleges (*curiae*) of grand estate owners, cities, chambers of industry and commerce, and rural communities. The reform of 1896 expanded the number of voters considerably by creating a fifth electoral class with universal (male) suffrage, which chose 72 of the 425 deputies. 1907 was the year in which the universal, equal, secret and direct suffrage for all men was introduced: one motive was to weaken the electoral weight of the non-German (especially Czech) bourgeois elites who were seen as the carriers of nationalistic ideas, and another being to mobilize voters for non-national, Catholic or socialist parties.[17] As for the Austrian crown lands, each area had its own regulations regarding its government and electoral representation (diet). All diets were indirectly elected in the form of electoral colleges, with a restricted franchise based on wealth and education that resembled the criteria used for the Reichsrat's Chamber of Deputies until 1907. The diets could be dissolved at the emperor's pleasure, and their legislation needed his approval.

The Reichsrat was responsible for many of those matters that were highly significant to some crown lands, such as the issue of language. From the turn of the century onwards, the Chamber of Deputies contained an ever-increasing number of parties, as all political groupings became additionally organized along ethnic lines. It was often prorogued due to tumultuous scenes between national blocs, in particular between German and Czech delegates; frequently parliament was paralysed to such an extent that the government had to resort to emergency decree. Although the Austrian constituencies were allotted in such a way that the Germans had a disproportionate advantage, they were still left with only 232 seats in the 1911 Chamber. Its overall total of 516 deputies included 259 Slavs, of whom 107 were Czech.[18] The growing ethnopolitical fragmentation led to more than 30 independent political parties in the Austrian Reichsrat. Even the Social Democrats, who one would have expected to adhere to a Marxist and supranational stance, formed separate national factions in 1911. This erosion of internationalism would also affect other socialist parties in Europe and culminate in their rallying to their respective fatherlands in 1914. Still, the Social Democrats in the Habsburg monarchy were among the most ardent supporters of a multinational empire. The ascendancy of radical German nationalism in the Vienna parliament is illustrated by the fact that the German-National Association, a fusion of the aggressively nationalistic and antisemitic Pan-Germans and the German People's Party, became the largest grouping in 1911. Due to the introduction of universal suffrage in 1907, the Social Democrats became the second strongest camp, which, along with the growing trade unionism, was an expression of the political emancipation of the working class. In third place was the conservative and antisemitic Christian-Social Party.

The ruling German elites in the Austrian half of the Habsburg Empire considered the nationalities problem as being even more perilous than the one posed by Social Democracy. Here, the Czech question was the most explosive of all. In 1900, German-speakers counted for 27.9 per cent of Moravia's population, and in Bohemia there were as many as 37.3 per cent.[19] Some areas – the so-called Sudetenland – were predominantly German, others were predominantly Czech, and others again had more equally mixed populations. Due to Bohemia's advanced stage of industrialization, and to the emergence there of a nationally conscious and economically powerful bourgeoisie, its Czech-speakers were no longer willing to play second fiddle in cultural and political affairs. On the eve of the war, there was still discrimination against the Czech language. Its partial emancipation had been enacted in 1880, when Czech joined German as one of Bohemia's two official languages. However, only those villages and towns with a substantial Czech population were administered bilingually. While primary schooling was undertaken in the respective mother tongue, provision for Czech at secondary level was much less satisfactory. Whereas, in the 1850s, Bohemian cities such as Prague had still been dominated by Germans, they became increasingly Czech towards the end of the century. In 1882, a Czech university seceded from the germanophone Charles University in Prague. The Bohemian Diet, which met in the same city, had a Czech majority, but many issues (including limitations on bilingual administration) were decided by the Reichsrat in Vienna. Proposals to give the Czechs autonomy comparable with that enjoyed by the Hungarians were fiercely resisted by Magyars and Germans alike. For similar reasons, the efforts made in the 1890s by the Austrian government to appease increasingly aggressive Czech nationalism by conceding fuller linguistic emancipation also proved unsuccessful.

In the 1870s, this national movement had split into two factions: the Old Czechs and Young Czechs. The former followed the conciliatory Austro-Slav policy mapped out by the Bohemian historian František Palacký. He had advocated turning the Habsburg Empire into a federation of eight states, each with its own diet, and giving equal rights to all the major nationalities. The failure to bring about a compromise between Czechs and Germans furthered the rival cause of the radical-nationalist Young Czechs who, from the 1890s onwards, dominated the political scene in Bohemia. They wanted to be liberated from the Habsburg straightjacket: some stood for an uncompromising Pan-Slavism under Russian leadership; many, however, followed the ideology of Neo-Slavism developed by Tomáš Masaryk. This aimed at bringing Czechs and Slovaks (the latter being under Magyar control) into a single state, which would be loosely associated with a Russia that would serve as a protective power against both Austria and Germany. The intransigence of the Young Czechs often led to riotous scenes in the parliament in Vienna, but it was also coupled with a certain realism. In 1909 Masaryk acknowledged that a federal arrangement was the only solution to the Czech question, as full independence was not a viable option for a people living next to a powerful Germany and having so many ethnic Germans in its own midst.[20] As for the latter, their fear of losing hegemony within the Czech lands made many of them adopt a fiercely nationalistic stance. For some, this meant embracing a Pan-Germanism that was hostile to the Habsburg monarchy and looked towards Berlin instead. This developed in other parts of Austria, too, and won the support of the young Adolf Hitler.

The nationality issue was also potential dynamite in the Hungarian-controlled part of the empire. Here the Magyars constituted the 'state people', even while forming barely half the population. The 1910 census recorded the major nationalities as follows: Magyar 48.1 per cent; Romanian 14.1 per cent; German 9.8 per cent; Slovak 9.4 per cent; Croat 8.8 per cent; Serb 5.3 per cent.[21] In 1868, the year after the Austrian-Hungarian *Ausgleich*, there had been a similar 'compromise' within Transleithania involving Hungary and Croatia-Slavonia. A Croatian Diet was created, but the leader of this provincial assembly was appointed by the emperor on the proposal of the Hungarian government. The subsequent policy of Magyarization throughout the Hungarian sphere of power made this 'compromise' a dead letter. Two-thirds of the population of Croatia-Slavonia were Croats, a quarter were Serbs; although their languages were very similar, Croats were Catholic and considered Serbs, with their Orthodox allegiance, as not belonging to the Occident. Common to both Croats and Serbs was their antagonism towards Hungary. The Serbs within the empire could also look outwards to the independent kingdom of Serbia as a national reference point. The Romanians in Transylvania and the Slovaks were given an even rougher deal in terms of disrespect towards their languages and cultures.

Transleithania had its own parliament and its own government, headed by a prime minister who was appointed by the Emperor Franz Joseph, acting here essentially as King of Hungary. In matters purely domestic to that part of the empire, the government made decisions that were approved by parliament and sanctioned by the monarch. The latter's position was also strengthened by the fact that no legislative proposal could be formally debated without his prior permission.[22] The Upper House of parliament was firmly in the hands of the aristocracy. Aided by gerrymandering, electoral laws with built-in property qualifications, rigging of elections, and blatant discrimination against the other nationalities, the Lower House was dominated by Magyars both from the landed aristocracy and gentry and, to a far lesser extent, from the slowly emerging middle classes. Although the latter were gaining more economic and financial clout, this was not directly translated into political power. Many within the middle classes were assimilated Jews: in the bigger cities, such as Budapest, they constituted over 20 per cent of the population, and the Hungarian *haute bourgeoisie* included a number of them who had been ennobled and who had acquired huge estates.[23]

Despite their powerful position in the empire, the Magyars generally thought of themselves as being oppressed; conversely, Austro-Germans deplored the Hungarians' overbearing impact on the Dual Monarchy.[24] It is fair to say that the Magyars were not unduly kept down. The only area where their influence was wanting was the army, which acted as an independent power within Transleithania. Until the 1980s, Hungarian historians spoke of the economic colonization of their country through Austro-German capital. Recently, however, a more positive interpretation of the economic benefits and disadvantages of the economic union has emerged, pointing out that both halves of the empire profited – an assessment now endorsed by most scholars.[25] Although there was not much love between Magyars and Austro-Germans, Hungary was only too aware of the great number of Slavs within Transleithania and beyond its borders in Eastern Europe, who were backed by the great power of Russia. Therefore the Magyar elites saw no alternative to the Habsburg Empire as a guarantor of Hungary's position and of their own power base in one half of the monarchy.[26]

Although the vast majority of non-Magyars were hostile to Hungary because they opposed political, economic, social and cultural discrimination, they still remained loyal to the Habsburg dynasty.[27] National antagonisms were also not clear-cut, as the case of Croatia-Slavonia illustrates. Two-thirds of its population were Croat and a quarter were Serb; while there were strong religious-cultural differences (Catholic versus Orthodox) between Serbs and Croats, the similarity of their languages and their common resistance to the Magyars formed a strong bond. Still, the Croatian nobility was attached to the Habsburg dynasty because this guaranteed their hegemony both over the Serbs and over their own peasants. A different situation prevailed in Transylvania, where, despite Magyarization, large sections of the Romanian population were apathetic and no organized opposition emerged.

Hungary was opposed to 'trialism' – the solution that would threaten the Magyar position by acknowledging the Southern Slavs as a third ethnic elite within the empire. In response, the Croats increasingly turned towards the independent kingdom of Serbia. This domestic development assumed international significance with the Bosnian Crisis of 1908–09, which threatened to escalate into general war and which pitted Austria-Hungary (backed by Germany thanks to the Dual Alliance) against Russia and Serbia. Bosnia and Herzegovina (where Serbs comprised 40 per cent of the population) had been occupied and administered by Austria-Hungary since 1878. The Habsburg regime became increasingly keen on a formal annexation, not least due to a desire to demonstrate that the monarchy was still strong enough to survive and even expand. Initially, the Russians were willing to play along, provided they were given free passage for their war fleet through the Dardanelles between the Mediterranean and the Black Sea. The Austro-Hungarians, backed by the Germans, got what they wanted, but the Russians did not. The ensuing international crisis not only further alienated Germany and Austria-Hungary from Russia, but also brought the Dual Monarchy into conflict with Serbia. The latter was harbouring hopes of uniting all the Southern Slavs of the Balkans into one state under its leadership, and of thus detaching Slovenes, Croats and Habsburg Serbs from the Dual Monarchy. It was this Southern Slav question that triggered World War One.

There had been several suggestions about how to tackle the Southern Slav problem and the other nationalistic antagonisms within the Habsburg Empire. Many of the so-called Austro-Marxists of the Social Democratic Party called for a federalism based on ethnicity rather than on the historic crown lands.[28] The Social Democrat Karl Renner did not want a federation of nation-states, but advocated instead a separation of territory (concerned with the rights and duties of a territorial citizen) and nationality (focused on cultural and educational requirements).[29] The idea of a 'United States of Greater Austria' in the form of 16 autonomous provinces, drawn up along ethnic lines, was put forward in 1906 by the Romanian jurist and politician Aurel Popovici. He was connected to the circle around the Archduke Franz Ferdinand, who advocated a compromise with the Slavs. As heir to the Habsburg throne, the latter aimed particularly at reducing the privileged position of Hungary and blocking its policy of subjugating the Transleithanian Slavs. The archduke's vision of trialism would have involved an autonomous Southern Slav state within the Habsburg Empire. This plan went counter to the Serbs' dream of leading their own union of Southern Slavs. This seems the main reason for Franz Ferdinand's assassination in Sarajevo in 1914. But it is worth noting that most Austro-Germans and Magyars were also resistant to trialist pressures that might have endangered their own hegemony.

It is uncertain whether the Habsburg Empire was close to break-up in 1914. Expectations of a possible dissolution were widespread: the German Emperor did not have a high opinion of the Dual Monarchy, and even some members of the Habsburg dynasty feared its collapse.[30] On the eve of war, there were signs of both crisis and consolidation. What is clear, however, is that Austria-Hungary had serious nationality problems and that its economic backwardness had not diminished. In 1911 it produced only one-fifth of the coal and one-sixth of the steel achieved by Germany's output.[31] Ultimately, it was the decision to attack Serbia and risk partaking in a world war that proved its downfall.[32] The gamble was grounded in fears that the empire might crumble under the weight of the nationality issue; Russia's support for the Habsburg Slavs was seen as a huge threat, and firmness against Serbia as the troublemaker in the Balkans was considered a necessity. In the July crisis of 1914 Austria-Hungary could also draw on the unconditional backing of the recently formed German Empire.

The Centre: (ii) the German empire

The Centre of Europe has long been its Germanic heartland, the crossroads of West and East, North and South. Until 1871, however, it had not constituted a united nation-state. Even then, this new creation did not include within its borders all those who, by virtue of their language, were normally defined as 'Germans'. Most notably, the new Reich left out the Austro-Germans. None the less, it became an increasingly powerful and militaristic state in the heart of Europe, one that engendered antipathy and fear among all its neighbours – most notably France, which was resentful of the recent German annexation of Alsace-Lorraine. Thanks to Bismarck's 'blood and iron' policies, it was a Prussian-dominated Reich that glorified the national principle and the role of the military. At the time, the famous philosopher Nietzsche warned of a growing hubris, which viewed the establishment of the new Reich as the triumph of German *Kultur* over French (Western) *civilisation* – an attitude that, in his opinion, threatened the annihilation of the true German spirit.[33] The Reich was dominated by Protestantism: only a third of its population was Catholic. The 1870s and early 1880s saw the so-called *Kulturkampf*, the (only partially successful) fight of the state against the Catholic Church, with the goal of diminishing the influence of Catholicism in public life. The birth of the new Reich as a result of war was mirrored by the fight against the Reich's presumed 'inner enemies', whether 'nationally unreliable' Catholics allied to the Vatican, or Social Democrats. By the turn of the century, Germany had become a major European economic power: it was at the forefront of many new industries, particularly in the electrical and chemical fields. By 1914, its annual output of steel was 16.24 million metric tons, as compared to Britain's 6.93 million, the Russian Empire's 4.20 million and France's 4.09 million metric tons.[34]

The *kleindeutsch* ('lesser German') Reich that excluded Austria was constructed as a federation under the leadership of Prussia, whose king received (in deference to the other rulers involved) the formal title of 'German Emperor' rather than 'Emperor of Germany'. Its holder, from 1888 until 1918, was Kaiser Wilhelm II. The empire that he headed was a constitutional monarchy, conceived as a federation of princes whose states retained many sovereign rights in the realms of taxation, domestic policing and culture. The largest of the 26 participants were Prussia, Bavaria, Saxony, Hesse, Baden and Württemberg. Prussia comprised some two-thirds of the Reich's territory and contained three-fifths of its total population, and thus was Germany's undisputed leader, with its king assuming the permanent presidency of the federal empire. The Federal Council (Bundesrat) was the formal sovereign body, representing the constituent states; the actual sovereign, especially in the people's eyes, was the emperor, who appointed the Imperial Chancellor as head of the Reich government. Prussia had only 17 out of the Federal Council's 58 votes, but due to the dependence of many of the smaller North and Central German states on its economy, Berlin's hegemony was always guaranteed. The Bundesrat was also part of the legislature, as its agreement, as well as that of the parliament (Reichstag), was essential for the passage of any new law. Only through this route could the emperor exert influence on legislation as, unlike the Habsburg ruler, he did not have a right of veto in this field. This same Federal Council could also dissolve the Reichstag: the threat to use that power was often sufficient to make parliament comply with the wishes of the Imperial government, especially during Bismarck's chancellorship until 1890. The franchise for the Reichstag was surprisingly democratic with its universal and equal male suffrage. But – apart from legislative and budgetary rights – the Reichstag had only limited political power as it could not topple the Imperial government. In that sense, the new empire was a constitutional state, but not a parliamentary one like Britain or France.

The emperor had a powerful position: he appointed both the Imperial Chancellor and the prime minister of Prussia, and generally both offices were in the same hands. As ruler, he was also advised by his personal Civil, Military and Naval Cabinets, all of which deliberated on the highest appointments and were not answerable to parliament. The emperor was the supreme commander of the army and navy, and his military chiefs (unlike ordinary government ministers) always had the privilege of direct access to him. Keen on exercising his own powers to the full, Wilhelm II forced Bismarck to resign in 1890. Thereafter, the Kaiser operated a 'personal regime' devoted to *Weltpolitik*, and to the task of compensating for Germany's late arrival on the international stage. This pattern of governance, however, was not autocratic when compared with his counterparts in Vienna and particularly St Petersburg. Some historians even claim that Wilhelm II's personal rule and authority were fairly limited. They suggest that Wilhelmine Germany had an authoritarian polycratic power structure, composed of various competing protagonists: the Imperial Chancellor; the military leadership; the higher Imperial and Prussian bureaucracy; and the Civil, Military and Naval Cabinets. Still, ultimately they all depended on the emperor; therefore it is not appropriate to speak of a 'weak Kaiser'.[35]

The post-1890 period was marked by a growing nationalism, the build-up of armaments, colonial projects, anti-British naval policies, ostentatious militarism, and a foreign policy that was determined by fears of encirclement. Germany's backing of Austria-Hungary over the Bosnian annexation, its sabre-rattling in the two Moroccan crises, its role in the European arms race, and, last but not least, its enormous population growth and economic success, created anxieties on the part of Britain, France and Russia, all of which viewed the Reich as a threat to the balance of power. In this context, some historians have highlighted Germany's particular domestic situation, speaking of 'social imperialism' as a manipulative technique. They argue that this was used by the Imperial government, and by the hegemonic elites behind it (especially the landowning aristocrats and the leaders of heavy industry), as a means of diverting into an assertive foreign policy the energies otherwise liable to be spent on domestic squabbles about the need for political and social change. The concept of 'social imperialism' forms part of the wider *Sonderweg* theory, which claims that Germany's history took a 'separate path' in the nineteenth and early twentieth centuries, especially when seen from a 'Western' perspective – a path that facilitated the coming to power of Hitler. Crudely put, Germany's failed bourgeois revolution of 1848 meant that, unlike in Britain and France, the middle classes underwent a process of 'feudalization'. This made them acquiescent about the rule of aristocratic, pre-industrial elites in the new Reich, and thus led them to abstain from fighting for a parliamentary regime while focusing instead on advancing their own economic interests. The authoritarian structures of Imperial German society – so the theory concludes – survived the collapse in 1918 and paved the way for Hitler.[36]

The *Sonderweg* thesis has attracted both acclaim and criticism from historians. It has certainly shed new light on Imperial Germany's sociopolitical structures. In domestic terms, the Wilhelmine Reich was not an autocratic state like Russia. However, its constitutionalism was not of a liberal kind, but one with authoritarian or (if one makes sufficient allowance for some progressive forces) semi-authoritarian traits. Many members of the political and military elites in the Reich generally, and in Prussia particularly, were aristocrats who stamped their values on the culture of governance. One symbol of the latter was the so-called Junker (member of the landed aristocracy) from the eastern half of Prussia, who managed to keep his power in the political and military realms despite a general decline of economic clout due to the agricultural crisis. This Junker power base was firmly grounded in the three-class franchise for the Prussian Diet, which also slowed the parliamentary advance of Social Democracy. Most members of the Imperial government, and of the federal state governments, were noble; so were the upper ranks of the bureaucracy and military, together with those who generally controlled the Upper Houses of the federal states' diets. Still, especially in the South German states, these diets were more liberal-oriented than the Prussian one. To progressive parts of the population in western and southern parts of Germany, 'East-Elbian' (east of the river Elbe) was a synonym for Prussian Junker authoritarianism and 'Eastern barbarism': they clearly saw within Germany a West–East gradient of civilization. Authoritarian traits included the glorification of the military in civil society, especially among the middle classes; enthusiasm for the navy knew no bounds. Reverence for the state and for its bureaucracy – here a much more autonomous and powerful institution than in Britain or France – was deeply engrained in people's minds. There was a German tradition, moulded by philosophers such as Hegel, that saw the state as a benevolent arbiter of antagonistic social interests and as a provider of reform 'from above' – a stark contrast to the relationship between state and society prevailing in the parliamentary West.[37] Whether this authoritarianism was also fed by a specifically German mentality of submissiveness and strict obedience is questionable, and is too much of a stereotype. While such traits were clearly present in institutions such as the army and the schools, criminality on the part of the lower classes and their strike activity would suggest otherwise. The contention that there was no German tradition of rebellion can also be refuted by countless examples in the revolutionary years of 1830 and 1848–49. But some historians in the 1960s maintained that there was a 'peculiar' German mind – marked by irrationalism, cult of inwardness, glorification of the military, mentality of strict obedience, and contempt for Western political ideas and values – a mind that was very different from the Western one, and that ultimately made 'Hitler' possible.[38] Many proponents of nationalism in Wilhelmine Germany certainly indulged in a kind of hubris: German *Kultur* was seen as superior to the Slavic 'barbarism' of the East and to the materialism and utilitarianism of the West.[39] Romantic notions of the Germans as an organic 'community', rather than a fragmented 'society', fed such a sentiment. However, with respect to the West, hubris and disdain often mixed with a rarely acknowledged admiration for aspects of French *civilisation*, as well as for the ideal of the English gentleman that contributed to Wilhelm II's love–hate relationship with Britain.

In order to create a politically and culturally homogeneous Reich, the Germanization of national minorities within its borders – especially the Poles, but also the Danes and even the German-speaking but Francophile Alsatians – took on an almost missionary zeal. This endeavour was far from unique, as similar processes of national homogenization were at work in the Russian Empire, Austria-Hungary, France and Britain, albeit in varying degrees of intensity. While there was hubris, Germany also had fears of international isolation and possible military inferiority in the long run. Bismarck's towering role in the unification process, and in the first two decades of the new Reich, contributed to a personality cult that reinforced the allure of charismatic leadership. Although the post-1890 period lacked anyone of the same calibre, the Bismarckian 'carrot-and-stick' technique of rule persisted. On the one hand, there was social welfare; on the other, elements tending towards an authoritarian political culture. The latter included attempts to contain *Reichsfeinde* (enemies of the Reich) such as the Social Democrats, threats to the Imperial constitution by means of a military coup to keep the Reichstag in check, repression through censorship, and penal laws on matters such as *lèse-majesté*.

There were also other forces shaping Wilhelmine society. Among these was the growth of trade unionism and of social democracy, which point to processes of social emancipation. Furthermore, due to unification 'from above', and to state policies that guaranteed the rule of law and encouraged industrialization through the homogenization of economic conditions throughout the Reich, the middle classes were assuming a dominant economic and social role. This was especially the case in western and southern parts of Germany, including areas that had been incorporated into Prussia through the Congress of Vienna in 1814–15 and through its victory in the German War of 1866; some of these regions had a liberal tradition, such as the Rhineland. Despite its use of radical rhetoric, even working-class culture was strongly influenced by bourgeois values, which became visible in the network of workers' associations.[40] Some historians see in the phenomenon of *embourgeoisement* a kind of 'bourgeois revolution'.[41] As for the argument highlighting middle-class feudalization, one can counter this with the observation that emulation of aristocratic patterns of behaviour by the wealthy bourgeoisie was widespread in liberal-parliamentarian Britain too. Popular politicization in the Wilhelmine period also increasingly found an outlet in economic and/or nationalistic extra-parliamentary pressure groups, such as the German-National Commercial Assistants' Association, the Society for Germandom Abroad, the Colonial Society, the radical-nationalist Pan-German League, the Navy League and the Army League. Nationalism, imperialism and anti-semitism were growing among the middle classes, notably among the petty bourgeoisie and parts of the intelligentsia. Although heavy industry certainly agitated through the Navy League, radical nationalization was not due to a manipulative 'social-imperialist' strategy 'from above'. Rather, it was an effort of political emancipation, especially on the part of the lower middle classes. Thus they exerted pressure on the Imperial government as well as on the parties of the Right and Centre-Right, which in turn responded by reinforcing the rising aggressive nationalism. On the eve of war the Conservatives (the 'old' Right) did indeed adjust their programme by embracing the radical new Right, so as to stem their electoral decline.[42]

Of particular importance – and a counter-argument to the *Sonderweg* model – is the fact that the Reichstag was gaining in influence due to three factors: through fiscal policies which affected the economic positions of agrarians, consumers and the different industrial sectors; through the rising volume of Imperial legislation due to the requirements of socio-economic homogenization; and through control over the public purse, which was increasingly relevant to Germany's military and naval policies. The 1912 Reichstag elections brought a landslide for the Social Democrats (SPD) and a collapse of the parties of the

Right. The Catholic Centre party (*Zentrum*) had to cede its traditional position as the largest parliamentary faction. The SPD won a third of the votes and gained 110 seats out of 397; it was not just a proletarian party, but attracted a share of opposition votes from the (mostly Protestant) bourgeois intelligentsia, which welcomed its reformist pledges.[43] Subsequently, the Imperial government could not rely on a secure parliamentary power base; instead it had to negotiate with groupings across the political spectrum. These all had widely differing party programmes, reflecting the incompatible interests of their voter clienteles, especially concerning taxes and tariffs. Rather than pulling the strings, the government was under mounting criticism from both Left and Right, as well as from the military and the increasingly powerful radical nationalist and economic pressure groups.[44] There was even a majority in the Reichstag that criticised the government's handling of the 1913–14 Zabern Affair in Alsace, which showed the ruthlessness of the military (backed by Wilhelm II) and, conversely, the cowardice of the civil authorities.

On the eve of war, German society was thus marked by an impasse between forces of progressive change on the one side and, on the other, those stemming both from traditional authoritarianism and from the newer radical-nationalist right dominated by the petty bourgeoisie. Even as the economic success story of the Reich unfolded, the Wilhelmine regime increasingly faced a state of crisis at home. It is small wonder that historians came to see domestic factors as crucial in pushing Germany towards war in 1914.

Conclusion

Our journey from West to East and back to the Centre suggests that there may be some virtue in the stereotypical assessment that rates the first of these regions as possessing a certain 'superiority'. On the eve of war, Britain and France were not confronting insuperable domestic crises. Their liberal parliamentarianism worked well and produced strong nations in both the political and economic sense. In the East, the governance of tsarist Russia was defined by autocracy, and, even in its final phase after 1905, by nothing better than mock constitutionalism. There the empire was in difficulties due to the continuing subjugation of recalcitrant countries such as Poland or Finland, which did not consider themselves as belonging to the East. Russia also found itself in a domestic crisis, due to the fragmentation of society and the misery of workers and peasants. It has been shown that industrialization and 'Western' ideas also served to undermine a regime whose problems were exacerbated by absence of efficient leadership. War as a 'social imperialist' answer to Russia's problems may not have been chosen deliberately, but it was certainly taken into consideration when assessing the international political and military situation in the summer of 1914. In the Centre, the same is true for the multinational Habsburg Empire, even if it could not have embarked on war without Germany's unconditional support. The nationality issue had the potential to push Austria-Hungary to breaking point. Each half of the Dual Monarchy had a constitutional system, but also showed (particularly in the case of Hungary) authoritarian traits. The Austrian Chamber of Deputies was finally elected by universal suffrage, but it exerted no real control over the government and it became ineffective after being paralysed by the national question. Even more obviously in the Centre was Germany, which embodied elements of West and East alike as the forces of progressive change competed with those of militaristic authoritarianism. The Reich also thrived economically, in a manner which suggested that liberal parliamentarianism was not the only way to ensure the triumph of bourgeois prosperity. Like the Russian and Austro-Hungarian Empires, the German one was in a political crisis on the eve of war. The question as to whether these states were propelled into war more through the 'primacy of domestic policy' and 'of social imperialism' than through the 'primacy of foreign policy' remains open-ended. In all three cases, these factors were essentially interdependent.

As for France and Britain, the further they peered eastwards across Europe the more 'uncivilized' did other states appear. Such an attitude did not, however, prevent them from allying with the Russians against the Central Powers. A gradient from West to East was perceived even within Germany, namely by representatives of a more liberal and progressive persuasion. The Reich as the 'heart' of Europe was Janus-faced, displaying characteristics of both West and East, while simultaneously indulging in the sentiment that the German model of state and society was not only 'special', but also superior to any other. The rival claim to distinctiveness, which came, in turn, from Russia, centred on belief in a nation more 'spiritual' than any of its rivals. Even so, the fate of the tsarist Empire was affected profoundly by ideas imported from beyond its western frontier. None proved more decisive than those developed by Marx and Engels, two Germans who spent most of their adult lives in Britain, but who then posthumously inspired Lenin to adapt their ideology for the purposes of undertaking communist revolution in Russia.

All the regimes we have been considering were imperialistic, and their respective alliances contributed to the dynamic that steered them towards war – a struggle seen as a legitimate means of pursuing political objectives. Each of the five powers thought of itself as being in some way 'special', and thus each pursued its own form of *Sonderweg* according to its distinctive historical conditions. Perhaps the most fundamental difference between them was that only one of their histories went on to feature Hitler and the Holocaust. Even so, the shortcomings of the Reich, as gauged by comparison with the West, did not lead inevitably to the German catastrophe of 1933–45: World War One, the defeat of 1918, and the ensuing political and economic problems faced by the Weimar Republic were also vital for the success of Nazism.

Further reading

There are two excellent, easy-to-read surveys on Europe between 1890 and 1914: John M. Merriman, *A History of Modern Europe: From the Renaissance to the Present* (2nd edn, New York: W. W. Norton, 2004) and Eric Hobsbawm, *The Age of Empire, 1875–1914* (London: Abacus, 1994, reprint 2002). Also recommended is Timothy C. W. Blanning (ed.), *The Nineteenth Century: Europe 1789–1914* (Oxford: Oxford University Press, 2000). See also Pamela M. Pilbeam, *The Middle Classes in Europe, 1789–1914: France, Germany, Italy and Russia* (Basingstoke: Macmillan, 1990).

On Britain: Robert Rhodes James, *The British Revolution: British Politics, 1880–1939*, 2 vols, Vol. 1: *From Gladstone to Asquith, 1880–1914* (London: Hamish Hamilton, 1976); Michael Willis, *Reading Historical Documents: Nineteenth-Century Britain, 1815–1914* (Oxford: Basil Blackwell, 1990); John Davis, *A History of Britain, 1885–1939* (Basingstoke: Macmillan, 1999); and Martin Pugh, *The Making of Modern British Politics, 1867–1945* (Oxford: Blackwell, 2002, 3rd edn).

On France: Eugen Weber, *Peasants into Frenchmen: The Modernization of Rural France, 1870–1914* (London: Chatto & Windus, 1977); Robert David Anderson, *France, 1870–1914: Politics and Society* (London: Routledge and Kegan Paul, 1977); Roger Magraw, *France 1815–1914: The Bourgeois Century* (London: Fontana, 1987); Jean-Marie Mayeur and Madeleine Rebérioux, *The Third Republic from its Origins to the Great War, 1871–1914* (The Cambridge History of Modern France, Vol. 4), transl. J. R. Foster (Cambridge: Cambridge University Press, 1987); Robert Tombs (ed.), *Nationhood and Nationalism in France: From Boulangism to the Great War, 1889–1918* (London: HarperCollins Academic, 1991); Theodore Zeldin, *A History of French Passions,*

1848–1945, 2 vols (Oxford: Clarendon, 1993); and Robert Gildea, *France 1870–1914* (2nd edn, London & New York: Longman: 1996).

On Russia and the Tsarist Empire: Hugh Seton-Watson, *The Russian Empire, 1801–1917* (Oxford: Clarendon, 1988 [1967]); Theodore R. Weeks, *Nation and State in Late Imperial Russia: Nationalism and Russification on Russia's Western Frontier, 1863–1914* (DeKalb: Northern Illinois University Press, 1996); Orlando Figes, *A People's Tragedy: The Russian Revolution 1891–1924* (London: Random House/Pimlico, 1996); Peter Waldron, *Between Two Revolutions: Stolypin and the Politics of Renewal in Russia* (London: UCL Press, 1998); John F. Hutchinson, *Late Imperial Russia, 1890–1917* (London/ New York: Longman, 1999); Dominic Lieven, *Empire: The Russian Empire and its Rivals from the Sixteenth Century to the Present* (London: Random House/Pimlico, 2003); Ian D. Thatcher (ed.), *Late Imperial Russia: Problems and Prospects* (Manchester: Manchester University Press, 2005); and Alexander Polunov, *Russia in the Nineteenth Century: Autocracy, Reform and Social Change, 1814–1914* (London: M. E. Sharpe, 2005).

On the Habsburg Empire: Jörg Hoensch, *A History of Modern Hungary, 1867–1994*, transl. K. Traynor (2nd edn; London; New York: Longman, 1996); John W. Mason, *The Dissolution of the Austro-Hungarian Empire, 1867–1918* (2nd edn, London/New York: Longman, 1997); and Alan Sked, *The Decline and Fall of the Habsburg Empire, 1815–1918* (2nd edn, Harlow/London: Longman, 2001). See also Dominic Lieven, *Empire: The Russian Empire and its Rivals from the Sixteenth Century to the Present* (London: Random House/Pimlico, 2003) for a comprehensive understanding of the Balkans.

For Imperial Germany and the discussion of *Sonderweg* the literature is extensive: Hans-Ulrich Wehler, *The German Empire 1871–1918* (Leamington Spa: Berg, 1985); Richard J. Evans (ed.), *Society and Politics in Wilhelmine Germany* (London: Croom Helm, 1978); David Blackbourn and Geoff Eley, *The Peculiarities of German History: Bourgeois Society and Politics in Nineteenth-Century Germany* (Oxford: Oxford University Press, 1984); Katherine A. Lerman, 'Bismarckian Germany and the structure of the German Empire', in Mary Fulbrook (ed.), *German History since 1800* (London: Arnold, 1997), pp. 147–67, and her chapter on 'Wilhelmine Germany', *ibid.*, pp. 199–226; Matthew S. Seligmann and Roderick R. McLean, *Germany from Reich to Republic, 1871–1918: Politics, Hierarchy and Elites* (Basingstoke/ London: Macmillan, 2000); and Wolfgang J. Mommsen, *Imperial Germany, 1867–1918: Politics, Culture, and Society in an Authoritarian State*, transl. R. Deveson (London: Arnold, 1995). Consult also the older literature on the 'German mind', even if the conclusions are too one-sided and general: Hans Kohn, *The Mind of Germany* (London: Macmillan, 1961); Fritz Stern, *The Politics of Cultural Despair: A Study in the Rise of the Germanic Ideology* (Berkeley: University of California Press, 1961); George L. Mosse, *The Crisis of German Ideology: Intellectual Origins of the Third Reich* (New York: Grosset & Dunlap, 1964/London: Weidenfeld & Nicolson, 1966). A radically new historical assessment of Wilhelmine Germany and 'war guilt' was given by Fritz Fischer, *Germany's War Aims in The First World War* (London: Chatto & Windus, 1967) and his *War of Illusions: German Policies from 1911 to 1914*, transl. M. Jackson (London: Chatto & Windus, 1975). Other, more specialized works worth consulting are: Geoff Eley, *Reshaping the German Right: Radical Nationalism and Political Change after Bismarck* (New Haven/London: Yale University Press, 1980); Mark Hewitson, *National Identity and Political Thought in Germany: Wilhelmine Depictions of the French Third Republic, 1890–1914* (Oxford: Oxford University Press, 2000); John C. G. Röl, *The Kaiser and his Court: Wilhelm II and the Government of Germany* (Cambridge: Cambridge University Press, 1994); Mark Hewitson's articles on 'The Kaiserreich in question: constitutional crisis in Germany before the First World War', *Journal of Modern History*, 73 (2001), 725–80, and 'Germany and France before the First World War: a reassessment of Wilhelmine foreign policy', *English Historical Review*, 115 (2000), 570–606. See also Geoff Eley, *From Unification to Nazism: Reinterpreting the German Past* (London: Routledge, 1992); Imanuel Geiss, *The Question of Unification, 1806–1996*, transl. F. Bridgham (London: Routledge, 1997); Peter Alter, *The German Question and Europe: A History* (London: Arnold, 2000); and Reinhard Rürup (ed.), *The Problem of Revolution in Germany, 1789–1989* (Oxford & New York: Berg, 2000).

Notes

1 Robert Gildea, *France 1870–1914* (2nd edn, London/New York: Longman, 1996), p. 31.
2 *Ibid.*, p. 32.
3 Dominic Lieven, *Empire: The Russian Empire and its Rivals from the Sixteenth Century to the Present* (London: Random House/Pimlico, 2003), p. 278.
4 On the topic of *zemstvo* and land captains, see John F. Hutchinson, *Late Imperial Russia, 1890–1917* (London/New York: Longman, 1999), p. 12; Orlando Figes, *A People's Tragedy: The Russian Revolution 1891–1924* (London: Random House/Pimlico, 1996), pp. 53–54.

5 See details on Stolypin's reforms in Alexander Polunov, *Russia in the Nineteenth Century: Autocracy, Reform and Social Change, 1814–1914* (London: M. E. Sharpe, 2005), pp. 223–37; and Peter Waldron, *Between Two Revolutions: Stolypin and the Politics of Renewal in Russia* (London: UCL Press, 1998).

6 Figes, *A People's Tragedy, op. cit.*, pp. 47–49.

7 Polunov, *Russia in the Nineteenth Century, op. cit.*, pp. 213–14.

8 *Ibid.*, p. 232. See also John M. Merriman, *A History of Modern Europe: From the Renaissance to the Present* (2nd edn, New York: W. W. Norton, 2004), p. 816.

9 Figes, *A People's Tragedy*, p. 231–32. See also Theodore R. Weeks, *Nation and State in Late Imperial Russia: Nationalism and Russification on Russia's Western Frontier, 1863–1914* (DeKalb: Northern Illinois University Press, 1996).

10 Figes, *A People's Tragedy, op. cit.*, pp. 248–49.

11 *Ibid.*, pp. 13–24.

12 Hutchinson, *Late Imperial Russia, op. cit.*, p. 69.

13 See discussion in 'Introduction' by Ian D. Thatcher (ed.), *Late Imperial Russia: Problems and Prospects* (Manchester: Manchester University Press, 2005), pp. 1–2; Polunov, *Russia in the Nineteenth Century, op. cit.*, p. 239; Waldron, *Between Two Revolutions, op. cit.*, p. 186.

14 See Alan Sked, *The Decline and Fall of the Habsburg Empire, 1815–1918* (2nd edn, Harlow/London: Longman, 2001), p. 191.

15 John W. Mason, *The Dissolution of the Austro-Hungarian Empire, 1867–1918* (2nd edn, London/New York: Longman, 1997), pp. 12, 86; Lieven, *Empire, op. cit.*, p. 180; Sked, *Decline and Fall, op. cit.*, p. 335.

16 Sked, *op. cit.*, p. 335.

17 Eric Hobsbawm, *The Age of Empire, 1875–1914* (London: Abacus, 1994, reprint 2002), p. 92.

18 Sked, *Decline and Fall, op. cit.*, p. 223.

19 Mason, *Dissolution of the Austro-Hungarian Empire, op. cit.*, p. 86.

20 *Ibid.*, p. 228.

21 *Ibid.*, p. 216.

22 *Ibid.*, pp. 195–97.

23 On the involvement of aristocracy and bourgeoisie in Hungarian politics see Jörg Hoensch, *A History of Modern Hungary, 1867–1994*, transl. K. Traynor (2nd edn, London/New York: Longman, 1996), pp. 27, 32, 37–38.

24 Sked, *Decline and Fall, op cit.*, p. 198.

25 *Ibid.*, pp. 202–5.

26 Lieven, *Empire, op cit.*, p. 175.

27 Hoensch, *History of Modern Hungary, op cit.*, p. 77.

28 Mason, *Dissolution of the Austro-Hungarian Empire, op cit.*, p. 37.

29 On socialist ideas in this regard see Sked, *Decline and Fall, op cit.*, pp. 232–33.

30 *Ibid.*, pp. 233–34.

31 Mason, *Dissolution of the Austro-Hungarian Empire, op cit.*, pp. 23, 88.

32 Sked, *Decline and Fall, op cit.*, p. 273.

33 Friedrich Nietzsche in O. Levy (ed.), *Unzeitgemässe Betrachtungen* (or *Thoughts Out of Season*), Vols 1–2, A. Ludovici and A. Collins (transl.) (Edinburgh/London: Foulis, 1909).

34 Merriman, *A History of Modern Europe, op. cit.*, p. 816.

35 See the discussion by Katherine A. Lerman, 'Wilhelmine Germany', in Mary Fulbrook (ed.), *German History since 1800* (London: Arnold, 1997), pp. 207–14.

36 The first and most prominent proponent of the *Sonderweg* model is Hans-Ulrich Wehler, *The German Empire 1871–1918* (Leamington Spa: Berg, 1985). For a good summary of the *Sonderweg* theory and its criticism, see David Blackbourn and Geoff Eley, *The Peculiarities of German History: Bourgeois Society and Politics in Nineteenth-Century Germany* (Oxford: Oxford University Press, 1984). See also Wolfgang J. Mommsen, *Imperial Germany, 1867–1918: Politics, Culture, and Society in an Authoritarian State*, transl. R. Deveson (London: Arnold, 1995), pp. 163–88, 205–16.

37 See Mommsen, *Imperial Germany, op. cit.*, pp. 207–13.

38 Hans Kohn, *The Mind of Germany* (London: Macmillan, 1961); Fritz Stern, *The Politics of Cultural Despair: A Study in the Rise of the Germanic Ideology* (Berkeley: University of California Press, 1961) George L. Mosse, *The Crisis of German Ideology: Intellectual Origins of the Third Reich* (New York: Grosset & Dunlap, 1964/London: Weidenfeld & Nicolson, 1966).

39 See Mommsen, *Imperial Germany, op. cit.*, chapter 11: 'The spirit of 1914 and the ideology of a German Sonderweg' pp. 205–16.

40 *Ibid.*, pp. 123–24.

41 See Geoff Eley and David Blackbourn, *Peculiarities of German History*; even Wehler now sees in the German unification process an (economic!) victory of the bourgeoisie: H.-U. Wehler, 'The German "Double Revolution" and the Sonderweg, 1848–79', in Reinhard Rürup (ed.), *The Problem of Revolution in Germany, 1789–1989* (Oxford/New York: Berg, 2000), pp. 55–65.

42 See Geoff Eley, 'The Wilhelmine Right: How it Changed', in Richard J. Evans (ed.), *Society and Politics in Wilhelmine Germany* (London: Croom Helm, 1978), pp. 112–35; Geoff Eley, *Reshaping the German Right: Radical Nationalism and Political Change after Bismarck* (New Haven/London: Yale University Press, 1980).

43 On the SPD see Katherine A. Lerman, 'Wilhelmine Germany', *op. cit.*, pp. 201–3; on pressure groups and other parties see Lerman, *ibid.*, pp. 203–7.

44 See Mommsen, *Imperial Germany, op. cit.*, pp. 75–100, especially 98–99.

2 Social and economic developments in Europe, 1890–1939

Pamela Pilbeam

Demographic change

In 1890, Europe dominated the world economy. Its population was still predominantly rural, but industrialization was proceeding rapidly. Political, social and economic frameworks seemed stable, although there was some concern among elites that worker organizations, expanding socialist parties and a growing population might threaten their control. The estimated population of Europe (including Russia) was 274 million in 1850, 423 million in 1900, and nearly 600 million in 1950. In some areas the rate of growth slowed towards 1900, and more noticeably after 1919. More babies were surviving to five years; life expectancy was improving. In France, average life expectancy at birth rose from 47 in 1900 to 60 in 1940. More reliable supplies of food might have helped. Improved water supply and sanitation reduced the virulence of waterborne diseases such as cholera, and some medical advances, particularly smallpox vaccination and the care of TB sufferers, also assisted. However, apart from the measures against smallpox, such improvements came too late to explain the period of fastest growth. Research into changes in the age at marriage and in the size of families has provided no conclusive explanations. Possibly the most significant factor in the shrinking death rate was the chance absence, apart from cholera, of the pandemics encountered in earlier centuries. Up to 1914 the population of the most industrialized nations grew fairly rapidly, 1.1 per cent a year in England and Wales, 1.2 per cent average in the German empire, slightly less elsewhere. The population of the regions that in 1871 became the new German empire grew from 24.5 to 58.5 million between 1800 and 1910, making it the most populous state after Russia.[1]

The growth of urban population was almost entirely due to migration from the countryside. Hence the virtual stagnation of the French population for nearly a century from the 1860s, in a country that possessed one of the most prosperous rural economies and the largest number of peasant landowners, seems illogical. There the total stood around 36.5 million in the mid-nineteenth century and, in 1914, hovered around 40 million, where it remained, despite losses in war and gains in treaties, until after World War Two. Deaths exceeded births in 11 years between 1850 and 1914. Numbers were sustained only by immigration. Russia, on the other hand, with acute land shortages, a famine that in 1891–94 caused 400,000 deaths, and enormous pressure on peasants to export grain in order to buy land, grew from 94.3 million in 1897 to 155.4 million in 1914, when all but 30 million of these were living in the European provinces.

Contemporaries believed that social factors were paramount. The Roman Catholic Church blamed *coitus interruptus* for demographic stagnation in France, but others attributed this to Napoleon's Civil Code of 1804, which decreed equal subdivision of property among surviving children on the death of the father. In France, with over 6 million peasant farmers in the nineteenth century, many units of cultivation risked becoming uneconomic if there were more than two heirs. Émile Zola's novel *The Earth* (1887) graphically describes the murder of one sister by another to avoid the subdivision of their farm.[2] In southern Germany, where the same rules of inheritance prevailed, the population rose very rapidly. The uniqueness of population stagnation in France was also put down to the popularity of wet nursing, a practice vehemently criticised in popular novels such as Victor Hugo's *Les Misérables* (1862). It was traditional for artisan families and those who ran small businesses to send their newborn children to rural wet nurses for up to five years. Many of these progeny died. The Roussel law (1874) ordered (reluctant) doctors to register and inspect wet nurses. Despite a campaign to promote breastfeeding at the turn of the century, wet nursing remained the norm.[3]

Migration

Rapid population growth forced people to migrate in search of work. By 1907, only 50 per cent of Germans lived in their place of birth. Migration was part of European culture: people had been moving to seasonal work, or as a stage in their artisan training, for centuries. Masons from the agriculturally poor Limousin trekked to Paris every spring to work in the building trades, returning to their families only when the weather was too bad for such labour. In the capital, they always congregated in the same lodging houses run by their compatriots.

Many Italian workers, too, spent the summer months employed away from their families. Farmers from a wide range of regions, including Normandy, Brittany and Wales, herded their animals to towns, especially to capital cities, for slaughter, arriving always in the same districts of Paris or London or wherever, *en route* to the meat markets of Les Halles or Smithfield. Towards the end of the nineteenth century, clusters of grocers' shops with Norman or Welsh names sprang up in the vicinity of the meat markets as members of the family settled. The French moved from poorer parts of the rural south to the towns of the north. By 1890, more than half of French departments faced declining numbers. Although seasonal movement did not disappear, there was a tendency for permanent migration to become the norm after the creation of rail networks in the second half of the nineteenth century. Up to the 1880s, many moved but a short distance. Young people left home to work in service, in the expanding bureaucracies, in retail trade and in industry, in both small workshops and factories. Russia experienced massive internal migration, both temporary and permanent. Many of those who crammed into fast-growing urban industrial centres continued to return home to help with the harvest. Russians moved east within the empire, not always willingly. Asiatic Russia housed 30 million by 1914, at least 10 million of whom were first-generation settlers. Only half a million Russians moved abroad between 1911 and 1914.

In addition to movement within countries, there was a huge increase of migration between states, often of single men who left their families back home. Much agricultural work in southern France was done by Italian or Spanish labour. By 1914, there were 1 million foreign workers in France. There were men from Belgium, and even Poland, working in the mines of the north-east. France's borders were porous; foreigners sometimes worked seasonally, returning to their homes in the winter. Some married local women and stayed. Legislation in 1889 encouraged the settlers to become naturalized, in the hope of making up the declining numbers of young Frenchmen in the army. Irish migrants worked in Britain as labourers, often in the building trades. From about 1880, Germany also attracted foreign workers, mostly male, and usually on a seasonal basis. In 1910 there were 1,236,000, mainly Ruthenians, Poles and Italians. Nearly 25 per cent of the population of Herne, a Ruhr mining town, spoke only Polish.[4]

Political oppression, motivated by nationalist notions, uprooted whole communities. In the mid-nineteenth century, two-thirds of the world's Jews lived in Russia. The Tsarist regime forced many into exile, mainly to Germany, France and Britain. The Communists attacked those who remained. During World War Two, the Nazis indulged in an unprecedented racial onslaught, against not only Jews, but also Slavs, gypsies, and anyone else they considered alien.

About 52 million Europeans went overseas between 1815 and 1930,[5] of whom 10 million returned. Their motives were economic or political, or both. Real poverty was not a factor; the very poor could not afford the sea passage, even though Australia, keen to remain British, began to offer free emigration in the 1890s. Migrants generally stayed in close touch with their families, sending money back. There was often a chain response, as relatives joined the earlier settlers and helped to create regional clusters. The British headed the list of emigrants to a variety of destinations with 11.4 million, followed by Italians and Germans. A million Germans left in the decade after the failure of the 1848 revolutions. The economic depression of the 1880s pushed another 1,342,400 more to leave, many for the prairie provinces of North America. By 1914, about 6 million Italians were sending money home, mainly from the USA.

Urban growth and social consequences

Towns grew at an unprecedented rate, crammed with country people who were in the 1890s mostly first-generation residents. Between 1850 and 1900, the number of German towns of 100,000-plus leapt from four (Berlin, Hamburg, Breslau and Munich) to 45, many of which were clustered in the Ruhr heavy industry complex. In 1897, only 14 million Russians were town-dwellers; by 1914, 26 million. The two biggest industrial cities were St Petersburg, the imperial capital with a population of just under 2 million, and Moscow, the capital of the Russian province with 1.5 million. Paris, the centre of French government, industry and culture, was a city of 2.75 million by 1910.

For centuries before unification in 1861, the Italian peninsula had been divided into city states, with long histories as commercial as well as cultural centres. Rome was a city of half a million in 1910, and 1 million by 1931. Most cities were clustered in the north, where in 1910 Milan had 519,000 and Turin 427,000 inhabitants; 13 others contained more than 100,000 people. With the exception of Naples, previously a capital city and still growing fast with 723,000, population change was intensifying the sharp contrast between an industrializing, urban north, and a predominantly agrarian and much poorer south. Mussolini's fascist regime (1922–43) talked in vain about reversing this trend.

Nineteenth-century middle-class Europeans were often horrified by the dirt, squalor and crime of these vastly enlarged cities. Rapid urbanization eventually obliged municipal governments to accept responsibility not only for some planning of transport but also, following the cholera epidemics of 1832, 1849 and 1892, of sanitation and water supply. In Paris, 18,000 died of cholera in 1832. In the 1850s, a model sewage system was developed, as well as the wide boulevards intended to hinder revolutionary uprisings. In 1892, the scandal of 9000 deaths from cholera in Hamburg obliged the city authorities to take charge of sewage. Cities were reworked into socially distinct districts. It became less common for the poor to live in less desirable parts of the same buildings as the better off. Instead, suburbs spread on a basis that segregated the dwellings and factories of the industrial workforce from the more salubrious areas that housed the middle classes, and offered the latter better transport links to their city-centre places of employment.

Demographic consequences of World War One

World War One, subsequent peace treaties, and the revolutions and civil wars in Russia and later in Spain had a huge impact on numbers as well as attitudes. About 10 million men died in the war, and many millions more were permanently injured. Every combatant country emerged from the conflict with a significant gender imbalance. Germany lost 3 million men. Although the French figure was less than half that, it still represented roughly 10 per cent of the country's young males – a devastating drain on a population already ageing on average long before 1914. Russia lost about 3 million to the war itself, and nearly 13 million more to the revolutions, famine and the civil war that ensued (1918–23). In *And Quiet Flows the Don*, the renowned Communist writer Sholokov describes villages petitioning the Communist government for permission to eat babies under the age of one. For Russia as a whole, the total demographic cost of war, famine, influenza and the more speculative calculation of the potential births denied is now calculated as between 20 and 24 million.[6] The war, peace treaties and civil wars also forced large numbers to move. The war eliminated the great dynastic empires of continental Europe: German, Russian and Austro-Hungarian. Collapse of Ottoman rule also soon followed. European borders were drastically revised, to some extent in line with what the peacemakers, especially President Wilson of the USA, thought of as 'national self-determination'. The upheavals left millions in search of a new home. The Russian Civil War forced possibly 7 million to become refugees. The treaties pushed 800,000 Germans back to Germany from the newly reinvented Poland, the Baltic States and Alsace-Lorraine.

During the early 1920s, there was an even larger population transfer involving the removal of more than a million Greeks from Turkey and Thrace together with a reverse flow of some 400,000 Turks. As for the New World, European migration to it fell after 1919. In 1901–10, nearly 15 million had left; between 1931 and 1940, only 1.8 million. In 1924, the USA shut the door to immigrants, apart from restricted quotas mainly concerning Britain and Germany. The World Depression of the early 1930s made former target countries for migration both less attractive and less welcoming. The USSR and Italy blocked emigration. The British government still paid assisted passages of migrants to Australia, New Zealand and Canada, although setbacks to agriculture in Australia meant that some families came back. French economic recovery depended, in part, on continued immigration from Spain, Portugal, Belgium and Poland. By the early 1930s, its immigrant population was around 3 million. In 1929, naturalization procedures were relaxed to allow citizenship to migrants after three years of residence, but the World Depression saw substantial forced repatriation.

Urbanization and its social consequences, 1919–39

Europe continued to become more urban. In 1910, there had been seven cities of 1 million-plus, by 1940 there were 16. In the USSR, the urban population rose from just under 16 to 31.6 per cent between 1920 and 1940, but towns were generally smaller than in the West. Europe's urban belt was still focused mainly on the old industrial areas ranging from northern France and Belgium through the Ruhr/Rhineland to Upper Silesia. The big change was the growth of suburbs and the siting of factories in them, rather than in city centres. Although horses remained important for the movement of such goods as coal, milk, bread and other foodstuffs, the key developments in urban transport now centred on trams, motorized buses and various forms of suburban railway. The London Underground dated from 1862. On the continent, the first similar provision appeared in Budapest in 1896, followed by the Paris Métro in 1900. The Berlin suburban rail network was built between 1924 and 1929, and the state-of-the-art Moscow Metro was completed in 1935.

Building homes helped European economies recover. By 1939, one-third of the housing in Britain postdated 1919. Three million dwellings were built in the 1930s, double the number of the previous decade. Much was private construction. Building societies expanded, interest rates fell from 6 per cent in 1931 to 4.5 per cent in 1935, and longer-term loans helped less well off people begin to own their own homes. The housing boom concentrated on the midlands and south, moving people from the still distressed northern cities. The buyers were mainly lower middle-class. The poor continued to rent, often having to settle for substandard rooms without basic private facilities.

Middle-class critics became concerned that unplanned urban sprawl led to anonymity, anomie and disorder. Fritz Lang's film *Metropolis* (1926) illustrated the bleak isolation of city life. The architect Le Corbusier warned contemporaries of the need to choose between 'architecture or revolution'. Like him, many German colleagues also opted for modernism. In the 1920s, Walter Gropius and the Bauhaus movement stressed 'form follows function' and used modern materials, steel, concrete and glass. In Germany, the hyperinflation of 1919–23 plus rent controls ruled out much private house-building. In the 1920s, two-thirds of the new housing built in Germany was publicly owned and of outstanding quality. A 'monumental' style for public buildings gained ground in totalitarian regimes, for instance in Moscow, and in Germany under the influence of Albert Speer. Speer was also influenced by modernism in his designs for the Berlin Olympic village of 1936. A third trend was the 'garden city' or 'new town', which introduced an idealized rurality. These were built Europe-wide, for example in Welwyn Garden City, Letchworth, Mantes-la-Jolie and Magnitogorsk.

Agriculture and rural society

In 1890 the proportion of people living on and by the land was still considerable; by 1945 the majority was urban in all but the most underdeveloped countries. There were huge variations. In 1910, in France 41 per cent worked the land, 35 per cent in Germany, under 10 per cent in Britain, but up to 75 per cent in Spain and 80 per cent in Bulgaria. Types of landownership and tenure were very varied in 1890. In East Prussia, southern Italy and southern Spain, large estates were the norm. In wheat-producing estates of East Prussia, noble Junker landowners gradually sold out to rich urban middle-class owners; the land was farmed by tenants. The owners of big farms (*latifundia*) in southern Italy and Spain were sometimes absentees and the workers were mainly insecure day-labourers. In Seville, 60 per cent of rural workers were in this tenuous state. Where monoculture, habitually either olives or cereal, prevailed, labourers might be employed for no more than 130 days a year.[7] Small-scale peasant agriculture predominated in much of France, although the nobility still owned 20 per cent of the land. Small farms persisted in southern and western Germany and north and central Italy. Many peasants also rented patches of land. The status of tenants varied enormously. Around the Paris basin, wealthy tenant farmers produced wheat for the market, whereas sharecroppers in the poorer lands further south struggled to survive. Elsewhere, there were huge mixed areas in Russia, Poland, Hungary, Austria and Bohemia.

Before 1914, falling agricultural prices made life tough for poor rural families as arable farming declined in profitability. Prairie and Russian wheat imports brought a dramatic fall in price, for instance in Great Britain from 126.5 to 69.9 grams of silver per hundred kilograms between 1871–80 and 1891–1900. Cheaper bread could have been a blessing to labourers; high food prices had brought much distress and upheaval among the poor earlier in the century. Unfortunately, cheap wheat also reduced rural wages, rents and land prices. Most governments, apart from Britain, which relied on its world financial dominance, responded with tariff walls to try to protect domestic production. As always, the poorest suffered most acutely. Richer landowners could diversify, buying estates overseas, in Australia, South America and elsewhere, or acquiring profitable business investments and directorships. Large tenant farmers in Britain and northern France could turn from wheat to dairying or other food crops in demand in urban areas, which could now be easily reached by rail. Small farmers might opt for market gardening if they were near a town. Otherwise they struggled to form cooperatives to buy fertilizers and tools.

Labourers sometimes moved to jobs in industry, notably in Germany, Britain and France. Those in less developed areas banded together to strike, with slightly more success in Italy than in Spain, but to no avail in Hungary, where 40 per cent of the agricultural population were landless labourers. A cheaper immigrant workforce, or indeed machines, took over. In some areas, animal-rearing or dairying replaced arable. Military service, which became ubiquitous, and which the poor could not avoid, at least meant one less mouth to feed. Increasing pressure to send children to school would have seemed less of an economic loss than in the past.

Russian peasants endured terrible privations. Emancipation in the 1860s had made them personally free, but obliged them to buy land their families had often farmed for generations. Half of noble-owned land was sold at emancipation, and half of the remainder had been disposed of by 1914. Peasants were obliged to take 49-year loans from a new Peasant Land Bank to buy communal holdings. Government reformers, fearful of the repetition of rural unrest, which had wracked the rest of Europe earlier in the century, partly as a result of the sale of communal land to individuals, dictated that the purchased land would then be owned by the village community or *mir*, not the peasant family. The dramatic rise in population put intense pressure on cultivable land, which, despite the vast size of Russia, was itself limited. Peasant participation in the 1905 revolution led to the abolition of redemption payments. Families who had already completed their payments could own their land outright. By 1916, a mere 6 million slightly more prosperous peasants had taken advantage of these decrees,[8] but the deprivation of the increasingly large number of landless peasants grew worse.

Impact of World War One on rural society

World War One brought chaos to the Russian countryside when traditional scorched-earth policies failed to halt the relentless advance of the German armies, which occupied all of Russian Polish land, and Russia itself as far as the Ukraine. After the February 1917 revolution, peasants, particularly the 16 million drafted to fight in the war, demanded land. When the provisional government hesitated and tried to continue the war effort, soldiers deserted in huge numbers and divided noble estates among themselves. In October 1917, the Bolsheviks seized power in alliance with peasants, promising to confirm their titles to the land they had taken. Instead, a month later, the Bolsheviks nationalized the land and deemed the farms of the nobles to be state property.

During the ensuing civil strife, 'war communism' meant peasants ran their holdings, but subject to draconian state requisitioning of grain. Many sold on the black market or refused to cultivate. In 1921, Lenin was forced to backtrack with a New Economic Policy (NEP), which promised peasants control of the land and their produce. Cultivation resumed, but rural social stratification intensified as the better-off peasants, reviled by Lenin as political enemies or *kulaks*, became the key producers. Conscious of the power a market economy would give the peasants, in 1928 Stalin introduced a state-run command economy, 'Socialism in One Country'. All rural land was collectivized, leaving only tiny allotments for individual cultivation. *Kulaks* were violently ejected, and those who resisted were rounded up into distant prison camps. Many dissident peasants slaughtered their animals rather than join collectives. The land was turned back into huge estates managed by party members, often with few rural skills. Some Bolsheviks argued that the solution lay in large-scale cultivation and mechanization, but machinery was in short supply. All peasants became landless labourers.

Up to 1914, Russia had been one of the bread baskets of the rest of Europe, supplying 25 per cent of its wheat imports. War, revolutions and civil war brought dearth and starvation, compounded by the devastating impact of collectivization. The USSR was unable to feed itself. The command economy meant that the Communists paid low prices and wages to the farmers, while attempting to focus resources on industrial growth. Sholokov's novels portraying collectivization, including *Virgin Soil Upturned* (1932), made the human misery tangible.

The impact of World War One on farmers elsewhere in Europe varied. Nearly 11 of France's departments, including some of its most productive arable land, were occupied by the Germans for all but the last few weeks of the war. Two million people were evacuated from the occupied departments, to spend the war as unwelcome guests in other parts of France. Otherwise, farming families generally prospered as food prices rose. Returning soldier-peasants often found their wives had amassed enough money to add to their small farms and buy new equipment. In Italy, the bulk of the soldiers were rural labourers, who believed government promises to give them land when the conflict was over. Returning soldiers, particularly the southerners, followed the example of the Russian peasants and in the 'two red years' of 1919–20 tried to break up the big estates and seize land. Politicians from the left and right alike made them unrealizable promises. In power from October 1922, Mussolini promised to make Italy self-sufficient in wheat, and attempted to boost production by schemes such as the draining of the Pontine marshes.

The deaths of so many Europeans, and the poverty of others, actually meant a big hole in the global market for primary products. Wheat prices slid from US$2.10 a bushel in 1924–25 to US$1.15 in the spring of 1929.[9] The prices of rubber, cotton, sugar and coffee followed the same trend, cutting the ability of primary producer areas to buy manufactured goods. The problem was exacerbated by bumper harvests in 1928. The closely interrelated World Depression, which was set off by the Wall Street Crash of October 1929, brought prices of all commodities tumbling down. Everywhere, the small farmer suffered. In 1933 Darré, Nazi agriculture minister, promised to make small peasant farms inalienable, but to little effect. As in Italy, it was the big farmer who commanded the attention of the government. In France in 1936, a left-wing Popular Front government of Socialists and Radicals, supported from the sidelines by the Communists, set up a Wheat Office to try to halt the collapse of agricultural prices, but with little success. When Spain became a republic in 1931, an Agrarian Reform Law was passed that set an eight-hour day for labourers and tried to make it easier for tenants of small plots to buy their land. Big landowners responded by 'eating the Republic'; in Seville, 66,000 hectares of land were left uncultivated. When the Spanish Popular Front government came to power to combat fascism at home and abroad, the agricultural workers' union mobilized 60,000 people to seize 3000 estates.[10] In 1936, a military-led rebellion against the republic set off a violent struggle over land. After three punishing years of civil war, the Franco state attempted to control the grain market, with disastrous results. Everywhere in Europe the interests of the rural poor went unheard as governments focused on heavy industry, particularly armaments, to pull their countries out of the World Depression.

The totality of warfare in World War Two, with heavy bombing and submarine warfare blocking imports, meant that food shortages became desperate. Rural areas were subject to unprecedented government regulation. In Britain, volunteer 'land girls' filled the gap left by men gone to war, and the population was relatively lucky to receive 2 oz of butter and cheese and half a pound of maggot-infested bacon a week. Public parks, such as Hampstead Heath, were divided into allotments to grow vegetables. For European agriculture at large, World War Two was a turning point. The lesson learned by governments was the need to promote more efficient productivity, which would require more mechanization, bigger units and a shrinking farming population.

Industrial change to 1914

Around 1890, the basic industries of the first 'industrial revolution', coal, iron and textiles, were still dominant. However, particularly in Germany, the development of chemical engineering and of steel processing accelerated. Europe was beginning to use oil and electricity alongside coal as sources of power, as well as enlarging its machine-tool capabilities and offering a wider range of industrial products (such as bicycles and typewriters) for mass consumption.

Rural industry, which had grown rapidly earlier in the century, declined. Although small family producers and artisan firms were still numerous in 1890, the large urban factory increasingly prevailed. Big firms were still family-dominated. In Britain, where company legislation favoured the continuance of family control, 80 per cent of firms were still privately owned in 1914. In Germany, family-led firms were able to secure investment from banks, but vertical concentration was leading to the growth of gigantic trusts such as Krupps, which by 1907 employed nearly 65,000 in steel, engineering and munitions.

The role of the state in economic development ranged from tariff and tax policies, as found particularly in France, to ones involving even more direct management. Before 1914, railways were taken over by the state in Germany, Russia, Austria, Hungary, Italy and Belgium. Governments intervened most in the less developed East European economies, where capital was scarce. In the Russian case, Witte – who as finance minister was particularly aware of the need for rapid modernization, as well as being fearful lest domestic investment from the small middle class might weaken Tsarist control – offered from 1892 competitive interest rates to attract loans from foreign banks. Between then and 1914, 60 per cent of industrial investment, concentrated first on a rail network to facilitate grain exports, came from abroad – chiefly from France, but also from Germany and Britain. Foreign engineers and managers were employed to run the huge factories and mines that emerged. Former peasants were recruited as workers and lived in barracks at the factories.

Foreign investment was crucial to industrial development elsewhere, especially in other parts of eastern Europe. Over half of German foreign investment in the years before 1914 was concentrated on its ally, Austria-Hungary, which relied on its neighbour for over 40 per cent of the capital for growth, notably in the coal and chemical industries of Bohemia. In 1914, almost the whole of Romania's oil industry was foreign-owned. In these years, when domestic markets were deemed to be near saturation, the main European industrial nations, Britain, Germany and France, became convinced that investment overseas was vital to their economic growth.

Although the USA was becoming a serious rival, world trade was still dominated by North-West Europe. Between 1900 and the outbreak of World War One, world trade doubled. European countries traded most with each other. Britain was the only European state that exported more to the rest of the world, and it was also Germany's best customer. France was dependent on its neighbours for nearly all the coal its industries consumed. The Ruhr imported nearly 60 per cent of the steel it smelted, mainly from Sweden and France. Britain exported coal to Germany. Although the European economies were competitive, and the British worried, with reason, that Germany had taken the lead by 1914, there was a close web of interdependence.

Workers' organizations

The proportion of the population defined as industrial workers increased, most dramatically in northern and western Europe, and in

Britain almost doubling between 1851 and 1914 to 18.4 million. In the same period, the agricultural sector in Britain dropped from 22 to 8.2 per cent of total labour. By 1907, 66 per cent of German workers were industrial wage-earners, whereas in France over 60 per cent of the working population were still employed on the land in 1914. There were five million working in French industry by 1914, but even in 1896, 88 per cent of firms were artisanal, employing no more than five workers.

Factory industry meant workers had no protection against sickness and unemployment. Workers banded together in organizations, ranging from traditional mutual aid or friendly societies to retail cooperatives and trade unions. The degree to which these were accepted by employers and governments varied hugely. In Britain, tolerable prosperity and the dominance of organizations run by moderate, highly skilled workers facilitated gradual, wary acceptance. France, with a long tradition of mutual aid societies, but also one of worker participation in revolution (1830, 1848, 1871) and some enthusiasm for Proudhon's anarchist notions, had governments that were more nervous. There, unions were legal from 1884, but strikes met violent military resistance. In Russia, unions were illegal, apart from a brief period after the 1917 revolutions. The first labour legislation in Russia in 1886 decreed imprisonment for those who organized or took part in strikes.

Skilled male workers took the initial lead in organizing trade unions in the traditional heavy industries. From the 1890s, unions developed among the highly skilled male workers in shipbuilding, engineering, mining, metallurgical and machine-building trades, including motor car production. Mechanization led to bitter strikes as workers fought against the elimination of their craft status and income. In 1897–98 in Britain, the Amalgamated Society of Engineers struck over new machine tools. In France, file-makers took similar action at St Étienne in 1910–11. Gradually, unskilled and semi-skilled men also began to form their own separate groups. In 1889 in Britain, gas workers and dockers went on strike.

By 1914, in both Britain and Germany, 4 million workers belonged to trades unions, which tolerated each other and operated within the parliamentary system, as was the case for instance with Kier Hardie and the Labour Party. In Germany, unions were closely linked to the *Sozialdemokratische Partei Deutschlands* (Social Democratic Party, SPD). Ninety per cent of its members were workers, and by 1914 it was the largest single grouping in the Reichstag. Close worker unity in Germany was partly a reaction to persecution between 1878 and 1890, when the SPD had been banned. In France, in contrast, unions and the socialist groups were mutually antagonistic. Although the majority of the million union members in France in 1914 were affiliated to the *Confédération générale du travail* (CGT, General Confederation of Labour), founded in 1895, this organization remained implacably hostile to the now united *Section Française de l'Internationale Ouvrière* (SFIO, French Section of the Workers' International). Unionism in France embraced a Proudhonist (federalist/anarchist) as well as a Marxist tradition. Although the SFIO included Marxist revolutionary notions, the unions argued that it did not represent their interests because a large proportion of its voters were white-collar workers, especially teachers, and its members of parliament were professional men, with a preponderance of lawyers. By 1914, there were 100 SFIO deputies in parliament. There were also 50 independent socialists. In Italy, the *Partito Socialista Italiano* (PSI, Italian Socialist Party), founded in 1892, was even more fragmented, but was well represented in parliament, although hostile to such 'bourgeois' institutions. No European governments included socialists before 1914.

By 1914, only a minority of workers belonged to trade unions. No foreign workers were welcome. In 1900, in Britain, no more than 40 per cent of workers were unionized, and even these were dispersed across more than 1200 different unions. Friendly societies had far more members, 7 million by 1914, but they were merely insurance schemes. Cooperative retail organizations, whose shops provided members with beneficial prices for food and household items, had 2.4 million members by 1905. They included a Women's Cooperative Guild.[11] In France, *bourses du travail* were set up by the government in 51 major towns to coordinate matters of concern to workers, especially employment, but also to try to moderate union demands.

Women workers

How did women fit into this changing world of work? For most, little altered; the largest number were still girls in domestic service in towns, striving to save up for marriage. The next biggest element were in agriculture, often unpaid, working in family units. What changed, and brought women workers into conflict with men, was that as traditionally highly skilled trades, such as clothing, footwear and potteries, were increasingly mechanized, they could manage with growing numbers of cheap, semi-skilled female operatives. Women also were taking low-paid clerical jobs in state and private organizations and in primary school teaching. By 1914 in Britain, the majority of primary school teachers were female. In 1866, 30 per cent of French workers were women; by 1906, 38 per cent. By 1903, the dominant power looms in the Lyon silk industry were 95 per cent female-operated. In the ready-made clothing trades, the newly invented sewing machine, light and easily operated by women, eliminated much of the hand-sewing and finishing previously done by highly skilled male tailors. In the early 1900s, a woman would be proud to work for a mere 5 shillings a week as a man's tailor, struggling to buy her own Singer treadle sewing machine, because the title of 'man's tailor' still carried status.

Women figured in the exponential growth of the new department stores. They joined the sales staff; female employees were cheap and tractable, in Britain in 1900 earning only 65 per cent of a man's wage, and working in excess of a 60-hour week.[12] The stores themselves were sometimes founded by husbands and wives in partnership, who had both worked their way up from the shop floor. Such a couple were the Boucicauts, who founded *Le Bon Marché* in Paris. Department stores, together with their catalogues and delivery services, were also an insidious element in the development of a consumer culture appealing to better-off women. The stores, with their polite staff, artistic displays and numerous counters, were a 'respectable', safe environment in which middle-class women were offered an alternative to religion. They were turned into consumers, idling the day, spending their husband's earnings. Stores like *La Samaritaine*, founded by the Cognacqs, another couple of humble origins, also surrounded themselves with a philanthropic and paternalistic aura. In 1914, the Cognacqs made their employees partners in the store. The Boucicauts provided accommodation, restaurants, education and leisure activities for their employees, within which the female element were the most 'protected', living in almost feudal 'comfort' on the upper floors of the store.[13] The lady shoppers could persuade themselves that they were contributing not just to the expansion of a capitalist enterprise, but also to a caring and charitable endeavour. Department stores did not cater just for the rich. They made consumerism available to the rapidly expanding middle and lower-middle classes. Their catalogues taught less well-off women how to dress and equip their homes in bourgeois style. Regular 'sales' convinced the gullible they were saving money. The shop girls, kitted out in decorous black gowns, were living proof that social graces could be learned.

Some traditional retail businesses were displaced by the new stores, a transition portrayed in Zola's novel of 1883, *Ladies' Delight* (*Au Bonheur des Dames*). However, the massive expansion in consumer goods generated by department stores often allowed independent shopkeepers to survive, especially in France. The small, specialist workshops of

Paris, which served a specifically luxury market for such items as furniture, clothes and jewellery, were sometimes busier than ever, but often now dependent on department stores for orders.

Enterprising women might turn the front room of their rented terrace house into a food shop when they started their family and could no longer manage factory work. Nearly every street in British industrial towns acquired such a shop, selling everything from bacon and washing soda to barley sugar sticks and patent medicines. The start-up cost was tiny and, if things went well, the family might begin to buy the property. The husband might leave the factory and acquire a small pony and cart to sell things himself, in industrial areas probably coal. From around the 1880s, these little shops became numerous. Working mothers or their children could reach them easily; their range of goods eventually included sterilized milk and wrapped bread (undercutting home deliveries); and some agreed to allow credit ('tick') until the next pay day, or operated as informal pawn shops when the money did not materialize. Families registered their ration books with them in World War Two, but the absence of things to sell during wartime and the development of cheaper cooperative shops often forced them to metamorphose back into houses after 1945. They can still be traced by the different shape of the front window. Statistics tell us that in Britain in 1911 there were 8 per cent fewer women workers doing semi-skilled jobs than 30 years earlier, but they do not reveal how many had become shopkeepers.

New semi-skilled jobs often made life worse for women workers. Men, who had defended the women in their family team, fought against them when they undercut men for work. Male workers encouraged restrictions on female employment and would strike to try to prevent women taking their jobs. In France, legislation in 1892 restricting the hours and conditions of female workers in factories forced seamstresses and others to decline into unprotected 'sweated' outworkers. Female workers earned little and had homes and families to care for, and thus little spare time or money to join mutual aid societies or the newer trade unions. Before 1914, fewer than 9 per cent of German trade union members were female.

Social welfare and worker society

Employers sometimes organized welfare schemes, such as that at Le Creusot and Decazeville, where schools, creches, houses, stores, clinics and pension funds were set up. By around 1900, 600,000 French male workers were covered by employer pension schemes, but workers resented the hold such paternalism gave employers. A protesting worker would risk his pension, if not his job. In Germany, the state began to take over private insurance schemes in the 1880s. Although this was initially a ploy by Bismarck to snuff out the fast-growing socialist vote, it helped to enable German workers to become the best protected in Europe. In Italy, in 1900, following nearly a decade of unrest and violent but ineffectual repression, Giolitti introduced state-organized sickness benefit, old-age pensions and legislation restricting child and female working, but these measures did not stop the escalation of strikes. British employers resisted state provision. The Workmen's Compensation Law (1897) made employers responsible for accidents at work. An Old Age Pensions Act of 1908 provided some money to elderly persons having less than 10 shillings a week to live on. The National Insurance Act (1911) ordered friendly societies to administer worker insurance, including sickness benefit based on voluntary deductions from wages. However, one-third of workers received nothing. The French also hesitated to set up state systems. In 1898, an Industrial Accident Compensation Act left decisions to judges. The French parliament introduced state-funded old-age pensions in 1910, but they included few types of worker, and most would be dead before the pensionable age of 65. French workers received only one-fifth of the sick pay of their British counterparts. Two-thirds of the citizens of the cotton town of Lille died virtually destitute.

Housing for workers was habitually poor and crowded, offering little privacy. In Britain, The Artisans' Dwelling Act (1875) defined a slum and gave the state the right to demolish it, but the legislation was rarely enforced. There was no check on the rents demanded by private landlords, and no security of tenure. Small terraced houses were likely to burst at the seams, often being occupied by three generations of a family. If a house had its own lavatory, it would be outside, and every morning family members would troop there with brimming 'jerries'.[14] Large tenement blocks, the norm from Glasgow to Kreuzberg in Berlin, often provided a family with one room, the sleeping area roughly curtained off from living quarters, maybe an open range for cooking, with communal water supplies and lavatories, normally outside. A revealing series of photographs dating from the German Empire before 1914, ranging from prosperous bourgeois homes to those of the almost destitute, show weavers and other artisans working, living and sleeping in the same room.

With little chance of private family life in such cramped circumstances, labourers found sociability in clubs and pubs. Workers built on artisan traditions of self-help to create what was almost an alternative culture of their own. They ran literacy and numeracy classes, as well as lectures on scientific, historical and political themes. Depending on the area, there were also male voice choirs, boxing, football, rugby, darts, dominoes, boules, allotments and pigeon fancying. Miners' choirs sang folk songs in south Wales, German ones also included Wagner and Beethoven. The introduction of bank holidays and cheap rail travel gave workers a chance of day trips to the seaside with their families. They might also afford the entry for popular entertainments such as Madame Tussaud's waxworks in London or the Musée Grévin in Paris. The Chamber of Horrors displayed models of convicted murderers dressed in the criminal's own clothes, often on the very day of the execution. These drew huge crowds now that executions, which had been hugely popular, were often no longer public spectacles. Family outings would be rare. Madame Tussaud's cost sixpence, a substantial sum from a worker's budget. Most worker sociability was exclusively male, and sometimes had a political edge. In Russia a sense of peasant-worker identity was sustained because the workers in a factory were usually recruited from the same village, where they had left their wives and families.[15]

The growth of industrial cities, unions and strikes, plus urban rebellions such as the Paris Commune of 1871, awakened better-off, educated sections of society to the threat that they feared the working classes might pose. Religion was promoted as an alternative to socialism. Churches provided reassuring social contact, although congregations contained more women than men. Under the papacy of Leo XIII (1878–1903), the Roman Catholic Church began to reconcile itself to modernity and democracy and tried to attract a worker clientele. In Britain, for example, it built huge churches in areas such as Kentish Town (London), and encouraged the formation of Catholic trade unions and social and recreational groups. Protestant churches already had Sunday schools for children, organized 'guilds' for men and 'Women's Bright Hour' gatherings, which provided sociability and some education. Often the only books in a worker's house would be prizes awarded by these organizations, dubiously desirable items such as *Happy Homes and How to Make Them*.[16] Freemasons began to form new lodges in the cities, while a myriad of charitable organizations, such as the Peabody Trust, built improved tenement blocks in which to house workers, as well as providing educational, social and healthcare opportunities. Their efforts brought huge social benefits, but also reinforced the divide between themselves and workers.

Relations between workers and employers boiled over in the years just before 1914, with a growing number of strikes and violent government responses. These years were mainly prosperous, although wage-earners saw proportionately less benefit than their bosses. Conflicts tended to be linked to complaints that changes in industrial methods were undermining formerly recognized skills. In Germany, in 1912, over 1 million workers, primarily skilled, were involved in 2834 strikes. In France, industrial disputes became increasingly confrontational. Employers paid gunmen to bully pickets, and leaders of the May 1906 general strike were arrested. An unarmed march of Lorraine iron-miners in 1905 was charged by cavalry when a police informer threw a stone at one of the horses. A witness wrote to the local paper, 'The ignoble conduct of some officers has done more than five years of antimilitarist propaganda. I myself, an old woman of 66 ... filled my apron with stones to hurl at them.'[17] In 1910, after a strike of formerly moderate engine drivers, those involved were forced to enlist in the army. A further 3000 were sacked. The drivers' union responded by joining the main French trade union, the CGT.

In Russia, any dispute was treated by the government as a rebellion against the state.[18] Anarchist ideas in the tradition of Bakunin had some impact on worker groups. Troops were habitually used against strikers, for instance in Moscow in 1905, where artillery and Cossack troops clashed with protesters – a scene vividly recalled in Pasternak's *Dr Zhivago* (and even more dramatically reconstructed in the film). Two hundred gold-miners were killed during the 1912 strike.

In the Catalan region of Spain and in the industrial north of Italy, anarchist ideas were laced with reformism among workers. In Italy, commercial and industrial recession in the early 1890s provoked confrontation. Military law was declared in 1894 to control Sicilian peasants and workers. Strikes, meetings, associations, freedom of the press were all declared illegal. In May 1898, Milan was put under military occupation after a strike at the Pirelli rubber factory. Socialists and strikers were rounded up, tried and imprisoned, often on trumped-up charges.[19] Such persecution helped to create a sense of worker identity. The Second International persuaded leading European socialists to pledge fraternal opposition to war. However, when it came to 1914, all governments played the defensive patriotic card and pacifist worker unity collapsed instantly.

Middle classes and elites

Economic change encouraged a growing section of society to define itself as lower middle-class. Perched uneasily between workers and traditional middle-class groups, these new elements worked in the massively expanding white-collar jobs in railway companies, banks, insurance, post, telegraph and telephone services, and as primary school teachers. In Britain they tended to be grouped with skilled workers, while in Germany social insurance regulations defined them as middle-class.

Economic growth made the rich richer. At the top end of the social scale, there were massive fortunes to be made in finance and specula-tion, and noble landowners when facing declining land prices often forgot old prejudices and became businessmen. In 1858–79, 75 per cent of British millionaires were landowners; by 1900 the figure was 27 per cent. Rich businessmen no longer felt obliged to buy landed estates to be socially acceptable. They sent their sons to Oxbridge, filled their mansions with expensive paintings, and sometimes married into titled families. To some extent, money overcame snobbery and united the elites. In 1885, Nathan Meyer de Rothschild became the first Jew to enter the House of Lords: Queen Victoria had successfully opposed his father's admission a generation earlier. Even in the midst of economic change, traditional elites proved capable of protecting their dominance, to absorb new wealthy families by financial and marriage alliances and seamlessly to impose their values on them.

Ruling elites used education to underline their own wealth and power and to reinforce social 'stability'. Schooling was expanded as a direct consequence of both the democratization of voting and the rapid growth of the white-collar service sector. Illiteracy fell in France, from 32 per cent in 1855 to 3 per cent in 1905. State primary provision began in 1833, but was made compulsory and free only in the 1880s. Prussia, which moved faster in the literacy stakes, claimed to have no illiterates by 1910, while at the same time 50 per cent of Italian and Spanish 10-year-olds, and 75 per cent of Russians, were unable to read and write. In 1880, Britain made attendance mandatory for children between five and ten, and provided free education to primary pupils (from 1891) and secondary pupils (from 1910).

Secondary and tertiary education were generally reserved for the better off. In France, primary and secondary schooling ran on parallel, non-intersecting lines. A clever poor student could progress from a higher primary school to a 'normal school' to train as a primary school teacher, or to a vocational school to learn a trade. The son of a peasant or worker might be enrolled in a 'little seminary' and train as a priest. Middle-class families who could afford the fees sent their sons to state-run high schools (*lycées*) or expensive colleges run by religious orders, such as the Jesuits or the Marists. The number of children in French secondary school quadrupled between 1875 and 1914 in response to government legislation, embracing mainly middle-class families. In Britain, 'public' boarding schools catered for the very rich, and grammar schools for the middle-classes, with a few scholarships for children of less prosperous families. In Russia, attendance at similar schools was restricted to sons of nobles or the rich middle classes. The Italian and German systems were more flexible, but everywhere high fees deterred poorer parents. The development of secondary school-leaving examinations (*baccalauréat, Abitur*), which still focused on Latin and Greek and were essential prerequisites for either civil service jobs or university places, excluded most sons of peasants or workers. Only 1 in 1000 German university students came from a working-class background. The French system was even more elitist, for above the universities were the *grandes écoles*, dating mostly from Napoleon's time, institutions such as the Polytechnic School, the School of Mines, the Superior Normal School, which, unlike universities, demanded two additional years of preparation beyond the baccalaureate, an entrance examination and high fees. Many graduates were sons of former students, and went on to senior government jobs. Thus schooling, buttressed by birth and money, reinforced established hierarchies and elitism.

The daughters of peasants did not fare much better than their sons. In France, nearly half of middle-class girls attended schools run by nuns, who taught them the social graces and basic literacy. By 1882, only 49 girls had managed to complete the baccalaureate. As a consequence of government reforms, in the next five years the number of secondary schools for girls rose from three to 111. Italian universities never made a gender-specific rule about university attendance, so a few women gained degrees and a handful became university teachers in the nineteenth century. The first university establishments for women were started by women in London, with Bedford College in 1849. From the 1860s, French universities and medical schools had began to offer courses to women. Women were allowed into Spanish medical schools in 1881.

Curiously, Russia seems to have been more willing than most European states to educate girls. In the eighteenth century, Catherine II had founded the first girls' secondary school, the Smolny Institute. By 1914, over 300,000 girls were attending secondary schools, and their curricula were accepted as equivalent to those in boys' schools. By 1881, St Petersburg University was running nearly 1000 courses that admitted women. In 1897, a Medical Institute for Women was founded in the capital, and its graduates were employed in the state system as doctors and as administrators. By 1904, there were 5000 women in higher education in Russia. In 1908, all Russian universities were running external courses for women. Six years later there were 20 higher institutes solely for women with 20,000 students. Out of a total of 90,000 students in higher education, 50,000 were women. Perhaps the tsarist system thought it was less dangerous to educate girls than boys.

In Britain, the years before 1914 witnessed growing pressure for votes for women, but in France the 'new woman' of *La Fronde*, a newspaper by and for women, was more preoccupied with extending other civil rights. French feminists struggled to modify the Civil Code of 1804, which left women with lower civil status than a child. The reintroduction of a divorce law in 1884 was followed by legislation in 1895 that allowed a married woman to open a savings account without seeking her husband's permission. However, fathers or husbands could still demand that a woman's earnings be paid to them.

The impact of World War One on European economy and society

On the eve of World War One – despite the activities of suffragettes, the waves of strikes, and the growth of socialism – the societies and empires of Europe still seemed basically secure at the centre of a prosperous world economy. That confidence was shattered, however, by the impact of the ensuing conflict and then by the global Depression triggered in 1929. The war flung all European economies into debt, while the USA became the only substantial creditor nation. Unemployment and inflation became apparently inescapable problems.

Economic upheaval in Russia was a direct consequence of war and the two revolutions of 1917. The Bolsheviks turned their promise of 'All Power to the Soviets', or workers' councils, into the nationalization of industry. In the name of war communism trade unions were turned into instruments of state control. Subsequent chaos led to some relaxation of the hand of the state during the years of NEP. Firms with fewer than 20 workers were privatized. Capital was desperately lacking, wages fell and unemployment grew. In the mid-1920s, consumer industries began to recover and a market economy started to emerge. Some theoreticians deplored the newly prosperous retail profiteers, the NEP men, and insisted that Communism could be developed only by the modernization of heavy industry. This, in turn, could be done only by forcing capital out of the agricultural sector through low agricultural wages and prices (presumably this assumption was a gloss on prewar growth in north-west Europe).

A series of five-year plans for industrial growth were designed to accompany the collectivization of agriculture. While the capitalist world suffered from the Depression, in the USSR production in heavy industries rose dramatically and many workers were enthusiastic. The Dnieper dam was built, and new cities such as Magnitogorsk emerged. Government propaganda vastly exaggerated industrial growth, especially in the second five-year plan, when expansion slowed down. The horrors of collectivization were ignored. Nine million peasants were compelled to become industrial workers, with the alternative of starvation. They were forced into an unprepared and extremely uncomfortable urban environment, with totally inadequate accommodation and services. The government was able to boast that the USSR was modernizing while capitalist economies seemed to be near to meltdown. Hopes of developing consumer industries, which might have made workers' lives slightly better, were put aside when Hitler came to power. Soviet industry focused on armaments. Defence expenditure rose from 3.4 to 16.5 per cent of the budget. Even so, Stalin's purges, which included engineers and workers, led to a slump in industrial production in 1937.

Elsewhere, a market economy prevailed, but the optimism, monetary stability and balance of the prewar world were shaken by the war, and virtually disappeared in the slump of the early 1930s. In 1914, the major European powers, with the exception of Russia, were creditor nations. The war stripped away the foreign reserves of the main protagonists. France lost half its foreign investments, suffering especially from events in Russia. Germany lost all but 10 per cent, and Britain sold roughly a quarter of its investments. No dividends on surviving foreign investments were paid. The war was funded at first by public loans and simply by printing more money. The inflationary consequences were catastrophic, and remained an uncontrollable nightmare throughout the interwar years. In 1914, the French franc was 25 to £1; by July 1926, 200. Inflation made the currencies of the defeated powers utterly worthless. What was even more destabilizing and inflationary was that a great deal of the cost of war was covered by bilateral loans. The combatants borrowed from each other. The British lent £1741 million to their allies, of which £568 million went to Russia and was never seen again. Britain borrowed £1365 million to cover these loans, £1027 million from the USA.[20] The French borrowed 45,000 million francs from the British and 18,500 million francs from the Americans. The USA, which had entered the war as a debtor and by 1918 was the sole creditor nation, demanded that repayment begin as soon as the war was over. It was the tradition that the defeated power pay an indemnity; France had been obliged to do this in 1815 and 1871. The Allies carefully wrote war guilt clauses into the World War One treaties and assumed that the defeated powers would pay.

However, World War One had been the most destructive conflict ever. A Reparations Commission was set up to decide how much Germany and its allies should pay. It did not report until 1921. One of the members was the young British economist John Maynard Keynes. In his influential *Economic Consequences of the Peace* (1919), Keynes warned that the attempt to punish Germany by demanding it pay massive reparations to its former enemies would damage all their economies. In 1914, Germany had been an integral part of the European economy, a major supplier to, as well as purchaser from, the other powers. Heavy reparation demands would prevent both its recovery and theirs. However, its enemies had promised their voters that the defeated powers, Germany and Austria, would pay the costs of the war. It was politically inconceivable in the postwar climate for any of the previous belligerents to try to solve their debt problem by raising taxes. The USSR was the only power to get away with refusing to recognize its debts, and only then because it cut itself off from the world economy.

All the defeated nations were asked to pay reparations. The German bill was £6600 million. Having lost Lorraine iron and the coal of the Saar, Germany struggled to recover economically. The successor states of the old Austro-Hungarian Empire were economically unviable. Austria, now a mere rump of 7 million, over 2 million of whom lived in Vienna, with a railway network that simply connected the city with a lost empire, had little hope of economic recovery. By 1923, rocketing inflation left both German and Austrian currencies worthless. It would take 4420 million deutschmarks to buy a single dollar. Wages bought nothing and middle-class savings were wiped out. The Germans defaulted on reparations and the French, suspecting that the Weimar regime had deliberately let inflation spiral to reduce the repayment burden, responded by occupying the Ruhr, which only made the situation worse.

The Dawes and Young Plans, dating from 1924 and 1929 respectively, negotiated smaller reparations payments over a much longer period. They were paid by yet more loans. Big US banks, particularly Morgan Stanley, attracted by high interest rates in Berlin, made short-term loans to Germany. Between 1924 and 1928, three times as much was lent by American banks as the Germans paid in reparations. Germany used this hot money for long-term economic recovery. A Ford plant in Cologne, and General Motors' purchase of the Opel works in Rüsselheim, presaged the adoption of assembly-line production. By 1928, almost the entire Ruhr coal industry had been mechanized.

French economic recovery was remarkable. Trench warfare and occupation had devastated nearly 11 of its most profitable industrial departments for all but a few weeks of the war. In 1918, iron and steel production was less than 50 per cent of prewar levels. In 1921, coal production was still only half that of 1913. Communications were seriously disrupted, and 2 million hectares of land were laid waste, leaving grain production a mere 60 per cent of prewar levels. Yet by 1925, France was third in the world table of metallurgical industries. It was also third in the world export league and had a favourable balance in foreign trade. Newer industries – including cars (where France led European production), aeroplanes and films – helped to make the country a leading European economic power in the 1920s.

The social impact of World War One on women

The impact of war on women was stark. Never before had so many men left for war, and never before were there so many casualties. A soldier's family had to survive on a fraction of his peacetime earnings, 50 per cent at best. Initially there were fewer jobs for women, as middle-class families 'did without' servants in the cause of the war effort. Luxury trades such as textiles, clothing, shoes and tobacco, where traditionally women were a substantial part of the workforce, were cut back to focus on war industries. In Germany, by 1918 fewer than half as many women had jobs in textiles and clothing as in 1914. However, by 1917 women's employment in mining, iron and steel, chemicals and engineering was 700,000, six times that in 1913.[21] In France, by 1918 119,966 women were involved in metallurgy, a rise of 650 per cent on 1914. One-third of the workers in the armaments' factories in the Paris area were women. The proportion of women at the Renault car plant rose from 4 to 32 per cent.[22] Women worked as railway guards, made grenades or drove army lorries, doing jobs that had always been reserved for men. Governments became more concerned about workers' welfare. They did not want to damage the health either of future worker mothers, or of the babies they were rearing in addition to their jobs. In 1916, French munitions factories restricted the working day to eight hours for women (and perforce for men). Although most women workers were single, firms also had to add creches, nurseries and mothers' rooms to try to retain their married workers, who were more reliable than single girls.

During the war, poorer women showed a militancy that harked back to a premodern world. In Germany in 1915, when bread, potatoes and butter became virtually unobtainable, women workers joined and ran food riots against government offices. Women were far more active than before in organizing and joining industrial protests, notably the 200,000-strong strikes and walkouts of Berlin munitions workers in April 1917 for 'Bread, Peace and Freedom', and the strikes of a million German workers in January 1918 for peace and democracy.[23]

Middle-class women, whose 'char' ladies did battle for them in the bread queues, often scorned such behaviour as unpatriotic. Those campaigning for the vote and women's rights declared a temporary truce and mobilized themselves in the war effort. At the outset, in Germany in August 1914, the *Nationaler Frauendienst* (National Women's Service) was set up, incorporating the existing middle-class women's organization, the *Bund Deutscher Frauenvereine* (Federation of German Women's Organizations), to do charitable work and run lectures to promote the war. Women, mostly middle-class, worked as nurses, serving close to the battle trenches on the Western Front. In the case of France, by 1918 these nurses numbered 120,000, the majority of them volunteers. Marie Curie and her daughter took their innovative X-ray equipment close to the front lines, while at home hundreds of thousands of wives, sisters and mothers ran French family farms with the help of older male relatives and children.

In many countries, women got the vote after World War One, for example in Britain (in 1919 at 30; in 1929 at 21), Germany, Italy and Soviet Russia (in 1919) and Spain (in 1931). In Germany, 10 per cent of the members of the new republican Reichstag in 1919 were women, and by 1932 there had been 111 female members, mostly for left-wing parties. In France, although all adult males were enfranchised in 1848, women did not get the vote until 1945. The Chamber of Deputies repeatedly voted in favour of votes for women in the interwar years, to find their proposals squashed by the Senate. In 1936, Léon Blum, Popular Front prime minister, included three women in his government. However, the enthusiasm for enfranchisement shown by Roman Catholic women's organizations, with several million members, did not help the cause thanks to Church hostility to the republican regime.

When the men were demobbed at the end of 1918, so too were almost all the women in war jobs. In 1925, 2.2 million of the 4.2 million women workers in Germany were doing unskilled or semi-skilled work. In the interwar years, the real revolution in women's employment centred on clerical jobs. In England and Wales, in 1914, 20 per cent of such workers were female, mostly from middle-class families. Working-class girls, a few of whom were staying at school for an extra year, or even winning scholarships to grammar schools, began to compete for such jobs, which paid the massive sum of £2 a week. By 1931, there were over a million female clerical workers in England and Wales, ten times the figure for 1911. Women also began to be employed in newer electrical and small engineering works, doing jobs regarded as too fiddly for men's fingers, helping to make bicycles, planes and electrical cables. By 1938, 235,000 women were working in these industries in England and Wales, earning about half what men were paid.[24] Middle-class women made some headway in the job market too. During World War One in France, Germany and Italy, women were appointed to supervise health and welfare services for women workers. In 1919, these developments were confirmed and women were allowed to compete for senior posts. This was also the year in which German and British women were allowed to enter legal practice.[25]

The family and depopulation

Fears about depopulation were intensified by the loss of so many men and the inevitable spinsterhood of many women. Pronatalist doctrines became popular. The fashion among single young women for short skirts, bobbed hair and 'flapper' styles was soon replaced by propaganda that single, childless women were selfish and unpatriotic. It was nothing new for women to be told it was their national or class duty to have children. In the 1880s, Charles Darwin's cousin, Francis Galton, urged middle-class women to have more children, with carefully selected mates, to balance the feared unrestrained growth in numbers of the poor and feckless. In 1911, Karl Pearson was appointed to the first Chair of Eugenics at University College, London. Real science, however, was offering women a more appealing choice. Mechanical and chemical contraception was improving and was publicized by women such as Nelly Roussel in France and Marie Stopes in Britain.

During the war, penalties against contraception and abortion were increased in Germany. A German Society for Population Policy was set up to encourage better care for working mothers and their babies. The French, already alarmed before 1914 at the lack of population growth, and with a population slightly smaller than in 1900 despite the return of 2 million Alsace-Lorrainers in 1919, were in no doubt that more babies were vital to the nation's survival. Contraception and abortion were banned in 1920. A Council on Natality distributed allowances for families of three or more children. Mothers with five or more legitimate children were awarded a 'medal of the French family'. However, French women do not seem to have been persuaded by medals. The abortion rate doubled to an average of 120,000 a year. Deaths continued to exceed births. In 1939, a Family Code gave extra benefits to couples who had a baby within two years of marriage.[26] Mussolini's Italy also gave financial incentives to marry and prizes for large families. The abortionist's business was boosted by unemployment. There were a million terminations in Germany in 1931. Concern became widespread that population growth had slowed too much, and that government initiatives were needed to prevent eventual depopulation. The middle-class Federation of German Women's Organizations urged 'organized motherliness', and campaigned against abortion and the spread of pornography.[27] The Weimar regime increased penalties for abortion. The Nazis created a Reich Mothers' Service in 1934 to run courses in cooking, nursing and racial hygiene, which by 1939 had been taken by 1.7 million women.[28] The *Bund Deutscher Mädel* (League of German Girls) encouraged their 'Aryan' members to forswear wicked French fashions, to wear plaits and plain clothes, and to avoid make-up.[29] The Nazis adopted a cult of the Aryan family. Engaged couples were offered marriage loans, and family allowances were introduced. Following a perverted version of eugenics, Aryans were forbidden to marry Jews and sterilization began to be imposed on the insane and incurable. The German birth rate went up between 1934 and 1939, not because families grew from an average of two children, but because there were more marriages, as presumably more people had jobs. In 1938, divorce was made easier after three years' separation. This was not intended to be liberal, but to facilitate procreative remarriage. Abortion was also made easier for Jews because their families were not valued by the state.[30]

In the USSR, after the desperate famines of the civil war years, abortion was legalized in 1927. Between 1924 and 1928, abortions rose from 5.5 to 31.5 per thousand births in Leningrad. From 1936, however, concern that the Soviet population had begun to decline led to a pronatalist policy. Across much of Europe, the biggest factor behind the slowdown in overall growth may have been persistent unemployment and consequent later marriage.

The social impact of the World Depression

The limited optimism of recovery in the 1920s was short-lived. Even during that decade, older industries such as coal, iron and textiles faltered and lacked investment. In Britain and Germany, these industries remained depressed throughout the interwar years, with around 1 million persistently out of work in Britain; between the two world wars, unemployment in Britain and Germany never fell below 9 per cent. Even in the prosperous years between 1925 and 1929, 2 million

Germans were out of work. In 1928, a buoyant US economy pushed interest rates so high that volatile short-term American investment in Germany was sucked back home. The subsequent essentially artificial boom in security prices on Wall Street was followed in October 1929 by bust. Share prices tumbled. Worldwide commercial and industrial recession ensued. By the first quarter of 1931, the value of international trade was less than two-thirds of that of the first quarter of 1929. By April 1932, 32 countries had suspended the gold standard and it was inoperative in 17 others. In May 1931, the Credit-Anstalt, Austria's biggest bank, which controlled two-thirds of the country's industry, collapsed with appalling consequences for its European neighbours, including the Reichsbank and other German banks. Governments attempted to deflate, cutting wages and unemployment pay and raising tariffs to try to protect their own economies. Germany defaulted on reparations, which were cancelled by the Lausanne Conference of 1932. The USA continued its attempts to recover war loans, but after December 1933 no-one paid. The Americans were the first to heed the advice of Keynes that the way out of recession was to boost, not reduce, government spending. Their New Deal policy improved the American situation.

Economic disaster and over-optimistic publicity about Communist Russia convinced some Europeans that capitalism was now defunct and that the future lay in socialism. Lenin had urged socialists everywhere to declare themselves communists and align themselves with his new Comintern, the Third International, established in 1919. European socialist parties, already divided over their response to World War One, fragmented yet again. Communist parties were formed in all the major parliamentary states, but the notion of a world revolution was never more than rhetoric. Workers' movements, despite high-profile activity such as the general strike in Britain in 1926, were seriously hobbled by unemployment.

Democratic parliamentary systems, often of post-1919 vintage, were threatened by the failure of coalition governments to agree on policies to cope with inflation and unemployment. In Italy, the unwillingness of the main parties to cooperate allowed Fascists to control the streets and mobilize elites, and the middle classes to destroy democracy. Mussolini's example was followed elsewhere. The World Depression added to fears (and in some cases hopes) that capitalism was finished and communist revolution a real possibility. In July 1932, the Communists became the third largest party in the German Reichstag. The SPD came second, but the Nazis came top, their meteoric rise being a direct product of middle-class fears that the 1923 currency collapse would repeat itself and that the consequence would be communism.

By 1932, there were 6 million unemployed in Germany. The government, advised by Schacht, president of the Reichsbank, embarked on a public spending programme. It might have worked, but the unwillingness of left and centre parties to work together climaxed in January 1933, with the appointment of Hitler as Chancellor, at the head of a right-wing coalition government dominated by the Nazis. The democratic system was speedily despatched by them, but they offered no radical alternative to capitalism, despite some threats to department stores. The Nazi economics minister, Schmitt, followed the policies of the previous government, providing tax reductions and exemptions to encourage capital investment in key industries such as steel and engineering. Firms received direct government subsidies and employers were encouraged to retain workers and take on more. Workers' rights disappeared. The Labour Front replaced trade unions. Strikes were banned, and wages and freedom of movement were restricted. Men were drafted into the German Labour Front (with its motto 'Strength through Joy'), which promised social benefits such as welfare programmes and holidays, but was a mere smokescreen to destroy individual rights. Within just over a year, unemployment had been halved. By 1936, it stood at 1 million; by 1938 there were no unemployed in Germany. Whether all were doing 'real' jobs or not, the publicity was positive. A year later, British unemployment was still 1 million.

The Nazis had a particular appeal to big business, at least when they took power. In 1934, businessmen's organizations were merged in a Reich Economic Chamber and, in 1936, government attempts to control prices were defeated by big producers. Schacht successfully fought off Nazi attempts to control the banks. In 1936, Göring introduced a four-year economic plan to make Germany economically self-sufficient through the development of synthetics and the use of low-grade iron ore. Conflict soon developed, however, between Göring and other interested parties such as Schacht, the generals, and the Ruhr industrialists. There were fears that Göring's plans were inflationary. The abandonment of disarmament quotas, subsequent rapid rearmament and the takeover of the economies of first Austria and then Czechoslovakia gave heavy industry and the cartels considerable freedom of movement. Any surviving Nazi radicals had to content themselves with attacking small Jewish retail shops and businesses, as occurred most notably in the *Kristallnacht* of 1938.

The World Depression affected France more slowly and less harshly than other states. Unemployment did not reach its peak of 400,000 until 1936, for a variety of reasons. Not only did France hold large gold reserves, its economy was more self-sufficient than those of its neighbours, and produced predominantly luxury goods that continued to sell to the rich. The jobless figures also remained low because of short-time working and the termination of work contracts for foreign labourers. It was left to the Popular Front coalition, formed initially in 1934 to combat fascism, to try to check the impact of the World Depression on France. The election of the Popular Front coalition government in May 1936 was followed by spontaneous strikes of industrial workers, expressing their delight that at last a Socialist-led government had been elected, but also trying to put pressure on Blum to ensure social reform. The Matignon agreements between workers and employers provided for immediate 10–15 per cent wage rises, and paid holidays were promised, along with a 40-hour week. Some modest industrial nationalization began. However, the Bank of France and other big financial interests were appalled at what they thought was an imminent communist revolution, and a major flight from the franc ensued. In September 1936, Blum was forced to devalue and soon the wage rises meant nothing. The French economy began to pick up, perhaps mainly because of the increase in defence spending decreed by the Popular Front. Even so, production was still below 1929 levels on the eve of World War Two.

Despite the serious economic setbacks of the 1930s and the enormous difficulties stemming from the civil war in Spain, for those in work, whether in one of the surviving democracies or in a totalitarian regime, even this decade seemed to offer much that was better than the way their parents had lived. The growth of consumer industries in the most developed states meant that a family might own a radio, a gramophone, a washing machine, bicycles, even a car, and possibly their own flat or house. The middle classes, and the rich especially, benefited from even more leisure opportunities. Recovery from the World Depression was tenuous, however, dependent on accelerated military spending and fierce economic protectionism. The inability of democratic societies to cope with enemies at home and abroad led inexorably to another world war, in which the peoples of Europe were again pawns to live or die at the behest of governments.

Further reading

T. C. W. Blanning, *Oxford Illustrated History of Modern Europe* (Oxford: Oxford University Press, 1996), is brief but wide-ranging, and brilliantly illustrated. Mark Mazower, *The Dark Continent: Europe's Twentieth Century* (London: Penguin, 1998) and Eric Hobsbawm, *Age of Extremes: The Short Twentieth Century, 1914–1991* (London: Michael Joseph 1994) cover the whole period and are stimulating. A readable and informative short account of the years before 1914 can be found in Robert Gildea, *Barricades and Borders: Europe 1800–1914* (Oxford: Oxford University Press, 1987). For the post-1919 period, Martin Kitchen, *Europe between the Wars* (2nd edn, London: Pearson, 2006) is brief and accessible. Tom Kemp, *Industrialisation in Nineteenth-Century Europe* (London: Longman, 1985) sets out a brisk account, mainly country by country. Social change is dealt with succinctly by Dick Geary (ed.), *Labour and Socialist Movements in Europe before 1914* (Oxford: Berg, 1992); Ute Frevert, *Women in German History: From Bourgeois Emancipation to Sexual Liberation* (Oxford: Berg, 1992); Susan K. Foley, *Women in France since 1789* (Basingstoke/New York: Palgrave Macmillan, 2004); and Pamela Pilbeam, *The Middle Classes in Europe, 1814–1914* (Basingstoke: Macmillan, 1990). Dudley Baines, *Emigration from Europe 1815–1930* (London: Macmillan, 1991) is also admirably brief.

Notes

1 D. V. Glass and E. Grebenik, 'World Population, 1800–1950', in H. J. Habakkuk and M. Postan (eds), *Cambridge Economic History of Europe*, Vol. VI, Part I (Cambridge: Cambridge University Press, 1966), p. 61.
2 Emile Zola, *La Terre* (1887) [*The Earth*] (Harmondsworth: Penguin, 1980).
3 E. Ackerman, *Healthcare in the Parisian Countryside 1800–1914* (New Brunswick/London: Rutger University Press 1990), p. 126.
4 D. Geary, 'Socialism and the German Labour Movement before 1914', in D. Geary (ed.), *Labour and Socialist Movements in Europe before 1914* (Oxford: Berg, 1992), p. 104.
5 D. Baines, *Emigration from Europe 1815–1930* (London: Macmillan, 1991), p. 7–9.
6 J. M. Roberts, *Europe 1880–1945* (London: Longman, 1989), p. 368.
7 A. Shubert, *A Social History of Modern Spain* (London: Routledge, 1990), p. 84.
8 A. Gerschenkron, 'Agrarian policies and industrialization: Russia 1861–1917', in *Cambridge Economic History of Europe*, Vol. VI, II (Cambridge: Cambridge University Press), p. 797.
9 D. Landes, *The Unbound Prometheus. Technological Change and Industrial Development in Western Europe from 1750 to the Present* (Cambridge: Cambridge University Press, 1970), p. 367.
10 Shubert, *A Social History of Modern Spain, op. cit.*, pp. 101–3.
11 D. Geary, 'The British Labour Movement before 1914', in D. Geary (ed.), *Labour and Socialist Movements in Europe before 1914, op. cit.*, pp. 36–37.
12 E. Roberts, *Women's Work 1840–1940* (Cambridge: Cambridge University Press, 1995), p. 27.
13 M. Miller, *The Bon Marché: Bourgeois Culture and the Department Store, 1869–1920* (Princeton: Princeton University Press, 1981).

14 P. Pilbeam, 'From Orders to Classes', in T. C. W. Blanning, *Oxford Illustrated History of Modern Europe* (Oxford: Oxford University Press, 1996), p. 117. This drawing, 'Over London by Rail', (Gustave Doré, 1872) clearly illustrates the outside 'facilities'.
15 R. E. Johnson, *Peasant and Proletarian:the Working Class of Moscow in the Late Nineteenth Century* (New Brunswick: Rutgers University Press, 1979).
16 By Dr J. W. Kirton (1883) – a popular gift on marriage.
17 Roger Magraw, 'Socialism, Syndicalism and the French Labour Movement before 1914', in D. Geary (ed.), *Labour and Socialist Movements in Europe before 1914, op. cit.*, pp. 65–69.
18 C. Read, 'Labour and Socialism in Tsarist Russia', in *ibid.*, p. 177–79.
19 J. A. Davies, 'Socialism and the Working Classes in Italy before 1914', in *ibid.*, pp. 189–91.
20 D. Landes, *The Unbound Prometheus, op. cit.*, pp. 362–63.
21 U. Frevert, *Women in German History. From Bourgeois Emancipation to Sexual Liberation* (Oxford: Berg, 1992), p. 156.
22 S. K. Foley, *Women in France since 1789* (Basingstoke/New York: Palgrave Macmillan, 2004), p. 166.
23 U. Frevert, *Women in German History, op. cit.*, pp. 158–60.
24 J. M. Roberts, *Europe 1880–1945, op. cit.*, pp. 28, 60.
25 L. Clark, *The Rise of the Professional Woman in France* (Cambridge: Cambridge University Press, 2000), p. 142.
26 P. Smith, *Feminism and the Third Republic. Women's Political and Civil Rights in France, 1918–1945* (Oxford: Oxford University Press, 1996), p. 249.
27 M. Stibbe, *Women in the Third Reich* (London: Arnold, 1993), p. 13.
28 *Ibid.*, p. 39.
29 U. Frevert, *Women in German History, op. cit.*, pp. 241–42.
30 *Ibid.*, pp. 234–36.

3 Intellectual and cultural upheaval, 1890–1945

Michael Biddiss

Among the nineteenth-century voices that expressed an optimistic view of the future, none was clearer than Thomas Macaulay's. Here we have this celebrated Whig historian writing about the march of science:

> It has lengthened life; it has mitigated pain; it has extinguished diseases; it has increased the fertility of the soil; it has given new securities to the mariner; it has furnished new arms to the warrior; it has spanned great rivers and estuaries with bridges of form unknown to our fathers; it has guided the thunderbolt innocuously from the heaven to earth; it has lighted up the night with the splendour of the day; it has extended the range of human vision; it has multiplied the power of human muscles; it has accelerated motion; it has annihilated distance; it has facilitated intercourse, correspondence, all friendly offices, all dispatch of business; it has enabled man to descend to the depths of the sea, to soar into the air, to penetrate securely into the noxious recesses of the earth, to traverse the land in cars which whirl along without horses, to cross the ocean in ships which run ten knots an hour against the wind. These are but a part of its fruits, and of its first-fruits; for it is a philosophy which never rests, which has never attained, which is never perfect. Its law is progress.[1]

Those words were first published in 1837. Over the next four or five decades, much of the intellectual and cultural life of Europe was characterized by this kind of confidence. Only after acknowledging the scale of its influence can we also properly appreciate the significance of the extent to which such consoling certainties fell under challenge towards the end of the nineteenth century, and how these then came to look increasingly frail as European society went on to experience an era of world wars and of deep ideological conflicts.

Perceptions of progress

The mid-nineteenth-century climate of confidence owed much to the remarkable economic and industrial expansion of Europe's 'railway age'. As critics such as Marx and Engels stressed, the financial and other benefits were spread very unequally. Even so, an increasingly large number of Europeans were coming to enjoy either the actuality or the early prospect of richer and more varied habits of material consumption. Advances in such fields as communications and food supply, sanitation and healthcare, education and literacy were all readily brought together within a single master image of 'progress'. In 1851, the variety and interdependence of its manifestations were well encapsulated inside Hyde Park's Crystal Palace, which housed the Great Exhibition of the Works of Industry of all Nations. Victorian Britain was prominent not just in matters of material improvement, but also as a source of progressive political inspiration. The prosperity associated with the application of *laissez-faire* economics served to enhance the prestige of other liberal commitments – especially those favouring parliamentary institutions backed by broadened franchise. Under those circumstances, the rebuffs to European liberalism suffered in 1848–49 looked all the more temporary. It became plausible – although not necessarily correct – to regard the new Italy of 1860–61, or Tsar Alexander II's reformist programme of the 1860s, or the Austro-Hungarian *Ausgleich* of 1867, or Britain's Reform Act of that same year, or the eventual ascendancy of republicanism in France, as each forming part of a broader force steadily advancing against the enemies of freedom.

Much of this optimism survived beyond the turn of the century. For example, even while economic growth slowed during the relatively depressed years from 1873 until the mid-1890s, certain countries engaged in a burst of colonial expansion more explosive than any previously recorded in the long history of European empire-building (see Chapter 11). While its motivations were complex, the principal intellectual consequence was simpler. In essence, this imperialistic surge reinforced familiar beliefs about the naturalness and permanence of Europe's political, technological, cultural, and indeed racial hegemony. Within domestic settings too, the ruling classes were over-reliant on the stability of old assumptions: a perilous complacency surrounded, for instance, the aristocratic glitter of Viennese society as it danced the last waltzes of the Habsburg age. As for the European bourgeoisie at large, Alan Bullock wrote:

> With light taxation, no inflation, cheap food, cheap labour, a plentiful supply of domestic servants, many ordinary middle-class

families with modest incomes lived full and comfortable lives. No wonder that so many who came from such families and survived the War, looking back, felt that there was a grace, an ease, a security in living then which has since been lost for ever.[2]

Nowadays, equipped with hindsight and haunted by indelible images from the battlefields of 1914–18, we can more readily grasp the significance of certain anxieties that undoubtedly surfaced during the prewar epoch, even if they remained under-rated at that time. Among them were fears about the disruptive dynamics of mass socialization, and about the violence associated with the anarchist, socialist and nationalist challenges to an old order whose rulers were locked into a potentially destructive arms race. The horrors of World War One would soon give a whole continent much more urgent cause to question the faith in progress, and much else that nineteenth-century Europeans had tended to take for granted. But how far, even before 1914, had intellectuals and imaginative artists themselves embarked on their own dissolution of confident expectations and familiar certainties?

Positivism under challenge

Changes within natural science form a fundamental part of any proper answer. As Macaulay's observations already hinted, this domain had become central to the whole paradigm of progress. Much of that material advance, which helped to inspire the nineteenth-century faith in human betterment, had depended on the practical exploitation of scientific knowledge, as exemplified in the deployment of germ theory to combat disease, or of electromagnetic principles to refine the dynamo. So striking was the capacity of scientists to harness their understanding of nature to the purposes of social improvement that their discipline had seemingly become destined to attain the kind of dominant status once enjoyed by theology or philosophy. Natural science was not simply supplying impressive answers to its own questions, but also extending its methods and achievements to other spheres. That enlargement of its authority is essential to our understanding of nineteenth-century 'positivism' – the term devised by Auguste Comte to denote a secularizing belief that science (as distinct particularly from theology) provided the supreme model for all reliable knowledge. It followed that the insights claimed by other disciplines were valuable only to the extent that they incorporated or imitated scientific habits of enquiry, observation, testing and commitment to rational causality. At the core of the cultural upheaval of the years around 1900, we find not simply a deeper questioning of such insistence on science as intellectual lodestar, but also a shattering of the established image of the physical world itself.

During the generation before 1890, the liveliest scientific debates had surrounded biological issues, especially those tackled in Charles Darwin's *On the Origin of Species* (1859) and *The Descent of Man* (1871). His achievement was not to discover evolutionary change itself, but rather to reveal its principal mode of operation in the form of 'natural selection'. This presented a relentless struggle for existence, occurring within and between species. In the context of a potentially hostile environment, the inherited variations which chanced to be most favourably adapted to the needs of the organism would tend to be those best preserved. The randomness of such variations seemed to negate conceptions of ideal form and purposive direction within nature. Thus the creation even of the remarkable human species ceased to need explanation by reference to some special act of God. Rather, men and women were being invited to acknowledge their own evolution from more lowly forms, according to a pattern of kinship that included the apes as their distant cousins.

Between 1890 and 1914, William Bateson, Hugo de Vries and Thomas H. Morgan filled some significant gaps in this theory. Above all, they developed a new science of 'genetics'. This involved belated recognition of Gregor Mendel's pioneering studies from the 1860s on particulate inheritance, and on the nature of 'mutation' as applied to 'leaps' in the evolutionary process. However, in another vital sense, Darwin's structure was actually looking less complete by the early twentieth century. Before his death in 1882, he had managed to achieve not just a remarkable synthesis of human, zoological and other biological studies, but also the integration of these with the geological and palaeontological discoveries of the earth sciences. On that basis, many had been confident about all this becoming subsumed within an even broader unifying theory of physics. This, precisely, was the prospect of ambitious synthesis that was plunged into doubt around 1900.

The nub of the matter was a revolution in physics that matched in scope, and challenged in substance, the transformation registered by Newton 200 years earlier. His was still the framework that nineteenth-century scientists sought to refine. They continued to treat the universe as being composed of material bodies existing in separate dimensions of time and space; to view the basic units of matter as billiard ball atoms of fixed weights that combined in various ways; and to describe the dynamic forces (such as gravitation) operating between them in terms of a mathematics whose own neatness crystallized the regularities supposedly essential to external reality. The principal achievements of the mid-nineteenth century – especially in the fields of thermodynamics, chemical elements and electromagnetism – served to confirm this tidiness of things. Even with Darwin, biology too seemed to be confirming the emergence of a harmonious overall structure. Such order, potentially consistent from microcosm to macrocosm, offered even the prospect of total description and explanation. As more of the master blueprint emerged, science – rather like that superb technological symbol, the Eiffel Tower of 1889 – would surely continue to drive upwards towards its own symmetrical pinnacle. Accordingly, whatever remained presently unknown was merely that which happened to be as yet undiscovered, rather than something that might be, in principle, unknowable. This confidence in the progressive unfolding of a systematic reality had provided positivism with its chief sustenance. Equally, it was this same faith that the new physics now imperilled.

One of the crucial triggers occurred in 1895, with Konrad Röntgen's discovery of phenomena that, in puzzlement, he labelled X-rays. They were rapidly publicized as a form of fluorescence stimulated by a discharge tube and capable of penetrating certain solids. Henri Becquerel and Marie Curie then detected other kinds of radiation, emanating from such elements as uranium. It was soon recognized, especially through J. J. Thomson's work at Cambridge, that the huge amounts of energy involved in these 'radioactive' transformations of matter must stem from processes operating within the structure of atoms hitherto deemed indivisible. Investigation of these unheralded subatomic levels, where scientists now encountered the electron and similar particles, thus become central to physics as further refashioned by Ernest Rutherford and Niels Bohr in the years down to 1914. Within their strange new world, the orbit of electrons – and much else besides – was characterized by jerky unpredictability, utterly at odds with the previous assumption that some regular pattern of continuity and determinacy must prevail through all the causal relationships of nature. The foundations for a very different view had been laid in 1900 by Max Planck. His ideas about 'the quantum' were pivotal to his formula for gauging the discrete discontinuities involved in the emission of energy, and in 1905 they were similarly central to Albert Einstein's particulate theory of light.

The range of Einstein's contribution to scientific revolution stretched even further, into the special and general theories of relativity propounded in 1905 and 1915–16 respectively. In the former, he presented time and space as interdependent aspects of a single fourth-dimensional continuum; insisted that light had a constant velocity, whatever the movement of its source or observer; argued for the mutual convertibility of mass and energy; and concluded that each particle of matter held energy (*E*) equivalent to its mass (*m*) multiplied by the square of the velocity of light (*c²*). Through his resulting and celebrated formula $E = mc^2$, Einstein expressed the vast power contained within the atom. As for his general theory of relativity, this focused on celestial motion and offered a very different model from Newton's. It was now argued that such movement must be understood in terms not of 'flat' Euclidean geometry, but of 'curved' space–time, which included distortions from the electromagnetic fields surrounding large bodies. Just as Planck had highlighted discontinuity and indeterminacy, so Einstein's relativity amounted to denial of any absolute frame of reference. Such revision called into question the very nature of scientific laws. Was it possible to continue viewing them as operating consistently across the whole spectrum from microcosm to macrocosm, or even as still possessing an objective existence independent of the scientist's own imagination? It was certainly plain that the new physics was dealing with phenomena less predictable, more mysterious, than the old. Here was a vast leap in knowledge – but one that raised more problems than it solved, and opened up vistas of uncertainty far beyond anything anticipated by nineteenth-century positivists.

Similarly perplexing was the work of Sigmund Freud, a Viennese specialist in nervous illness whose creation of 'psychoanalysis' well exemplified the ambiguities encountered around the turn of the century along the borderlands between scientific and imaginative endeavour. While he did not discover the unconscious, he certainly made unprecedented claims about its sheer power, as an active force embracing concepts and memories literally too terrible to contemplate. He encouraged his patients to engage in relaxed narration. While serving them as a form of therapy, this also provided Freud himself with material that he could analyse (through often speculative procedures of verbal association) for the purpose of probing into the depths of the mind. He developed a particular concern for dream-experiences, believing that, as 'a disguised fulfilment of repressed wishes', they provided keys for unlocking an individual's past. Here, so he argued in his epochal *Interpretation of Dreams* (published late in 1899), was 'the royal road to a knowledge of the unconscious activities of the mind'.[3] What guaranteed Freud's notoriety, however, was his insistence that, even from infancy, those activities were dominated by sexuality. He stressed particularly that every child harboured a passion for the parent of opposite sex. Moreover, he contended that its thwarting produced a universal condition of 'neurotic' guilt which was all the more powerful precisely because it remained uncomprehended, and that the degree to which it was successfully managed through unconscious processes of repression conditioned society's perceptions of the essentially hazy frontiers between 'normality' and 'abnormality'. Thus, while the physicists were finding curves in time and space, the more dubious science of psychoanalysis appeared to be warping the customary categories of sanity, morality and rationality, too. However, despite the claims of his opponents, Freud was not a wrecker aiming to unleash a riot of primal urges. True, on the map of mind which he was replotting, the domains of reason were much reduced. Yet he believed that the revised chart, covering even the logic of the dreamily illogical, would reflect reality far more accurately. In this sense he aimed to help preserve rationality in human affairs precisely by attacking the more uncritical positivistic exaggerations of its effective scope.

Misinterpretation of Freud's intent was all the easier because his efforts coincided around 1900 with two major forms of philosophical reorientation, each of which seemed to reinforce moral confusion. One of these, associated particularly with Bertrand Russell in Cambridge and with his younger associate Ludwig Wittgenstein in Vienna, continued within the positivist tradition. However, it abandoned many of the previous aspirations towards grandiose systems not simply of intellectual synthesis, but of ethical prescription too. This refined positivism would involve, instead, a more self-absorbed and tightly limited concern with the precise mathematical, logical and linguistic mechanisms appropriate to making philosophy essentially scientific. As for the rest, according to Wittgenstein's most celebrated maxim, 'Whereof one cannot speak, thereof one must be silent.'[4] In contrast, the second brand of reorientation, which had much the wider influence during the years before 1914, was not a retreat from philosophy's traditional engagement with ethics, but an even more alarming assertion of a new morality aimed at radical subversion of the old.

Here, the writer who made most impact was Friedrich Nietzsche, notwithstanding the fact that he was incurably insane by 1890 and dead by 1900. Indeed, who better than a mad philosopher to inspire 'the new irrationalism'? Its supporters challenged positivism by drawing from the wells of an earlier romanticism. They declined to acknowledge the omnipotence of reason, and instead assigned greater value to unconscious instinct and vitalistic intuition. Upon that basis, and through aphoristic and semi-poetical prose, Nietzsche launched his attempt 'to philosophize with a hammer'.[5] Among his targets was the cosy assumption that advances in literacy and rational refinement would serve to improve humanity. True history was a tale not of linear ascent, but of cyclical 'eternal recurrence'. Moreover, just as it denied relentless secular progress, so too did it confound all hopes of religious fulfilment. 'God is dead!', Nietzsche famously declared, 'God remains dead! And we have killed him! How shall we comfort ourselves – we who are the greatest murderers of all?'[6] Thus the real challenge was to accept, and then benefit from, loss of illusions both secular and sacred. The Christian 'pity-ethic' must yield to 'the Will to Power', which would operate so as to give meaning to virtue only within the context of a quest for quasi-Darwinistic survival. Those so converted must spearhead a revaluation of all values. In doing so, they would take humanity 'beyond Good and Evil' as hitherto conceived, and themselves aspire to the condition of *Übermenschen*, or superior beings. All this was plainly heady stuff, and by 1914 Nietzsche's legacy had become a focal point of cult and controversy among intellectuals nearly everywhere in Europe. What mattered most was not their agreement or disagreement with him. Rather, it was their experience of catalytic engagement with a figure who, like Freud, had scourged the complacencies of a whole era.

The legacies of Darwin and Marx

Nietzsche's was not the only personal legacy that those bent upon analysing society around the turn of the century found themselves almost unavoidably addressing. Darwin and Marx (who had died in 1882 and 1883, respectively) also set posthumous challenges that stirred widespread controversy. Both had laboured during the heyday of positivism, each invoking science to underpin theories of social development which were at odds with religious orthodoxy, which emphasized group struggle (whether between species or classes), and which suggested that human destinies owed less to conscious choice and rational effort than to the impersonal forces of a biological or economic determinism. It was Engels who, at Marx's funeral, bracketed his friend together with Darwin by virtue of their shared achievement in connecting the general laws that governed organic nature and human history. However, such a Marxist reading of the social and political implications of the English naturalist's work never went uncontested, and dispute was all the more vigorous because so many others were also keen to claim the benefit of this scientific cachet, even at the expense of severely distorting his own intentions.

The outstanding feature of 'social Darwinism' was indeed its plasticity – its adaptability to multiple and often mutually inconsistent purposes. Liberals, for example, were apt to decode 'struggle' as a justification for individualistic competition within the free market of capitalism, whereas socialists tended to annex it to class warfare. By the turn of the century, Darwinistic rhetoric was also permeating debates on the dynamics and outcome of national and racial rivalries within and beyond Europe. The liberal version of nationalism prominent in 1848–49 had progressively weakened in the face of something fiercer, which could now be adapted to the supposedly Darwinian jungle of *Realpolitik*, where right was derived from might, and where morality was assessed principally according to its contribution towards survival. The schism from liberalism ran all the deeper as the vogue developed – most notably, but far from exclusively, in the form of Germanic 'Aryanism' – for treating racial essence as the leading criterion for nationhood. Darwin's phrase about 'The Preservation of Favoured Races in the Struggle for Life' (the subtitle to *Origin of Species*) was incorporated into assertions not simply about difference, but also about immutable inequalities of worth. Such racism, imbued with biological determinism, plainly aspired to be the ultimate embodiment of a truly scientific politics. Yet, as its later history increasingly demonstrated, it was equally capable of flourishing amid the Nietzschean and antipositivistic worship of instinct and intuition – as part of a culture where 'thinking with the blood' seemed all too natural. This potent brew of gut feeling, mixed with quasi-scientific rationalization, was already frequently encountered among Europeans during the generation before 1914. One prime example was the rapid intensification of racial antisemitism, while another was that belief in the superiority of white over 'coloured' stocks which pervaded the most recent and dramatic advances in colonial domination.

This imperialism was less problematic to social Darwinists than to those now extending the Marxist tradition. The latter needed to ask whether such colonial ventures were merely symptomatic of capitalism's terminal decay, or something more troubling to a revolutionary – that is, a means of postponing collapse by transferring overseas much of the burden of economic exploitation. During the epoch of the Second International (launched in 1889), Marxist thinking also needed to adapt to other developments that might be interpreted as bids for capitalistic self-protection, including wider franchise, state-sponsored welfare schemes, and legal recognition of trade unions. Did these features indeed strengthen the case for a 'gradualist' alternative to the pursuit of socialism by essentially revolutionary means? The dilemma was such that towards 1914 the largest of all parties championing Marxism – the German Social Democrats, inspired by Karl Kautsky – still seemed unable to escape, in practice, from the gradualism for which the 'revisionist' Eduard Bernstein (author of *Evolutionary Socialism*, 1899) had been so roundly criticised.

In autocratic Russia, much of this debate seemed irrelevant, especially because parliamentary institutions were absent before the revolt of

1905 and only feebly present thereafter. However, while broadly agreeing on resort to violence, the left-wing intelligentsia still wrangled over issues of leadership and timing, and over the specific roles assignable to peasants and proletarians. The 'populists' argued that the rural masses held the key to success. The response of Lenin, Marx's most renowned revolutionary heir, focused instead on the pivotal role of an industrial proletariat, albeit far smaller in its overall numbers. Lenin's elitist propensities were even more sharply suggested by his insistence that urban workers would need to be stimulated not simply by their own sufferings, but by an injection of heightened Marxist consciousness from a tightly disciplined cadre of professional revolutionaries. He also attacked gradualism by stressing that any tsarist concessions simply made urgent militancy more, rather than less, imperative. The split of 1903 within the Russian Social Democratic Labour Party was occasioned by the resistance of the so-called Menshevik faction to the organizational elitism of Lenin and his Bolshevik grouping. The divide deepened when the latter went on to castigate their rivals for collaborating with liberal-bourgeois elements, and thus for delaying the hour of revolution. Among Lenin's own critics, none was more perceptive than Rosa Luxemburg, a Pole prominent within the German Marxist movement. She contended, in essence, that Leninism was threatening to crush the spontaneity of the exploited beneath the overcentralized dictatorship of a vanguard Bolshevik Party. In Luxemburg's view, the result would be effectively to strip the working class even of its fundamental entitlement to ownership of the forthcoming revolution.

Fears about communism's authoritarian potentialities were also prominent in the anarchist movement. Back in 1872, the First International had collapsed amid accusations from Mikhail Bakunin that Marx was devaluing spontaneous action and becoming overkeen on exploiting, rather than destroying, state structures. By the years around 1900, writers such as Peter Kropotkin were helping to bring about the heyday of European anarchism. Though actual bomb-throwers remained a minority, the movement's ideas attracted quite widespread intellectual sympathy. Its endeavours to expose the moral suffocation entrenched within the bourgeois order were both uncompromising and timely. Equally so were its pleas for revolt through seemingly irrational violence which, as a means of spontaneous self-expression, allegedly restored individual freedom, identity and dignity. Thus anarchism, when interpreted as a critique of rational constraints and as a philosophy of will applied to politics, becomes relevant to those strange new worlds of the mind being explored by Freud or Nietzsche.

Towards a science of mass society

Similar concerns also confronted 'sociology', which in these years began to assert stronger claims to academic status. This term, like positivism, had been coined by Auguste Comte in the early nineteenth century, and many of the issues central to the subject had subsequently been addressed by Marx as well. Their efforts to expound the 'laws' of society had reflected a positivistic confidence in grand systems of scientific explanation that looked more questionable by 1900. By then, sociology was coming to appreciate that the sources of human action might be far more mysterious than previously thought. One important line of questioning, inspired by anthropology, called into doubt whether European experience alone could provide adequate criteria for judging the value of particular social practices. For example, despite the complacent belief of the white races in their own supremacy, there was evidence that alien and 'primitive' cultures could satisfy complex needs and sustain communal harmony on bases that were seemingly instinctual and remote from Western rationalistic constructs.

Reconsideration was all the more urgent under circumstances associated with the rising influence of the masses everywhere in Europe itself. Even if Marx welcomed their approaching triumph, many other analysts were more fearful. Two French authors, for example, were particularly notable for their pioneering, and disturbing, studies of mass behaviour. In *The Crowd* (1895), Gustave Le Bon showed how, through 'mental contagion', apparently rational individuals might lapse into irrational behaviour once placed within a herd context; and the criminologist Gabriel Tarde highlighted in *Opinion and the Crowd* (1901) the manipulative potential of mass communication, particularly as directed towards securing the 'imitation' of superiors by inferiors. Such works heightened doubts as to whether, despite all the fashionable progressive rhetoric about egalitarian democracy, a gullible populace was fated to remain permanently in thrall to manipulative elites. The issue soon became central to political sociology. Here, in *The Ruling Class* (1896), Gaetano Mosca suggested that an elite could perpetuate its authority through astutely chosen 'political formulas', almost regardless of whether these reflected empirical truth. From Robert Michels there came *Political Parties: A Sociological Study of the Oligarchical Tendencies of Modern Democracy* (1911), a work whose title hints at its argument about an 'iron law' operating towards a professionalization of leadership, and thus towards elitist expertise and dominance. Then, in *Socialist Systems* (1902) and in the more general treatise translated as *Mind and Society* (1916–23), Vilfredo Pareto explored how elites 'circulated', with success going to whatever group might devise, from time to time, the most topical and alluring rhetorical structures based on its grasp of the interplay between rational and non-rational behaviour.

Among those who were now setting sociology's future agenda, pride of place is shared between a Frenchman and a German, Emile Durkheim and Max Weber. The former's works include *The Division of Labour in Society* (1893), a refutation of Marx's view that this process must be inevitably an 'alienating' one; *The Rules of Sociological Method* (1895); *Suicide* (1897), a study of the social dysfunctions conditioning a type of behaviour usually misinterpreted as being supremely individualistic; and *The Elementary Forms of Religious Life* (1912), in which gods are treated as the symbolization of social interests, and especially of a craving for community. Durkheim remained enough of a positivist to try to find a scientific basis for identifying the form of morality most conducive to harmony within a mass society which was now (rightly, in his view) rejecting Christianity – and he believed that the price of failure would be the growth of *anomie*, a pathological absence or confusion of norms. As for Weber, his *Protestant Ethic and the Spirit of Capitalism* (1904–05) countered Marx not simply by showing how religious factors might rival economic ones as social influences, but also by dismissing any kind of monocausal determinism. Other writings expanded his analysis of the 'rationalization' process, which he had discerned in capitalism and Calvinism alike, and which was now evident in the spread of bureaucracy. Here, like Michels, he feared lest the linkage between expertise and power might endanger individual freedom. Would people react to this threat by attaching their hopes to 'charismatic' heroes, deemed to possess exceptional, almost magical qualities? And might the leadership of such figures provide psychological compensation for what otherwise seemed, under conditions of secularization, a diminished sense of purpose and a soulless demoralization? These anxieties stemmed from Weber's view that rationalization also entailed 'disenchantment' – a liberation from magic that is inseparable from a feeling of loss, and indeed of 'disillusionment' as commonly conceived. The ebbing of traditional belief, the crisis of disorientation, and the value of some functional substitute for religion remained for him, as for Durkheim, central issues. No less than Nietzsche or Freud, Weber was querying just how much reality humankind could bear.

Horizons of imagination

In all the domains surveyed so far, we have encountered a radical questioning of previous assumptions. During the quarter-century before 1914, this was no less evident in the sphere of imaginative creativity, particularly as expressed through the literary and visual arts. Here, again, positivism had left a firm imprint on the work of the previous generation, when 'realism' and 'naturalism' had dominated the scene in their pursuit of what the French novelist, Emile Zola, called 'the exact study of facts and things'.[7] His own 20-volume sequence entitled *Les Rougon-Macquart* (1871–93), a family saga detailing the interaction of heredity and environment, was the greatest literary monument to this attempt to dignify art by converting it into a documentary supplement of science. It was largely by movement against and beyond such positivistic constraints that the culture of 'modernism' took shape towards the end of the century.

One of the most seminal modernist figures was Henrik Ibsen, a Norwegian dramatist famed throughout Europe by 1900, whose plays first embodied and then transcended naturalism. For example, his treatment of female revolt against the asphyxiating hypocrisies of male-dominated society becomes subtler – especially in evoking those inner forces most defiant of capture by quasi-scientific description – as between *A Doll's House* (1879) and *Hedda Gabler* (1890). The latter set the tone for the consummate psychological and spiritual explorations that pervaded Ibsen's final achievements, such as *The Master Builder* (1892) and *When We Dead Awaken* (1899). A similar shift is evident in the case of the German novelist Thomas Mann. 'Naturalistic' was the term that he applied to *Buddenbrooks* (1902), his first major work, dealing with the fortunes of a Hanseatic merchant family similar to his own. Yet, even there, the treatment of the tensions between artistic and bourgeois values was hinting that introspective exploration of individual creativity might properly take precedence over more mundane concerns with social documentation.

Mann's growing preoccupation with this theme was most famously crystallized in his novella of 1911 entitled *Death in Venice*. That story, where the author-hero dies amid obsessive contemplation of the golden boy Tadzio, prompted questions not just about the corruptive power of art, but also about the degree of frankness permissible in discussions of sexuality. As Freud had also emphasized, here was the domain within which respectable society could be most readily shocked and its hypocrisies most explosively punctured. Attacks on the 'normal' sexual conventions of polite society thus became central to the wider revolt against customary assumptions. The call of 'art for art's sake' was also increasingly heard. Did this mean that it could now impose its own terms and supplant conventional values by offering society some counter-morality, Nietzschean or otherwise? Or did such a slogan imply that artistic endeavours of every kind must now renounce all social and moral engagement whatsoever? Those favouring the latter conclusion turned inward to create a private world of symbolic expression and pure form, accessible only to fellow initiates. They found beauty not in nature, but in the artifice that transcended it. This 'aestheticism' involved making one's own life into a work of art, so as to proclaim the delights of the extravagant, the useless and the effete – the allure of everything exotic, occult and perverse. It was encapsulated in Joris-Karl Huysmans' *A Rebours* (1884, sometimes translated as *Against Nature*), which offered to the pre-1914 generation the model for a lifestyle that writers and artists such as Oscar Wilde and Aubrey Beardsley sought directly to embrace. To condemn this as 'decadent' merely encouraged its practitioners to convert that same label into a badge of pride.

If prose supplied the most obvious medium for naturalism's positivistic pretensions, it was often poetry that best reflected the introspective concerns of *fin-de-siècle* writers. Pre-eminent here was the French 'symbolist' movement, associated particularly with Arthur Rimbaud, Paul Verlaine and Stéphane Mallarmé. Their wider influence was apparent also from work in German by such poets as Stefan George and the Austrian Rainer Maria Rilke. Symbolist truths sprang not from science, but from what Rimbaud called 'a disordering of all the senses'.[8] Thus inspired, these poets contributed to that heightened interest in the mystical and the irrational that we have already observed elsewhere. They immersed themselves in the flow of language and in the magical properties of sound. Particularly in Mallarmé's final works of the 1890s, the grammatical and typographical eccentricities appeared to suggest that the strategy of insulating the artist from the philistine world had reached the point where the communicative power of words stood in peril of exhaustion.

By the start of World War One, no author had managed better than Marcel Proust to encapsulate within a single volume most of those concerns that we have seen moulding literature's contribution to the cultural upheaval of this epoch. *Swann's Way* (1913), the opening instalment within a long-planned cycle of novels focusing on French society since the late nineteenth century, embodied a precision of observation that certainly drew upon naturalistic techniques. Yet it also went beyond them – reflecting, for example, the symbolists' sense of fragile language under strain, and their concern with the tensions between artistic introspection and exposure to the harsh realities of the everyday world. Like Freud, Proust was probing into the mysteries of different levels of consciousness, and into the complex memory processes through which we recapture fragments of largely forgotten past experience. For him, remembrance is an essentially active force, which gives us our sense of identity and releases from the prison of the subconscious something of our own past that then becomes vital to our present. Contentment stems only from the recapturing of time gone, from the recontemplation of paradises lost. This is a world where the multiple refractions between past and present warp all ordinary chronology, and where every perspective endlessly shifts. Thus, while Proust's work was never directly inspired by science in the manner of Zola's, it possessed vertiginous and disorientating qualities that seemed similar to the new physics in offering what his first major biographer called 'the picture of a relativistic universe, expanding and contracting in a curved space–time continuum'.[9]

In painting, as in literature, much of the urge towards innovation around the turn of the century stemmed from revolt against the limitations of naturalism. Even when Claude Monet and Auguste Renoir launched their own challenge in the 1870s, it was upon the quasi-scientific merits of the new 'impressionism' – as 'this study of light in its thousand decompositions and recompositions'[10] became known – that Zola based his influential support. Over the longer run, however, this was not the emphasis that prevailed. The eventual success of impressionism and 'post-impressionism' flowed not from an ability to complete an experiment, but from a capacity to convey intensely subjective perceptions of mood and atmosphere. In his great 'series' paintings of the 1890s – repeatedly exploring such subjects as Rouen cathedral under rapidly changing conditions of light and weather – Monet was repudiating any idea of definitive version or final answer. Here 'reality' is the sum of countless different appearances, each spatially and temporally personal. A century – and millions of reproductions – later, the works inspired by impressionism in the years before 1914 now seem so familiar that we can easily underestimate how radically they explored new ways of seeing. Those in the vanguard of innovation were asking, for example, what might be learned from the forms through which children, or the insane, or those living in 'primitive' and exotic cultures depicted external reality – and indeed expressed their own internal worlds of feeling too. The latter point was particularly vital in helping to highlight the most fundamental issue of all: a rethinking of what art itself should be about.

That question dominated the final prewar years, when – during perhaps the most stimulating single decade in the history of modern European art – the movements of cubism, futurism and expressionism made their mark. The towering figure among cubists was Pablo Picasso, whose *Demoiselles d'Avignon* (1907) constituted their first great statement.

While its mask-like faces reflected his debt to African and other exotic art, the depersonalization of its female figures was even more deeply conveyed by the angular and fragmented manner in which the painting presented them. As with Proust, a plurality of viewpoints accentuated an uncertainty of identity; as with Einstein, space was being conceptually remodelled. Soon Picasso and his closest associate, Georges Braque, were repeatedly shattering the rules of single-point perspective. They superimposed planes, and flouted the conventions of opaqueness and transparency. Their splintering of form became such that by 1910–11 cubism was coming close to losing all identifiable contact with those objects from the external world that still served as its alleged points of departure. Although Picasso and Braque then turned to collage, together they had certainly helped to stimulate debate as to whether art might now best fulfil its potentialities by concentrating on non-representational themes and techniques. Towards 1914, futurism too was probing these borderlands between the perceptual and the conceptual, between form seen and form thought. Originally launched from Italy in 1909 as a literary movement, it advocated a focus on the dynamism of the city and the machine, the habit of energy, the beauty of speed, and the pursuit of struggle (with war as the supreme manifestation of a mechanized culture). The painters who adopted these ideas based themselves on industrial Milan, and repeatedly wrangled with the task of simultaneously freezing and conveying rapid motion. Umberto Boccioni and Carlo Carrà were prominent as refiners of a technique, already engaging the cubists as well, analogous to multiple or continuous exposure in photography. With Giacomo Balla, who was particularly stimulated by the new physics, one encountered pictures (such as those of 1913 devoted to *Abstract Speed*) where the conversion of matter into dynamic light and colour has, yet again, almost reached the point of abandoning any representation of objects as such.

This was the issue upon which expressionist painting went furthest of all, in its preoccupation with inner feeling and a laying bare of the soul, in its assertion of spirit and imagination against the crushing forces of materialism. Within its pedigree there is a significant place for the Dutchman Vincent Van Gogh (who killed himself in 1890) and the Norwegian Edvard Munch, both of whom superbly communicated states of anguish through their work. In the early twentieth century, expressionism became centred on two artistic groups, one formed as 'Die Brücke' (The Bridge) at Dresden in 1905, and another as 'Der Blaue Reiter' (The Blue Rider) at Munich in 1911. The latter included the Russian Vasily Kandinsky, who arguably did more than any other single figure to complete the breakthrough into a radically non-representational artistic idiom. His own awareness of the revolutionary nature of this undertaking was amply apparent from his commentary of 1911, *Concerning the Spiritual in Art*. It pleaded for liberation from an excessive preoccupation with external phenomena, and sought instead to inspire the kind of creativity that would enable the expression of 'a slowly formed inner feeling'.[11] This was the philosophy behind a series of paintings that Kandinsky entitled *Compositions*. There he explored, between 1910 and 1913, the communicative qualities inherent within colours and forms to the point where any residual influence from external objects was purely incidental. As a reflection of the interior forces of the mind operating at different levels of consciousness, the work of art – in itself – now constituted 'reality'.

Blood and darkness

Everything we have surveyed so far serves to suggest that, even before the guns began to fire in 1914, many far-reaching changes of attitude and perception were already rapidly developing in Europe. Their scale was such as to justify a later view that they should be rated among 'those overwhelming dislocations, those cataclysmic upheavals of culture, those fundamental convulsions of the human spirit that seem to topple even the most substantial of our beliefs and assumptions'.[12] If intellectual turmoil was indeed amply present by the eve of World War One, then the nature of the ensuing struggle could only increase that same sense of upheaval. What the novelist Henry James called 'this abyss of blood and darkness'[13] made it all the more difficult to avoid confrontation with doubt and disorientation. The conflict accentuated the potential relevance and even the acceptability of many of the new trends and concepts that had been emerging even before 1914. In sum, much of the intellectual and cultural history of the 1920s and 1930s deals with ideas that were projected from the turn of the century and were then refracted, first through the experience of general warfare and subsequently through that of economic collapse and authoritarian dictatorship.

The war that ended in 1918 was, in a crucial sense, quite different from the one that had started four years previously (analysed further in Chapter 5). At that earlier and more innocent epoch, the German Crown Prince had talked of a swift, and even 'jolly', combat. During 1915, however, Europeans began to realize that they had become bogged down – often quite literally – in a conflict characterized not by rapid mobility, but by slow attrition. This was especially apparent across the desolate landscape of the Western Front – the world not of

Rupert Brooke's poetic romanticization of war, but of Wilfred Owen's anguished lamentations. By the time of the Armistice, most surviving Europeans, whatever their own particular experience or interpretation of the hostilities, saw the conflict as forming a decisive temporal landmark. The idiom of 'prewar' and 'postwar' became almost immediately current as an expression of the widespread modulation of consciousness engendered by the recent battles – ones in which the wonders of industrial advance once cited by Macaulay had suffered gigantic conversion from productive to destructive purposes.

What price, now, the idea of progress that had previously seemed so plausible? The question was all the more pressing because, in the course of its fighting, the war had assumed a far deeper ideological significance than Europe's leaders had anticipated at the outset. The victorious Western powers might take comfort from the fall of the more autocratic Hohenzollerns, Habsburgs and Romanovs. However, the task of securing the future of the domains previously ruled by the first two dynasties was complicated by the fact that the battered empire of the third was now governed by Lenin. He certainly had ideas about progress, but not ones that readily tallied with the liberal-democratic aspirations of France, Britain or the USA. The spectre of his Bolshevism would haunt the peacemakers who gathered in 1919 at Paris. There President Woodrow Wilson offered the alternative formula of 'national self-determination' as a basis for freedom and felicity. But how practicable was this, granted especially the unstable power vacuum created in central and eastern Europe by a war that surprisingly ended with all three of the region's great powers – Germany, Austria-Hungary and Russia – being, in one sense or another, defeated? It is arguable that Wilson's rhetorical flourishes simply embodied a Mazzinian innocence without the excuse of belonging to the Mazzinian age, when the illiberal potentialities of nationalism had not yet become so apparent. Clearer still is the fact that the President implemented self-determination inconsistently, and failed to rally either the US Congress or his allies properly to its cause. The gaps between, on one hand, the professions of principle surrounding the negotiations and, on the other, the realities of the outcome undermined confidence in the legitimacy of the settlement – and, even more generally still, in the liberal-democratic values that it claimed to uphold. The tragedy of the Versailles treaty, in particular, was not that it annoyed Hitler and his fellow-extremists (for nothing more reasonable would have satisfied them), but that it alienated many more moderate Germans and, even more remarkably, failed to retain the respect of so many within the victor nations themselves.

Ideological confrontations

Among the earliest liberal critics was John Maynard Keynes. His *Economic Consequences of the Peace* (1919), highlighting the shortsightedness of massive reparation demands, rapidly proved to be an international bestseller. By the mid-1920s, this had helped to spur some measure of revisionism. Amid the atmosphere of the Locarno and Kellogg–Briand Pacts, and of the Dawes and Young Plans, there were hopes of refurbishing the idea of progress on the basis of the liberal conviction that, in Karl Bracher's words, 'politics is the art of the peaceful settlement of diverging interests, and that its method is democratic decision by the majority, ensuring protection for the minority and the right of opposition'.[14] But the Great Depression of the early 1930s, triggered by the Wall Street Crash of October 1929, transformed the whole scene. For the second time within a generation, vast forces appeared to be escaping from human control, even from all rational understanding. The catastrophe of 1914 had been readily blamed on autocratic emperors. Now these were no longer available as scapegoats for the unprecedented scale of collapse that seemed to shatter every familiar orthodoxy about the essentially self-regulating mechanisms of liberal capitalism. At this juncture, Keynes was once again prominent – now in advocating the need to generate a more symbiotic relationship between the values of individualism and the pressures for greater governmental involvement in economic planning. He was right to declare in *The General Theory of Employment, Interest, and Money* (1936) that this epoch-making work crystallized a 'struggle of escape from habitual modes of thought and expression'.[15] Meanwhile, however, it was not only the dole queues that had been growing – so, too, through much of Europe, had the allure of more radical substitutes for the seemingly discredited principles of political and economic liberalism.

Communism (see also Chapter 6) provided the first of two principal sources of new inspiration. Most Marxists had barely anticipated a situation in which early twentieth-century Europe would march into general warfare on the basis of national rather than class rivalries. Yet Lenin, in particular, was to prove adept at exploiting the unexpected. He and his comrades were aided by the fact that they were not only blameless for the horrors of World War One, but were also offering a comprehensive humanitarian ideal that promised to restore substance to the idea of progress. Until the Bolshevik revolution, the main thrust of Marxism had been a critical and negative one, potentially subversive of all established governments. Having lost this political virginity in 1917, communist ideology now formed the basis for actual rule in Europe's most populous state. How well would it survive that translation from theory to practice, especially within a far less industrialized society than Marx had envisaged for such a pioneering revolutionary role? Any answer was sure to be marked with the Bolsheviks' most distinctive stamp – the organizational elitism already strongly justified in Lenin's earlier polemics. Once in power, his party machine maintained a certain distance from the proletariat in whose name, but beyond whose control, it operated. Such autonomy eased its embarkation upon a task whose theoretical status was disputable – that of using political power as the instrument of radical transformation in Russia's supposedly substructural economic conditions. There was no prospect here of the state 'withering away' in fulfilment of the most utopian of Marxist expectations. Particularly after the suppression of the Kronstadt rising in February 1921, it was evident that the Bolsheviks would be ruthless in pursuit of their objectives. They would tolerate no rival organization, socialist or otherwise, nor any separation between party and government. Even the much vaunted federal constitution of the new USSR could not obscure the realities of imperial-dictatorial centralization.

Both within and beyond Bolshevik Russia, a major issue was that of revolution's likely spread. While the Paris peacemakers were fearful, the new Third Communist International was conversely confident about the outcome of further risings. However, once those of 1919 in Berlin, Munich and Budapest had failed to take permanent root, Lenin needed to improvise responses to an unexpectedly protracted period of revolutionary isolation. By the time of his death early in 1924, there were deep divisions on this topic between Joseph Stalin and Leon Trotsky. While the former wished to prioritize the consolidation of 'socialism in one country', the latter dismissed this as a recipe for bureaucratic stagnation, and advocated instead a strategy of 'permanent revolution' requiring urgent and ceaseless activism on an international scale. By 1929, when he secured the deportation of Trotsky, Stalin had already launched the first of his Five-Year Plans. This embodied massive industrialization, coupled with agricultural collectivization. The dynamism of the first made more immediate propaganda impact than the follies of the second. Thus it was not surprising that, at the very epoch when the Great Depression was ravaging the capitalist system, the USSR's version of idealistic progress seemed all the more attractive to many foreign observers.

The persistence of such appeal thereafter is perhaps harder to explain. It clearly helped that the full scale of Stalin's tyranny was, as far as possible, hidden by a huge apparatus of secrecy and censorship. Moreover, whenever suffering could not be concealed, his regime depicted it as the unavoidable price for survival in a world of hostile capitalist states. By 1936–38, the Soviet Union lay in the grip of a Stalinist reign of terror. Millions suffered arbitrary arrest, followed by condemnation to labour camp or to death or – in effect – to both. These purges, preceding the worst of the Nazis' own barbarities, swept even through the Party itself, 'liquidating' not least those comrades (including Trotsky and Nikolai Bukharin) who dared to question Stalin's ideological primacy. This was also the decade when Soviet communist discourse accelerated its descent into the crudest versions of dialectical materialism. The survival of any more self-critical Marxist tradition thus became dependent during the interwar period on thinkers operating beyond Russia: for instance, the Hungarian György Lukács (up to 1930, the date of his 'recantation' in Moscow), the Italian Antonio Gramsci, and in Weimar Germany such figures of 'the Frankfurt School' as Max Horkheimer, Walter Benjamin and Theodor Adorno.

The fact that Gramsci spent the last 11 years of his life in one of Mussolini's jails symbolizes the emergence of fascism (explored further in Chapter 7) as a second major threat to the politics of moderation. The elements of novelty in its style of thought and action confused not only liberals, but many communists and democratic socialists too. Those on the Left who viewed the various fascist movements emerging across Europe in the 1920s and 1930s principally as symptoms of decay within the capitalist system were often inclined to leave such activists temporarily free to hasten the destruction of liberal-democratic values. Orthodox Stalinists were among those who – both initially and then again in the period of the Nazi–Soviet Pact from 1939 to 1941 – underestimated the scope of the threat to themselves as well. At such points, analysis based solely on polar opposition between the 'extreme Left' of Stalin and the 'extreme Right' of Mussolini and Hitler does insufficient justice to their points of resemblance. Each of the three dictators used both propaganda and violence to mobilize mass support behind regimes that expressed contempt for representative democracy and consensual compromise. All three sought to impose, through the power of the single-party state, a standardized mode of life and thought, where distinctions between the public and private realms would be annihilated and every prompting of individual conscience nullified. Furthermore, the various ideologies that justified these aims, and offered a reinvigorated sense of purpose and progress, became closed intellectual systems, built on assumptions of absolute certainty about the past struggles and future destinies of the particular class, or race, or nation-state championed, respectively, by Stalin, Hitler, and Mussolini.

During the 1920s, it was the Italian 'Duce' who set the tone for fascist activism. Imitative movements of a minority nature then developed in parts of western Europe, while in such countries as Spain, Hungary and Romania there was a tendency for similar techniques of political mobilization to be absorbed within stronger forces of traditional authoritarianism. Most significantly of all, by the 1930s contemporaries were readily viewing Nazism as Germany's particular contribution to a broader European phenomenon. The various fascist movements generally aspired to go beyond the familiar rhetoric of 'left' and 'right', so as to transcend both socialism and capitalism as hitherto understood. They aimed to make irrelevant the habitual confrontation between conservative and revolutionary, by offering a higher form of shared community. However, they also treated such fellow-feeling in a spirit of national or racial exclusiveness that set it apart from the universalistic ideals preached not just by liberalism, but by socialism and communism too. Fascism's violent cult of elitist domination never embodied that note of apology – those allusions to temporary expediency – intermittently observable even in Stalinism. Moreover, Mussolini and Hitler, in particular, proved more adept than most of their opponents at exploiting mass psychology and propaganda, and at harnessing the power of mass emotion in ways foreshadowed by the analyses of Le Bon and company. The measure of support that fascism obtained from intellectual circles was indeed largely attributable to its ability to draw from the wells of irrationalism enlarged before World War One. In this sense, the aggressive modernity of its elite-inspired myths helped to encourage within the mass of its supporters an epic and redemptive state of mind.

With Mussolini, whose intellectually pretentious 'Doctrine of Fascism' was elaborated only in 1932, theory tended to follow practice and to be focused principally on a glorification of the state as 'the synthesis and unity of all values'.[16] While Hitler's ideas were similarly anti-individualistic, they differed in being well formed from a much earlier stage, and having at their core a racist worldview based on the crudest type of social Darwinism. Within the Nazi interpretation of history, race played the same pivotal and deterministic role as class did for the Marxists. As the Führer asserted in *Mein Kampf* (1925–26), 'All the human culture, all the results of art, science, and technology that we see before us today, are almost exclusively the creative product of the Aryan ... He alone was the founder of all higher humanity, therefore representing the prototype of all that we understand by the word "man".'[17] From this it was easy to conclude, conversely, that non-Aryans were something less than fully human – even to the point of suggesting that certain races embodied essentially bestial features. By 1945, Europe's Jews had become the principal – although not the only – victims of this ideology centred on racial hierarchy. Debate continues about whether full-scale genocide was, even from the outset, the fate that Hitler had in mind for them. What is less disputable, though, is the logic behind the eventual annihilation of something contemptuously designated as an 'anti-race', as a lethal biological threat to Aryan mastery. While any brand of racism must depersonalize its victims, the exterminatory thrust of the Nazi version involved subjecting them to an even more radical dehumanization.

Those mass murders were not the work of 'savages' in the sense that Europeans had usually given to that word. Instead, they were perpetrated from the heartlands of supposed civilization. Amid all the turmoil of the first half of the twentieth century, the Third Reich was certainly unique in the pitch that its barbarities attained. Even while inflicting his own vast terror, Stalin had never forsworn certain humane aspirations; and not even he had brought theory and practice so perfectly into murderous alignment as did Hitler. Thus it is easy to see why, after its defeat in 1945, Germany became the object of such universal condemnation. Even so, this should not obscure the senses in which Nazism had simply intensified a mood of antisemitic and other brutality already endemic within much of Europe. As Alan Bullock wrote of the Führer, 'The condition and state of mind which he exploited, the *malaise* of which he was the symptom, were not confined to one country ... Hitler's idiom was German, but the thoughts and emotions to which he gave expression have a more universal currency.'[18]

The authoritarian politicization of culture

If the experience of a generation that had stumbled from Ypres to Auschwitz was hardly reconcilable with simple faith in political or social improvement, it was similarly obvious by 1945 that any assumptions about the steady advance of intellectual and cultural achievement must be severely questioned. Back in August 1914, many writers and artists had shared in the patriotic intoxication of the moment. Some, such as the Italian futurists, or the German novelist Ernst Jünger (author of a semi-autobiographical 'diary', *The Storm of Steel*, published in 1920), continued, even to the end, their celebration of bracing conflict. However, especially as the battles of attrition took increasing toll, the dominant tone became more sombre. From France there came Romain Rolland's *Above the Battlefield* (1915), a Nobel Prize-winning essay advocating international pacifist solidarity amongst intellectuals, and the novel *Under Fire* (1916), in which Henri Barbusse detailed the grim realities of trench warfare. The theme of revulsion from mindless slaughter was similarly pursued after the war by the German novelist Erich Maria Remarque, whose *All Quiet on the Western Front* (1929) attracted swift international celebrity and was promptly adapted in Hollywood for the cinema. The path by which, ten years later, Europe became again a battlefield was partly shaped by each of those two broad mentalities. The enthusiasts who believed in struggle as a whole way of life would never have got as far as they did by the late 1930s without the appeasing propensities of others who were prepared to pay almost any price in order to escape the horrors of renewed warfare.

Viewed as a whole, the period from 1914 to 1945 was characterized by an increasing politicization of cultural endeavour. This was all the more remarkable as it ran counter to much of the original modernist impulse. Part of the legacy from the pre-1914 epoch was a questioning as to whether the creative activity that went on *amidst* public events should also be directed *towards* them. In short, how essential was social engagement? We have already noted within modernism the many elements of abstraction and introspection, including a criticism of positivistic realism and an advocacy of 'art for art's sake', that served to support initially negative answers. However, the era following World War One was not one in which it was easy to sustain for very long any position of creative neutrality or disengagement. The pressures towards politicization obviously proved strongest within the countries that fell directly beneath the control of authoritarian dictators. Under Hitler and Stalin especially, the fanatical political party became central to the operation of the repressive state. Every channel of propaganda was mobilized in support of ideological orthodoxy, and the new media of cinema and radio broadcasting were exploited to particularly striking effect. The dictatorships also politicized the rapidly developing spheres of mass sport and leisure, as well as every level of the formal education system. Such authoritarian regimes sought to make independent thought itself unthinkable, and to erase the individuality of literary or other creative activity. Thus by the mid-1930s virtually any habit of behaviour or expression on the part of those subject to such rule – whether they adopted this in a spirit of dissent, or of enthusiastic commitment, or simply of conformist acquiescence – assumed a political meaning.

From its earliest days, the Soviet regime insisted that culture should serve the purposes of communist advance. Initially, this approach preserved some potential for experimentation with those *avant-garde* forms that had developed, even in the West, as part of the modernist critique of bourgeois civilization. The Bolsheviks urged Kandinsky into a temporary return to Russia so that he might supervise picture purchasing for the state museums, and on May Day 1918 they bedecked Moscow with the 'suprematist' abstract images of Kasimir Malevich and his followers. Creative innovation was also outstandingly characteristic of early Soviet film-making, inspired by directors such as Vsevolod Pudovkin and Sergei Eisenstein. Cinema was a genre technological in its basis, industrial in its organization, and popular in its appeal – not least, it formed a medium as uncluttered as the Bolshevik regime itself by any associations with tsarist or bourgeois values. When Eisenstein completed *Battleship Potemkin* in 1925, it was still possible to argue for some congruence between political revolution and cultural experimentation. However, as Stalin consolidated his authority, the remaining scope for literary and artistic independence rapidly vanished. The regime increasingly demanded conformity of production in terms of 'socialist realism', a revamped naturalism concerned with easily accessible depictions of fascist enemies, proletarian muscles, hard hammers and sharp sickles. Novelists were encouraged to glorify the technological achievements of the Five-Year Plans, but without referring to the forms of Stalinist terror that accompanied their implementation. A similar blight fell upon theatre, film and the visual arts. Even music could not escape: when the communist newspaper *Pravda* condemned modernistic 'chaos' and advocated more popularly attractive tunes, the USSR's two leading composers of the later 1930s and 1940s, Dmitri Shostakovich and Sergei Prokoviev, found it only prudent to comply.

On the fascist side, Mussolini never attained a comparable degree of control. It is true that, from early on, those who proposed to earn their living from intellectual or artistic activities within Italy's new corporatist state were obliged to join the appropriate *sindacato* or union. Yet it was only after 1935, with the formation of the Ministry of Press and Propaganda (soon relabelled as Ministry of Popular Culture), that such controls meshed into a sustained campaign directed towards standardization of content and technique. By then, it was the Führer rather than the Duce who was setting the tone for cultural fascism in Europe. Quite simply, from 1933 the Nazis were just as rapid and ruthless in matters of intellectual purging as in the other spheres where they similarly pursued *Gleichschaltung*. That policy – essentially one of crushing everything into a flat uniformity – brought a swift end to the creative excitement characteristic of the Weimar period, when political and aesthetic innovation had run hand-in-hand, and Berlin had begun to rival Paris as a cosmopolitan focal point for European culture.

Many exiles from the Third Reich endeavoured to salvage something of worth elsewhere. Inside Germany, however, only the hollow heroic and the sickly sentimental survived as weapons with which to combat the perceived menace of *Kulturbolschewismus*. An assault was launched even on language itself, by a regime that made the discourse of 'Nazi-Deutsch' ('final solution', 'protective custody', and much else besides) a means not of clarifying but of obscuring thought and action alike. Literature and painting, music and film, broadcasting and every form of popular culture were all dragooned into celebrating the sacredness of Aryan blood and soil, the imminent triumphs of the master race. Led by Joseph Goebbels, Nazi cultural propagandists thrust modernism aside – for example, condemning Van Gogh and Picasso as representatives of 'degenerate art' – and returned to forms of pedantic naturalism in order to project their ideas of strength and joy. As favoured by Hitler and Stalin, respectively, depictions of Nazi-Aryan muscle and of Soviet-proletarian muscle looked all too similar; and in both German and Russian cases this was often the kind of art preferred for decorating new public buildings whose architecture appeared notable only for its bombastic monumentality.

These two leading dictatorships also aimed to extend their 'totalitarian' control across other intellectual domains. From the outset, the Bolsheviks had conferred an unhealthily monopolistic status upon Marxist approaches to knowledge. Under Stalin, these were further narrowed into a particularly arid version of dialectical materialism. Thus the method that Lenin had commended for every context now became the only one tolerated within each, whether involving the study of philosophy or history, linguistics or genetics. In Nazi Germany, it was antisemitism and the rest of racist biology that similarly tainted every area of scholarship, often producing an alluring mysticism semi-disguised by the mantle of scientific pretension. Here the corruption of intellect penetrated even to the superficially apolitical sphere of theoretical physics, which had become the centre ground of scientific revolution in the years around 1900. The consequences for the Reich were essentially counterproductive. Condemnation of 'Jewish physics' would have been indefensible at any time; but in an era when Jewish scientists deserved their prominence among the best in the field, such attacks were also, in a precise sense, self-defeating. Nazi racism spurred a flight of talent from those universities – most notably Göttingen and Berlin – that during the 1920s had rivalled Cambridge at the leading edge of research into the structure and potency of the atom. By the time the military relevance of this was becoming plainer, many of those exiles were working in countries hostile to Hitler. It was fitting that his regime, so contemptuous of real scholarship, should have debilitated those same centres of excellence that might otherwise have helped to produce – through alliance between science, technology and ruthless military ambition – a uniquely powerful instrument for the domination the Führer craved.

Varieties of response

By the later 1930s, these developments were concentrating minds on major public issues, even in the countries still lying beyond the direct ambit of authoritarian control. Heightened political consciousness was speeded by the migration of refugees. The retreat of Jews and others from actual or imminent Nazi rule grew in scale, and included a significant proportion of artists, writers and scientists. Overall, the rising numbers of the persecuted, whether or not they reached shelter abroad, helped to stimulate greater social engagement among those European intellectuals who still enjoyed freer conditions of expression. Even within the ranks of the latter, there were some who did willingly succumb to the spell of fascism. A rather larger number saw it as a threat that needed to be countered by allegiance to a Marxism more humanely inspired, and many of these tended to treat whatever there might be of substance in tales of Stalinist terror as a matter of temporary aberration or transient necessity. But among others – probably most numerous of all – a distaste for fascism and communism alike prompted renewed awareness of the interdependence between political liberties and creative freedoms. For them, the ideological confrontations of the 1930s strengthened what the Great Depression had already served to encourage: a realization that, at this epoch, any intellectual or imaginative activity that simply spurned social commitment might well be viewed as mere frivolity.

In such a climate, the churches too were under increasing pressure to offer guidance. But who or what would they identify as the real enemies of 'Christian civilization'? The anticlerical and secularizing force of liberalism was undoubtedly a longstanding foe. However, the atheistic values associated with the USSR were now even more plainly menacing. So great was the communist threat that Hitler's anti-Bolshevism won him an otherwise inexplicable degree of ecclesiastical acquiescence, from Protestant and Catholic circles alike. Despite the evident tensions between Nazism and Christianity, both the Führer and the churches at large found themselves playing for time, with neither side eager to enter prematurely into a situation of total and open hostility. These compromises, accepted by religious leaders for the sake of limiting institutional damage, were bought at high moral cost to Christianity. According to James Joll, 'The Churches in general did not, and perhaps could not, rise above the prejudices of most of their members, who had welcomed or accepted the rise of National Socialism, just as other Germans had done and for the same reason.'[19] In Italy, moreover, the Vatican strove harder to accommodate Mussolini's regime than it had done to support any of the governments that had operated within the 'liberal' era beginning from the 1860s. Similarly, General Franco's victory over 'red' republicanism in the Spanish Civil War of 1936–39 – earned with vital help from the Führer and the Duce – was a triumph that the Catholic Church took for its own.

Where, finally, did imaginative literature – so central to the European cultural tradition throughout half a millennium – become most significantly engaged by the ideological conflicts that increasingly absorbed this generation? During the earlier 1920s, especially, some of the most stimulating work did remain politically detached, or at least politically ambiguous. The poetry of Rilke in German and of Paul Valéry in French continued the symbolist disdain for worldly involvement. After the American-born T. S. Eliot had published *The Waste Land* from Britain in 1922, he felt obliged to hint at its essentially private meanings in answer to those who treated it too simply as a public statement about the aridity of contemporary civilization. The Sicilian playwright Luigi Pirandello also won sudden postwar renown through dramas suggesting that no single reading of reality could ever be deemed authoritative. As for the novel, Proust's progress through the cycle started by *Swann's Way* certainly confirmed his virtuosity, but also his lack of enthusiasm for registering directly political messages. The year in which he died, 1922, was also the year in which the Irishman James Joyce issued from Paris his own principal contribution to the modernist upheaval. *Ulysses* was narrated through forms of prose-poetry that blended naturalistic detail with symbolist inspiration, and carried the art of interior monologue ('streams of consciousness') to new heights. With *Finnegans Wake* (1939), Joyce's assault on literary convention stretched even to the radical fracturing and luxuriant recreation of language itself. The author of these works was plainly involved in a cultural revolution, but hardly a political one. Nor could straightforward ideological intent be attributed to the paradoxical tales written in German by Franz Kafka, who died in 1924. Only later would hindsight allow readers to marvel at how, while living originally under Habsburg rule, this Czech Jew had succeeded in prefiguring so much of the world of nightmare necessity that eventually unfolded during the 1930s and early 1940s. As time passed, such works as *Metamorphosis*,

The Trial and *The Castle* (published during the period 1915–26) looked ever more chillingly relevant. Soon – in reality, and not just in anguished imagination – millions did become identified as vermin, distinctions between guilt and innocence did get wilfully confused, and vast bureaucratic labyrinths were indeed constructed at dictatorial whim.

Even in countries still free from these terrors, the poiliticization of literature rapidly increased from the late 1920s onward. Most of what resulted was antifascist in tone. Yet this is not to say that the minority of authors sympathetic to the radical Right was derisory either in number or quality. For example, among writers in English, Eliot came to share some of D. H. Lawrence's enthusiasm for Italian fascism as regenerator of a civilization that was rightly disillusioned with liberalism, but also wrongly enchanted by socialist or communist visions. In France, Henri de Montherlant and Charles Maurras similarly encouraged the same kind of authoritarian solution to the problem of protecting culture from mass debasement. There, the Vichy regime (1940–44) soon confirmed the hollowness of attempts to use broadly fascist values for the purposes of reconciling creative spontaneity with the need for order in art and politics alike.

Among the antifascists, none asserted literature's social responsibility more stridently than Bertolt Brecht. Through such pieces as *The Threepenny Opera* (1928), with its laboured parallels between capitalism and criminality, this German Marxist developed a new form of epic theatre. Didactic slogans and interpolated commentaries 'distanced' Brecht's audience from any habitual empathy with the characters portrayed. Here drama was 'real', not in managing some illusory imitation of the external world, but in so far as it created within the theatre an occasion that intensified social and ideological awareness. For another major German literary figure, who similarly exiled himself from Nazi rule, the road even towards a less radical politicization was much more tortuous. We previously noted how Thomas Mann, in his pre-1914 stories, had expressed anxiety about creative activity becoming endangered by excessive concern with social issues. Now his emphasis was shifting, albeit painfully. The sanatorium of *The Magic Mountain* (1924) supplied the setting for a great debate about the dilemmas of a civilization behind whose own tubercular bloom there ravaged forces of inner decay. In 1930 Mann published *Mario and the Magician*, alluding subtly to the dangers of fascism's hypnotic potential. Then, through the quartet of *Joseph* novels (1933–43) about exile, as well as in *Doctor Faustus* (1947), with its allegorical treatment of Germany's diseased condition, he revealed still more of his growing conviction that creativity needed to be reconciled with democratic political commitment. By gradually accepting that the season for what he had earlier defended as 'unpolitical man' was now over, Mann epitomized the most significant shift in the cultural history of the 1930s and 1940s.

During the three years immediately prior to the renewal of general armed conflict in 1939, the civil war rampant in Spain had served to sharpen responses to the ideological confrontations of the era. The struggle that brought Franco to power inflicted deep wounds on his country's cultural life. Fascist brutality spurred Picasso into painting the huge masterpiece of *Guernica* (1937), but it was now as exiles that he and such other distinguished figures as José Ortega y Gasset (especially notable for *The Revolt of the Masses*, 1930) would pursue their careers. Even more tragically, the young Republican poet and dramatist Federico García Lorca was only the most renowned of many talented Spaniards who suffered political murder or died in action. Foreign writers also felt greatly involved, and many (such as George Orwell, Arthur Koestler and the American Ernest Hemingway) came to the battle zones as participants or observers. As the left-wing English poet Stephen Spender recalled, the Spanish Civil War 'offered the twentieth century an 1848'[20] – a revolutionary opportunity to stand and be counted. Even so, the hostilities also underlined the ambiguities still remaining within the essentially triangular relationship between fascism, communism and liberal or moderate socialist democracy. In countries where freedom to choose still survived, most support from intellectuals went to Franco's opponents. Yet the war also did much to compel many on the Left to revise the naive idealism with which they had hitherto assessed the Soviet experiment. The most perceptive of them realized that a genuinely popular Spanish movement had become cynically exploited for Stalinist purposes. Of all novels, it was Koestler's *Darkness at Noon* (1940) – a vivid depiction of revolutionary hopes corrupted within Russia itself – that best conveyed an author's personal experience of disillusionment with the communist faith as preached from Moscow.

Nevertheless, a mere five years later, much of central and eastern Europe found itself under Stalin's control. From mid-1941, when Hitler violated the non-aggression agreement that he had shocked the world by making with his fellow-dictator in August 1939, the USSR was linked to Britain (and soon to the USA as well) in the task of defeating the Third Reich. The cessation of open warfare that followed their victory was, however, destined to be insecure. From the liberal-democratic standpoint, one kind of dictatorial threat had been removed only at the price of enlarging another. In 1945, Orwell published *Animal Farm,* which transposed Stalin's betrayal of revolutionary idealism into an allegorical setting where pigs could suffer no more hideous fate than that of becoming indistinguishable from humans. More complex was the message of his final novel, *Nineteen Eighty-Four* (1949), in which Orwell warned not only against authoritarianism, but also against mass capitalist society's own drift towards unthinking conformism. During the later 1940s, the prospects for liberal-democratic regeneration across Europe at large looked generally less favourable than they had done in 1918–19, at the peak of President Wilson's revivalist rhetoric. The fact that the conquest of Nazism had been followed by the rapid onset of Cold War between the capitalist and communist victors produced a new configuration of ideological tensions. Although simpler in form, this was now rendered all the more perilous by the invention of atomic weaponry. The realignment did not, however, reverse the tendency, which had been developing since around 1930, for some brand of confrontation between ideologies to constitute the principal feature of Europe's political, intellectual and cultural condition. This was a situation that would indeed outlast Hitler's fall by more than 40 years – until, at the end of the 1980s, an internal collapse of the communist system of ruling and thinking brought the next major phase of European history to its own dramatic close.

Further reading

The themes pursued in this chapter can best be followed up by reading the various primary sources directly mentioned in the text. As for secondary works, nearly all that follow contain detailed bibliographies of their own.

Particularly useful items within the general reference literature are P. P. Wiener (ed.), *Dictionary of the History of Ideas* (four vols, New York: Scribner, 1973–74); Alan Bullock, O. Stallybrass and S. Trombley (eds), *The Fontana Dictionary of Modern Thought* (2nd edn, London: 1988); Alan Bullock and R. Woodings (eds), *The Fontana Biographical Companion to Modern Thought* (London: 1983); M. Levenson (ed.), *The Cambridge Companion to Modernism* (Cambridge University Press, 1999); and two works edited by J. Wintle: *Makers of Nineteenth-Century Culture, 1800–1914* (London: Routledge, 1982), and *Makers of Modern Culture* (London: Routledge, 1981).

Broad surveys of intellectual and cultural developments include J. W. Burrow, *The Crisis of Reason: European Thought, 1848–1914* (New Haven: Yale University Press, 2000); M. D. Biddiss, *The Age of the Masses: Ideas and Society in Europe since 1870* (Harmondsworth: Penguin,

1977); Peter Gay, *Modernism: The Lure of Heresy* (London: Heinemann, 2007); G. Masur, *Prophets of Yesterday: Studies in European Culture, 1890–1914* (London: Weidenfeld, 1963); J. Romein, *The Watershed of Two Eras: Europe in 1900* (Middletown: Wesleyan University Press, 1978); and W. R. Everdell, *The First Moderns: Profiles in the Origins of Twentieth-Century Thought* (Chicago: University of Chicago Press, 1998). Although focused on one country, Orlando Figes, *Natasha's Dance: A Cultural History of Russia* (London: Penguin, 2003) is another lively work marked by ambitious breadth of coverage. Note also N. Rzhevsky (ed.), *The Cambridge Companion to Modern Russian Culture* (Cambridge: Cambridge University Press, 1998); and C. Kelly and D. Shepherd (eds), *Constructing Russian Culture in the Age of Revolution, 1881–1940* (Oxford: Oxford University Press, 1998).

The remarkable cultural contribution of the Habsburg capital in the pre-1914 period is examined in C. E. Schorske, *Fin-de-Siècle Vienna: Politics and Culture* (London: Weidenfeld, 1980); and that of the French one in R. Shattuck, *The Banquet Years: The Origins of the Avant-garde in France, 1885 to World War I* (revised edn, London: Cape, 1969) and E. Weber, *Fin de Siècle* (Cambridge, MA: Harvard University Press, 1986). See also G. Masur, *Imperial Berlin* (London: Routledge, 1971). The role of early twentieth-century science in the intellectual upheaval is well covered by J. Bronowski, *The Ascent of Man* (London: BBC, 1973); C. C. Gillispie, *The Edge of Objectivity: An Essay in the History of Scientific Ideas* (Princeton: Princeton University Press, 1960); and S. Kern, *The Culture of Time and Space, 1880–1918* (revised edn, Cambridge, MA: Harvard University Press, 2003).

Among rewarding analyses of the impact of 1914–18 are P. Fussell, *The Great War and Modern Memory* (Oxford: Oxford University Press, 1975); M. Eksteins, *Rites of Spring: The Great War and the Birth of the Modern Age* (Boston: Houghton Mifflin, 2000); and A. Roshwald and R. Stites (eds), *European Culture in the Great War, 1914–1918* (Cambridge: Cambridge University Press, 1999). Good treatments of the intellectual and artistic scene during the interwar period include Peter Gay, *Weimar Culture: The Outsider as Insider* (Harmondsworth: Penguin, 1974); Walter Laqueur, *Weimar: A Cultural History, 1918–33* (London: Weidenfeld, 1974); G. Steiner, *In Bluebeard's Castle* (London: Faber, 1971); and G. Brantlinger, *Bread and Circuses: Theories of Mass Culture as Social Decay* (Ithaca: Cornell University Press, 1983).

Although more detailed suggestions about further reading relating to the major dictatorships can be found at the end of Chapters 6 and 7, certain items are worth highlighting here. Hannah Arendt, *The Origins of Totalitarianism* (2nd edn, London: Allen & Unwin, 1958) remains a splendidly provocative point of departure for comparative discussion of the authoritarian systems. Visual aspects of their propaganda are strikingly brought together in D. Ades *et al.* (eds), *Art and Power: Europe under the Dictators, 1930–1945* (London: Hayward Gallery, 1996). Roger Griffin (ed.), *Fascism* (Oxford: Oxford University Press, 1995) provides a geographically wide-ranging 'reader' that combines source texts and commentary. In the huge literature about the Nazi leader's ideas, J. P. Stern, *Hitler: The Führer and the People* (London: Fontana, 1975) still occupies an outstanding place. Rewarding material on the USSR includes B. Thomson, *The Premature Revolution; Russian Literature and Society, 1917–1946* (London: Weidenfeld, 1972); Sheila Fitzpatrick, *The Cultural Front: Power and Culture in Revolutionary Russia* (Ithaca: Cornell University Press, 1992); and P. Kenez, *Cinema and Soviet Society, 1917–1953* (Cambridge: Cambridge University Press, 1992).

Regarding political and social ideas, H. S. Hughes, *Consciousness and Society: The Reorientation of European Social Thought, 1890–1930* (London: MacGibbon, 1959) retains its classic status. Note also, from the same author, *The Sea Change: The Migration of Social Thought, 1930–1965* (New York: Harper & Row, 1975). T. Ball and R. Bellamy (eds), *The Cambridge History of Twentieth-Century Political Thought* (Cambridge: Cambridge University Press, 2003) provides comprehensive expert coverage. Other interesting contributions are W. M. Simon, *European Positivism in the Nineteenth Century: An Essay in Intellectual History* (Ithaca: Cornell University Press, 1963); K. D. Bracher, *The Age of Ideologies: A History of Political Thought in the Twentieth Century* (New York: St Martin's, 1984); J. Joll, *The Anarchists* (London: Methuen, 1964); L. Kolakowski, *Main Currents in Marxism: Its Origins, Growth, and Dissolution* (revised one-volume edn, New York: Norton, 2005); and N. Harding, *Lenin's Political Thought* (two vols, London: Macmillan, 1977–81).

The European literary scene is well surveyed in M. Bradbury and J. McFarlane (eds), *Modernism, 1890–1930* (Harmondsworth: Penguin, 1976). The first of these authors has also written a series of stimulating essays entitled *The Modern World: Ten Great Writers* (London: Secker & Warburg, 1988). Still outstanding among the older commentaries is E. Wilson's much reprinted work, *Axel's Castle: A Study in the Imaginative Literature of 1870–1930* (original edn, New York: Scribner, 1931). Artistic developments are skilfully reviewed in G. H. Hamilton, *Painting and Sculpture in Europe, 1880–1940* (Harmondsworth: Penguin, 1967), and R. Hughes, *The Shock of the New: Art and the Century of Change* (2nd edn, London: Thames & Hudson, 1991). One vital aspect is brilliantly illuminated in P. H. Tucker, *Monet in the '90s: The Series Paintings* (New Haven: Yale University Press, 1989). Standard studies of specific movements include J. Rewald, *Post-Impressionism: From Van Gogh to Gauguin* (3rd edn, New York: Museum of Modern Art, 1978); D. Cooper, *The Cubist Epoch* (London: Phaidon, 1971); R. Cardinal, *Expressionism* (London: Paladin, 1984); and, for futurism, E. Braun (ed.), *Italian Art in the 20th Century* (London: Royal Academy, 1989).

Especially valuable biographies include: M. Meyer, *Ibsen* (abridged edn, Harmondsworth: Penguin, 1974); G. Painter, *Marcel Proust* (two vols, London: Chatto, 1959–65); and two studies by R. W. Clark, *Einstein: The Life and Times* (London: Hodder, 1973) and *Freud: The Man and the Cause* (London: Weidenfeld, 1980).

Notes

1 T. Macaulay, 'Lord Bacon' [1837], in *Critical and Historical Essays* (London: Longman, 1883), pp. 403–04.
2 A. Bullock, 'The Double Image', in M. Bradbury and J. McFarlane (eds), *Modernism, 1890–1930* (Harmondsworth: Penguin, 1976), p. 62.
3 Sigmund Freud, *The Interpretation of Dreams*, in *The Pelican Freud Library*, Vol. 4 (Harmondsworth: Penguin, 1976), pp. 244, 769.
4 L. Wittgenstein, *Tractatus Logico-Philosophicus* (London: Routledge, 1981), Proposition 7, p. 189.
5 F. Nietzsche, *Ecce Homo: How One Becomes What One Is* (Harmondsworth: Penguin, 1979), p. 37. This work was written in 1888, and first published posthumously in 1908.
6 F. Nietzsche, *The Joyful Science* (1882), in W. Kaufmann (ed.), *The Portable Nietzsche* (New York: Viking, 1954), p. 95.
7 Quoted by L. Nochlin, *Realism* (Harmondsworth: Penguin, 1971), p. 41.
8 Rimbaud to Paul Demeny, 15 May 1876, quoted by R. Stromberg (ed.), *Realism, Naturalism, and Symbolism: Modes of Thought and Expression in Europe, 1848–1914* (New York: Harper & Row, 1968), p. 188.
9 G. D. Painter, *Marcel Proust: A Biography* (Harmondsworth: Penguin, 1977), Vol. 2, p. 329.
10 E. Zola, 'The Impressionists' (1880), quoted by R. Stromberg (ed.), *Realism, Naturalism, and Symbolism, op. cit.*, p. 156.
11 V. Kandinsky, *Concerning the Spiritual in Art* (New York: Dover, 1977), p. 57.
12 M. Bradbury and J. McFarlane, 'The Name and Nature of Modernism', in M. Bradbury and J. McFarlane (eds), *Modernism, 1890–1930, op. cit.*, p. 19.
13 Quoted by M. Bradbury, *The Modern World: Ten Great Writers* (London: Secker & Warburg, 1988), p. 16.
14 K. Bracher, *The Age of Ideologies: A History of Political Thought in the Twentieth Century* (London: Methuen, 1985), p. 166.
15 *The Collected Writings of John Maynard Keynes*, Vol. 7 (London: Macmillan, 1973), p. xxiii.
16 B. Mussolini, 'The Doctrine of Fascism', in A. Lyttelton (ed.), *Italian Fascisms: From Pareto to Gentile* (London: Cape, 1973), p. 42.

17 A. Hitler, *Mein Kampf* (London: Hutchinson, 1961), p. 263.
18 A. Bullock, *Hitler: A Study in Tyranny*, revised edn (Harmondsworth: Penguin, 1962), p. 808.
19 J. Joll, *Europe since 1870: An International History* (Harmondsworth: Penguin, 1976), p. 341.
20 Quoted by H. Thomas, *The Spanish Civil War* (Harmondsworth: Penguin, 1965), p. 291.

4 Explaining World War One: debating the causes

Gordon Martel

People began asking themselves what caused war to break out from the moment the first shots were fired in August 1914, and historians have continued to ask questions about it ever since. The earliest explanations were offered by the governments of the warring states: Austria-Hungary – the first to declare war, against Serbia, on 28 July – insisted that it was to bring to justice the state-sponsored terrorists who had assassinated the heir to the Austro-Hungarian throne in Sarajevo on 28 June. Germany – the next to declare war, against Russia, on 1 August – insisted that it was the mobilization of the Russian army, which began on 28 July, that had forced it to act in self-defence; and then that the terms of the Franco–Russian alliance left it with no choice but to declare war against France on 3 August, after the French government had refused to declare its neutrality in the Russo–German conflict. Britain – which declared war against Germany on 4 August – professed to do so because German troops had invaded Belgium and thus violated the neutrality agreements that had been in place since the creation of Belgium in 1830. By the end of August, the circle had widened, with each of the great powers declaring war on the allies of its enemy: France and Britain on Austria-Hungary, Austria-Hungary on Russia and Belgium. Smaller states soon joined the fray: Montenegro declared war on both Austria-Hungary and Germany, as did Japan. By the close of 1914, the only significant states not engaged in the war were Italy and the USA – and they too would enter, in 1915 and 1917, respectively.

Thus the first explanations for the outbreak of war were loaded with the baggage of national self-interest. Obviously, the enemy (whoever it was) was to blame; one need look no further than across the frontier to discover terrorists or militarists who left the blameless innocent with no choice but to defend themselves against the aggressors. In order to sustain this position, each of the great powers soon began to publish collections of official documents: Britain published a 'blue book'; Germany a 'white book'; France a 'yellow book'; Austria-Hungary a 'red book'; Belgium a 'grey book'; Russia an 'orange book'; and, when Italy finally entered the war in May 1915, it joined the throng with the publication of a 'green book'.[1] Thus the battles with which the war began were quickly followed by the Battle of the Coloured Books, as propagandists in each of the combatant states utilized carefully selected documents to justify the war to their people. In grappling with competing explanations of the cause(s) of war, this phenomenon was not insignificant: people – especially the educated and the politically active – on what came to be called 'the home front' perused these collections and contemplated the debates they precipitated.

Most of the documents submitted to an eager public focused on the July crisis. Each of the combatant states sought to demonstrate that it was not responsible for the outbreak of the war, that its own actions were defensive, and that it had had little choice but to go to war in order to save itself from the consequences of defeat on the battlefield. Thus the Austrians sought to show that their ultimatum to Serbia was a fair and measured response to the continuing threat of state-sponsored terrorism; and the Germans that Russia intended to use the excuse of the Austro–Serb conflict to destroy the Austro-Hungarian empire, which would then enable Russia to dominate south-eastern Europe. The Russians maintained that it was Austria-Hungary that was determined to turn Serbia into its satellite, which they had to defend partly because their fellow-Orthodox Christians would suffer under a Catholic domination, partly because Serbia was the only barrier to Austro-German control of the Balkans. The French insisted that their only defence against a German hegemony in Europe was a strong Russian ally – thus their independence would be jeopardized if the Dual Alliance of Austria-Hungary and Germany were to defeat Russia. The British pointed to the invasion of Belgium to prove that Germany would stop at nothing – including the violation of longstanding international agreements – in its determination to reduce France to a second-rate power.

These were the positions that were first debated at the beginning of the war, with governments and their critics utilizing the published documents to demonstrate the legitimacy of their responses to the crisis that had been precipitated by the assassination of Archduke Ferdinand. Questions of who said what to whom at which moment in the crisis, and of who gave the first orders to begin the mobilization of armed forces, were vital in determining whether actions were aggressive or defensive, which in turn would determine who was deemed to be responsible for the outbreak of war. And this occurred at a time when it was still possible to believe that the war would be relatively brief, along the lines of European wars since the defeat of Napoleon in 1815. The interest and the arguments intensified as the war was prolonged and as the carnage mounted: between the July crisis of 1914 and the armistice of November 1918, over 600 books were published on the subject of responsibility for the war's outbreak.

Questions of causation would almost certainly have continued to be asked once the war ended, but it was the Treaty of Versailles that was responsible for stimulating a new round of controversy, which proved to be no less emotional than the one conducted during the war itself. The famous 'war guilt clause' – article 231 of the treaty – charged Germany and its allies with 'sole responsibility' for the war, a charge that was immediately taken up by the German representatives at Paris.[2] There the argument over responsibility became indissolubly linked with the reparations clauses, thus connecting forever in the minds of the German public the money that they were to be obliged to pay, and the arguments concerning the conduct of each of the governments concerned in the July crisis. Pamphlets and books refuting the charge of guilt quickly began to pour out of Germany: *Deutschlands 'Schuld' und recht*;[3] *Die Grosse Lüge*;[4] *Wer ist schuldig?*;[5] *Frankreichs Kriegs-schuld*;[6] and *Die Verantwortung der Entente am Weltkriege*[7] are titles typical of the genre.

The controversy over war guilt became an international phenom-enon almost immediately. Governments found it impossible to contain the debate as interested parties translated works that supported their views almost as quickly as they appeared. The German 'Save the Honour' League was particularly active in translating German works into English, and English works into German.[8] The Germans were joined by those dissidents in the victorious states who had been suspi-cious of their own government's complicity in the outbreak of the war, and were now horrified that such errors of judgement were to be com-pounded in the peace settlement. The Independent Labour Party (ILP) in Britain published E. D. Morel's pamphlet *Pre-War Diplomacy: Fresh Revelations* (a sequel to his wartime *Truth and the War*);[9] in the USA, Stewart E. Bruce published *The War Guilt and Peace Crime of the Entente Allies*,[10] and Albert Jay Nock reproduced articles he had first published in *The Freeman* as *The Myth of a Guilty Nation*.[11] Before long, those who had participated in the fateful decisions of July and August 1914 joined the controversialists and pamphleteers; by the end of the decade, presidents, prime ministers, foreign secretaries, dip-lomats and soldiers had joined the debate by publishing their recollections of the crisis or, in some cases, complete autobiographies.[12]

Although World War One did not create the subdiscipline of diplomatic history, the controversy stimulated by the competing selections of documents (which, for the most part, consisted of official correspondence between diplomats and foreign offices) gave it a vitality during and after the war that placed it at the pinnacle of the historical profession. Previously regarded as arcane specialists pursuing antiquarian interests, diplomatic historians found themselves at the centre of a whirlwind of controversy. Historians who had previously focused on the middle ages, or constitutional history, or the history of ideas turned themselves into students of modern diplomacy. Careers were made – or unmade – according to the extent of success in expounding a convincing position on the question of war guilt. Degrees of responsibility were debated at public meetings, articles and essays written for the popular press and, in Germany, an entire journal, *Die Kriegschuldfrage* ('The War Guilt Question') was devoted to the subject.[13] In Germany, too, the government of the new 'Weimar' republic undertook the most ambitious official historical publication project ever mounted when it appointed Johannes Lepsius, Albrecht Mendelssohn Bartholdy and Friedrich Thimme to publish all of the essential German diplomatic correspondence from the creation of the German empire in 1871, following the Franco–Prussian conflict, to the outbreak of war in 1914. Between 1922 and 1927, 40 volumes of documents were published as *Die grosse Politik der europäischen Kabinette, 1871–1914*. The amount of detail available for studying the outbreak of World War One was, by the latter part of the 1920s, unprecedented. Nevertheless, no-one yet had free and untrammelled access to the archives, and students of the subject still had to rely on published materials that were usually government-sponsored.

The first full-length 'academic' treatments of the subject appeared against the background of a decade of controversy, but in the midst of the new 'spirit of Locarno' that, emotionally at least, was considered by many to mark the 'real' end of the war. They viewed Germany's entry into the League of Nations and its willingness to recognize the legitimacy of its new frontiers in the west without the intimidation it had faced in 1919 as signs of the country's readmission into the comity of nations. The arguments offered in books such as Erich Brandenburg's *Von Bismarck zum Weltkriege; die deutsche Politik in den Jahrzehnten vor dem Kriege*,[14] Pierre Renouvin's *Les origines immédiates de la guerre (28 juin–4 août 1914)*,[15] Harry Elmer Barnes's *Genesis of the World War*,[16] and R. W. Seton-Watson's *Sarajevo, A Study in the Origins of the Great War*,[17] were less strident and more detailed than those that had preceded them. Nevertheless, each of them – in a somewhat more dispassionate manner – continued to focus on the search for a guilty party (or parties). They also, for the most part, maintained a focus on the decisions that immediately preceded the mobilizations and declarations of war, providing fresh grist for the controversialist mill. Barnes, for example, soon found his work countered by a German-American: Bernadotte Schmitt, who had been a Rhodes scholar at Oxford before the war, countered Barnes's assertion that it was Russia, not Germany, that was primarily to blame for launching the world on the path to war. Schmitt debated Barnes and his views in public and in the press for several years before publishing his own *The Coming of the War, 1914.*[18]

Thus, for approximately a decade after the outbreak of war, most of those who sought to explain the event attempted to assign blame, although a growing mountain of evidence meant that their arguments became more detailed and more sophisticated. Nevertheless, most of these accounts focused on the diplomacy of the immediate prewar period – or, as one critic of the genre, the English social historian G. M. Young, put it – 'what one clerk said to another'. This approach changed significantly with the appearance of two remarkably successful (and quite different) books: *The International Anarchy* (1926)[19] and *The Origins of the World War* (two volumes, 1928).[20] The first was written by a Cambridge classicist, Goldsworthy Lowes Dickinson, who had opposed Britain's participation in the war. He was a moving force in the Union of Democratic Control (UDC), a friend of John Maynard Keynes, and one of the 'Bloomsbury Group'. He had no background or training in the field of diplomatic history, which perhaps accounts in part for the different approach he took to the subject. Rather than assigning guilt to one party or another, he attacked the system itself (and thus the 'anarchy' of the title). In essence, he argued that, despite the professions of peace made by European governments in the era before the war, they were pursuing objectives that could be achieved only by war or by the threat of war. Most of those who had heretofore written about the war's origins had concentrated on the superficialities of diplomatic exchanges – when the real, 'fundamental conditions' that produced war ought to be the focus of their interest, not the immediate events that simply occasioned it. In this view, Germany and its allies were absolved of any special responsibility. The true causes were to be found in the system itself: in the alliances, the secret diplomacy, the imperialist ambitions, and the armaments race that made Europe the powder keg that exploded when the Austrian archduke was murdered at Sarajevo. The analysis was prescriptive: the only chance Europe had to avoid a repetition of the tragedy of 1914–18 was through the League of

Nations – which, through collective security and procedures for the peaceful resolution of international disputes, offered an alternative to the 'anarchy' of the prewar system.

Lowes Dickinson was a classicist and political activist with little background in modern history and little first-hand knowledge of politics outside of Britain. His book was a passionate – if rather amateurish – plea to 'do politics' in a new way. The American Sidney Bradshaw Fay, by contrast, was a trained and well established historian before 1914, representative of the new professionalism of the discipline that had developed in the late nineteenth century. After receiving his PhD from Harvard in 1900, he engaged in further study at the Sorbonne and at the University of Berlin, wrote several textbooks on modern European history, and taught at Dartmouth College before the war and at Smith College from 1914 to 1929. It was the success of his two-volume *The Origins of the First World War* that took him back to Harvard as a faculty member for the rest of his career. Like Dickinson, Fay did not lay blame for the war on any one state, but placed it on 'the system' instead. Although he maintained that Austria-Hungary, Russia and Serbia bore a greater degree of responsibility than Germany, France or Britain, he argued that too much emphasis had been placed on the question of guilt, and not enough on what he referred to as the 'underlying' causes of the war: the system of secret alliances, militarism, nationalism, economic imperialism and the newspaper press. His first volume began with an explanation of why these factors were paramount, which he then used as the foundation on which to erect the narrative of events in European diplomacy from 1871 to 1913. The second volume was devoted entirely to the diplomacy of 1914 – with most of it again focused on the July crisis. Notwithstanding the continuing fascination with the immediate crisis itself, it was Fay's emphasis on the underlying causes that made it the standard work in the field for the next 30 years. Practically every survey of European history, almost every textbook on the subject, began to repeat the mantra of 'alliances, militarism, nationalism and imperialism' as the causes of World War One. The search for 'guilty men' lost its steam; blame was no longer assigned to either side, or to any one state; historical work on the war's origins began to focus on particular alliances, the role of military organizations and preparations for war, the nature of nationalist aspirations, and the place of imperial rivalries. Partly as a result of this shift in attention to 'impersonal forces', the public lost interest. When, in the 1930s, Hitler succeeded in tearing the treaties of peace to shreds, the relationship between the 'war guilt debate' and real politics disappeared. The subject was relegated to the academies as a subject for antiquarians – as remote from the issues of contemporary politics as the Peloponnesian or Punic Wars.

It seems entirely likely that historians would have continued the quiet work of assessing the relative importance of the various underlying factors that were now assumed to have been the root causes of World War One, had it not been for Hitler and the Holocaust. In one of the most unusual inversions of thinking about causation, World War Two turned things upside-down. Where most students of the subject had, by 1939, come to believe that no one party was guilty for the first war, that the causes were 'systemic', almost everyone believed the reverse was true of the second war: Hitler was guilty. It was Hitler who aimed to dominate Europe and then the world, it was Hitler who conducted a race war against Jews, Slavs and all those deemed to be inferior to the German master race. In this view, the immediate events that led up to the outbreak of war in September 1939 were almost immaterial: it was only a matter of time until Hitler got his way and launched his war of aggression. The crises of the 1930s – the remilitarization of the Rhineland, the *Anschluss*, the Munich affair – were of interest only in illustrating how the spineless appeasers of western Europe had failed to take the opportunity to fight Hitler and Nazism while Germany was still relatively weak. Thus, those 'guilty men' in the west were deemed responsible for not going to war soon enough; everyone knew and everyone ought to have known – that Hitler was going to launch his war. The Nuremberg trials would eventually serve as a vivid and visceral demonstration of Nazi guilt – in stark contrast with the failure to bring Kaiser Wilhelm II 'to justice', and with the gradual acceptance of the argument that no one was really to blame for the outbreak of war in 1914.

But how did this affect our understanding of the origins of World War One? It did so because, to begin with, a small clutch of dissident historians questioned the widespread assumption that Hitler and Nazism were aberrations. In Britain, A. J. P. Taylor had produced an essay on German history for the Political Warfare Executive (PWE) in 1944. When they declined to publish it because it was deemed to be too inflammatory, he turned it into a book entitled *The Course of German History*. This argued that the Third Reich was merely the fulfilment of the historical wishes of the German people as a whole.[21] And the deepest of these wishes was to dominate Europe and enslave the Slavs. 'Good Germans' were few and far between: the liberals of Wilhelmine Germany, the republicans of Weimar and the socialists of the *Sozialdemokratische Partei Deutschlands* (Social Democratic Party, SPD) shared the vision of a dominant Germany – they disagreed only on the question of who was to be responsible for its achievement. Thus the real origins of both world wars were the same.

Taylor was joined by a German and an Italian in forming a most curious *troika*. Ludwig Dehio, a German archivist and specialist in the thirteenth century, published a thoughtful and wide-ranging essay in 1948 entitled *Gleichgewicht oder Hegemonie* that examined four centuries of the 'balance of power' in Europe.[22] Luigi Albertini, an Italian journalist, wrote – over a period of almost 20 years – an account more detailed than anything that had preceded it (or that has followed it) of the diplomacy that led up to World War One. His three-volume *Le origini della guerra del 1914* was published in the midst of World War Two, in 1942–43, shortly after his death in 1941.[23] Their personal histories stretched back to the war of 1914–18 itself: Dehio had served as a frontline officer and had been a supporter of the annexationist *Vaterland* party; Albertini had supported Italy's war against Turkey and the annexation of Libya, opposed Italian neutrality in the crisis of 1914, successfully advocated intervention as editor of the influential Milan newspaper *Corriere della Sera*, and (despite considering himself to be a 'conservative' liberal) had then gone on to become an early supporter of Mussolini's Fascist party. In rather different ways, the three broke with their own past and with the consensus on the war's origins that had emerged in the 1930s. Dehio, in surveying successive challenges mounted by Charles V, Philip II, Louis XIV and Napoleon to the balance of power in Europe, argued that Wilhelm II and Hitler were the heirs to this tradition of those who attempted to establish hegemonic rule. Thus World War One came when Germany decided that the crisis of July offered the most opportune moment for mounting its challenge, and when the Powers on the periphery (Britain and Russia) decided to resist. Albertini – although he died before he could compose the conclusions to his three volumes – had already laid the detailed foundation for this argument when he determined that Germany had precipitated the war by encouraging Austro-Hungarian intransigence during the July crisis and by miscalculating Britain's response to Berlin's determination to settle, 'finally', the Balkan question in favour of the Dual Alliance.

Thus from three different perspectives – 1000 years of German history, 400 years of the balance of power in Europe, and a minutely detailed study of the prewar crisis – the consensus of the 1930s came to be challenged during, and immediately after, World War Two. All three authors made a connection between the imperialist designs and hegemonic ambitions that led to World War One and the more ruthless – and obvious – policies of Hitler and Mussolini and the ideologies that underpinned Fascism and Nazism. Nevertheless, these works did not cause much commotion in the historical world, and they came nowhere close to reviving the animosities of the debate that had raged during the 1920s. 'Denazification' and the Nuremberg trials were supposed to have eradicated the fanatics responsible for World War Two, and a 'good' demilitarized and constitutional West Germany could serve as a respectable ally in the new Cold War struggle to restrain the hegemonic aspirations of the Soviet Union. Although there were some positive responses to the work of Albertini, Dehio and Taylor among their fellow historians, the response was muted and low-key; no new debate began.

Things changed dramatically when, in 1961, Fritz Fischer, a professor of history at the University of Hamburg, published an exhaustive account of the war aims of Germany in World War One: *Griff nach der Weltmacht: die Kriegszielpolitik des Kaiserlichen Deutschland, 1914–18.* In an immensely detailed book of almost 900 pages, Fischer dismantled the assumptions about the war that had predominated in Germany since 1919 (and possibly since 1914):[24] German policy was not defensive in 1914; Germany had not been the victim of an organized assault; Germany would not have been satisfied with a rectification of frontiers that would have incorporated all German peoples within the Reich had it won the war. Fischer argued that Germans had suffered under an illusion since their defeat in 1918 and did not comprehend 'that in reality Germany had followed for four years aims the realisation of which would not only have destroyed for ever the European balance of power, but which would have also infringed the liberties of peoples who were either previously independent or had won their independence during the upheavals.'[25] In other words, the war launched by Germany in July 1914 was an aggressive war of annexation.

This argument alone may have been sufficient to ignite a new debate within Germany, but it was Fischer's 'continuity thesis' that enraged many of his fellow historians, and pushed the debate outside the confines of the academy and into the public sphere. At the outset of his study, he suggested that it contained 'pointers' to fields wider than its own, 'for it indicates certain mental attitudes and aspirations which were active in German policy during the First World War and remained operative later. Seen from this angle, it may serve as a contribution towards the problem of the continuity of German policy from the First World War to the Second.'[26] The suggestion that Hitler was not an aberration in German history had been made before, but Fischer made it in a different way: instead of taking Hitler 'back' into the German past and looking for his 'roots' in the demagogues, militarists and imperialists of German history, he took the Kaiser and his advisors 'forward' into the German future, arguing that it was the particularities of their ambitions, successes and failures that inspired and shaped the Third Reich under Hitler's direction. Ironically, when A. J. P. Taylor had made similar arguments in his *Course of German History*, he was largely ignored – but in 1961 he created a furore when he published his *Origins of the Second World War* which, among other things, asserted that Hitler was merely a traditional German statesman who, like his predecessors, dreamt of dominating Europe by establishing German hegemony in the east. Thus two of the most famous historians of the postwar era published, in the same year, profoundly revisionist works that caused readers to reconsider the causes of both world wars.

In a bizarre concatenation of circumstances, *Griff* appeared a few months after the trial of Adolf Eichmann in Jerusalem had begun. Therefore, to suggest – as Fischer had done – a line of continuity that stretched from the accession of Wilhelm II on to Auschwitz was emotionally explosive in Germany. Hitler and the Nazi phenomenon was supposed to be *sui generis*: an aberration from the normal 'course of German history', accountable in part to the unjustifiable *Diktat* imposed upon a defeated and helpless Germany in 1919. If Fischer's work unravelled this narrative by documenting the kind of peace settlement that the Germans would themselves have imposed on their enemies, and suggesting that this was not dissimilar from the actual rule imposed by the Nazis in Europe during the next war, it would prove to be deeply unsettling, because it would suggest that there was something profoundly 'German' about the wars of the twentieth century.

The arguments made by Fischer were not fundamentally dissimilar to those made a decade or so earlier by Albertini, Taylor and Dehio. What distinguished his work from that of his predecessors was the mountain of irrefutable documentary evidence that he marshalled in its support. Taylor and Dehio had not really gone beyond argumentative essays; Albertini relied entirely upon published sources. Fischer not only utilized the vast array of published documents available by the late 1950s, but was the first to make extensive use of materials in the archives of the German Democratic Republic (East Germany) in Potsdam. This difference was crucial to the debate that followed, because Fischer's critics found it extremely difficult to criticise the evidence that he had assembled. Instead, they focused on two things: first, that the aims that emerged in German decision-making circles once the war broke out did not necessarily demonstrate that they were the reasons for which Germany went to war; second, that treating German aims alone meant that readers were deprived of a balanced view that would have shown that every state at war between 1914 and 1918 had similar 'annexationist' war aims.[27]

The debate that commenced in 1961 raged for years – ironically dragging it back to where it had begun in 1919, by once again arguing over relative degrees of responsibility for the catastrophe. Suddenly, there was much less talk about the 'system', about alliances, the balance of power and the arms race, and much more about the personalities and intentions of the Kaiser, Bethmann Hollweg *et al.* In Germany, historians focused their attention on the relationship (or lack thereof) between prewar diplomacy and war aims, with Fischer's critics dismissing the relevance of the so-called 'September Programme' of 1914 to an understanding of the diplomacy that preceded the outbreak of war, and attacking his portrayal of Bethmann as a determined expansionist who shared a significant degree of responsibility for the war.[28] Fischer responded by producing another book that scrutinized German diplomacy in the immediate prewar years. *Krieg der Illusionen* (War of Illusions) argued that Germany had been intending to utilize an opportune moment to achieve its expansionist aims in the east at least since 1912, when a 'war council' was held to decide whether the Bosnian annexation crisis offered such a moment.[29] While some of those present at the Council wanted to go to war then, others argued that Germany needed more time to prepare for it. Thus, Fischer argued, the underpinnings of the July crisis were established: Germany was preparing to launch a war before Russia grew any stronger. It was the German readiness to launch such a war that emboldened the Austrians to present an ultimatum to Serbia that they knew the Serbs could not accept.

While the debate raged once again over the precise meaning of minutes of meetings, diary entries and various diplomatic documents – making the arguments of the 1960s reminiscent of the Battle of the Coloured Books in the autumn of 1914 – the controversy took another turn that was to prove a significant stimulus to new research. In *Illusions,* Fischer took up a line of argument first advanced by a young German historian 30 years before: Eckart Kehr had proposed in *Schlachtflottenbau und Parteipolitik 1894–1901* that the roots of Germany's ambitious 'world policy' (which set it on the path to war) were to be found in deep-seated sociopolitical dilemmas within the *Kaiserreich*.[30] In essence, he argued that the authoritarian, agrarian, Prussian-dominated empire centred in Berlin purchased the support of potentially liberal industrialists and financiers in western and northern Germany, by promising them the profits to be made from the vast battleship-building programme that was the vital component of an imperialist world policy. Although the arguments over direct responsibility for the war were intensely emotional, splitting the historical profession in Germany into two camps, the heat gradually dissipated, and it was Kehr's assertion of the 'primacy of domestic politics' (*Primat der Innenpolitik*) that established a new line of enquiry into the war's origins. German historians, particularly of the Left, began talking about the 'structures' of German history and society that 'determined' the directions of policy. In this view, policy was but the tip of the socio-economic iceberg; events were but the superficial products of profound continuities. So, gradually, the focus on the personalities and policies of the immediate prewar period began to fade once again, and historians started to investigate the social composition of political parties, interest groups and military organizations.

Outside Germany, in response to the Fischer debate, historians began to take up the challenge posed by Fischer's opponents of analysing the war aims of the Entente powers. Numerous works detailing various aspects of British and French war aims and peace plans tended to support the point made by Fischer at the outset of the controversy: that, unlike the German ones, these were neither mysterious nor hidden – the treaties of peace in 1919 were in fact the logical culmination of their aims. An array of studies on British policy demonstrated that the British had no desire to subjugate or encircle Germany in the future; rather, they aimed to restore a balance of power on the continent, to remove the causes of nationalist discontent by supporting the independence of nationalities 'struggling to be free', and – most demonstrably – to remove the likelihood of future friction with Germany by scuttling its fleet and depriving it of its colonies altogether.[31] What was hidden was the diplomacy of allied aims that culminated in the peace treaties: British interests were mitigated by French demands for security and Woodrow Wilson's wartime promises of an 'internationalist' settlement.[32] Studies of French war aims have demonstrated a surprising lack of interest in imperial expansion – in spite of colonialist interest groups – in fact the showpiece of colonial gains, Syria, did not emerge as an aim until six weeks before the end of the war.[33] David Stevenson, in an impeccably researched study of French war aims, suggested that nothing comparable with the 'September Programme' of 1914 existed in France; until the summer of 1918 the French aimed only to defeat Germany and to make another successful invasion less likely by recapturing Alsace-Lorraine and strengthening the provisions for Belgian neutrality.[34] An impressive study of French, British, American and German economic war aims, by Georges-Henri Soutou, argues that each of the powers sought to restructure finance and trading regimes in order to bolster their security in the future.[35]

In essence, the detailed investigations of allied war aims that emanated from the Fischer controversy have reinforced his arguments. With the possible exception of Russia,[36] the defensive war aims of the Entente powers reflected the defensive nature of their prewar diplomacy. But perhaps as instrumental in stimulating new research into studies of war origins was the opening of additional archival sources for exploration. With Fischer's opponents in Germany insisting that detailed research in the archives of the Entente would demonstrate little difference between German aims and theirs, governments found it difficult to withstand the growing demands for openness in investigating those wartime records that remained closed.[37] From the mid-1960s onwards, historians began to have almost untrammelled access to both prewar and wartime materials. Since the 1990s, with the disappearance of the Soviet Union and the reunification of Germany, the availability of materials has been unprecedented. Thus the Fischer controversy fortuitously coincided with relatively easy access to materials that might finally settle the argument in favour of one side or the other. The two phenomena of renewed debate and unprecedented access to original documents resulted in a wave of new research on the origins of World War One.

The war aims controversy proved to be short-lived outside of Germany. What proved to be more enduring was the interest in the role of *Innenpolitik*. Did the decision-makers of July 1914 succumb to the temptation of going to war in order to avert a domestic revolution – to forestall socialists, syndicalists and radicals at home? Was there a clique, cabal or conspiracy of special interest groups that succeeded in twisting the interests of the nation as a whole to its particular aims? What was the nature of the relationship between soldiers and the state: between the press and politics; between industrialists, financiers and politicians? Did the 'structures' of society, the bureaucracy and/or the processes of military planning leave the decision-makers of July 1914 with little or no room to manoeuvre? A series of dissertations, monographs, articles and essays attempted to answer these questions for each of the European great powers in the era preceding the outbreak of war.

Between 1973 and 1994, a number of distinguished historians attempted to synthesize the research that had been generated on each of the Great Powers. In Macmillan's 'Making of the Twentieth Century' series, Volker Berghahn, Zara Steiner, Dominic Lieven, John Keiger, Richard Bosworth and Samuel Williamson investigated the policies of Germany, Britain, Russia, France, Italy and Austria-Hungary, in the light of both the Fischer debate and the new interest in the role played by domestic political and social structures in determining policy.[38] While each of them examined the policies pursued during the

July crisis itself, they also considered the nature and composition of the diplomatic and foreign service, the evolution of military strategy and planning, the role of financiers and industrialists in politics, the popularity of imperialism, the ethos of nationalism, and the question of whether or not there was a 'domestic crisis' that made war a more attractive option than peace. A synthesis of these syntheses was produced in 1984 by one of the twentieth century's most distinguished (and wide-ranging) historians of Europe, James Joll. It was enlarged slightly in 1992, then considerably revised and further expanded by Gordon Martel in 2006.[39] The following summary analysis reflects the conclusions to be found in these works.

***

Most historians agree that the system of alliances that characterized European politics after the Franco–Prussian war played a significant role in the July crisis and in the decisions made to go to war in August. After World War One, critics of the system argued that the alliances grew out of a more fundamental cause: the 'balance of power' politics that had long permeated European diplomacy. According to this view, the unification of Germany disturbed the European balance. Despite Bismarck's subtle diplomatic strategy of ameliorating Austria-Hungary, emphasizing the ideological harmony between Germany and tsarist Russia and encouraging France to focus its attention on expansion outside Europe, the 'realities' of the balance-of-power equation eventually broke it down.[40] After the formation of the Dual Alliance between Germany and Austria-Hungary in 1879, Russia gradually came to regard itself as threatened by the alliance's growing strength and overcame its ideological aversion to republicanism. The result was the Franco–Russian alliance of 1891–94. For a time, this appeared to be the quintessence of balance-of-power politics – and, because the competing alliances matched one another so closely in terms of their ability to mobilize military forces, the system created a peaceful equilibrium that endured for over 20 years. The balance began to be disturbed when Russia was defeated by Japan in 1905, giving the Dual Alliance an advantage in Europe and encouraging both Germany and Austria-Hungary to become more ambitious and to take more chances. This new equation pushed Britain into Europe: the growing power of the Dual Alliance forced the British to reach an accommodation with their traditional rivals, France and Russia. By the time of the July crisis, the Franco–Russian alliance was airtight and likely to be strengthened by the addition of Britain.

In this view, the alliance system and balance-of-power politics had produced a 'powder keg' in Europe that needed no more than a match, a lightning bolt or an assassin's bullet to ignite it. In other words, as soon as one side perceived itself to be strong enough to defeat the other, it would take advantage of what might be its only opportunity to win, then reduce the enemy to permanent subordination or servitude. Given the dangers involved in losing such a struggle, none of the great powers was prepared to risk the consequences of abandoning its allies, which might well amount to a virtual defeat. The commitments made within the alliances meant that peace in Europe could be jeopardized by a single state prepared to run the risk of war. The states singled out after the war as having been prepared to run such a risk were Germany, Austria-Hungary and Russia. Some believed that an aggressive Germany had encouraged Austria-Hungary to use the assassination as an opportunity to defeat Russia while the Dual Alliance still enjoyed a military superiority that would diminish over the years; others believed that Austria-Hungary had used the assassination to squash forever the Serb nationalist threat to the Dual Monarchy and had succeeded in dragging a reluctant Germany along with it; still others argued that Russia had used the promise of French support in order to establish its hegemony in the Balkans once and for all. Whichever state is singled out for responsibility, in this scenario it was the existence of the alliances that encouraged the risk-taking that led to war.

No historian denies the importance of the arrangements made through the alliances, but there are a number of ways in which the alliance 'system' fails to explain the decisions that led to war. In the first place, the language used in the agreements left room to abandon allies, should this be deemed to be in a state's interest. All the treaties spoke of commitments in response to an 'act of aggression' (or even 'unprovoked aggression' in some instances).[41] This meant that the only thing a reluctant ally needed to assert was that the other side had not engaged in an act of aggression, thus rendering its own commitment null and void. Certainly, there was nothing in the Dual Alliance that committed Germany to go to war in support of the Austrian demands on Serbia contained in the ultimatum of 23 July. Other provisions referred to 'consultation' among the allies; here, too, a state could assert that such consultation had not occurred, or that it had been insufficient, thereby nullifying the arrangements. This was the reason – or excuse – that Italy gave for failing to support its allies in the Triple Alliance. Most famously, it was repeatedly asserted by British diplomats in the midst of the July crisis that the ententes with France and Russia were nothing like alliances, and that they entailed no promises on the part of Britain to support either of them in the event of war. There are critics of the British foreign secretary, Sir Edward Grey, who argue that it was precisely his reluctance to commit Britain to its Entente partners during the crisis – and his failure to warn Germany that Britain would support France and Russia in the event of war – that caused the hitherto effective balance of power to break down during the July crisis.

In other words, the decisions made by each of the Great Powers in July 1914 were made on the basis of their perceived interests at that moment, not because they had committed themselves on paper 35, 32, 22, ten or seven years previously.[42] As Bismarck had expressed it at the height of his career, all treaties should contain the phrase '*rebus sic stantibus*'.[43] If this is the case, one needs to consider the nature of the interests as they were perceived at the moment in 1914, thus making paramount the questions of who was interpreting these interests and how they made their decisions. Thus another explanation offered for the outbreak of war is that the 'old diplomacy' accounts for the attitudes and postures adopted by those who made the fateful decisions of July. This approach does not contradict the 'balance-of-power–alliance system' and is usually treated as a subsidiary to it. The diplomatic system that pertained prior to the war, according to this interpretation, was dominated by the old guard in Europe: the old, privileged aristocrats who dominated the embassies and the foreign offices operated in secret, away from the increasingly glaring lights of publicity, and according to their own standards. This meant, in practice, an old-fashioned, vestigial view of national honour and the part played in it by war. One of the primary exponents of this explanation, Arno J. Mayer, asserts that 'the decision for war and the design for warfare were forged in what was a crisis in the politics and policy of Europe's ruling and governing classes.'[44] Those responsible for the conduct of secret diplomacy enthusiastically arranged their alliances and managed the balance of power in order to retain the old social and political order in their state. These advocates of the old order believed that the July crisis offered them the opportunity to crush the forces that threatened their privileged position – and the system of secrecy enabled them to ignore those democratic and progressive elements that might have prevented them from launching such a war.

President Woodrow Wilson popularized this view when he made his famous declaration of war aims in the 'Fourteen Points' speech to Congress on 8 January 1918. He began by declaring that when the peace process began, it would be 'absolutely open': 'The day of conquest and aggrandizement is gone by; so is also the day of secret covenants entered into in the interest of particular governments and likely at some unlooked-for moment to upset the peace of the world.'[45] The very first of his 14 points stipulated that this would be the case, that henceforth 'diplomacy shall proceed always frankly and in the public view.' Although Wilson was not the first to point to the secretiveness of the old diplomacy as a significant factor in 'upsetting the peace of the world', he gave it the seal of respectability as official US policy, and publicized the idea of secret diplomacy as a cause of war.

In the same speech, Wilson pledged to continue the fight until a 'just and stable peace' could be secured 'by removing the chief provocations to war'. He insisted that there was nothing in his programme that would impair German greatness if only Germany would limit itself to 'legitimate influence or power'. German achievements in learning and pacific enterprise 'have made her record very bright and very enviable' and it was his wish that this nation should occupy a place of equality among the peoples of the world – 'instead of a place of mastery'. Finally, he insisted that before negotiating an end to the war, he needed to know who spoke on behalf of Germany: was it the majority of those (democratically elected) to the Reichstag, or was it 'the military party and the men whose creed is imperial domination'? Thus a causal linkage was asserted that has resonated ever since: secret diplomacy, militarism and imperialism were inextricably connected in a struggle for 'mastery' that provoked war.

Here Wilson built on a foundation first constructed by British propagandists at the outset of the war: the true cause of the war, they had proclaimed, was 'Prussian militarism'.[46] Reduced to its fundamentals, this explanation asserts that a culture in which military values predominate, and in which military men prevail over elected officials, will invariably be aggressive and pursue warlike policies. The military enjoy a place of privilege in a 'militaristic' society – their organization is hierarchical, their ethos authoritarian – and this combination isolates them from those forces in society that promote the peaceful resolution of disputes. In contrast with the non-violent inclinations of traders and merchants, the military elite benefits from the threat of war and the preparations made for it, and thus has a vested interest in sabre-rattling and warmongering. If the state is constructed in such a way as to give the military a special place in decision-making and to allow it to make war plans without civilian oversight, there will be a significantly increased likelihood of scales being tipped in favour of war. This thesis was first applied to Prussia, where the argument was that its armed contribution to the unification of Germany had secured for its generals a special place – one that enabled them to promote aggressive war planning across the wider Reich from 1871 to 1914. Although the thesis was later applied to both Austria-Hungary and Russia, few have argued that it can be used to explain the policies of Britain, France or Italy, even if some of their military figures, too, have been identified as particularly bellicose.[47]

Historians who apply the militarism thesis to the July crisis point especially to the role played by the generals and their staffs in producing the conditions that led to a 'war by timetable'.[48] The argument here is that the political crisis was pushed past the tipping-point when the civilians discovered that the strategic plans of the military left them with little or no room for manoeuvre. Crucial to the hypothesis is the German general staff's famous 'Schlieffen Plan', the successful application of which depended on mobilizing more quickly than Russia and France, and then delivering a quick 'knock-out blow' against France by launching a surprise attack through neutral Belgium. After that, they would be free to turn east and defeat Russia (which would be a much more dragged-out affair).[49] Because this was the only plan that Germany had, and because the general staff succeeded in convincing the Kaiser and the chancellor that any delay in implementing it would result in defeat, it turned what might have been a localized conflict limited to the Balkans into a general European war. When Russia, on 30 July, decided to mobilize its forces the next day, the Schlieffen Plan left Germany with no choice but to mobilize and declare a 'state of imminent war' [*Kriegsgefahrzustand*]. But the military interpretation also spreads the blame: the tsar, who had intended only a partial mobilization as a 'political' response to the Austrian declaration of war on Serbia, was persuaded by his general staff that this was impossible, that there was no alternative to a general mobilization. And what had precipitated the Russian decision was the success of Austria's chief of general staff, Conrad von Hötzendorf, in persuading the politicians that a military 'solution' of the Serb problem was the only one that made sense.

In a fascinating essay written in 1919, an Austrian economist, Joseph Schumpeter, extended the military interpretation in an unexpected direction. Rather than point to the mobilization schedules of the military planners, he argued that it was the expansionist ethos of the military that produced the imperialist spirit which then resulted in war.[50] Instead of asking 'what is imperialism?' as others had done, he asked 'who are the imperialists?'. What he found was a vestigial remnant of a precapitalist, pre-industrial past – a professional military caste that was atavistic in the modern world. This caste derived its *raison d'être* from its skill in perpetrating violence against others, which distinguished it from the progressive, purposeful aims of the entrepreneurs, industrialists and financiers who set the standards of modern capitalism. Militarists would present clear, concrete aims and objectives to the politicians and public in order to justify themselves, but in reality what they pursued was objectless: what they craved was expansion for expansion's sake. 'Hence the tendency of such expansion to transcend all bounds and tangible limits, to the point of utter exhaustion.'[51] Thus, the cold, calculating rationale presented by the military to the politicians in July 1914 was an illusion – they wanted war because it suited their view of the world as a place to exercise their skills in the arts of violence. In this sense, imperialism, perpetrated by its militarist advocates, was the ultimate cause of war.

Ironically, Lenin, writing in exile in Zurich in the spring of 1916, had also concluded that 'imperialism' was the cause of war, but for the opposite reason. Where Schumpeter had argued that capitalism was by nature peaceful and anti-imperialist, Lenin argued that imperialism was its 'highest stage' – a stage unforeseen by Karl Marx. After 1870, capitalists had discovered that they could continue maximizing profits and accumulating capital by acquiring colonies that would provide them simultaneously with cheap resources and new markets; this also enabled them to stave off the inevitable social revolution of their pro-letariat at home, as they were in a position to bribe their workers into believing that capitalism benefited the latter as well. Every highly developed bourgeois state, Lenin argued, was working towards a system of 'monopoly capitalism' in which the syndicates, cartels, trusts and banks of the financial oligarchy became the norm, and in which the state itself was transformed into an instrument designed to fulfil their imperialist requirements. World War One was the inevitable result of these national bourgeoisies coming into conflict with one another as they sought to seize for themselves what remained of the precapitalist world – and to grab the possessions of their competitors.

Historians have found it impossible to prove or disprove these grand theories of causation. While evidence can be found to support either or both, one cannot agree simultaneously with Schumpeter that 'capital-ism is by nature anti-imperialist' and with Lenin that 'imperialism is the monopoly stage of capitalism'. Schumpeter's assertion that wher-ever capitalism took root, rationalism grew and peace movements flourished, has much to sustain it – as does his argument that militarist elements encouraged an irrational, emotional nationalism that traded in symbols and legends in order to garner the support of ordinary people for its violent ambitions.[52] Lenin's insistence that imperialism was not a policy, but an inevitable phase in the evolution of capitalism that would lead to its demise, had much to recommend it in the atmosphere of war and its aftermath – when the treaties of Brest–Litovsk and Versailles seemed to prove that the partitioning of the world had been the object of the capitalist warmongers all along. Neither theorist attempted to make visible and verifiable connections between the decisions taken in July 1914 and the socio-economic interests that were supposed to lurk behind them. But historians have found a wealth of evidence to support Schumpeter's arguments when they examine the attitudes of the military during the crisis: the few who struck a cautionary note were overwhelmed by those who, like Moltke, Conrad, Sukhomlinov and Joffre, beat the war drum and convinced civilians that they could win the war if they fought now – and that such a favourable opportunity was not likely to arise again.[53]

Almost as strong is the evidence supporting Schumpeter's arguments concerning the 'rational' instincts of most businessmen that led them to calculate that peace and stability were more profitable than war and chaos. Research into organizations such as the World Peace Foundation, *Conciliation Internationale*, the Inter-Parliamentary Union, *Verband für internationale Verständigung* and the International Peace Bureau, on gatherings such as the peace conferences at the Hague in 1899 and 1907, has confirmed the extent to which these were 'bourgeois' movements led by bankers, traders, entrepreneurs and prosperous middle-class professionals. Moreover, in his diagnosis of the imperial phenomenon, Schumpeter pointed to the attraction of protective tariffs as offering opportunities for short-term profits, and to imperialism as a diversion from social problems at home. But these motives paled in comparison with the appeal to national sentiment that 'alone arouses the dark powers of the subconscious, calls into play the instincts that carry over from the life habits of the dim past. Driven out everywhere else, the irrational seeks refuge in nationalism – the irrational which consists of belligerence, the need to hate, a goodly quota of inchoate idealism, the most naïve (and hence also the most unrestrained) egotism.'[54] Research into a variety of nationalist, imperialist and militarist organizations before World War One has confirmed this conclusion. The sentiments and aspirations of the *Alldeutscher Verband*, the *Wehrverein*, the *Kolonialverein*, the *Jungdeutschlandbund*, the *Ligue des Patriotes*, the *Comitè d'Afrique Française*, the Navy League, the Army League, the Imperial Maritime League, the *Associazione Nazionalista Italiana*, the Dante Alighieri Society, the *Istituto Coloniale*, and of course the *Narodna Odbrana*, overwhelmed the fledgling internationalist organizations handicapped by their tedious legalistic schemes for the arbitration and mediation of disputes. These sentimental appeals established the foundations of what James Joll famously referred to as the 'unspoken assumptions' that lay beneath the decisions taken in July 1914.[55]

It is impossible to prove the part played by assumptions that were, by definition, 'unspoken'. Nevertheless, most historians who have engaged in the difficult and time-consuming labours involved in unearthing the archival materials that have produced an unparalleled knowledge of who said what to whom, when and where in July and August would agree that beliefs concerning national honour, manliness, duty, heritage, faith and fears for the future were essential ingredients in the atmosphere of Europe in 1914. Most of these sentiments looked backward, to the heroes – whether glorious or tragic – of national lore; to the battles – whether triumphant victories or noble defeats – of a legendary past. But mixed among these were new notions arising from the biological and social sciences of the nineteenth century. 'Darwinism' had, by the turn of the century, been transformed into 'social Darwinism' by writers and publicists such as Herbert Spencer, Emile Zola and H. G. Wells. Although Spencer himself (who coined the phrase 'survival of the fittest' to describe how Darwin's theory of natural selection applied to human society) believed that the evolution of human society would eventually lead to the disappearance of the state altogether, others turned the idea into one that applied to ethnicities, races or civilizations. In this view, the struggle for survival applied not to individual human beings, but to the competition among their social organizations. Only the strong would survive; the day of the small had passed; the twentieth century would belong to those who were vigorous enough and bold enough to expand and grow. This joined together the backward-looking view of national sentiments with the forward-looking view of scientific theories. Both encouraged the prevailing belief that the crisis of 1914 was the moment of truth in the great struggle for survival.[56]

Against these pervasive ambitions and fears, the organizations and movements committed to peace proved to be no match. The international socialist movement, which had condemned war as an instrument of the bourgeois-capitalist state in a series of pronouncements emanating from its meetings and theorists, disintegrated as a force in 1914. Although some efforts were made to convince the workers of Europe that they ought not to take up arms, socialist parties everywhere lined up with their nation-states in support of the war. Their bourgeois compatriots in the growing pacifist movement fared no better: some pleas that the crisis be arbitrated or mediated were issued, but these had no effect.

Although both movements failed to avert disaster at the time, they did succeed in creating their own legends concerning causation after the war. Socialist parties after 1919 repeatedly condemned war as the product of capitalist imperialism and succeeded in convincing most of their followers that war was merely the by-product of this phenomenon (and therefore only the triumph of international socialism could produce the conditions necessary for a lasting peace). Pacifist organizations committed themselves more fervently than ever to the view that armaments were themselves a cause of war. The conferences held at the Hague in 1899 and 1907 – both inspired by the belief that, unless a process leading to disarmament was initiated, war would inevitably erupt – had accomplished little more than the laying down of a few limits on how wars ought to be fought. Looking back on this failure after 1914, the movement became more fervently committed than ever to the principle that wars were caused (and not prevented) by the existence of arms and armies. And through advocates of this view, it gradually came to be accepted by many that the arms race had propelled Europe down the path to war, and that behind this lay the self-interest of those involved in the armaments industry. As this view – which verges on a conspiratorial interpretation of history – does not apparently contradict the socialist view of capitalists as bearing the burden of guilt, it has often merged with it in an inchoate way. Although the work of David Stevenson ought to have dispelled the myth forever, it has continued to attract adherents ever since.[57]

***

Paul Schroeder has argued that, if we are to understand why a general European war broke out in August 1914, it is necessary to understand not only the forces that pushed people into confrontation, but why the systems and devices that had previously succeeded in resolving disputes peacefully failed to do so in this instance. In the succession of crises that preceded 1914, those who made the decisions between going to war and remaining at peace had no aversion to the idea of war itself; rather, in each case, one side or the other decided that the risks involved outweighed the benefits and, at the moment of decision, backed down from the prospect of an armed confrontation. In the long succession of crises that began with Morocco in 1905 and stretched through the Bosnian annexation crisis of 1908, the Agadir crisis and the Italian declaration of war on the Ottoman Empire in 1911, and the first and second Balkan wars of 1912–13, at least one of the great powers involved had calculated that it had more to lose by risking war than it had to gain from it. In other words, those crises proved that the balance of power and its crucial ingredients – the alliance system and the arms race – functioned successfully in maintaining the peace.[58]

What had changed by the time of the July crisis was neither the system of international relations, nor the underlying beliefs, sentiments, ideologies, pretensions, fears or aspirations of those involved. A series of fateful, calculated decisions were made by men who were no less rational, no more quixotic, than those who had made the decisions that preserved the general European peace since 1814. When Serb terrorists succeeded in assassinating the heir to the throne of Austria-Hungary, the Austrians concluded that this was the best opportunity they would ever have to end the nationalist menace that threatened to destroy the empire – and therefore issued the ultimatum to Serbia. When the Serbs considered the ultimatum, they concluded that, if they were to give in to all of its demands, their dream of a Great Serbia would be lost forever – and therefore refused to accept the ultimatum without reservations. When the Russians contemplated the humiliation of their Serb ally, which raised the possibility of it returning to its earlier status as an Austrian satellite, they concluded that their position in south-eastern Europe and at the Straits would be fatally jeopardized – and therefore decided to mobilize in order to force the Austrians to back down. When the Germans contemplated the possibility of their ally being defeated by the Russians in a 'localized' war, they concluded that they would be reduced to the status of a second-rate European power, alone and encircled in the centre of the continent – and therefore gave their ultimatum to Russia, insisting that it demobilize. When the French considered the consequences of failing to promise their full support to Russia, they concluded that this would fatally jeopardize the alliance, on which they depended for their security against Germany – and therefore refused to comply with Germany's demand that they declare their neutrality in the event of a Russo–German war. The least important decision was made by the British, whose only stake in the July crisis was that the European balance should somehow be maintained, and who thus prevaricated until all the others had declared war and Germany had invaded Belgium – at which point they decided that a victory of the Dual Alliance would imperil the security of the empire. In essence, the conflict broke out when the statesmen of Europe decided that failing to fight was riskier than going to war.

Notes

1 Most of these were conveniently published in a single volume by the British government in 1915: *Collected Diplomatic Documents Relating to the Outbreak of the European War* (London: HM Stationery Office, 1915).
2 See Sally Marks, 'Smoke and Mirrors: In Smoke-Filled Rooms and the Galerie des Glaces', in M. F. Boemeke, G. D. Feldman and E. Glaser (eds),

The Treaty of Versailles: A Reassessment after 75 Years (Washington, DC: Cambridge University Press, 1998), pp. 337–70.

3 [Germany's 'Guilt' and Truth], Walter G. A. Otto (Marburg: N. G. Elwert, 1919).

4 Otto Harwich, *Die große Lüge: Beitrag zur Kriegsschuld-Frage* [The Great Lie: A Contribution to the War-Guilt Question] (Bremen: Zentrale, 1921).

5 [Who is Guilty?], Gustav Stresemann (Berlin: Staatspolitischer Verlag, 1921).

6 [France's War Guilt], Louis Guétant (Bremen: Volksbund 'Rettet die ehre', 1922).

7 [The Responsibility of the Entente for the World War], Georg Karo (Halle: Niemeyer, 1921).

8 For example, Stewart Bruce's *War Guilt and Peace Crime of the Entente Allies* was translated as *Kriegsschuld und Friedensverbrechen der Entente* (Berlin: H. Bousset [1921]); E. D. Morel's *Pre-War Diplomacy* as *Ein gerechter Engländer über die Schuld am Kriege: genehmigte Uebersetzung der Schuldkapitel aus E. D. Morel 'Truth and the War'* (Berlin: Engelmann, 1920); Georg Karo was translated as *The Responsibility of the Entente for the War in the Showing of their Own Statesmen* (Halle: Niemeyer, 1922).

9 London, [1919].

10 (New York: F. L. Searl, 1920).

11 (New York: B. W. Huebsch, 1922). The Library of Congress has, in its 'Third Reich Collection', Adolf Hitler's personal copy of this book.

12 For example: Graf Franz Conrad von Hötzendorf, *Aus meiner Dienstzeit 1906–18*, four vols (Vienna: Rikola Verlag, 1921–25); Kaiser Wilhelm II, *Ereignisse und Gestalten aus den Jahren 1878–1918* (Leipzig: K. F. Koehler, 1922); Raymond Poincaré, *The Origins of the War* (London: Cassell, 1922); H. H. Asquith, *Genesis of the War* (London: Cassell, 1923); Maurice Paléologue, *An Ambassador's Memoirs*, three vols (London: Hutchinson, 1923–25); Viscount Grey of Fallodon, *Twenty-Five Years, 1892–1916*, two vols (London: Hodder & Stoughton, 1925); Sergei D. Sazonov, *Fateful Years, 1909–16* (London: Jonathan Cape, 1928).

13 (Berlin: Zentralstelle für Erforschung der Kriegsursachen, 1923–28).

14 Berlin: Deutsche Verlagsgesellschaft für Politik und Geschichte, 1924; translated by A. E. Adams and published as *From Bismarck to the World War: A History of German Foreign Policy 1870–1914* (Oxford: Oxford University Press, 1927).

15 (Paris: A. Costes, 1925). English edn: *The Immediate Origins of the War* (New Haven: Yale University Press, 1928).

16 Subtitled *An Introduction to the Problem of War Guilt* (New York: Knopf, 1926).

17 (London: Hutchinson, 1926).

18 (New York: Scribner's, 1930). His book won both a Pulitzer Prize (1931) and the American Historical Association's George Beer Prize (1930) for the best book in European international history since 1890.

19 (London: G. Allen & Unwin, [1937, 2nd edn]).

20 (New York: Macmillan).

21 (London: Hamish Hamilton, 1945).

22 (Krefeld: Scherpe-Verl., 1948) – *Precarious Balance: Four Centuries of the European Power Struggle* (1962); see also his lectures and essays collected in *Germany and World Politics in the Twentieth Century* (London: Chatto

& Windus, 1959). On Dehio, see Sergio Pistone, *Ludwig Dehio* (Naples: Guida Editori, 1977).

23 (Milano, Fratelli Bocca, [1942–43]).

24 When the English translation of the book was published as *Germany's Aims in the First World War* (London: Chatto & Windus, 1967) (dropping the title of the original German 'Grab for World Power' and using only the subtitle), Fischer cut out approximately one-third of the original text – mainly extended quotations from archival sources.

25 *Ibid.*, pp. 637–38.

26 *Ibid.*, p. xxii.

27 The most important German critics of Fischer included Gerhard Ritter, Karl Dietrich Erdmann and Egmont Zechlin, whose criticism is most readily accessible in the collection edited by H. W. Koch, *The Origins of the First World War: Great Power Rivalry and German War Aims* (Basingstoke: Macmillan, 1984).

28 The debate can be traced in: John A. Moses, *The Politics of Illusion: The Fischer Controversy in German Historiography* (London: George Prior, 1975); John W. Langdon, *July 1914: The Long Debate, 1918–1990*, (Oxford: Berg, 1991); and Annika Mombauer, *The Origins of the First World War: Controversies and Consensus* (London: Longman/Pearson, 2002).

29 The book was subtitled *die deutsche Politik von 1911 bis 1914* (Düsseldorf: Droste, 1969; English translation, New York: Norton, 1975).

30 (Berlin: E. Ebering, 1930). The subtitle is indicative of the argument: *Eines Querschnitts durch die innenpolitischen, sozialen und ideologischen Voraussetzungen des deutschen Imperialismus* – 'A Cross-section of the Domestic Political, Social and Ideological Preconditions of German Imperialism'. A translated version was published as *Battleship Building and Party Politics in Germany, 1894–1901* by the University of Chicago Press in 1973.

31 Of course these comments oversimplify a wide range of hugely detailed studies, but these are, in essence, the arguments of: Harold I. Nelson, *Land and Power: British and Allied Policy on Germany's Frontiers, 1916–1919* (London: Routledge & Kegan Paul, 1963); W. R. Louis, *Great Britain and Germany's Lost Colonies, 1914–1919* (Oxford: Oxford University Press, 1967); V. H. Rothwell, *British War Aims and Peace Diplomacy, 1914–1918* (Oxford: Clarendon Press, 1971); R. E. Bunselmeyer, *The Cost of the War, 1914–1919: British War Aims and the Origins of Reparation* (Hamden: Archon, 1975); K. J. Calder, *Britain and the Origins of the New Europe, 1914–1918* (Cambridge: Cambridge University Press, 1976); B. Hunt and A. Preston (eds), *War Aims and Strategic Policy in the Great War, 1914–1918* (London: Croom Helm, 1977); David French, *British Strategy & War Aims, 1914–1916* (London: Allen & Unwin, 1986). On France see W. A. McDougall, *France's Rhineland Diplomacy, 1914–1924: The Last Bid for a Balance of Power in Europe* (Princeton: Princeton University Press, 1978); Marc Trachtenberg, *Reparation in World Politics: France and European Economic Diplomacy, 1916–1923* (New York: Columbia University Press, 1980).

32 On Wilson and Wilsonianism see: Laurence W. Martin, *Peace without Victory: Woodrow Wilson and the British Liberals* (New Haven: Yale University Press, 1958); Lawrence E. Gelfand, *The Inquiry: American Preparation for Peace, 1917–1919* (New Haven: Yale University Press, 1963); Antony Lentin, *Lloyd George, Woodrow Wilson, and the Guilt of*

Germany: An Essay in the Pre-history of Appeasement (London: Methuen, 1984).

33 Christopher Andrew and A. S. Kanya-Forstner, *The Climax of French Imperial Expansion, 1914–1924* (Stanford: Stanford University Press, 1981).

34 David Stevenson, *French War Aims against Germany, 1914–1919* (Oxford: Clarendon Press, 1982). Only when victory appeared to be in sight did Clemenceau envision other measures to enhance French security in the future: crushing reparations, an independent Rhenish state on the left bank of the Rhine, and ruling out a future *Anschluss* between Germany and Austria.

35 In this, he disputes Fischer's argument that the September Programme represented well established, long-term aims on the part of Bethmann Hollweg; the 'Programme' itself was a momentary response to immediate circumstances; what Bethmann really aimed at was an economic union with Austria-Hungary that would enhance German security by strengthening the German economy within Europe. Georges-Henri Soutou, *L'Or et le Sang: Les Buts de guerre économiques de la Première Guerre mondiale* (Paris: Fayard, 1989).

36 There is, unfortunately, no comparable study of Russian aims. C. Jay Smith Jr's *The Russian Struggle for Power, 1914–1917: A Study of Russian Foreign Policy during the First World War* (New York: Philosophical Library, 1956) preceded the Fischer controversy and relied almost exclusively on published materials put together by the Bolsheviks after the revolution in order to discredit the tsarist regime.

37 On 3 September 1965, for example, a letter to the Editor of *The Times* declared that 'We, historians of many countries, have attended the discussions of the International Congress of Vienna on German war aims in the First World War. We feel strongly that British war aims, as well as the war aims of other belligerents, should be discussed with the same frankness, and therefore appeal to the British Government that they should open the British archives for the First World War without delay or restrictions.' The signatories of the letter included Bernadotte Schmitt, Vladimir Dedijer, Hugh Seton-Watson, Fritz Fischer, A. J. P. Taylor and Immanuel Geiss.

38 This Macmillan series includes the following: Volker R. Berghahn, *Germany and the Approach of War in 1914* (2nd edn, London: 1993); Zara S. Steiner and Keith Neilson, *Britain and the Origins of the First World War* (London: 2003, 2nd edn); Dominic C. B. Lieven, *Russia and the Origins of the First World War*, (London: 1983); John F. V. Keiger, *France and the Origins of the First World War* (London: 1983); Richard Bosworth, *Italy and the Approach of the First World War* (London: 1983); Samuel R. Williamson Jr, *Austria-Hungary and the Origins of the First World War* (London: 1994).

39 James Joll and Gordon Martel, *The Origins of the First World War* (London: Pearson/Longman, 2006).

40 The classic account in English is J. V. Fuller, *Bismarck's Diplomacy at its Zenith* (Cambridge, MA: Harvard University Press, 1922); see also the views of A. J. P. Taylor in *Bismarck: The Man and the Statesman* (London: Hamish Hamilton, 1955) and in *The Struggle for Mastery in Europe* (Oxford: Oxford University Press, 1954); and of W. L. Langer in *European Alliances and Alignments, 1871–1890* (New York: Knopf, 1931) and *The Diplomacy of Imperialism* (New York: Knopf, 1935). See also Bascom Barry Hayes, *Bismarck and Mitteleuropa*, (Rutherford: Farleigh Dickinson

University Press, 1994); and, in German: Fritz Fellner, *Der Dreibund: europäische Diplomatie vor dem Ersten Weltkrieg* (Munich: Oldenbourg, 1960); Wolfgang J. Mommsen, *Grossmachtstellung und Weltpolitik. Die Aussenpolitik des deutschen Reiches 1870–1914* (Frankfurt am Main: Propyläen, 1993); Klaus Hildebrand, *Das vergangene Reich. Deutsche Außenpolitik von Bismarck bis Hitler* (Stuttgart: Deutsche Verlags-Anstalt, 1995); Jürgen Angelow, *Kalkül und Prestige. Der Zweibund am Vorabend des Ersten Weltkrieges* (Cologne: Böhlau, 2000); and Holger Afflerbach, *Der Dreibund* (Vienna: Böhlau, 2002).

41 The terms of the treaties may be found in Michael Hurst (ed.), *Key Treaties for the Great Powers 1814–1914, Vol. 2, 1871–1914* (London: David & Charles, 1974).

42 The Dual Alliance was signed in 1879; the Triple Alliance was formed in 1882; the terms of the Franco–Russian military convention were agreed in 1894; the Anglo–French convention established the 'entente' in 1904; the Anglo–Russian convention completed the entente in 1907. The Dual Alliance and the Triple Alliance were renewed a number of times, usually with some alterations in the arrangements, but there is insufficient space to describe these here.

43 'Things remaining as they are.'

44 Arno J. Mayer, 'Internal crises and war since 1870', in Charles L. Bertrand (ed.), *Revolutionary Situations in Europe* (Montreal: Centre inter-universitaire d'études européennes, 1977), p. 231. See also his 'Domestic Causes of the First World War', in Leonard Kreiger and Fritz Stern (eds), *The Responsibility of Power* (London: Macmillan, 1968). For a fuller development of Mayer's view that the war was a last attempt by the old European aristocracy to preserve its position, see his *The Persistence of the Old Regime: Europe to the Great War* (London: Croom Helm, 1981), especially Ch. 5. A detailed criticism of the thesis as it applies to Britain can be found in Donald Lammers, 'Arno Mayer and the British decision for war', *Journal of British Studies* 12 (1973), 137–65.

45 Arthur S. Link *et al.* (eds), *The Papers of Woodrow Wilson*, Vol. 45 (Princeton: Princeton University Press, 1984), p. 536.

46 Michael Sanders and Philip M. Taylor, *British Propaganda during the First World War 1914–1918*, (London: Macmillan, 1982).

47 Some of the more important works on this theme are: Lancelot L. Farrar, *The Short-War Illusion* (Santa Barbara: University of California Press, 1973); John Gooch, *The Plans of War: the General Staff and British Military Strategy, 1900–1916* (London: Routledge & Kegan Paul, 1974); Paul M. Kennedy (ed.), *The War Plans of the Great Powers 1880–1914* (London: Allen & Unwin, 1979); Douglas Porch, *The March to the Marne: The French Army 1871–1914* (Cambridge: Cambridge University Press, 1981); Jack Snyder, *The Ideology of the Offensive: Military Decision Making and the Disasters of 1914* (Ithaca: Cornell University Press, 1984); Holger H. Herwig, *'Luxury' Fleet: the Imperial German Navy 1888–1918* (London: Allen & Unwin, 1980); John Gooch, *Army, State, and Society in Italy, 1870–1915* (Basingstoke: Macmillan, 1989); István Deak, *Beyond Nationalism: A Social and Political History of the Habsburg Officer Corps, 1848–1918* (New York: Oxford University Press, 1990); Arden Bucholz, *Moltke, Schlieffen, and Prussian War Planning* (Oxford: Berg, 1991); Bruce

W. Menning, *Bayonets before Bullets: the Imperial Russian Army, 1861–1914* (Bloomington: Indiana University Press, 1992); Graydon A. Tunstall Jr, *Planning for War against Russia and Serbia: Austro Hungarian and German Military Strategies, 1871–1914* (Boulder: Social Science Monographs, 1993); Annika Mombauer, *Helmuth von Moltke and the Origins of the First World War* (Cambridge: Cambridge University Press, 2001).

48 A. J. P. Taylor, *War by Timetable: How the First World War Began* (London: MacDonald, 1969).

49 The very existence of a Schlieffen 'plan' has recently been challenged by Terence Zuber in *Inventing the Schlieffen Plan: German War Planning, 1871–1914* (Oxford: Oxford University Press, 2002). But his argument has won few adherents.

50 The essay first appeared as 'Zur Soziologie der Imperialismen' in the *Archiv für Sozialwissenschaft und Sozialpolitik* in 1919, although it is clear that it was written during the war years. It was translated by Heinz Norden, edited and introduced by Paul M. Sweezy, in Joseph A. Schumpeter (ed.), *Imperialism and Social Classes* (Oxford: Blackwell, 1951).

51 *Ibid.*, p. 7.

52 The literature on these themes is vast and continues to grow. On the peace movements, see A. J. A. Morris, *Radicalism against War 1906–1914* (London: Longman, 1972); Roger Chickering, *Imperial Germany and a World without War: The Peace Movement and German Society 1892–1914* (Princeton: Princeton University Press, 1975); J. D. B. Miller, *Norman Angell and the Futility of War* (London: Macmillan, 1986); Nicholas Stargardt, *The German Idea of Militarism: Radical and Socialist Critics, 1866–1914* (Cambridge: Cambridge University Press, 1994). On popular militarism see: Paul M. Kennedy and Anthony J. Nicholls (eds), *Nationalist and Racialist Movements in Britain and Germany before 1914* (London: Macmillan, 1981); Roger Chickering, *We Who Feel Most German: A Cultural Study of the Pan-German League* (London: Allen & Unwin, 1984); M. C. C. Adams, *The Great Adventure: Male Desire and the Coming of World War I* (Bloomington: Indiana University Press, 1990); M. S. Coetzee, *The Army League: Popular Nationalism in Wilhelmine Germany* (Oxford: Oxford University Press, 1990); Jeffrey Verhey, *The Spirit of 1914: Militarism, Myth, and Mobilization in Germany* (Cambridge: Cambridge University Press, 2000).

53 In addition to the works referred to in note 45, see: Steven E. Miller (ed.), *Military Strategy and the Origins of the First World War* (Princeton: Princeton University Press, 1985); W. Jannen Jr, 'The Austro-Hungarian Decision for War in July 1914', in Samuel R. Williamson Jr and Peter Pastor (eds), *Essays on World War I: Origins and Prisoners of War* (New York: Social Science Monographs, 1983), pp. 55–81; Stephen J. Cimbala, 'Steering through rapids: Russian mobilization and World War I', *Journal of Slavic Military History* 9 (1996), 376–98.

54 Schumpeter, *Imperialism, op. cit.*, p. 14.

55 See his essay in H. W. Koch, *The Origins of the First World War, op. cit.*

56 On the connections between social Darwinism and the mood of 1914, see: Alfred Kelly, *The Descent of Darwin: The Popularization of Darwinism in Germany, 1860–1914* (Chapel Hill: University of North Carolina Press, 1981); David P. Crook, *Benjamin Kidd: Portrait of a Social Darwinist*

(Cambridge: Cambridge University Press, 1984); Paul Crook, *Darwinism, War and History: The Debate over the Biology of War from the 'Origin of Species' to the First World War* (Cambridge: Cambridge University Press, 1994).

57 Although there were numerous prewar works that suggested a connection between armaments manufacturers and imperialism and war, the most influential (in English) were probably J. A. Hobson's *Imperialism: A Study* (London: Nisbet, 1902), and Norman Angell's *The Great Illusion* (London: Heinemann, 1910).

58 See his 'World War I as Galloping Gertie: a reply to Joachim Remak', *Journal of Modern History* 44 (1972), 319–45; and, more recently, 'International politics, peace and war, 1815–1914', in T. C. W. Blanning (ed.), *The Nineteenth Century: Europe 1789–1914* (Oxford: Oxford University Press, 1981), pp. 158–209.

5　World War One: conduct and consequences

Frank Tallett

For many in our own epoch, the Third Battle of Ypres, more commonly referred to as Passchendaele, has come to epitomize World War One. It signifies the mud and squalor of the trenches, the courage of the rank-and-file soldiers, the stupidity of the High Command, and the futile sacrifice of life in a conflict that was, according to one of its leading historians, both 'tragic and unnecessary'.[1] Such a perspective would not have been adopted by those living at the time of the conflict, and is potentially misleading. Of course, there is no denying the horrors of trench warfare. However, it should also be recognized that there was little alternative; that trenches saved lives; and that fluid and mobile warfare exposed men to the greatest hazards, with a consequent rise in casualties.[2] The focus on the Western Front is understandable, given that it so profoundly marked the French and British psyche, and is to some degree justifiable, given that it was so decisive to the final outcome. Yet it distracts attention from the fact that the conflict was a global one, with many fronts. The Central Powers (Germany and Austria-Hungary) were joined by Turkey in November 1914 and Bulgaria in September the following year. Ranged against them were the members of the Entente, initially comprising France, Britain and Russia, who were joined by Japan (August 1914), Italy (May 1915), Portugal (March 1916), Romania (August 1916) and Greece (June 1917). The USA entered the war in April 1917, though it was never technically an ally of the Entente, and insisted upon being called a co-belligerent 'Associated Power'. China, too, joined the war in 1917, as did some South American states. And as much of the globe comprised colonies of the Western powers, they too came into the conflict on the coat-tails of the original belligerents. The focus on the Western Front also underplays the contribution of sailors and airmen, as well as the impact of the conflict on civilians and their role in its outcome. Finally, any suggestion that the war was futile neglects both the principles that inspired so many of those who fought, and the tenacity with which they were held; while the contrast between maps of Europe in 1914 and in 1919 confirms that this was emphatically not a war without results. This chapter grapples with a number of these issues, by looking at the military dimensions of the conflict, its broader impact especially on the home fronts, and some of its longer-term results.

The fighting front

1914–15: the opening rounds

Germany's High Command had long recognized that the country was unlikely to prevail in a protracted attritional war fought by coalitions, and had therefore sought a 'short war solution'.[3] The particular plan chosen for use in 1914, based loosely on a scheme formulated by Alfred von Schlieffen, was predicated upon securing a rapid victory over France in a decisive offensive operation, before turning east to deal with Russia.[4] The strong defensive French positions, stretching from Belfort to Toul and then along the line of the Meuse, were accordingly bypassed. The main attack, begun on 18 August, swung round in a great arc from the north through the Low Countries, and aimed at enveloping and then destroying the French armies. By early September, German forces had advanced to within a few miles of Paris, but they were weary and outrunning their supplies. Displaying great coolness, Joffre, the French Commander-in-Chief, redeployed his forces and successfully counter-attacked. The battle of the Marne (5–11 September) checked the advance of the Germans, who were forced back to the Aisne, where they would remain for the next four years. Few battles in the history of warfare are truly decisive. The Marne was one such – even though this victory would have been merely a pyrrhic one if the French front had given way at any other point. The Germans had overrun most of Belgium and France's industrial heartland, and occupied territory that favoured the defensive. They would accordingly be difficult to dislodge. But, barring some unexpected collapse of the Entente Powers, Germany could no longer win the war. Each side now tried unsuccessfully to outflank the other, with the result that by Christmas the battle lines stretched from the Swiss border to the Channel ports. The front, characterized by an interlocking and complex network of trenches and barbed wire, remained largely static until spring 1918.

Germany had planned for a war on two fronts; its armed forces had been expanded accordingly, and the rail network was designed to shift troops from west to east and *vice versa*. However, it depended on its ally, Austria-Hungary, to hold back the Russians in the initial weeks of a war in order to give time for its offensive against France to succeed. Despite the importance of Austria-Hungary's role in German strategic planning, there was no mechanism for joint control of the forces of the two states, no joint operational manoeuvres had been practised, and Austria-Hungary remained convinced that Germany would shoulder the burden of dealing with the Russians. On 28 July, the Vienna government declared war only on Serbia, in the belief that this would be a localized, two-state conflict, but was then pushed into mobilizing against Russia too. Austria-Hungary accordingly had to divide its forces when it was scarcely strong enough to fight on one front, and this, coupled with incompetent leadership, resulted in shattering defeats. Against the much smaller Serb forces, it lost 200,000 men and much equipment; against the Russians, who had mobilized more quickly than many observers had anticipated, it lost twice that number, and the Galician front was rescued only with help from the Germans. By the end of the year, the fighting had cost Austria-Hungary over 950,000 men, more than twice the army's prewar strength. Russian forces also enjoyed initial success in East Prussia as well as in Galicia, but matters changed after the arrival of Hindenburg, recalled from retirement, with Ludendorff as his Chief-of-Staff. The two men took over a plan originated by Colonel Max Hoffmann, and a mixture of German brilliance and good fortune led to Russian defeats at the battles of Tannenberg (27–28 August) and the Masurian Lakes (7–10 September). The Eastern Front was stabilized, but to achieve this the Germans had been obliged to draw substantial numbers of men from the west.

At the start of 1915, the first instincts of Falkenhayn, who had succeeded the discredited Moltke as Army Chief of Staff in September 1914, had been to renew the offensive in the west. But the failure at Ypres in November 1914, the fluidity of warfare on the Eastern Front, which seemingly offered the possibility of fighting the type of envelopment battles for which German Staff officers had been trained, the pressure from Hindenburg and Ludendorff who had become national heroes after their recent victories, and finally the need to offer continuing support to Austria-Hungary, meant that priority was accorded to the East. At first, the policy appeared to pay dividends. At Gorlice-Tarnow (2 May 1915), the Austro-German forces broke through the weak Russian defences; German troops rampaged through the Baltic states in the north; and Warsaw fell on 5 August. By December, most of Galicia, Poland, Lithuania, Latvia and Byelorussia had changed hands. Serbia, too, had been overrun, and the Bulgarians – recently allied to the Central Powers – had occupied Macedonia. However stunning these territorial gains might be, the very size of the Eastern Front rendered them indecisive. Even though it had lost around 1.4 million men since May,[5] Russia showed remarkable resilience and was not forced into making the separate peace that would have allowed Germany to concentrate upon the West. Meanwhile, Austria-Hungary remained unable to support independent operations, thus continuing to drain its ally of men and resources.

Austrian difficulties were compounded by Italy's entry into the conflict on 26 April 1915. Its declaration of war was against Austria-Hungary alone, but was premised on Allied promises of large parcels of Habsburg territory; like most of the war's other late entrants, the Italians were open to the highest bidder. In the course of the next six months, they launched four major offensives along the line of the River Isonzo. By the end of the year, the Italians had suffered 235,000 casualties, the Austrians not many fewer. By 1917, a further seven offensives would have been undertaken, with the total casualties exceeding 1 million even though the front scarcely moved a dozen miles. Yet so long as the domestic integrity of its Austrian ally was not threatened, Germany was quite content to accept this stalemate. 'Basically, it does not matter a hoot to us whether Italy hacks another piece of the tail off the dying camel Austria', the Prussian War Minister noted cynically.[6]

1915 also saw the intensification of fighting on another set of fronts, initially created the previous year by Turkey's entry into the war. It had signed a treaty with Germany on 2 August 1914, keen to acquire an ally that might help to bolster its position in the Balkans. For their part, the Germans had overcome earlier doubts about Turkey's value as an ally. They hoped that Turkey would reinforce the military position on the Eastern Front and, by a call to *jihad*, rouse the 120 million Muslims living under British and French colonial mastery. In the event, nobody's expectations were fulfilled. Turkey began hostilities on 29 October, and everywhere met with failure. A move into the Caucasus immediately ran into difficulties, the troops falling victim to the climate and inadequate supplies as well as to Russian bullets. Meanwhile, a British-led force of mainly Indian troops in Mesopotamia made easy initial progress towards Baghdad. These Entente successes confirmed a belief that the Ottoman military would be a soft touch, and encouraged calls for an amphibious operation to force open the Dardanelles through landings at Gallipoli. This, it was argued, would knock Turkey out of the war, open up a supply route to Russia, set alight the Balkans, where the Entente and the Central Powers were competing for allies, and ease pressure on the deadlocked Western Front. Sometimes regarded as a potentially war-winning strategic masterstroke, the operation, launched in March 1915 and comprising troops from Britain, Australia, New Zealand and France, was a tactical and operational failure, redeemed only partially by a skilfully executed withdrawal during December 1915 and January 1916. The blow to Allied prestige was enormous, and Bulgaria now judged it timely to join the Central Powers. In Mesopotamia, too, things began to go wrong for the Allies. The force that had advanced so confidently into Basra province became bottled up at Kut Al-Amara, and would surrender in April 1916 after four attempts at relief had failed. The only bright spot for the British in the war with Turkey was the retention of the Suez Canal in February 1915. They would similarly defend it in July of the following year, thus maintaining a link vital to communications across their empire.

In 1914–15, the fighting also spread overseas. In some respects this was inevitable because of European colonial interests. On the eve of World War One, Ethiopia and Liberia were the only African states not under foreign rule. To be sure, Britain and France had no interest in extending the war, except in so far as they wished to draw on the resources of their colonies and dominions. But Germany, as a minor player in the colonial game with less to lose, sought to relieve pressure on the Western and Eastern Fronts by threatening its enemies' overseas territories. Best known are the exploits of Colonel Paul von Lettow-Vorbeck, who operated through the length of East Africa, eluding his opponents and not surrendering until after the Armistice was signed. His activities have tended to distract attention from the fighting in the German colonies of the Cameroons, Togoland and south-west Africa. It would be wrong to label these conflicts as imperial sideshows, as they involved more than 2 million Africans. Most served as labourers and carriers in mobile campaigns very different from warfare on the Western Front, characterized as they were by long marches and the use of human porters. This fighting did not, however, have a significant impact on the European conflict. Lettow-Vorbeck liked to believe that he had tied down his opponents' forces. But although he occupied the attention of some 160,000 British and Belgian troops, few would have been available for use on the Western Front; Britain was resolved that only local forces should be used in Africa, although the French took a different view. Moreover, at the outset of the overseas conflicts, the British successfully secured their major objective, the capture of the German wireless stations and ports that posed a threat to their naval mastery. Thus the key wireless station at Kamina in Togoland was captured in

August 1914; Douala in the Cameroons fell in the following month. Thereafter, Britain had little interest in acquiring German colonies. Elsewhere, however, other regional powers took a different view, exploiting opportunities to pursue their own territorial ambitions. Japan declared war on Germany on 23 August 1914 and immediately occupied the German naval base on the Chinese Shantung peninsula. Japan then pressured China for economic concessions. In the Pacific, Japanese, Australian and New Zealand troops captured German colonies to which they laid claim, generally with minimal fighting, in the opening months of the war.

1916–17: deadlock on land and at sea

By the end of 1915 there was, then, a stalemate of some kind on all fronts, mainly because the contestants could make no further progress or, otherwise, because they had achieved their major objectives. However, Falkenhayn was sufficiently confident about the achievements of the Central Powers on the Eastern Front to turn his attention to the west at the start of 1916. He had become convinced early on that final victory was impossible, but hoped to fight the Allies to a draw and to conclude separate peace treaties with each. Russia had disappointed him in this respect by refusing to make peace, but he wrongly believed that it was too exhausted to conduct further attacks. He therefore proposed in 1916 to weaken the Entente's resolve by forcing the French, in particular, into costly counter-attacks – or at least that was how he later justified the operation. Accordingly, German forces attacked Verdun in February. Over the following ten months, each side expended around 10 million shells, the Germans lost 337,000 men, and the French only slightly more (377,231). For France, Verdun became a symbol of national survival.

Meanwhile, the strategy of the Allies in 1916 was to continue joint offensives on all fronts, thus nullifying the advantage Germany had of operating on interior lines while making best use of their own superiority in men and resources. To the complete surprise of Falkenhayn, the Russians under Brusilov attacked in Galicia, and by 6 June they had advanced over 75 km in two days, capturing 200,000 prisoners and shattering the Austro-Hungarian Fourth Army. So encouraging were these advances that Romania joined the Entente, tempted by the Allied promise of Transylvania and Bukovina, and keen to be in quickly to finish off Austria-Hungary. On the Western Front, an Anglo–French offensive began on the Somme on 1 July. Because of the defence of Verdun, the French contribution to the attack had to be scaled back and the British forces increased, with the result that the latter henceforth played a major role in land operations, as well as at sea. Their small professional prewar army had now been transformed by mass conscription, and Haig commanded over 1 million men. However, the British artillery in particular was ill-prepared for the role it was asked to play, and by November, when the Somme campaign concluded, there had been negligible territorial gains. The losses, however, were staggering: up to 650,000 German casualties, 420,000 British and around 200,000 French. One further consequence of the Allied offensives in 1916 was Falkenhayn's replacement by Hindenburg and Ludendorff.

This change of leadership did not imply an alteration in overall policy. The Central Powers remained committed to bringing their enemies, one by one, to the conference table: hence the attacks on Russia in 1915, then at Verdun the following year. In 1917, they sought to achieve their aim by sea, through unrestricted submarine warfare and economic blockade. From the very outset, the naval war had not unfolded quite as anticipated. The British Grand Fleet refused to conform to German expectations. Rather than maintaining a traditional close blockade in the Heligoland Bight, where it would have been exposed to mines and torpedoes – the new weapons of naval warfare – it operated out of Scapa Flow in the Orkneys. From there, it denied the main German fleet access to the North Sea and hence to the rest of the world's oceans. Outside the European theatre, German naval bases and shipping had quickly been put out of action. None the less, both the British and German navies still anticipated a major engagement that would at some point decisively determine command of the sea. However, the only occasion on which this came close to happening, at Jutland on 31 May 1916, resulted in a draw. While the British fleet suffered disproportionately heavy losses and expectations of another Trafalgar were disappointed, the German fleet was again bottled up and the strategic situation in the North Sea remained unaltered. With German maritime commerce largely eliminated from the outset, Britain now proceeded to tighten its blockade by limiting the freedom of neutrals to trade with the Central Powers.

Germany had itself announced a submarine blockade of Britain in 1914. The essential difference was that it could be enforced only by sinking shipping and leaving crew and passengers to their fate. After the attack on the *Lusitania* in 1915, with the loss of almost 1200 lives, the Kaiser, fearful of US entry into the war, suspended unrestricted submarine warfare, and in 1916 refused Falkenhayn's pleas to reinstate it to coordinate with the assaults on Verdun. However, Hindenburg,

Ludendorff and the naval command, displaying a wilful disregard for the wider implications of such a campaign, continued to press the issue, believing that only through attacks on its economic substructure could Britain be driven to negotiate. In February 1917 they had their way, and unrestricted submarine warfare resumed. Losses of Allied merchant vessels, which peaked at 841,118 tons in April, were initially extremely heavy, and for a while British economic survival appeared threatened. But the introduction of convoys, on the insistence of David Lloyd George, together with the employment of 'spotter' aircraft in coastal waters, countered the underwater threat and reduced losses to manageable levels. They were down to 200,000 tons in September, and U-boat losses were growing.[7] Just as significant for the long-term outcome of the war, the USA was provoked by Germany's use of unrestricted submarine warfare, and its ham-fisted offer of an alliance to Mexico, into declaring war in April 1917. German submarines would prove unable to prevent the transport of men and resources across the Atlantic in the spring and summer of 1918.

While the Central Powers had shifted the emphasis from land to sea in 1917, the Entente strategy remained largely unchanged from 1916 – simultaneous, large-scale offensives on all fronts. In the event, this proved impossible to implement fully. The strains of war had taken a toll on Russia's armed forces and on its civilian population. Early in March, workers and soldiers in its capital (now patriotically relabelled 'Petrograd' to replace Germanic-sounding 'Petersburg') took to the streets, and soon forced the Tsar's abdication. Brusilov launched a final desperate offensive in July, but the Russian forces were routed and the Germans occupied the symbolically significant city of Riga. Although designed as much to stave off domestic revolution as to make military gains, Brusilov's action had the opposite effect. By early November, the Bolsheviks had seized power, and in December they agreed an armistice. Russia was out of the war, leaving the Entente without an active Eastern Front and thus undermining the basis of its strategy. When Romania, too, signed an armistice in December, another front was gone. On the Italian Front, a series of engagements in the summer of 1917 had drained both sides of men, resources and morale, prompting fears that Austria-Hungary would not survive. In response, the Germans moved troops to assist, the first time they had intervened in strength on the Italian Front, and in October they broke through at Caporetto. Significantly, over 600,000 Italians were captured or deserted, as against 40,000 who were killed, an indication that the rank and file had had enough of the poor supplies, futile offensives and defective leadership. Equally important, however, they rallied on the River Piave in defence of the homeland, although 11 British and French divisions had to be redeployed to provide backing. Like Germany, the Entente Powers were learning the costs of propping up a feeble ally. On the Western Front, the Germans had pulled back in March 1917 to a heavily defended position, the so-called Hindenburg Line, evacuating the very salient which the Allies had intended to make the focus of their attack. In the event, only the British were able to mount a major offensive, doing so in the Third Battle of Ypres (July–November). There was confusion at the highest levels about the purpose of the attack, and it petered out at the cost of 275,000 casualties. The only bright spot for the Allies in 1917 was the USA's entry into the conflict in April. America's declaration of war prompted others to do the same: Greece on 2 July and China just over a month later, while the South American countries either formally joined the Entente or broke off relations with Germany.

1918: the year of decision

The American involvement would prove decisive. This was partly because the industrial/technological superiority enjoyed by the Allies now became overwhelming,[8] partly because of the advantage US manpower reserves gave to the Entente, although the number of American troops on the ground did not become significant until the summer of 1918.[9] More immediately, it was also because German strategy in the west shifted from defensive to offensive in a bid to win the war before American intervention became fully effective. In November 1917, Ludendorff stressed the need to strike at the earliest possible moment 'before the Americans can throw strong forces into the scales'.[10] Since the autumn of 1914, it had been well nigh impossible for Germany to win the war; but a failed offensive operation meant that it could now lose it. Troops were moved westward in large numbers, although fewer than had been hoped for, as over 1 million had to be left on the Eastern Front, largely to police the troublesome populations. None the less, in March 1918 German forces applied in the west techniques similar to those so effective at Caporetto – above all, the sophisticated use of the artillery in close support of small squads of infantrymen trained to penetrate soft spots in the enemy positions and to maintain momentum in attack. This enabled them to take the offensive on the old Somme battlefield, then in Flanders, along the Aisne and in Champagne. Morale was initially high, and tactically the attacks scored significant successes. Operation 'Blücher' brought German troops to within 90 km of Paris, which came under artillery fire. But as many local commanders had feared, operationally and strategically the offensives achieved nothing; indeed Ludendorff had set no objectives in this respect. There was no breakthrough; the lead troops could not be reinforced; and the attacks created salients that were difficult to defend. As the *Friedensturm* (last push for peace) ran into the sands, morale plummeted. Losses stood at around 800,000, most of them among elite forces; desertion from units being sent to the front ran at 20 per cent; and as new recruits were drafted in, grievances from the home front merged with those of the serving soldiers. The German army had shot its bolt.

The Allies now counter-attacked in a series of coordinated offensives, designed to keep the German forces off balance. On 8 August (Ludendorff dubbed it 'the black day of the German army'[11]), the British forces made major gains around Amiens. Nearly half of the German casualties surrendered – an unprecedentedly high proportion and a key indicator of collapsing morale – while retreating troops tried to stop reinforcements from joining the front. French and American troops captured the St Mihiel salient, and American forces subsequently joined French units in advancing through the Argonne forest. The Hindenburg Line was breached at the end of September; the Canadians crossed the canal du Nord; and Allied forces pushed into Flanders. Around 1 million German casualties were suffered between March and June. Away from the Western Front, there was also collapse. The Austrians were defeated in June on the Piave and again in October when half a million men surrendered, as the Italian front crumbled. Anglo–French and Serbian forces in Salonika successfully attacked over mountainous territory, and by November had reached the Danube and retaken Belgrade. These victories not only drove Bulgaria out of the war – terms were agreed on 29 September – but shattered the Central Powers' Southern Front. The Turkish war effort collapsed as the British pushed through Palestine and Mesopotamia, as well as towards Constantinople from the west. Turkey surrendered on 30 October. An armistice was concluded with Austria on 3 November and with Hungary on 13 November – two days after the most decisive one, made with Germany itself.

The achievement of victory

The military collapse of the Central Powers is often obscured by the myth of betrayal on the home front (the *Dolchstoss* or 'stab in the back'), and by the decision of the Entente not to press home its advantage and advance into Germany. Nevertheless, since the defeat was real enough, how can we account for it after nearly four years of stalemate? On the

Western Front, apart from two occasions (the assault at Verdun in 1916 and the spring offensives of 1918), the Germans had largely been content to stand on the defensive after their initial assault had been checked in 1914. They enjoyed the advantages that trench warfare conferred on the defender: one calculation suggests that they killed 35 per cent more men than they lost.[12]

The Entente Powers could not exercise this defensive option, for two reasons. First, their war aims involved expelling the Germans from the extensive territories in northern France and Belgium that were occupied in 1914. Second, their grand strategy was to use their greater resources of men and *matériel* to best advantage by keeping up pressure on every front. This meant they were committed to the offensive in the west. But if attacks were to achieve anything, the stalemate of trench warfare had to be broken. Tactically, the problem was to regain mobility by reintegrating firepower and movement. To achieve this, the Allies tried a number of initiatives based on the available technology. In 1915 and 1916, infantry advances were preceded by heavy artillery bombardments (ironically, the stability of the trench system allowed the build-up of large quantities of artillery and ammunition). These all failed. The artillery was insufficiently powerful to destroy the opposing defences completely; it proved impossible to coordinate infantry and artillery; and prolonged bombardments ruined the element of surprise. Attacks employing gas briefly seemed to offer some possibility of breakthrough. Sixty-three varieties were used by both sides, ranging from chlorine through hydrocyanic acid to mustard gas. But although gas had some initial local impact, it caused relatively few casualties (perhaps 6 per cent of all fatalities), and counter-measures rapidly proved effective. More promising were tanks, a weapon most enthusiastically adopted by the Allies. Designed to cross no-man's land, crush wire and bridge trenches, tanks were rapidly improved following their introduction in 1916, one indication of the spur to technological invention provided by the conflict. Over 3000 came into French service alone in 1918. The deployment of tanks certainly proved significant in some localized situations. However, their high rate of breakdown, restricted range and tendency to 'bellying', as well as their vulnerability to artillery fire and anti-tank rifles, meant that they did not generally prove to be the war-winning weapons that advocates had promised.

Ironically, given its shortcomings early in the conflict, artillery would be the single most important tool of the Entente victory.[13] By 1918, accuracy of fire had been dramatically improved as a result of sound-ranging techniques, flash-spotting and the use of aerial reconnaissance. Ninety per cent of the Canadian Corps' fire was directed from the air by 1917. Arguably, this was the most crucial contribution of airpower to the war, although air-to-ground attacks supported the German advances in 1918 – specialist squadrons had been formed to strafe enemy lines – and also helped the Allies to stem the German attacks. By 1918, artillery was not only more accurate, but more effective. Better fuses meant that the shells actually exploded (30 per cent of British shells had failed to detonate at the Somme), while high explosives proved capable of destroying wire and trenches in a way that shrapnel had not. Quantity was also important. A dramatic increase in production, especially of heavy guns, meant that by 1918 the artillery could deliver a greater weight of fire in a shorter space of time than previously; and simultaneous attacks were possible at several points on the front. Surprise need no longer be sacrificed to the artillery bombardment. By 1918 the infantry, too, was much more heavily armed.[14] Moreover, its evolving tactics now stressed stealth, dispersal and rapidity of movement. Finally, and perhaps most crucially, if the Allied offensives of 1918 were largely predicated on artillery capabilities, they were combined-arms battles in which guns, infantry, tanks and aircraft all had a role to play. Thus at Amiens there was one gun for every 25 metres of trench; over 400 tanks took part; almost all the German batteries had been located in advance thanks to the 1800 aircraft employed by the Allies; and the firepower of the infantry battalions had increased by a factor of six compared with the first two years of the war.

Even though both sides had groped towards a combined-arms type of warfare that was, by 1918, capable of penetrating deep (up to 12 km in places) and flexible defensive positions, neither had the capacity for sustainable breakthrough and breakout. This meant that Entente victory was not just down to battlefield tactics, but was achieved through attrition. Germany's fear of defeat in an extended coalition conflict had led to the initial decision to seek a 'short-war solution', yet it had allowed itself to be sucked into a war of attrition. Casualties of 434,000 at Verdun, 650,000 at the Somme and up to 1 million in March–June 1918, for example, represented unsustainable losses given the greatly superior numbers available to the Allies.[15] To be sure, the Entente had lost the resources of Russia in 1917, but this was eventually outweighed by American involvement. The Allied achievement of 1918 would thus not have been possible without the wearing down of German forces over a period of four and a quarter years. Moreover, with the possible exception of Africa, no front stood in isolation during World War One. The attrition of its resources meant that by 1918, Germany could no longer assist its weaker allies on the Middle Eastern–Ottoman, Italian and Central European fronts. Here, too, Allied superiority of men and resources accordingly proved decisive. The German fear, at the start of the conflict, of the likelihood of defeat in an attritional war was thus vindicated in 1918.

Explanation of the Entente victory must perforce include matters away from the battlefield. The war could not have been fought on such a scale, nor for such an extended period, without the mobilization of industry and civilian manpower. Moreover, by 1917–18, conditions on the home front were proving crucial to the ability of the combatants to continue the struggle. In Russia, most obviously, discontent with the way the war was being prosecuted and with the hardships that it brought in its wake led to the revolutions of March and November 1917, which took Russia out of the conflict by the end of that year. In Germany, industrial and agricultural production had slumped to new lows, civilian discontent had grown alarmingly, and there was political chaos. When sailors at Kiel mutinied and refused to engage in a suicide mission against the Royal Navy, events quickly spiralled out of control. There were strikes and other demonstrations across Germany in support of the sailors and of an immediate end to the war, followed by the proclamation of a republic, which agreed an armistice on 11 November. In Austria-Hungary, too, the strains of war had become unbearable by 1917–18, as strikes, demonstrations and industrial unrest added to the multinational fissures in the Empire. The Habsburg monarchy disintegrated in a welter of civil disorder and ethnic strife, although the ruler, Karl, refused to abdicate, agreeing only to 'withdraw from government'. It mattered little what he said: Hungary instituted a republican government, while Czechoslovakia and Yugoslavia declared their independence. In all these examples, grievances of civilians and soldiers had blended together. It is therefore important at this juncture to consider the war on the home front. What was war's impact on civilians? How effectively were states able to mobilize for war? And why did the war-induced tensions common to all states prove unmanageable in some?

The home front

An uncertain distinction

It is important to note at the outset that it remains possible to distinguish between the home front and the fighting one during World War One. Even so, the distinction was generally more blurred than it had been in earlier conflicts – something that Ludendorff acknowledged when referring to a 'total war', which drew on all the resources of the nation.[16] One indication of this blurring was the large number of civilians who were directly caught up in the fighting. Among the first civilians to come into contact with an advancing army were the populations of Belgium and northern France in 1914. German forces, often poorly controlled by their officers and afraid of *franc-tireurs*, interpreted Belgian and French hostility to their advance as military resistance, and this became the justification for a series of atrocities, with almost 4500 Belgian and over 700 French civilians being killed in so-called 'reprisals'. Sooner than be overrun, some civilians chose flight. Up to 1 million inhabitants of Brussels fled after its occupation on 20 August 1914. Yet such numbers were dwarfed by the scale of population movement in the east, which resulted in a refugee problem of unprecedented proportions. The ebb and flow of the fighting on the Eastern Front had created some 3.3 million refugees in Russia by the end of 1915; by 1920 there were around 10 million refugees in eastern Europe. Here the Germans hoped to use the territories they overran to provide wheat, livestock, textiles and manpower. The result of this 'brutal, arbitrary and violent rule', as Vejas Liulevicius has termed it, was disastrous for the populations of Lithuania, Latvia and Kurland, as their resources were plundered and they were organized into labour battalions, leaving their lands untilled, the inevitable result being famine in 1916–17.[17]

Civilians fled not just from occupying forces, but to avoid long-range artillery bombardments of cities. This had occurred during the Franco–Prussian War (1870–71), but not on anything like the scale that was now witnessed. Belgrade became the first major city to experience bombardment. The population of Rheims fell from 100,000 to a mere 20,000 in 1915 as a result of the exodus, and around 800 inhabitants were killed during 1000 days of shelling. Half a million people fled Paris when it was bombarded in March 1918. Naval action and aeroplanes also brought civilians into the frontline of the fighting for the first time. One hundred and thirty-three deaths were caused when the German High Seas Fleet shelled West Hartlepool, Scarborough and Whitby in December 1914. Although outlawed by the Hague Conventions, aerial bombardment of civilians was used by all sides during the conflict. The Channel ports, Paris and Great Yarmouth were attacked in the first two years of war. Altogether, German airships caused almost 5000 casualties in England; around 350 British reprisal attacks, using 2319 planes, killed 700 German civilians and injured a further 1800. A leading prewar theorist of air power was the Italian Giulio Douhet, and it is scarcely surprising that Italy was at the forefront of its use, attacking ports in the Adriatic; the Austrians responded with attacks on Venice, Padua, Milan and elsewhere. The overall failure of anti-aircraft measures – for instance, the Germans lost more aircraft to accident (37) than to air defence (24) in operations over England – apparently reinforced the judgement of advocates of air power that the bomber would always get through, and would have important consequences for the conduct of World War Two.

Where there were ethnic tensions, civilians were at even more risk from the invading forces. Austro-Hungarian troops moving into Serbia in 1914 were reminded that 'all humanity and all kindness of heart are out of place' with regard to the local population.[18] Civilian hostages were taken and homes destroyed: one estimate suggests that as many as 4000 people were killed or disappeared during the opening invasion. These actions, like those by German troops in Belgium, were justified as reprisals against guerrillas. In 1915, retreating Russian forces took the opportunity to purge 'undesirable' elements, including Jews. Most notorious were the mass killings, conducted with the connivance of the Turkish authorities, which were inflicted on the Ottoman empire's own Armenian subjects, whose loyalty was suspect. An order in May 1915 for their deportation from war zones led to what is now reliably estimated to have been at least a million deaths, including those related to hunger and disease.

Adjusting to the demands of war

Despite the large numbers of civilians caught up in the fighting, certainly greater than in any previous European conflict, most of those on the home front had no direct experience of the war. For them, its realities were conveyed through newspapers, letters from soldiers, and government propaganda. They also experienced its effects through loss of civil liberties, conscription, rationing, the mobilization of the labour force, and higher taxes.

The outbreak of war was marked in most states by a flurry of emergency legislation suspending the normal operation of government and some civil liberties. In Germany, legislation could be passed without parliamentary consent; in Hungary, Parliament continued to sit but new elections were postponed; and in Britain, elections to Parliament were suspended and it ceased to scrutinize the military estimates. Although slack drafting complicated the operation of the Defence of the Realm Act, passed in August 1914, it none the less conferred sweeping powers on the British government; while in Italy, civil rights were dramatically curtailed in a panicky response to the defeat at Caporetto. In Austria-Hungary, the War Service Law, passed in 1913 at the time of the First Balkan War, effectively allowed the military to supersede civilian government. The army took full advantage of this, eventually extending its control throughout the empire. In this multinational polity, ethnic minorities quickly came under suspicion and over 2000 Bosnians were deported or interned within months of the war's outbreak. Far beyond Europe, Australia legislated for the deportation of groups believed to be subversive, while the Espionage and Sedition Acts of 1917 and 1918 in the USA were, in some respects, even more draconian. Even in liberal states there was, perhaps surprisingly, little initial protest at the erosion of long-cherished liberties, so enthusiastic was the support for the war. But subsequent and more insidious measures, such as the growth of agencies for monitoring suspect groups and individuals, did occasion hostility. A secret police was already well established in Russia pre-1914; less well known are the Special Branch and Military Intelligence services of France and Britain, which investigated subversive intellectuals and trade unionists (as well as Irish Nationalists in the second case). And even less welcome was the state's intrusion into private life: wives of British serving soldiers had to show they were faithful and rearing their children properly in order to qualify for the Separation Allowance.

The enthusiasm for war that permitted the passage, or revival, of emergency legislation also produced a rush of volunteers at the start of the conflict. Recruiting offices in Austria-Hungary could not cope with the numbers presenting themselves, and many had to be turned away. To be sure, the eagerness for war was less than is often portrayed. The press everywhere was jingoistic, but the big demonstrations in favour were urban phenomena, and largely restricted to the major cities: Berlin's hysterical pro-war rallies were not replicated in Bremen, for example. Among Europe's rural inhabitants there was little bellicose fervour, rather a mood of resignation; and in Russia, with its overwhelmingly peasant armies, there were rural protests in almost 50 of the provinces as mobilization was announced. Nevertheless, most people seem to have accepted the necessity of a war for self-defence, the line peddled by governments and the media. Accordingly, conscription rates were high. Only 1.5 per cent of reservists became draft dodgers in France; the High Command had anticipated 10 per cent. Even in Russia, 96 per cent of reservists reported for duty. The inability of trade unions, socialist parties and the Second International to persuade workers to oppose the war may have been one reason for the high turnout. Another was the support offered by local churches. They justified the conflict on grounds similar to those proffered by governments, but additionally made reference to divine sanction for 'their' side, while some even turned the war into a crusade. Despite the professed neutrality of Pope Benedict XV, French and German Catholics alike rallied to their respective national causes, in each case seeing the war as an opportunity to end their political isolation. In France, young clerics were called up, and around 4500 would lose their lives. Pacifists and religious opponents of the war were thus thin on the ground.

The percentage of draft-dodgers remained small, and the number of volunteers stayed relatively buoyant down to 1916.[19] The decision of Britain, which alone of the great powers had no system of compulsory enlistment in 1914, to move to conscription two years later was not so much a result of shortage of volunteers, as a move towards a system that the public perceived as fairer and that enabled the government to improve distribution of manpower as between industry and the forces. Yet, by then, casualty rates were weakening the enthusiasm for military service, most especially in Russia. Here, losses of almost 6 million (including prisoners of war) since the start of the war obliged the government in 1916 to call up 'second-category recruits' – that is, sole breadwinners. The result was to deepen hostility to the conflict at home, and to bring into the forces thousands of discontented conscripts. As would also be the case in Germany, the grievances of the home front and of the army fused together, and this would help to produce the disintegration in the fighting and home fronts witnessed in 1917–18.

States varied widely with regard to the proportion of potential recruits who were actually mobilized. For example, Russia did best in absolute terms, raising 15 million men, although this represented only 39 per cent of eligible males. By contrast, France drafted 79 per cent of its male population totalling 8.4 million, including 475,000 from its colonies. Britain recruited nearly 50 per cent of its 15–49-year-olds, around 4.9 million for the army, and half a million for the navy and air force. Germany conscripted around 13.2 million men, representing around 85 per cent of those of military age. In every state, however, there were serious economic consequences stemming from the large numbers of men under arms, from the initial concern to call up as many recruits as possible for the expected short war, and from governments' subsequent unwillingness or inability to make hard choices about manpower allocations.

It is normally assumed that industry suffered most from labour shortages. Yet agricultural productivity was affected at least as much, if not more, partly because the damaging effects of diminished manpower were compounded by the requisitioning of horses for the armies and the diversion to industry of chemicals hitherto used for fertilizers. The result was a sharp decline in food supplies and spiralling inflation, which sapped civilian morale. France had always produced an agricultural surplus in peacetime; by 1917 it faced a food crisis. Italy, too, was a net exporter prewar, but now suffered severe food shortages. Russia was probably the world's largest exporter of agricultural products pre-1914, but mismanagement and the appalling transport system would reduce whole sections of the population to starvation by 1917. In Austria, agricultural production had fallen by 1918 to around 40 per cent of prewar levels. In Germany, production of cereal crops and potatoes declined by around one-third. To be sure, governments intervened in agriculture, just as they would do in industry, to enhance productivity. In Britain, it became illegal after 1916 to leave land fallow; and in France local boards were established to bring uncultivated land into use. In Germany, food agencies proliferated. The Wartime Cereal Company and the Imperial Potato Office were given a commercial monopoly over these two staples in 1914–15; the War Food Office was set up the following year. However, here and in the other belligerent states, such initiatives were piecemeal at best, and proved largely ineffectual. Moreover, food shortages in Germany and Austria-Hungary were made worse by the Allies' economic blockade. Although only 10 per cent of Germany's food supply had been imported prewar, one-third of its agricultural fertilizers had been brought in from abroad. Its difficulties deepened as resources were channelled to industry in almost madcap fashion after the announcement of the *Hilfsdienstgesetz* (the so-called Hindenburg programme) in 1916, starving agriculture of men and horses, as well as of chemical fertilizer. By contrast, the submarine blockade proved less damaging to Britain, which was still able to import food, chiefly from the USA, Australia, New Zealand and Argentina, although at the cost of an escalating foreign debt. Ironically, Britain, which could sustain itself from domestic production for only 125 days per year prewar, suffered least from food shortages because of its access to overseas produce. France, too, benefited from the American connection. When the harvest failed in 1917, disaster was averted by diverting grain shipments previously intended for Britain.

One way to even out the effect of food shortages was through price controls and rationing. All states resorted to these mechanisms, at different times and in different ways. Germany took the lead, fixing the price of staples – potatoes, sugar and grain – in 1914. Farmers responded by switching production to non-controlled goods, and the staples became virtually unobtainable outside the black market. Food rationing therefore had to be introduced in 1915, an acknowledgement both of the need to bring some semblance of fairness into the system, and also of the Reich's declining agricultural productivity. Meagre from the outset, by 1918 the ration covered barely half of the required nutritional intake. In Austria, too, bread rationing was introduced in 1915, although again the system worked poorly. Bread prices were fixed in France soon after the outbreak of war but, as in Germany, farmers shifted production, in this instance to non-wheat cereals. A more developed system of rationing did not emerge until later. Sugar and bread were rationed in April 1917, and meat sales were reduced to two days per week, although in practice the bread ration card was employed only fitfully until the following year. Food rationing was introduced in Britain only in 1918, and even then on a restricted range of products. All governments, through their disregard of agricultural production and their ill-coordinated policies of rationing and price-fixing, failed to respond effectively to the demands of war; the neglect of civilian needs would have especially disastrous consequences for the Central Powers.

Yet if states did badly with regard to agricultural production and distribution, they showed a surprising ability to produce huge quantities of war materials. Modern warfare made prodigious demands on resources. Merely to take the example of munitions: more artillery shells were fired during the First Battle of the Marne than were expended by both sides during the Franco–Prussian war (1870–71). The longer World War One progressed, the greater its logistical demands. In a ten-day bombardment before the Somme, the British fired over 3 million shells, more than had been used in the whole Russo–Japanese war of 1904–05. All the belligerents recognized the need to outproduce the enemy and thus to give priority to managing industry; but as the war was initially expected to be short, no plans were readily to hand for this sector. Consequently, like agriculture, industry suffered initial disruption as a result of military mobilization. More than half of French companies were temporarily closed in August 1914, while British factories were short of 14,000 skilled workers by the summer of 1915.

One way of dealing with the labour shortage was to return soldiers to the factories. By June 1916, France had sent back 287,000 of them to civilian work, although they remained under martial law (an important consideration as this prevented them from striking). In Germany, the *Zurückstellung* (recall for work) returned around 1.2 million men from military service in September 1916, and a further 1.9 million the following July. Gradually, all the belligerents introduced more systematic schemes to decide categories of exempt and non-exempt workers. Another solution to industrial labour shortages was to employ prisoners of war or workers deported from occupied areas. Germany made greatest use of this expedient, using 900,000 prisoners of war and over 400,000 foreign workers, many of them plucked reluctantly from Belgium. However, their erratic deployment and their unwillingness meant that they made poor substitutes for workers lost to mobilization. A third, and more promising, alternative was the employment of unskilled workers, including women and children. The increasingly repetitive nature of the industrial process that had emerged prewar permitted such a dilution of the labour force. A Patriotic Auxiliary Service law was accordingly passed in Germany at the end of 1915, funnelling women and children into employment, and a Women's Labour Office was also established. Joffre's typically overblown comment, that if the women in France's factories stopped working for 20 minutes 'we would lose the war', none the less contained a grain of truth.[20]

Governments sought not only to enlarge the labour force, but also to control it. In Germany and Britain, laws prevented workers from changing jobs; German males were obliged to accept employment in war work; and there were prohibitions on the right to strike. It is far from clear that this legislation served much purpose. In Germany, for example, strikes actually proliferated after 1915 as skilled workers in particular used their improved bargaining position to push up wages. Governments in all the belligerent states showed little inclination to resist demands for higher wages from such key workers, much to the annoyance of the bosses. Intervention in the labour market also brought governments up against the trade unions. In Britain, opposition to the use of women in factories was overcome only when Lloyd George agreed that any replacements would be a wartime expedient and limited to the arms industry. Here and in France, trade unions demanded some restrictions on company profits, although the legislation proved hard to enforce; while in Germany the powerful trade unions accepted the employment of women, but retained extensive control of hiring and firing with the connivance of both government and the bosses.

The war also witnessed government intervention aimed at securing some greater general command over the manufacturing and industrial sectors. This resulted in the proliferation of new ministries and departments. In Britain, a Ministry of Munitions was created in May 1915, which would eventually employ 25,000 staff and oversee 20,000 establishments. Ministries of Labour, Shipping and Food were also set up, and after Lloyd George became Prime Minister in 1916, central government control of the industrial war effort increased. There was already a prewar trend in Britain towards greater government oversight of industry, which eased the process after 1914. Austria-Hungary was even more unusual in that prewar legislation allowed the state to take over strategic industries. By 1917–18, over 900 firms in Hungary, employing 50,000 workers, were under military supervision and the rule of martial law, up from 263 enterprises in 1915; while in Austria the main vehicles for state intervention were the General Commissariat for the War Economy and the War and Transitional Economy Commission, both offshoots of the Trade Ministry. Arguably, competition between rival ministries, as well as the habitual tensions between Hungary and Austria, stifled initiative and harmed industry. Germany lacked the prewar legislative framework found in the Habsburg Empire to enable state intervention, but the High Command was acutely aware from the outset of the lack of raw materials essential to modern warfare. A committee was consequently established in 1914 to plan the manufacture of artificial substitutes; the *Kriegsrohrstoffabteilung*, part of the War Ministry, was also set up to ascertain the availability of raw materials, both inside the Reich and in the occupied territories, and to oversee their procurement and allocation. Further government/military oversight of the economy was bedevilled by the proliferation of competing agencies, most notably by the rivalry between the Prussian War Ministry and the *Kriegsamt*, a creation of the army. To be fair, this lack of coordination was probably no worse in Germany than elsewhere, although the degree of military control was unusual. However, the Hindenburg programme dating from August 1916, which introduced tighter controls over industry, probably did real damage to the economy as it was concerned obsessively with munitions to the detriment of the rest of manufacturing.

It should be stressed that this *dirigisme* was at odds with the liberal economic theories of the time, and in no country was the drive to greater state oversight the result of ideology. Rather, it was accepted as a necessary short-term measure, which would be reversed once the war was concluded. Even in the USA, where distrust of the federal government and the attachment to *laissez-faire* principles was strong, the need for greater central involvement was acknowledged, and there was a concomitant growth in the number of government agencies. Moreover, the trend was not towards state capitalism, but towards a partnership between government and business which left the capitalist system untouched, and which operated largely through a system of incentives rather than through direct state control. In practice, prominent businessmen were frequently brought in to staff the government agencies. In the USA, for instance, the leading banker, Bernard Baruch, headed the War Industries Board, which co-coordinated government purchases. Such men were often seen as providing the kind of drive needed to energize government departments. In Britain, where the pragmatic Lloyd George was anyway sceptical of the quality of the bureaucracy and always preferred to work with cronies, the ship-owner Joseph Maclay became Minister of Shipping, the coal-owner Lord Rhondda became Minister of Food, and a railway executive, Eric Geddes, served in the Ministry of Munitions and elsewhere before becoming First Lord of the Admiralty.

There is little doubt that businessmen who infiltrated the state apparatus were unscrupulous in maintaining high prices for war-related material, and were far from impartial in awarding contracts. In Germany, Walther Rathenau and Richard von Moellendorf, both executives in the electronics giant AEG, ran the raw materials agency which operated 25 cartels for each commodity. These secured materials below cost price and then overcharged for their products. In France, after initial meetings between the Minister for War and a number of industrialists in September 1914, monthly sessions were arranged to share out government orders. Thus, for those businesses already engaged in war work, or for those that could switch production, these years were a boom time. Well established firms, such as Krupps and Schneider, flourished; the French Michelaud company switched its manufacturing from porcelain to spark plugs; and Renault, founded as recently as 1898 for car-making, thrived on the production of aircraft engines and tanks.

The reallocation of manpower, better labour management and the development of improved production methods eventually brought about extraordinary rises in the output of war-related materials. In Britain, manufacture of heavy guns went from 91 in 1914, to 3390 in 1915, to 8039 in 1918; while the production of machine guns jumped from 300 to almost 121,000. Aircraft production soared from 200 to 32,000 in the same period. In France, machine-gun production went up 170-fold, rifles 290-fold. The French experience was especially impressive, given the initial loss of industrially significant territory, but by no means exceptional. In Austria-Hungary, production went up dramatically until the end of 1916, despite regional disputes and ministerial friction. Even in Russia, normally thought of as economically backward, after a slow start shell manufacture went to 1 million rounds per month by September 1915, and had topped 4 million a year later. Russia's munitions output compared favourably with the Germans' 7 million shells and the Austrians' 1 million, while its aircraft production topped that of France. Russia's difficulties lay not so much in the manufacture as in the transport and distribution of goods, which meant that its troops often remained short of equipment that had been produced in abundance. In all belligerent states, increased output was initially due, at least in part, to a decrease in quality: hence the large number of shells that failed to explode and the number of weapons that blew up (600 French artillery pieces in 1915 alone). Nevertheless, the staggering output of guns and munitions not only extended the length of the conflict, but also permitted the dramatic improvements in fire-power which contributed to the Allied tactical victory in 1918.

Financing the war

Those in authority, both civilian and military, were to be surprised by the levels of production of war materials. The ability to finance the conflict caused them even greater astonishment. The Hungarian Finance Minister judged in 1914 that he could pay for the war for three weeks at most. Similar assessments characterized the cabinets of all the belligerent powers. In practice, however, just as states were able to adjust their economies to match the demands of industrial warfare, so too did they discover their capacity to raise money on a scale hitherto undreamt. This is not to suggest that the process was simple. The costs of war were staggering: $43.8 billion for Britain; $13.4 billion for Austria-Hungary; $14.7 billion for Italy; $28.2 billion for France; $47 billion for Germany; $36.2 billion for the USA. Where did the money come from? In Britain, where direct taxes already comprised a major element of government income, they were increased still further. The level of income tax went up more than fivefold, and around 2.4 million workers who were previously exempt were caught in the tax net by 1918–19. The modern tax state had arrived with a vengeance. However, Britain was unique in the degree of its reliance on direct taxation. In France, an income tax was introduced in 1914, but not collected until two years later, and the state continued to draw on indirect levies for the bulk of its tax revenues. This pattern was even more pronounced in Germany and, above all, in Russia, where the significance of direct tax was negligible. The Tsar was resolute in his long-standing refusal to countenance any levy on income.

However, taxes, both direct and indirect, raised only a proportion of the funds needed for the war effort (in Britain around 23–26 per cent, in Italy 23 per cent, in France 24 per cent and in Germany 16–18 per cent). The rest was found through a variety of means. All the belligerents resorted to borrowing, raising loans both at home and abroad. Domestically, the favoured method was the issue of war bonds (although these were also marketed overseas), which at the start of the conflict were eagerly subscribed, a reflection not just of patriotism, but also of the solid interest rates on offer. However, as shortages hit home and wages declined in real terms, the bonds became less attractive. Although they continued to attract investors in Britain, in Germany the ninth bond was substantially undersubscribed – a contrast indicating the different economic impact the war was having on these two civilian populations. 'Outside' loans accounted for the bulk of state borrowing. Austria-Hungary obtained $2.96 billion from Germany, while France borrowed $3.6 billion from Anglo–American sources. The Entente's ability to raise overseas loans from Australia, Argentina and, above all, from the USA proved to be a major advantage. In theory, the USA's credit resources were equally available to the Central Powers until 1917, but in practice US banks made few loans to Germany from 1915. The Entente Powers had not only a bigger overseas credit pool to draw on, but also the advantage of Britain's still extensive financial and industrial strength. This allowed it both to raise loans in its own right and to guarantee those raised by its allies. Thus almost 90 per cent of the inter-Allied war credits of $4.3 billion in April 1917 were underwritten by Britain. But Britain's financial resources were far from inexhaustible, and like the rest of the Allies it became increasingly reliant on US funding. The advantages to the USA were enormous. American credit was used to purchase American-manufactured products, a virtuous circle that brought benefits to the nation's whole financial and business community. Arguably, the USA was so economically tied into the Entente war effort by 1916–17 as to be in effect a co-belligerent who could not afford to see the Allies beaten. Germany reckoned, therefore, that there was little to lose through the use of economic blockade in 1917 – a fatal error, as things turned out.

For governments, an easier option than borrowing was simply to print the money needed to finance the war effort. This expedient was employed, notably in France and Germany but above all in Russia, even though it clearly made inflation inevitable. Shortages, hoarding and a reluctance to use cash also fed into the inflationary spiral, with the result that the cost of living rose dramatically. National comparisons must be regarded with caution as the figures tend to be unreliable, but Beckett suggests that in Britain the cost of foodstuffs went up by 61 per cent; in France by 74 per cent; in Italy by 84 per cent; in Germany by 300 per cent; and in Belgium and Austria-Hungary by over 1000 per cent.[21] In Russia, prices had quadrupled by the start of 1917, before becoming 'stratospheric' thereafter; and in Turkey there had been a 26-fold increase by the time of the Armistice.[22] The contours of these statistics, crude though they are, align with the map of civil and political discontent at the end of the war.

A universal and a unique experience

In some respects, the lived experience of civilians outlined above was universal – inflation, higher taxes, food shortages, rationing, labour controls and mobilization affected nearly everyone. Yet it was also profoundly mediated by a range of variables including wealth, social class, gender, employability and region. Thus wage earners and those on fixed incomes suffered most from the war-induced rise in the cost of living, while indirect taxes, generally reckoned to be regressive in their impact, hit the poorest hardest. The well-to-do were not only better placed to withstand the ravages of higher taxes, they also could more readily alleviate the effects of rising prices and, by resort to the black market, the effects of food shortages and rationing. Such difficulties must also be understood in terms of social status. In Germany, one response to shortages was the establishment of communal feeding stations. These ensured a more equal distribution of food, but to appear at them proved demeaning for many 'blue-collar' workers, whose social status was already under threat from a combination of fixed incomes and rising prices.

Gender was a further important determinant of war's impact. Women were generally expected to wait in the bread queues. One observer noted that production at the National Projectile Factory in Hackney fell, 'due to the fact that women had to stand in food queues during the day.'[23] In Russia's provincial cities, women took the lead in mass anti-conscription protests and soldiers' wives led the riots against non-payment of the separation allowances in 1915–16. Women headed the food protests in Milan and Turin that turned into anti-war rallies in 1917, thus continuing a leadership role in social protest that went back at least to the eighteenth century. The entry of women into the labour market altered their traditional roles and status, albeit not as profoundly as is generally believed. The proportion of women in the workforce certainly increased. There were two-and-a-half times more female employees in American factories in 1918 than in the previous year. In Germany, an additional 5.2 million women entered the labour market, and they accounted for 55 per cent of the workforce in 1918 compared with 35 per cent in 1914. In Britain, around 1.5 million women took up paid employment during the war, between 1.5 and 2 million in France. In these two states, females accounted for almost 37 per cent of the workforce in 1918 compared with 26–30 per cent in 1914. These increases were significant, but not as large as is often imagined. Moreover, the war was more important in marking a shift within that section of women who were already employed, from rural and domestic jobs into industry (predominantly munitions work), than in bringing women into the workplace *de novo*. Thus only a quarter of the wartime female workers in Bavarian factories had not previously been employed. Although their wages were higher than women had previously enjoyed (but not on a par with those of the men they replaced), they faced additional risks from the toxic chemicals and the danger of explosion; for instance, significant numbers were killed or injured filling shells at the plants at Avonmouth, Chittening, Amequin and Armentières. Additionally, long hours and Sunday working, which was 'optional in theory but compulsory in practice', had a detrimental impact on family life.[24] Finally, any wartime gains proved transient as women workers were ousted by men at the end of the conflict, a move they did little to contest. The postwar female component of the industrial labour force was actually lower in Britain and Germany than prewar.

Leaving aside the chequered experience of women, we should not forget that some elements in society did relatively well out of the war. This most obviously applies to the owners of war-related businesses. Yet, equally, those employed in essential industries, especially if they had key skills, were able to use their enhanced bargaining position to secure higher wages. In Germany, for instance, pay in war industries went up by almost 150 per cent, although this was not matched in civil industry, where the increase was of the order of 65 per cent. Accordingly, average real wages declined overall: by 15 per cent in Britain, by 23 per cent in Germany, by 33 per cent in Italy and by almost 60 per cent in Russia. Skilled workers had little compunction in deploying their industrial muscle in the struggle for higher wages, and strikes proliferated in Germany after 1915 as they fought for, and obtained, higher wages. By contrast, striking German miners in May 1916, and the 18,000 French women involved in the textile industry who downed tools the following year to support demands for wage increases to match inflation, did not have the same bargaining power. In this respect, the war proved profoundly divisive of the working class. Black marketeers are generally assumed to have displayed even less patriotic fervour than striking workers. However, it is not always easy to see the moral boundary between the former and others seeking to exploit the new circumstances: where, for instance, does one put the Normandy horse dealers who responded to the army's insatiable demands by passing off colts as full-grown animals? Others for whom the war provided an unlooked-for bonus included relatives of those French farmworkers now transferred into the armed forces. Similarly, in Britain the payment of Separation Allowances, which cost the government about as much as the soldiers' wages, scarcely made the recipients rich, but did at least lift many working-class families out of their prewar poverty.

There was also a marked regional texture to the war's impact. Most obviously, the experience of civilians whose homes lay in the path of an invading army or close to the frontline was very different to that of those living well back from the fighting front. The former might have their houses and barns destroyed or requisitioned and their daughters propositioned by licentious soldiers; but equally, they might profit from their proximity to the front by opening an *estaminet*, a sort of bar-*cum*-brothel, for off-duty servicemen. There was also an urban–rural dichotomy in the experience of the war. Dramatic fluctuations in the populations of Paris, London and Berlin, caused by successive waves of emigration and immigration, severely disrupted food-supply systems. And townspeople generally suffered more than rural inhabitants from food shortages because they were wholly dependent on market supplies. Significantly, retail prices in Berlin rose well above the national average, and by 1917 the Russian cities were in desperate straits as rural producers refused to put their goods onto the open market. Above all, there was a national dimension to war's impact. Broadly speaking, Britain and France were most successful in maintaining tolerable material conditions for their populations. Russia and Austria-Hungary stood at the other end of the spectrum, with Italy somewhere in between. The situation in Germany declined sharply after 1916, with working-class conditions in particular deteriorating much more sharply here than in the two main Entente powers.[25] There was no simple relationship between material deprivation and the social unrest which, as we noted earlier, helped to bring about the end of the war. As Bonzon and Davis put it, there was no 'material threshold for protest'.[26] Domestic support for the conflict depended not only on the perception that the sacrifices which everyone expected to make were equally shared, but also on the maintenance of an accord among the political and intellectual elite regarding the legitimacy and necessity of the war. It is hard to resist the conclusion that, whatever the difficulties in Italy and Russia, the two key Entente powers of France and Britain proved more capable of supporting and managing their civilian populations than did the Central Powers.

The conflict also had an impact on the home front in ways that historians are only just beginning to grapple with. For example, there are indications of increased sexual permissiveness. There was a rise in illegitimate births, from 8.4 per cent (1913) to 14.2 per cent (1917) in the case of France; and reported levels of venereal disease increased, although the latter may have resulted in part from closer medical surveillance and better methods of detection. Such statistics reflected not merely the greater opportunities for recreational sex generated by wartime conditions and a 'live-for-the-day' attitude; they also owed something to the increased number of women involved in prostitution, not as a full-time occupation, but in intervals of need. Crime rates also rose, especially petty theft by children, reflecting both the need to make ends meet at a time of shortages and a decrease in parental control. At the outset of the conflict, the realities of the fighting front remained obscure to most civilians. Censorship operated in all states, and front-line soldiers writing home were chiefly concerned to reassure their families. Moreover, the repatriated wounded were generally confined to hospitals away from the main centres of population. Families accordingly tried to connect with the fighting front in a variety of ways. One was by dressing in military style – braided jackets were all the rage for a time in Paris – and there was a healthy trade in knick-knacks such as supposedly bullet-proof cigarette cases, as well as ashtrays and lighters made from spent shells and cartridges. Most military deaths occurred far distant from relatives and friends, thus bringing to a close traditional forms of grieving that had centred on the body of the deceased, and leading to a bifurcation of mourning. It was now both intensely private, yet also coupled with state observances that placed loss on the national stage. All states debated (with variable outcomes) what forms of war grave might be most appropriate for their own fallen, as well as the question whether corpses that had been recovered after death on foreign soil should be repatriated.

The aftermath of the war

If World War One was unprecedented in its scale and immediate impact, its broader consequences were no less significant. The physical costs of the conflict were enormous. Most damage had been sustained by those territories that had witnessed the fighting. In Belgium, 250,000 acres of agricultural land had been rendered unusable, and three major towns had been completely devastated. In the military zone of northern France, almost 300,000 houses had been destroyed. In Poland, over 90 per cent of the territory had been fought over, 10 per cent of properties wrecked and 11 million acres of agricultural land put out of service. Not surprisingly, all belligerents had in mind claims for financial reparation. Away from the combat zone, four years of neglect had reduced much of the housing stock – which was anyway in poor condition – to dire straits. Booming wartime industries had drawn in immigrants who occupied overcrowded and often unsanitary districts, and would fall easy victims to the ravages of Spanish influenza in 1918–19.

The human costs of the conflict, the inevitable result of the pursuit of decisive military victory in an industrialized war, were even more staggering. The fighting forces of the Entente suffered 17.3 million casualties, the Central Powers 15.5 million, of whom just over 5.4 million and 4.0 million, respectively, were deaths, overwhelmingly among males aged 19–35. It is easy to forget that the losses were not sustained in Europe alone. Around 10 per cent of the 2 million Africans who had served as soldiers and labourers died from one cause or another. Quite apart from the fighting forces, the conflict had cost the lives of at least 6.6 million civilians. The social consequences of all these losses were traumatic. France and Germany had sacrificed around 10 per cent of their 'active' male population, costing the former perhaps 2 million and the latter perhaps 3 million in potential births denied. Both countries were left with ageing populations. The war created some 6.5 million invalids in Europe, around 8 million orphans, and well over 4 million widows. Social pressure often prevented a widow from remarrying, even when she wished to find a new husband; similarly, social tradition meant that many young women whose fathers had been killed stayed at home with the mother. In France, they were referred to as the 'spinsters of 1914'.

The social dislocation caused by the war went beyond what is suggested by a mere cataloguing of the numbers. Contrary to what is sometimes claimed, the shared experience of the trenches had not broken down class barriers. How could it, given the class-based system of military ranks, and the deeply traditional outlook of the army as an institution? Indeed, class animosity was sharpened by the experience of war. Unsurprisingly, there had been complaints about the cosy relationship between big business and government, and anger at the huge profits being made by captains of industry. When other war-induced changes were fed into the equation – including the employment of women and other unskilled workers, the use of non-unionized labour, plus the re-ordering of traditional pay and hierarchical differences – the upshot was increased tensions in the workplace. These developed between bosses and workers, between skilled and non-skilled, between organized and non-unionized labour, and between those able to demand higher wages and those who could not. World War One was emphatically not a time when everyone in the workplace pulled together. To be sure, everyone had expected to make sacrifices, but there was a perception that these had been shared unequally. In particular, the middle classes saw themselves caught between labour and the bosses, both of whom had received privileged treatment. They believed that they had suffered some greater share of losses as they provided the officer class, and had paid for the war through taxation. And they were irked and threatened by the apparent decline of deference from their social inferiors. Consequently, they were in no mood to fund the social reforms which the workers demanded as their reward for sacrifices in the trenches and endurance at home. The burgeoning of organizations such as the Liberal Party in Germany and the Middle Class Union and Anti-Waste League (as well as strike-breaking during the General Strike) in the British case, were examples of what may be termed a postwar middle-class reaction. The modest progress made towards integrating the Left into politics during the conflict made it easier to envisage radical, if not socialist, governments after 1918. Nevertheless, the war's legacy of class conflict would make interwar politics turbulent.

The politicians who assembled at Paris in January 1919 to decide the postwar settlement were acutely aware of the wider significance of these domestic difficulties. All the prewar regimes in the belligerent states – and they ranged from autocratic through authoritarian to pluralistic and liberal – had been severely tested by the conflict. While the Ottoman regime was now approaching its extinction, the three empires of Germany, Austria-Hungary and Russia, which had dominated central and Eastern Europe before 1918, had already collapsed. An array of smaller, weaker and often contending states came into being. These included Poland (back on the map for the first time since 1795), Lithuania, Latvia, Estonia, Finland, Czechoslovakia and Yugoslavia (initially as the Kingdom of the Serbs, Croats and Slovenes), together with a truncated Austria, a fully independent Hungary and an enlarged Romania. The development of these new polities was, to some extent, legitimated by the principle of national self-determination, particularly as enunciated by Woodrow Wilson in January 1918. In practice, however, some of these successor states were just as multi-national and as racially intolerant as the empires they replaced, making them potentially unstable. Moreover, the viability of these polities depended on the continuance of the new power vacuum created by the collapse of German and Russian influence. Whether they had the capability to maintain their independence in the face of a resurgent Germany and Russia remained an open question.

Five separate treaties, between the victorious Allies and the defeated powers, were produced by the Paris Peace Conference: those of Versailles (with Germany, June 1919), St Germain (with Austria, September 1919), Neuilly (with Bulgaria, November 1919), Trianon (with Hungary, June 1920) and Sèvres (with Turkey, August 1920 but eventually superseded by the Lausanne Treaty of July 1923). The pivotal German settlement was flawed, even if not for the reasons usually advanced. True, the Treaty of Versailles was a *Diktat*, and it imposed reparations that were justified by a war-guilt clause. It disarmed Germany, demilitarized the Rhineland, and stripped it of some European territory as well as all colonial holdings. These terms added insult to injury for many Germans, especially given that the country had not unconditionally surrendered, as distinct from suing for peace. Yet after four years of gruelling conflict, it is scarcely surprising that the victors lacked magnanimity, particularly after the predatory terms of the Brest–Litovsk settlement that the Germans had sought to impose on Russia were revealed in March 1918. In practice, the new Weimar Republic was able to evade most of the reparations payments. Moreover, the losses of European territory, population and resources inflicted on Germany were relatively modest.[27] Thus, as Colin Gray notes, the treaty 'offered maximum offence while inflicting minimal long-term damage'.[28]

It was only natural that Germany would seek redress. This would not have mattered had the victors enforced the terms of the peace, but they were unwilling or unable to do so. The USA withdrew into isolationism, declining to ratify the Versailles Treaty. It also failed to join the League of Nations, newly established to maintain the peace through a system of collective security, and thus fatally weakened the organization. Meanwhile, Britain's attention was fixed overseas. More importantly, its financial power had been undermined by the war. As Germany increasingly evaded reparations, Britain (like France) found repayment to the Americans of its own war borrowings all the more crippling. As its financial power drained away accordingly, Britain was replaced by the USA as the world's banker. As for Russia, Lenin's Bolshevik state was a pariah. To make matters worse, two of the victorious powers – Italy and Japan – felt cheated by their limited gains from the Paris settlement and wanted revisions. In practice, France was left as the policeman of the new European political order. This was unsatisfactory because it had not won the war strategically. Before 1914, France had been able to confront Germany with a powerful Russian ally and the threat of a conflict on two fronts. During the war, it had a firm ally in the shape of Britain and (even as Russia's war effort was collapsing) finally won US support as well. It had taken their combined might to defeat Germany. But things were very different after 1918. Although France did construct treaties with states in eastern Europe, it was the latter that anticipated deriving much the greater benefit from them. Thus, in practice, the French found themselves standing virtually alone.

Given that the peace settlement 'rested not so much on French strength as on German weakness',[29] it might be assumed that a new round of conflict was inescapable. As Marshal Foch put it, 'This is not a peace, but an armistice for twenty years.'[30] Yet such a judgement would be erroneous. It ignores, for example, the effects of the Great Depression and the significance of Hitler himself in bringing about World War Two. The Paris peace settlement may have made further conflict more likely; it did not make it inevitable.

World War One and the peace settlement had a similarly ambiguous effect on Europe's relationships with the wider world (see Chapter 11). Europeans controlled 84 per cent of the globe in 1914, with Britain as the leading player. In 1919 Germany's colonies were shared among the victors, and in this respect their existing colonial dominance was entrenched. Moreover, during the campaigns in Africa, Europeans had mapped previously unexplored areas, spread their cash economy and eroded traditional tribal and familial patterns. In the short term, then, imperialism was promoted by the war. In the longer term, however, the conflict did much to undermine it. The Gallipoli experience proved formative in the development of Australian and New Zealand national identity. But it was also crucial for the formation of a new post-Ottoman brand of national identity among the Turks. Atatürk, the hero of resistance at the Dardanelles, would be the founder of the modern Turkish state. Another consequence of rupture within the Ottoman Empire was the emergence of Zionist and Arab nationalist movements. Even further afield, the war had demonstrated the vulnerability of the Europeans and helped to erode the self-serving myth of their invincibility. The very significant colonial contribution to the war effort raised expectations of reward, as did President Wilson's doctrines of self-determination, which were so warmly welcomed by many emerging nationalist leaders. However, it would take World War Two, and its political and economic consequences, for the European powers to realize that colonialism was unsustainable and to begin in earnest their imperial withdrawal.

Today, hardly anyone survives who can directly recall the events of 1914–18. Even so, some wider memory of World War One has remained strong. This has certainly not been fixed with respect to either place or person, and it has altered – and continues to alter – with the passage of time. Indeed, it is only in very recent decades that historians have begun to deconstruct some of the myths about 1914–18. Memories of World War One, however variable their form or their accuracy, have certainly exercised a pervasive influence on succeeding generations. And this is not the least of the reasons for keeping in mind

Gary Sheffield's bold assertion that World War One was indeed 'the key event of the twentieth century, from which all else flowed.'[31]

Further reading

The literature on World War One is large and unwieldy. A good short introduction is to be found in K. Robbins, *The First World War* (Oxford: Oxford University Press, 1984). H. Strachan, *The First World War: A New Illustrated History* (London: Free Press, 2006) presents an accessible digest of his magisterial *The First World War* (Oxford: Oxford University Press, 2001); and his edited *The Oxford Illustrated History of the First World War* (Oxford: Oxford University Press, 1998) brings together some splendid essays by leading historians. David Stevenson, *1914–1918. The History of the First World War* (London: Penguin, 2005) is outstanding. N. Ferguson, *The Pity of War* (London: Penguin, 1998) is also good, although self-consciously revisionist. I. F. W. Beckett, *The Great War, 1914–1918* (London: Longman Pearson, 2001) is a mine of factual information; while G. De Groot, *The First World War* (Basingstoke: Macmillan, 2001) offers a structured approach. Norman Stone, *The Eastern Front, 1914–1917* (London: Hodder and Stoughton, 1975) has stood the test of time. The military side of the conflict is well treated by Tim Travers, *How the War Was Won: Command and Technology in the British Army on the Western Front, 1917–1918* (London: Routledge, 1992); and R. Prior and T. Wilson, *The First World War* (London: Cassell, 1999). The experience of the home front and civilians can be approached through R. Chickering and S. Förster (eds), *Great War, Total War. Combat and Mobilisation on the Western Front, 1914–1918* (Cambridge: Cambridge University Press, 2000) and J. Horne (ed.), *State, Society and Mobilization in Europe during the First World War* (Cambridge: Cambridge University Press, 1997). On France, see J.-J. Becker, *The Great War and the French People* (Leamington Spa: Berg, 1986) and P. Fridenson (ed.), *The French Home Front, 1914–1918* (Oxford: Oxford University Press, 1992). On Germany, see R. Chickering, *Imperial Germany and the Great War* (Cambridge: Cambridge University Press, 1998) and G. Feldman, *Army, Industry and Labor in Germany, 1914–1918* (Princeton: Princeton University Press, 1996); while H. H. Herwig, *The First World War. Germany and Austria-Hungary, 1914–1918* (London, 1997) extends the coverage to the Habsburg lands. On Britain, see J. Bourne, *Britain and the Great War* (London: Hodder Arnold, 1989) and G. De Groot, *Blighty. British Society in the Great War* (London: Longman, 1996). The experience of cities is thoughtfully approached by J. Winter and J.-L. Robert (eds), *Capital Cities at War. London, Paris, Berlin, 1914–1919* (Cambridge: Cambridge University Press, 1997). On the material devastation, Hugh Clout, *After the Ruins. Restoring the Countryside of Northern France after the Great War* (Exeter: University of Exeter Press, 1996) is an outstanding local study. Gender issues are dealt with by S. Grayzel, *Women's Identities at War: Gender, Motherhood and Politics in Britain and France during the First World War* (Chapel Hill: University of North Carolina, 1999). The memory of the conflict is treated by J. Winter, notably in his *Remembering War. The Great War and Historical Memory in the Twentieth Century* (New Haven: Yale University Press, 2006); and by Gary Sheffield, *Forgotten Victory. The First World War: Myths and Realities* (London: Headline, 2001).

Notes

1 J. Keegan, *The First World War* (London: Pimlico, 1998), p. 3.
2 For example, casualties were high in the opening, mobile phase of the war: David Stevenson, *1914–1918: The History of the First World War* (London: Penguin, 2004), pp. 92–93. British casualties at the Third Battle of Ypres, which peaked at 81,800 in August 1917, soared to 122,272 in the more open fighting of the following year: Hugh Strachan, *The First World War: A New Illustrated History* (London: Free Press, 2006), p. 160.
3 Hugh Strachan, *ibid.*, p. 46.
4 Schlieffen, too, had argued that 'a strategy based on attrition is unworkable': cited by G. Hardach, *The First World War, 1914–1918* (London: Penguin, 1977), p. 55.
5 Hugh Strachan, *The First World War, op. cit.*, p. 140. G. De Groot, *The First World War* (Basingstoke: Macmillan, 2001), p. 61 puts the figure at 2 million.
6 Cited by H. H. Herwig, *The First World War. Germany and Austria, 1914–1918* (London: Arnold, 1997), p. 153.
7 Total Allied losses for the war were 11.9 million tons, while Germany lost 178 of its 335 submarines: H. Herwig, *'Luxury' Fleet: the Imperial Navy, 1888–1918* (Atlantic Highlands, NJ: Ashfield Press, 1987), pp. 247, 291.
8 For an illustration of this point, compare tables 22 and 24 in P. Kennedy, *The Rise and Fall of the Great Powers: Economic Change and Military Conflict from 1500 to 2000* (London: Unwin Hyman, 1988), pp. 258, 271.
9 N. Ferguson, *The Pity of War* (London: Allen Lane, 1998), pp. 312–13; notes also that American troops had limited fighting abilities and were most useful in replacing French and British forces on quiet sectors of the front.
10 Cited by G. Martin, 'German strategy and military assessments of the American Expeditionary Force', *War and Society* 1 (1994), 179.
11 Cited by T. Travers, 'The Allied victories, 1918', in H. Strachan (ed.), *The Oxford Illustrated History of the First World War* (Oxford: Oxford University Press, 1998), p. 282. The German Army's Official History called it the worst defeat since the war's start: J. Terraine, *Douglas Haig, The Educated Soldier* (London: Hutchinson, 1963), p. 458.

12 N. Ferguson, *The Pity of War, op. cit.*, p. 294.
13 Around 70 per cent of battlefield casualties came from shellfire, compared with some 10 per cent in the Russo–Japanese conflict and 8.4 per cent in the Franco–Prussian War: Hugh Strachan, *The First World War, op. cit.*, p. 309, De Groot, *The First World War, op. cit.*, p. 167.
14 Thus each British infantry battalion carried 30 Lewis guns as against four in 1915; eight trench mortars as against two; and 16 grenade-throwing rifles. The size of the battalion had been reduced by half, thus multiplying the effective firepower. See R. Prior and T. Wilson, *Command on the Western Front: the Military Career of Sir Henry Rawlinson, 1914–1918* (Oxford: Oxford University Press, 1992), ch. 27.
15 In 1914, the main Entente Powers (including their colonies) had a combined population of around 656 million, compared with 144 million for the four Central Powers; the former mobilized over 32 million men, the latter some 25 million.
16 Cited by Richard Overy, 'Warfare in Europe since 1918', in T. C. W. Blanning (ed.), *The Oxford Illustrated History of Modern Europe* (Oxford: Oxford University Press, 1996), p. 211.
17 V. G. Liulevicius, *War Land on the Eastern Front. Culture, National Identity and German Occupation in World War I* (Cambridge: Cambridge University Press, 2000), p. 81.
18 R. A. Reiss, *How Austria-Hungary Waged War in Serbia: Personal Investigations of a Neutral* (Paris: Armand Colin, 1915), p. 46, cited by Hugh Strachan, *The First World War, op. cit.*, p. 27.
19 Although it should be noted that the volunteer generally chose which branch of the services he entered. As life expectancy was higher in the artillery than in the infantry, volunteering probably incorporated some element of pre-emptive self-preservation.
20 Cited by M. Ferro, *The Great War, 1914–1918* (London: Routledge & Kegan Paul, 1973), p. 170.
21 I. F. W. Beckett, *The Great War, 1914–1918* (London: Pearson, 2001), p. 255. On the use of wartime statistics, see J. Manning, 'Wages and purchasing power', in J. Winter and J.-L. Robert, *Capital Cities at War: Paris, London and Berlin, 1914–1919* (Cambridge: Cambridge University Press, 1999), pp. 255–56.
22 N. Stone, *Europe Transformed, 1789–1919* (London: Fontana, 1999, 2nd edn), p. 279; David Stevenson, *1914–1918, op. cit.*, p. 115.
23 Cited by J. Manning, 'Wages and purchasing power', *op. cit.*, p. 283.
24 *Ibid.*, p. 279.
25 David Stevenson, *1914–1918, op. cit.*, p. 279, ch. 11 generally.
26 T. Bonzon and B. Davis, 'Feeding the Cities', in J. Winter and J.-L. Robert, *Capital Cities at War, op. cit.*, p. 339.
27 Six million ethnic Germans, Alsace-Lorraine, Eupen-Malmédy, West Prussia and Upper Silesia.
28 C. S. Gray, *War, Peace and International Relations* (London: Longman, 2007), p. 102.
29 S. C. Tucker, *The Great War, 1914–1918* (London: UCL Press, 1998), p. 227.
30 Cited by P. M. H. Bell, *The Origins of the Second World War in Europe* (London: Longman, 1997, 2nd edn), p. 216.
31 Gary Sheffield, *Forgotten Victory. The First World War: Myths and Realities* (London: Headline, 2001), p. 221.

6 The Soviet Union and Bolshevism abroad

Matthew Worley

'Give us an organization of revolutionaries, and we will turn Russia upside down.'[1] So wrote Vladimir Ilich Ulianov – better known as Lenin – in 1902, as he endeavoured to realize a means by which to transform the revolutionary theories of Karl Marx into effective political practice. Fifteen years later, Lenin's prophecy seemed to have been realized. First, in February 1917, the people of Petrograd (formerly St Petersburg) took to the streets to overturn 300 years of autocratic Romanov rule, dismantling the hated structures of the Tsarist state in the process. Then, in October, Lenin's Bolsheviks responded to the crumbling authority of the interim 'provisional government' by seizing power in the name of the *soviets*: the workers' and soldiers' councils that had emerged in the streets, barracks and factories as a supplementary locus of authority during the earliest revolutionary days. In so doing, the world's first workers' state was ushered in under the 'dictatorship of the proletariat', before the Bolsheviks renamed themselves the communist party and set about the task of 'building socialism'.

Yet the Russian Revolution did more than turn its host country 'upside down'. Coming, as it did, in the midst of World War One (1914–18), the overthrow of Nicholas II seemed to symbolize both a decisive challenge to the old ruling elites who had plunged the world into a conflict of unprecedented slaughter, and the beginning of a new age based on the enlightened motifs of freedom and democracy. As Marxists, Lenin and his comrades saw revolution in Russia as being – in Marx and Engels' own words – 'the signal for a proletarian revolution in the West'.[2] In its wake, they looked to the workers of Germany, Britain and elsewhere to follow their lead, to shake free their chains and push history onto its next, and highest, stage. Indeed, for many militant workers, young idealists and not a few intellectuals, the Russian Revolution became the defining event of the early twentieth century. In the words of Harry Pollitt, a Lancastrian boilermaker and future general secretary of the Communist Party of Great Britain (CPGB), it 'sent a thrill of excitement through every revolutionary worker … I pounced on everything that dealt with the Russian Revolution, and the knowledge that workers like me and all those around me had won power, had defeated the boss class, kept me in a growing state of enthusiasm.'[3] Simultaneously, socio-economic and political tensions exacerbated by the war provided the context for a period of widespread industrial and political unrest that did much to raise the Bolsheviks' high hopes. Across Europe, factories were occupied, demonstrations were held and revolutionary organizations formed, as the 'old order' convulsed and, in many cases, collapsed. In Germany, for example, a revolution built partly on workers' and soldiers' councils brought down the Second Reich, while soviet republics – modelled loosely on the Russian example – formed briefly in Bavaria, Hungary and Slovakia. Less productively, as the war drew to a close and the European map was redrawn, so the influence of the Bolshevik revolution could be gleaned from the splits that ravaged the socialist and labour movement across the continent, and in the fierce – but evidently fearful – response of those ruling elites who survived (and emerged from) the war to even the faintest whiff of socialism.

Of course, the internationalist aspirations of the Bolsheviks were thwarted: the worldwide revolution failed to materialize, political reaction – rather than social revolution – became the dominant creed of the 1920s and 1930s, and the Soviet Union was forced to improvise its own 'road to socialism'. This, in turn, came at great cost, ushering in the era of Stalin and its associated horrors. Nevertheless, those inspired by the events of 1917 continued to look to Russia for hope and direction throughout the interwar period. Most importantly, they gathered in national communist parties affiliated to the Communist International (Comintern), the world communist party established by the Bolsheviks in 1919 to disseminate revolution. For so long as the inequalities, inequities and repression associated with capitalism and imperialism existed, so the socialism preached and promised in the new Soviet capital of Moscow continued to resonate beyond. This chapter outlines the broad development of communism inside and outside the Soviet system from 1917, looking at the objectives, methods and frustrations of an ideology that helped define the twentieth century.[4]

Days of revolution, 1917–21

Soviet communism was a product of Bolshevism, which itself was a product of ruptures within the exiled leadership of the Russian Social

Democratic Labour Party. Thus, at the second party congress held in Brussels and London in 1903, the Russian Social Democratic Labour Party divided into two distinct factions: the Bolsheviks (under Lenin) and the Mensheviks. Very crudely, the disagreements revolved around aspects of the party programme, the rules of party membership and control of the party newspaper, with the Bolsheviks adopting a militant approach to Marxist theory and practice that contrasted with the relatively more temperate methods of their Menshevik counterparts. Although Lenin did not win all of the congress decisions in 1903, he nevertheless adopted the term *bol'sheviki*, meaning majority, to describe his supporters, labelling his opponents the *men'sheviki*, or minority.

So, what was Bolshevism? Put again in rather crude terms, Bolshevism was an assertive revolutionary ideology based on the theories of Karl Marx and applied, initially at least, to the prevailing socio-economic and political conditions of Tsarist Russia. This, in turn, acknowledged the revolutionary potential of the peasantry. The objective was the seizure of state power in the name of the proletariat (working class) and the economic reconstruction of society, so paving the way, eventually, for a worldwide communist community in which all worked collectively for the common good. To do this, Lenin and his comrades rejected the possibility of achieving their aims via peaceful or gradual socio-economic and political reform, thereby distinguishing themselves from more moderate – or constitutional – socialists gathered within parties such as the British Labour Party, German Social Democratic Party (*Sozialdemokratische Partei Deutschlands*, SPD) and, as became clear during the revolutionary days of 1917, the Mensheviks. Nor would Bolsheviks rely on the 'spontaneity' of the workers to achieve revolution, as argued most notably by the Polish-German Marxist Rosa Luxemburg. Integral to Bolshevism was the concept of a highly centralized, disciplined and committed 'vanguard party': a party of 'professional revolutionaries' trained in Marxist theory and dedicated to directing the working class movement towards revolutionary action. Such a party was to be organized, moreover, via a system of 'democratic centralism', by which communist theory and practice was discussed throughout the party until the leadership issued a definitive ruling that was binding on all members thereafter. Over time, such a *modus operandi* became more and more regimented and hierarchical, transforming from a system in which – theoretically – power flowed, through inclusive debate and elected representation, to one in which leadership decisions were taken directly, ratified by appointed party officials, and dictated to the wider membership. Conceived, too, within a mindset that regarded Marxism as a science, the rulings of the party were tantamount to a systematically reasoned 'truth'; to query or oppose the party line was not merely to disagree, but to question the validity of Marxism and serve as a fetter on the revolution.

The distinctive features of Bolshevism became more pronounced following the October Revolution. They now served as an explanation for the Bolsheviks' success in seizing power and as a means to distinguish their revolutionary policies from those of socialists who doubted the legitimacy of Soviet authority. From here on, the Bolsheviks perceived their revolutionary communism – based on Soviet power and the dictatorship of the proletariat – to be fundamentally opposed to a social democracy tied to forms of 'bourgeois' parliamentary politics deemed antithetical to the interests of the working class. In Lenin's words, speaking in 1919:

> The main thing that socialists fail to understand and that constitutes their short-sightedness in matters of theory, their subservience to bourgeois prejudices and their political betrayal of the proletariat is that in capitalist society, whenever there is any serious aggravation of the class struggle intrinsic to that society, there can be no alternative but the dictatorship of the bourgeoisie or the dictatorship of the proletariat. Dreams of some third way are reactionary, petty-bourgeois lamentations. That is borne out by more than a century of development of bourgeois democracy and the working class movement in all the advanced countries, and notably by the experience of the past five years. That is also borne out by the whole science of political economy, by the entire content of Marxism, which reveals the economic inevitability, wherever commodity economy prevails, of the dictatorship of the bourgeoisie that can only be replaced by the class which the very growth of capitalism develops, multiplies, welds together and strengthens, that is, the proletarian class.[5]

As this suggests, the Bolsheviks retained their internationalist perspective in the wake of revolution, enabling the renamed Communist Party to universalize its experience and provide the basis for a revolutionary model that could be exported – or at least adapted to conditions – beyond Russian boundaries. Accordingly, the interrelationship between communism in Russia and the emerging international communist movement was clear from the outset. From a Soviet perspective, the defence and advancement of Soviet power in Russia was indistinguishable from the furtherance of the worldwide revolution. For communists outside Soviet territory, Russia retained a prestige and encapsulated a successful model of revolution that merely gained in credence as time went on. It was, therefore, on the Bolsheviks' initiative and in the Bolshevik image that the Communist International was built, and it was through Bolshevik spectacles that international communist theory and practice were understood and formulated. And while it would be wrong to assume that the Comintern was created simply to protect the Russian national interest, the lack of a successful socialist revolution elsewhere combined with the wider movement's reliance on the Soviet regime for financial and political support to ensure that the Moscow-based leadership dominated the International from its formation.

To understand better the connotations of all this, it is helpful to utilize Marx's method of delineating distinct historical periods: an approach the Bolsheviks naturally continued from 1917. This, in turn, was based on analysis of prevailing class relationships and socio-economic conditions throughout the world. As circumstances changed, so communist theory and practice would do likewise, thereby shaping and responding to historical forces. Accordingly, the history of the Soviet experiment and the international communist movement can be divided into a series of self-determined stages, each of which encapsulated the objectives of the wider communist movement and reflected the priorities of the emerging Union of Soviet Socialist Republics (USSR), which formally came into being at the end of 1922.

The first of these began with the upheavals of 1917 and continued through until 1921. It was defined by the Russian revolution and the widespread sociopolitical unrest that accompanied the end of World War One. So, in the letter of 24 January 1919 that invited various socialist parties and worker organizations to the founding congress of the Comintern, the central committee of the Russian Communist Party (Bolshevik) could proclaim: 'The present period is that of the decomposition and collapse of the entire world capitalist system, and will be that of the collapse of European civilization in general if capitalism, with its insurmountable contradictions, is not overthrown.' To this end, workers were called upon to seize state power and establish a dictatorship of the proletariat as a means to expropriate capital, abolish private property, and establish a new system based on the 'self-administration of [the] masses by their elected bodies'.[6] As the Bolsheviks looked out across the 'debris and smoking ruins' of a war-ravaged Europe, so the opportunity for the working class to unite under the 'communist banner' and forge revolution appeared to have arrived.[7]

Not surprisingly, the Bolsheviks' own experience greatly informed such a perspective. By the summer of 1918, revolution in Russia had segued into a bloody civil war as the heady enthusiasm with which all power had been transferred to the soviets gave way to more practical concerns. Not only was Russia still embroiled in World War One, but the country's economic and political infrastructure had all but collapsed amidst the revolutionary upheavals of the previous months. It was imperative, therefore, that the Bolsheviks moved quickly and ruthlessly to consolidate their position as the true representatives of the indigenous working class and establish the framework for an effective workers' state. To this end, Russia was withdrawn from the war, power was centralized, potential and actual opposition was repressed, and the authority of the communist party was affirmed through its domination of the soviets and the fledgling state apparatus based on a Council of People's Commissars (*Sovnarkom*). Such a process would take time, but Lenin's intentions were made clear with the forcible dispersal of the constituent assembly elected in November 1917, in which the Bolsheviks represented just 10.9 million of the 48.4 million votes cast, having come second to the peasant-backed Socialist Revolutionaries.[8] This was justified on account of the Bolsheviks winning the majority of the working-class vote and with the assembly's sovereignty being deemed to conflict with that of the soviets, in whose names the party had seized power. But it revealed, too, both the fragility of Bolshevik support beyond the urban centres and military, and the lengths to which Lenin was prepared to go in order to retain power. Indeed, throughout 1918 the Soviet government sought to acquire more and more extensive state authority in order to protect and augment its position. As civil war loomed, the infamous All-Russian Extraordinary Commission for Combating Counter Revolution and Sabotage (*Cheka*) was created in tandem with the formation of a disciplined (and conscripted) Red Army. For all Lenin's talk of the dictatorship of the proletariat being 'the forcible suppression of the resistance of the exploiters, i.e., an insignificant minority of the population, the landowners and the capitalists', its remit evidently spread further once the extent of the Bolsheviks' task became apparent to the party leadership.[9]

The Bolsheviks won the Civil War at great cost. Fought primarily between the Red Army and the White armies formed by nationalist officers, the war also pitted both against peasant resistance to the grain requisitioning introduced to ensure food supplies; against 'leftist' opposition from the Socialist Revolutionaries and Mensheviks; and against nationalist movements in the former empire territories; and the Red Army against foreign (Allied) intervention on behalf of the Whites. In the process, some 12 million people died from the fighting, disease and famine that consumed Russia between 1917 and 1922; by the end of the war, the proletariat in whose name the Red Army fought had been depleted, dispersed and demoralized as a result of industrial collapse, food shortages, death and conscription.[10] Nevertheless, the civil war was a defining experience for the Soviet regime.[11] Victory had been assured by a combination of effective military strategy, geographical position, and superior political expediency, coherency and organization – qualities that the Bolsheviks held onto as they surveyed the socio-economic chaos that the war left in its wake. By its end, the communist party was hardened rather than weakened by the experience of war; its language had become more militaristic, and the Bolshevik 'uniform' of workers' cap, leather jacket, boots and revolver had become commonplace. The party had fought the class war and won; its methods had proven effective. The state had been wielded as a weapon of class dictatorship, directed from the centre by the communist leadership and executed by a party of committed, disciplined cadres. The means of production had been brought under state ownership, industrial management replaced direct workers' control, the population had been mobilized and revolutionary terror utilized to defend the revolution. And while Soviet policy would be realigned from 1921, the underlying methods of the Civil War victory became an entrenched part of Soviet rule.

Of course, the Bolsheviks hoped that revolution in the West would help ease their situation. As the Allies sought to redraw the European map and assert a new balance of power through the League of Nations, so national, socio-economic and cultural tensions sparked a protracted period of unrest. In among all this, communist parties inspired by the Bolshevik example began to form, often splitting away from existing social democratic parties – as in Germany, France and Italy – to join the Comintern over the course of 1919–21. At the same time, revolutionary aspirations did not always translate into proletarian power. In Germany, the fall of the Second Reich in November 1918 brought not a soviet republic but – in Marxist terms – a bourgeois democracy, in which the SPD formed part of an elected coalition government. Attempts to push the revolution further, such as the Spartacist uprising of January 1919 and the shortlived Bavarian Räterepublik of the same year, were repressed, thereby consolidating divisions within the German labour movement that would have severe repercussions come the rise of Nazism in the early 1930s. In Hungary, too, a brief soviet republic existed between March and August 1919, before collapsing as a result of internal and external pressures, while factory occupations across Italy, general strikes in Eastern Europe and worker protests in Britain and France similarly failed to bring the expected revolutionary outcome.[12] By early 1921, following yet another disastrous attempt by the German communist party (*Kommunistische Partei Deutschlands*, KPD) to mobilize for revolution (the March Action), it seemed clear to many communists that the historical moment had passed. Speaking to the third Comintern congress in July 1921, Trotsky suggested that '[the] first period of the revolutionary movement ... may be regarded by and large as terminated.'[13]

What had gone wrong? From the Comintern's Marxist perspective, conditions had been ripe for revolution; the 'capitalist' world had been devastated by war, the Bolsheviks had taken the initiative and subsequently held onto power, workers had revolted and communist parties had formed across Europe (and beyond). But although capitalism was still deemed to be in its death throes at the start of the 1920s, the 'mighty wave' of unrest had not brought the proletariat to power beyond the old Tsarist Empire.[14] Typically, as it would turn out, the Comintern sought to lay the blame for such an outcome on the actions of others. If the party line had been correct, as demonstrated by the Bolsheviks in Russia, then it must have been the interpretation and practical expression of communist policy that failed to harness the historical forces to enact effective revolutionary change elsewhere. Many of the communist parties formed from 1918 remained small and fractious throughout the 'first period', allowing their 'treacherous' and 'opportunist' social democratic rivals to retain the support of the majority of organized workers. Similarly, as the Comintern soon came to realize, the fledgling communist parties were often loosely organized, thereby negating the principles of unity and discipline deemed central to the Bolsheviks' success. So, for example, the Italian party (*Partito Comunista Italiano, PSI*) was reprimanded in 1921 for its 'opportunistic' policies, fractiousness and failure to transform 'spontaneous action into well-prepared campaigns'.[15] Tellingly, too, the failure of the KPD's March Action in 1921 was located in the party's portraying the campaign as a revolutionary 'offensive' rather than a 'defensive action' in response to capitalist attacks on the working class. The answer? Centralize, discipline, unify and establish firmer links with the 'mass' of the working class – in other words, 'Bolshevize'. More to the point, talk of a 'defensive struggle' suggested that class forces were realigning, and that communist policy would necessarily have to do the same.

Stabilization, New Economic Policy and the United Front, 1921–28

Communist analysis of the years between 1921 and 1928 was subject to change in emphasis and tone. Nevertheless, certain basic assumptions underlay the Comintern's and the Soviet Union's worldview for much of the 1920s. Speaking in late 1926, Nikolai Bukharin insisted that:

> [Commencing] from the first steps towards the stabilization of capitalism, we had a new phase. A certain shifting in the balance of forces took place. This shifting consisted in that the communists had to make a slight retreat, while the social democrats experienced a certain renaissance; a certain growth and they consolidated themselves to some extent. This proceeded along with the stabilization of capitalism.[16]

In other words, the revolutionary period had passed (temporarily); capitalism had survived the upheavals of World War One and was seeking to re-establish itself. This, in turn, meant the onset of a 'capitalist offensive' against the working class, leading to lower wages, longer hours, higher taxes, the curtailment of workers' rights and, in certain circumstances, the emergence of fascism. With regard to the Russian case, it meant that the 'workers' state' was 'encircled by capitalism', ensuring that it would have to begin to build its economy without the benefits of European revolution. Consequently, in this 'second period', communists had to adopt a new economic course in Russia and fight for workers' 'transitional demands' in the West.[17]

Let us take the Soviet regime first. The New Economic Policy (NEP) was launched in 1921 and was designed primarily to ease the tensions that existed between the party, the urban centres and the peasantry. As noted above, the Bolsheviks had won the civil war at great cost. By the turn of the year, unrest in the countryside was widespread, the economy remained in disarray, and even those closely associated with the Bolshevik Revolution, such as the Kronstadt sailors who mutinied in early 1921, were showing their displeasure. The NEP, then, was presented initially as a necessary – or strategic – 'retreat'; a means by which to save the revolution in a country that, in Marxist terms, remained economically 'backward'. To this end, Lenin insisted that an alliance (*smychka*) between the workers and the peasants was required to build the economic basis for socialism, thereby transforming policies of 'retreat' into the means by which to advance the revolution.

In practice, the NEP evolved over time. Originally, it was based on the replacement of grain requisitioning with a tax in kind calculated on a percentage of the harvest, before further measures were then introduced, including a stable currency based on gold, the rationalization of industry, and a limited market wherein peasants were able to sell their surplus produce and individuals were allowed to lease small-scale enterprises.

The 'commanding heights' of the economy – large-scale industry, transport, banking, etc. – remained in state hands, but foreign investment was invited and more conventional budgetary practices were introduced. There was no return to workers' control either. Although labour discipline was relaxed and the working class expanded as the economy improved (with the burgeoning party and state apparatus becoming a means of social mobility), managerial authority remained and a reliance on so-called 'bourgeois specialists' continued to characterize the proletarian dictatorship. Culturally and socially, the Bolsheviks – as during the Civil War period – sought to establish an extensive welfare state that provided for (and created) a cultured and literate people, extending healthcare and education, legislating for sexual equality, and channelling the arts in the service of revolution. Lest we forget, communism was inspired by a vision of equality, opportunity and enlightenment – motivations that bound many to the revolution amidst the upheavals and hardships of the dictatorship. Nevertheless, the NEP period was distinguished by continued differentials across society, with specialists, party-state officials and skilled workers appearing to gain most.

Inevitably, perhaps, the 'concessions' and ambiguities associated with the NEP caused some unease. For many communists, the achievements of the revolution risked being undermined by such apparent compromise. Significantly, therefore, the economic policies of the NEP were accompanied by a further tightening of Bolshevik discipline within the communist party and throughout Soviet Russia. As Lenin put it in 1922, 'when an army is in retreat a hundred times more discipline is required than when it is advancing.'[18] With regard to the Communist Party, wherein various 'opposition' groups had formed in response to an array of political and organizational issues, the tenth party congress of 1921 passed a resolution 'on party unity' that banned such 'factions' organizing against the prevailing party 'line'. This contained a secret clause that allowed the leadership to expel persistent offenders, including elected members of the central committee. Simultaneously, a purge of the party sought to remove 'careerists' and ineffectual members from the growing party ranks, while 1922–23 saw the final rout of those openly opposed to the Soviet regime. Mensheviks, Socialist Revolutionaries and others were arrested, tried, imprisoned or deported, leaders of the Orthodox Church were publicly tried, and the dictatorship of the proletariat was emphatically reaffirmed. By the time of the USSR's formation in 1922–23 and Lenin's death in January 1924, the Communist Party's position was unassailable.

Famously, the main benefactor of this was Stalin (Josef Vissarionovich Djugasvili). As the party simultaneously expanded and centralized its internal structure, so Stalin's administrative skills came to the fore, enabling him to cultivate his position as General Secretary in order to influence the agenda of the party leadership (in the *politburo* appointed by the central committee) and oversee the selection of party personnel (through the organization bureau: *orgburo*). By aligning himself closely to Lenin and drawing on the values of unity and discipline so integral to Bolshevism, he emerged from a series of internal party political struggles over the course of the 1920s to become the pre-eminent communist leader. During the NEP period, and despite warnings from the ailing Lenin, Stalin consolidated his position; marginalized Trotsky and other leading Bolsheviks such as Zinoviev and Kamenev; and, with Bukharin, propagated a theory of 'socialism in one country' that prioritized the construction of socialism in Russia in the interim between the Bolshevik revolution and the victory of the international proletariat.

Beyond the Soviet Union, the communist movement similarly readjusted itself to the changed circumstances of the 1920s. With revolution no longer deemed imminent, the Comintern oversaw a shift towards the policy of a 'united workers' front'; meaning joint action with non-communist workers inside social democratic parties and trade unions. The objective was to defend workers' interests in the face of the capitalist offensive, and to cultivate communist support among the 'mass' of the working class by popularizing communist methods and 'unmasking' the shortcomings of the social democratic leadership. As this suggests, such a strategy was generally envisaged to be a united front 'from below', with members rather than leaders of social democratic organizations, although there were certain circumstances whereby communist parties could establish (temporary) united fronts 'from above' with social democratic hierarchies. So, for example, the CPGB was praised by the Comintern in early 1926 for its work inside the wider British labour movement, having formed a National Minority Movement of communist and non-communist trade unionists to agitate for a more militant trade union policy, a 'left-wing movement' inside the Labour Party, and a joint advisory council with the Trades Union Congress (TUC) on the question of unemployment.[19] Internationally, an Anglo–Russian trade union committee had also been established between the TUC and its Soviet equivalent. When the revolution arrived, so the Comintern reasoned, the workers would fall in line behind the communist leadership, shed their remaining social democratic illusions, and forge a Soviet-style dictatorship of the proletariat.

Such 'successes' were limited and rare.[20] As with the NEP in Russia, the united front was seen by many as a political 'retreat' and thus proved a difficult pill for revolutionaries to swallow, particularly as economic conditions seemed far from stable in many instances. At its heart, too, lay the incongruity of calling for unity with a social democracy that communists openly acknowledged they wished to destroy. Opposition to the change of line was therefore extensive, particularly among sections of the German, French and Spanish parties.[21] Indeed, the Comintern was forced throughout the second period to rebuke its sections for veering away from the 'correct' interpretation of the united front; in 1926, the Bulgarian and Polish parties were even accused of harbouring terroristic tendencies.[22] Not surprisingly, the policy remained somewhat vague; its criteria and emphases shifted over time in accord with Soviet priorities, power struggles and wider sociopolitical developments. The French occupation of the Ruhr in January 1923, for example, convinced a section of the Soviet leadership, KPD and Comintern that revolution was still possible in the heart of Europe. By October 1923, a KPD-led uprising had been planned and subsequently aborted, leading to a damaging round of recriminations that became entangled with disputes raging simultaneously inside the Soviet party. Once again, the Comintern sought to apportion blame for the KPD's failure on political errors rather than its own misreading of the 'objective conditions'; this time, 'opportunism' and an over-reliance on social democratic support were diagnosed.

In many ways, therefore, the defining characteristic of the international communist movement in the second period was its transformation from a diverse range of communist parties shaped by indigenous forces and an admiration for Bolshevism, into an apparently monolithic, strictly disciplined organization explicitly loyal to a Soviet leadership increasingly dominated by Stalin. According to the Comintern, Bolshevization meant 'studying and applying in practice the experience of the RCP [Russian Communist Party]', the 'application of the general principles of Leninism to the concrete situation of [a] given country', and the recognition that 'iron proletarian discipline' and a 'unity of will and action' were essential to the 'victorious proletarian dictatorship'.[23] Officially, such a process was not to be applied 'mechanically'; in reality, communist parties became ever more reliant on – and subservient to – the Soviet party representatives who dominated and oversaw the Comintern. Democratic centralism became bureaucratic centralism.[24]

Of course, Bolshevization was bound up in the struggle between Stalin, Trotsky and others in the Soviet party, with the victor (Stalin) necessarily extending his authority into the international field in the name of communist unity. This, as noted above, was clear in the recriminations that followed the failed 'German October', and paved the way for the Comintern's adoption of the 'Bolshevization' slogan at its fifth congress in the summer of 1924. From here on, the Comintern sought to exert the authority ingrained in its constitution: namely the executive's right to direct communist activity, expel groups and individuals from national sections, and enforce party discipline. As a result, party leaderships were overhauled, Trotskyism and other deviations were purged from the various national party ranks, and the already extensive ties that bound the national sections to the Comintern were tightened. In the process, hardened revolutionaries were castigated, expelled and replaced by those the Comintern supposed to be avowedly loyal to its (and, by extension, Soviet) authority. Yet some qualifying remarks are worth making. Although the process of Bolshevization became synonymous with Stalin's rise to power, it was also informed by other factors. Most obviously, the fractious nature of many national sections cried out for the Comintern to exert its discipline. Disunity, infighting and political ineptitude were genuine problems within the international movement. Second, as McDermott and Agnew have demonstrated, Bolshevization was 'to a certain extent an interactive process with exogenous and indigenous pressures co-mingling to produce subtle variations from country to country.'[25] Thus the achievements of the Bolsheviks garnered genuine respect, and communists coveted their methods. Similarly, association with both Bolshevism and the Soviet Union provided a source of strength and resilience for communists across the world. In addition, 'the tendency to bureaucratization in modern organizations; the expanding role of the state that seemed to confirm the centralist propensities of Marxism–Leninism; and the underlying social, economic and cultural changes that were threatening to fragment and reshape the structure of the European working class', meant that communists were receptive to Bolshevization.[26] That said, the process proved to be a protracted one, with opposition, indifference and misunderstanding evident in many instances.[27]

Looked at in late 1927, communism had confirmed itself as a major global force. The NEP had helped stabilize and rebuild the Russian economy, the USSR had been established and the Soviet communist party appeared secure in power. Globally, national parties had developed throughout the world and a coherent international movement was in place. Yet tensions existed within the apparent monolith. In Russia, debates over the NEP were about to unleash another round of internal struggle and a major realignment of Soviet policy, while the limitations of the united front and the repercussions of Bolshevization paved the way for a correlated 'turn' in Comintern theory and practice.

The 'third period' was set to be one of the most eventful and controversial in communist history.

Class-against-class, 1928–35

The origins of the third period were varied. On a general level, previous Comintern analysis had consistently regarded 'capitalist stabilization' as a temporary phenomenon. By late 1926, therefore, Bukharin could inform the Comintern that:

> I believe we have a new phase – a phase in which the process of the stabilization of capitalism brings forward its contradictions in ever sharper form. The relations between the classes are sharpening ... capitalism is attacking. The working class is daily becoming more convinced of the necessity of active and determined struggle. The leftward trend within the working class is an eloquent expression of this process.

Given such circumstances, Bukharin predicted that 'an immediate revolutionary situation' would soon appear in Europe, thereby necessitating an eventual shift in Comintern policy in 1927–28.[28]

Bukharin's reasoning related to perceived developments within the international capitalist economy, particularly Germany, Britain and the USA. In Bukharin's mind, as in Marx's, the advances of capitalism led dialectically to its 'inevitable' downfall: the bourgeoisie were to be their own gravediggers. In other words, technological innovation, increased production and capitalist competition led to crises of productivity, the extension of the bourgeois state, international tensions, structural unemployment, worker regulation, depressed working-class living standards and intensified class struggle.[29] The position of social democracy in such a context was contentious. For Bukharin, he looked to Weimar Germany as an acute example of the ongoing relationship between communists and social democrats, where the SPD's leading role in the Weimar system meant that workers regularly came into conflict with authorities that functioned under social democratic jurisdiction.[30] In line with its reformist nature, the Comintern reasoned, social democracy was ever more clearly revealing itself to be on the side of the bourgeoisie. Elsewhere, Bukharin pointed to Britain's declining economic prowess and the events surrounding the 1926 General Strike and miners' lockout to bolster his theoretical reasoning. In response, Bukharin talked of the 'English' [sic] working class moving onto the 'next stage of progress', from where the CPGB was to ruthlessly expose 'reformist treachery' in preparation for British capitalism's 'imminent collapse'.[31] In China, meanwhile, where Chinese communists were bound up in a fateful united front with the Nationalist Kuomintang, Bukharin was convinced that the 'Chinese revolution is one of the most important and powerful factors disrupting capitalist stabilization.' The disproportionate and competitive development of capitalist national economies encouraged global rivalry, Bukharin maintained, so paving the way for imperialist war and revolution.[32]

Over the course of 1927, various events – from Chiang Kai Shek's slaughter of the CCP to the uprising of Austrian workers in Vienna to the unravelling of the Comintern's united front initiatives in Britain and elsewhere – compounded such a worldview. That said, Soviet determinants were obviously fundamental to Bukharin's thesis; the position of the Soviet Union was indelibly linked to the development of international capitalism. First, deteriorating diplomatic relations between Russia and Britain helped fan the flames of a 'war scare' inside the Soviet Union. On the one hand, this 'proved' that capitalist stabilization was being undermined; in 'crisis', the bourgeoisie would turn to war, fascism and repression to maintain their power and profits. On the other, it raised questions as to the Soviet Union's ability to defend itself. Second, Bukharin's analysis was designed to deflect the criticism of Comintern policy made by Trotsky and Zinoviev. Finally, and concurrently, Comintern thinking was a by-product of the intensifying debate concerning the future development of the NEP. This, in turn, would precipitate a falling out between Stalin and Bukharin and pave the way for the so-called 'great turn' in Soviet history from 1928.

The debate over the NEP is perhaps the most important for our purposes. Basically, by 1926–27, economic recovery had more or less been achieved, but concerns remained within the Soviet leadership. Despite increased outputs, improvements in the terms of trade for agriculture and lower industrial prices, grain sales began to stall in 1927 and by the autumn there was a shortage of food reaching the towns.[33] Concerns, too, were mounting about the re-emergence of 'bourgeois elements' within the Soviet Union and the country's vulnerability to capitalist hostility. All within the party agreed that Russia needed to step up the pace of its industrialization; the question was how best to proceed. For Bukharin, it was important to keep cordial relations with the peasants and maintain the moderate NEP course instigated by Lenin. For those to his left, including Trotsky and – more acutely – Preobrazensky, industrialization should be rigorously pursued, with pressure applied on the *kulaks* (richer peasants) and NEP men (private entrepreneurs) to facilitate the move to a more centrally planned economy. As for Stalin, he publicly sided with Bukharin until the end of 1927, but was resistant to any further compromise with the peasantry. By mobilizing support within the *politburo*, therefore, he prepared to unleash his own programme of rapid industrialization and collectivization of agriculture over the course of 1928–29.

Our third period, then, is defined by Stalin's 'revolution from above' inside the USSR and the policies of 'class-against-class' within the Comintern. In both instances, the relatively moderate prognoses of, respectively, the first five-year plan drafted over 1926–28 and the 'left turn' in policy launched officially at the sixth Comintern congress in the summer of 1928, were eclipsed by a lurch towards extreme political and theoretical positions tied to the factional struggle inside the Soviet Union. This was then tempered, gradually, between 1930 and 1933, from which point the threat of fascism became too acute for the Comintern to downplay amidst a general theory of capitalist crisis. The result was the final victory of Stalin as the undisputed leader of the international communist movement, and the adoption of policies that would have violent repercussions for both the people of the Soviet Union and the working class of Europe.

Within the Soviet Union, the processes of industrialization and collectivization were evidently entwined. To proceed with the first five-year plan, it was essential to ensure reliable grain procurement to fund the industrialization drive, to provide for Soviet exports and to feed the growing proletariat. Drawing on his Marxist heritage, moreover, Stalin saw the issue in class terms: the problems of the NEP had been caused, in large part, by wealthy peasants hoarding grain and holding the workers' state to ransom. The solution, therefore, was class struggle and the collectivization of agriculture. As the urban economy industrialized, so the rural economy was to be controlled and made subordinate to the interests of the working class, with force if necessary.

The political-economic model that emerged from all this has become synonymous with the concept of Stalinism. Put simply, it comprised a highly centralized, planned economy, directed by the party leadership, coordinated by the state, and implemented by the various state branches of industry. Virtually all vestiges of the market were removed; targets were set for each sector of the economy; and heavy industry was given priority status in order to build Russia's industrial basis, to provide a dominant proletariat and to ensure national defence. The objective was to lay the foundations for a genuinely socialist, and modern, society. In the event, the impact of the five-year plan was certainly far-reaching, although its broader objective was effectively buried beneath the pursuit of short-term targets and a preoccupation with the pace of development. 'To slacken the tempo would mean falling behind', Stalin said, and 'those who fall behind get beaten.'[34] So, although production output increased throughout key sectors of the economy, it did so at the cost of, for example, textile and consumer goods production. Even more contentiously, there was a return to strict labour discipline (the authority of the factory manager increased), while the party and secret police became ever more integrated into the day-to-day management of the economy, with the latter developing its archipelago of forced labour camps and ensuring that 'wreckers' did not succeed in jeopardizing Russia's historic march. Over time, the targets, pace and extent of the plan passed through a number of changes, although its 'completion' in only four years was obviously more propaganda than actual achievement.

The debates over grain requisitioning continued throughout 1928–29. The previous two winters had seen a return to forced seizures of grain, but in 1929 the party finally resolved to enact its long-term objective of collectivization, meaning the seizure of land and machinery by the state, the formation of collective and state farms, and the full absorption of the agrarian sector into the planned economy. In effect, the party instigated a class war within the peasantry, deporting and executing those designated as *kulaks*. In the process, Stalin reasoned, Russia would overcome its backwardness (symbolized by the peasantry), modernize, and push the peasants along a 'socialist path of development, which squeezes the rich, the capitalists, and arms the poor and middle peasants with modern equipment, with modern implements, with tractors and agricultural machinery, thus enabling them to climb out of poverty and ... of bondage to the kulaks.'[35] In reality, chaos ensued. The label *kulak* was applied arbitrarily, and coercion bred discontent rather than a belief in the socialist future. And although Stalin claimed Russia to be 'dizzy with success' in early 1930, and blamed overzealous officials for the brutality inflicted on the countryside, the process continued throughout much of the decade.

The impact of Stalin's revolution was immense. Within the party, those associated with Bukharin were condemned for their 'right deviations' and replaced by comrades close to the general secretary, a process that extended into the Comintern (see below). In the cities, peasants fleeing collectivization, or simply attracted by the promise of work, brought with them problems of overcrowding, shortages and cheap labour. Food rationing was introduced, internal passports were issued in an attempt to control the shift in population triggered by the 'great turn', and the living conditions of most people fell over the course of the first five-year plan. Across the Soviet Union, new cities were built around huge industrial plants, such as Magnitogorsk in the southern Urals. Simultaneously, the regime sought to break its reliance on 'bourgeois specialists' by initiating policies of proletarian promotion, providing education opportunities for young workers and installing trained cadres into key positions. Most devastatingly, collectivization led to severe famine in parts of the USSR, not to mention the complete overhaul of rural life. The peasants now lived within the collective farm, holding their land and machinery in common, and farming set quotas of produce for the state. Modernization was slow, agricultural levels of output remained low, and party officials oversaw the management of the farms and ensured central control. For many peasants, they had simply been returned to serfdom.

Despite such problems, the achievements of Russia's industrialization and collectivization drive were trumpeted by the Comintern sections. Indeed, the onset of the 'Great Depression' following the Wall Street crash of October 1929 appeared both to validate Comintern predictions of growing capitalist crisis and to demonstrate the political-economic superiority of the USSR. In theory, too, the 'objective situation' provided a new revolutionary opportunity for the various national parties: class tensions were mounting as unemployment increased, both capitalism and bourgeois democracy were in 'crisis', social democrats were revealing themselves to be apologists for capitalism and, worse, acting as a block on the workers' revolutionary aspirations. 'Objectively', therefore, social democrats were no better or worse than fascists; they were, in fact, 'social fascists' actively opposed to the interests of the workers. Similarly, bourgeois democracy and fascism were merely different forms of bourgeois dictatorship; the former, the Comintern instructed its sections, should not be regarded as some kind of 'lesser evil'. Given such reasoning, the Comintern enacted a series of policies under the banner of 'class-against-class', by which communists were to prepare for revolution, rally the masses 'from below', break from any formal united front with social democracy, and establish the communist party as the 'independent' leader of the working class. Yet, despite the very real depression and political crises that afflicted capitalism in Europe and beyond from 1929, communists searched in vain for proletarian revolution during the third period. For most parties, the years of class-against-class were characterized by internal division, persecution and a declining influence.

Although Bukharin initiated the political shift to class-against-class in late 1927, the theoretical basis and practical expression of his 'new line' were realigned amidst the struggle against the 'right danger' in 1928–30. Most clearly, the theses presented to the tenth plenum of the

Comintern executive in July 1929 portrayed an exaggerated and somewhat distorted version of Bukharin's original conception of the third period, whereby revolution no longer appeared to be emerging from capitalism's advance but from its rapid decay.[36] The imminence of capitalism's final crisis, evident in Bukharin's thesis, was brought even more to the fore, while the Comintern now denoted clear confirmation of the 'fascist transformation of the state apparatus of the bourgeoisie' and the 'intensification of repression and white terror' in countries such as Yugoslavia, Germany, Poland, Italy and India. 'In the situation of growing imperialist contradictions and sharpening class struggle', the Comintern reasoned, 'fascism becomes more and more the dominant method of bourgeois rule.'[37] Linked to this, the theory of 'social fascism' was finally endorsed at the tenth plenum, a concept that Bukharin had refuted the previous summer.

What did all this mean in practice? First, the Comintern and its sections were wracked by a period of internal strife. This time, those associated with Bukharin, or deemed to be holding onto 'social democratic tendencies' acquired during the previous period, were purged from their respective parties. In their place emerged leaders deemed unequivocally loyal to the Soviet (Stalinist) leadership, such as Ernst Thälmann in Germany and Maurice Thorez in France. Throughout the Comintern, memberships declined and political effectiveness was jeopardized as the various parties realigned themselves to the changing circumstances. Many sections, including the Swedish, Yugoslav and Czechoslovakian parties, were wracked by intensive internal divisions, while others – such as the British and the Italian parties – were plunged into a period of protracted reorganization. The Comintern itself lost seven executive members between 1928 and 1930, while Stalin's ally Viacheslav Molotov was drafted in to oversee what amounted to the 'Stalinization' of the Communist International.

Second, communist policy became focused on the 'treachery' of social democracy, leading to the formation of 'red' trade unions and preventing even tactical alliances with social democrats for election or industrial purposes. Once again, the ramifications of such a policy were most acutely exposed in Germany. Although it must be remembered that social democrats detested communists just as much as communists detested social democrats, the Comintern's adoption of class-against-class effectively denied the German labour movement any chance of resisting the assault of Nazism in 1929–33. With Weimar democracy breaking down, and both the KPD and Nazi Party gaining in members and support, the Comintern saw the SPD as part of the problem rather than part of the revolutionary solution. The KPD – at the

Comintern's (and Stalin's) behest – even resolved, in certain circumstances, to ally with the Nazi Party to defeat the SPD, as in the Prussian referendum of August 1931. Of course, the KPD more generally engaged in physical and political confrontation with Nazism, with its members rallying under a slogan of 'hit the fascists whenever you meet them'. Yet Hitler's rise to power led only to the destruction of the KPD and the wider German labour movement; the KPD leader, Thälmann, was to perish in a concentration camp. Elsewhere, as in France and Britain, communist footholds in parliament and the labour movement were further damaged by the 'left turn'. The formation of red trade unions was generally ineffectual throughout the Comintern, while attempts to foster industrial unrest in the deleterious economic circumstances of the depression led to a series of defeats and, more often than not, initiatives that barely got off the ground. In Spain, meanwhile, where there was a revolution in 1931, the small Spanish party (*Partido Comunista de Español*, PCE) was left on the political sidelines as a result of its recalcitrant policy.

Finally, as a result of structural economic factors, detachment from the mainstream labour movement, and (in many cases) political repression, communist parties moved out of the workshops and factories to mobilize in the street or to operate as underground movements. Such a process preceded the third period, but was now exacerbated. Many parties, including the German and the British, were based largely on unemployed membership in the early 1930s, while others – including the Italian and Hungarian – adopted clandestine methods and functioned with exiled leaderships. In 1933, just 16 of the 72 parties attending the thirteenth plenum of the Comintern executive were functioning legally.[38] For all the Comintern's attempt to universalize and centralize its theories and methods, its policies were continuously refracted through varied sets of circumstances and contexts.

Evidently, the revolutionary aspirations of the third period proved fallacious; the strategy pursued by the Comintern had, at best, failed to prevent the emergence of fascism and reaction. For many historians, the Comintern actively contributed to such a scenario.[39] Yet we should be wary of too teleological an argument. The 'ultra-leftist' period of class-against-class was relatively shortlived (reference to the 'left' as well as 'right' danger was *de rigueur* by 1931); structural factors also impinged on communist policy and influence, which – in certain cases – began to revive in the early 1930s; and many others besides the communist movement can be held accountable for the rise of fascism. Even so, the third period was a difficult and often calamitous time for the Comintern. By its official end, in 1935, the international communist movement was in some disarray. In the Soviet Union, meanwhile, a second – less impetuous – five-year plan was under way; Stalin's position seemed imperious; and a recognizably modern society appeared to be emerging. And then came the terror ...

Fascism and terror, 1933–39

The appointment of Adolf Hitler as German Chancellor on 30 January 1933 provoked a shift in communist politics. The complete abandonment of class-against-class would take some time, but March 1933 saw the Comintern belatedly reply to social democratic overtures of cooperation against the fascist threat. In this, communist parties were 'recommended' to approach social democratic organizations with a view to taking joint action against fascism, while simultaneously reminding the working class that social democracy continued to act as the principal obstacle on the path to socialism.[40] In very specific circumstances, and in strict conditions, the united front 'from above' was back on the Comintern agenda; but it took a further 18 months for the policy to be officially endorsed within a realigned theoretical analysis of the 'international situation'.

By drawing on the work of Julian Jackson, McDermott and Agnew have suggested that a 'triple interaction' of national, Comintern and Soviet forces combined to facilitate the transition from class-against-class to a politics focused primarily on combating fascism.[41] Thus, at a local and national level, certain communist parties began to advocate a broader interpretation of the united front 'from below' and initiate anti-fascist actions with non-communist and social democratic workers. Although tentative attempts to further realign Comintern policy – by Georgi Dimitrov in 1932, and by Klement Gottwald and Thorez in 1933 – were rejected, the reality of the fascist threat encompassed in the Nazi's crushing of the KPD eventually led to a formal change in communist thinking over the course of 1934. In particular, the joint response of communist and socialist workers in France on 12 February 1934 to fascist demonstrations held a week earlier helped push the Comintern towards a more collaborative policy. This, in turn, was assisted by the rise of Dimitrov inside the Comintern, following his successful defence against Nazi charges that he was responsible for the burning of the Reichstag in February 1933. Once acquitted, the Bulgarian comrade was warmly received in Moscow in February 1934, and was promoted to general secretary of the Comintern at Stalin's behest. From such a position, Dimitrov was eventually able to convince the reluctant Soviet leader of the need to overhaul existing Comintern policy.[42] As this suggests, Stalin's personal approval was by now essential to any change of Comintern line, and Soviet determinants were therefore integral to the Comintern's adoption of the popular front at its seventh world congress in 1935. Accordingly, the potential threat of an aggressive Nazi Germany, along with an array of internal Soviet factors, underlay the realignment of Comintern policy in 1934–35.

Clearly, Stalin took his time in recognizing the challenge of Nazism. Initially, he believed Hitler to be preoccupied with reversing the postwar Treaty of Versailles, and so focused on the West. A closer reading of *Mein Kampf*, however, would have awakened Stalin to the very real threat posed to the USSR by a man who considered Bolshevism to be part of a wider Jewish conspiracy, as well as by the connotations of *Lebensraum*. As it was, it took until 1934 before the Soviet leader began to take Hitler seriously, from which point Nazis were added to the list of anti-Soviet elements working in and against the USSR. In other words, the rise of Hitler added momentum to the politics of terror evolving within the Soviet Union over the 1930s.

Stalin's recalcitrance was, in part, due to his preoccupation with specifically Soviet concerns. By the mid-1930s, the USSR had ostensibly left the worst excesses of the 'great turn' behind. The second five-year plan (1933–37) encompassed more realizable targets than its predecessor; the cultural provisions promised under socialism spread across the USSR, literacy levels and educational opportunities continued to rise, communications improved, and measures were even taken to ensure that consumer goods became more widely available. To use Robert Service's description:

> Russian towns whose houses had been chiefly of wooden construction were becoming characterized by edifices of brick and stone; and most new dwellings were apartments in immense blocks whose heating was supplied by communal boilers … The internal combustion engine took the place of horse-drawn vehicles for people going about their working lives. Goods were transported in lorries. In Moscow, the first section of the underground railway came into operation in 1935.[43]

According to Stalin, as he introduced the new constitution of 1936, socialism had basically been realized in the USSR. Yet the Soviet Union was really still in the midst of transition. Life remained hard for most Soviet citizens, with shortages and queues a fact of everyday life; the collectivized peasants would hardly have concurred with Stalin's announcement that 'life has become better, life has become more joyful.'[44] At the same time as Stalin was publicly celebrating the achievements of the Soviet Union, therefore, anxieties remained within the Kremlin walls. The result was the unleashing of the Great Terror: a wave of repression that swept across the Soviet Union between 1936 and 1938 in an attempt finally to purge the USSR of potential and actual opposition.

The roots of the Great Terror were manifold. Of course, the Bolsheviks had used terror as a political weapon to win the civil war; the dictatorship of the proletariat was built on the notion of the state as a weapon in the hands of the ruling (working) class. What differentiated the policies of the mid-1930s, however, was the fact that terror was used not just against those openly opposed to the Soviet regime, but against members of the Communist Party itself. Equally, the scale of the Great Terror took on momentous proportions. Officially, 681,692 people were executed in 1937–38, although millions were caught up in the arrests and deportations to the *Gulag* that reached into every corner of Soviet society. First, those associated with former oppositions within the party (Trotskyists, etc.) were rounded up, before attention turned to anyone else whose actions – real or imagined – were deemed to impede the fulfilment of Soviet policy. Local party bosses, regional secretaries, and then members of the central committee were targeted, show trials of well known Bolsheviks were held, the military leadership was culled on the basis of a supposed plot against the party leadership, and arrest quotas were issued to the People's Commissariat of Internal Affairs (*Narodny Komissariat Vnutrennikh Del*, NKVD) to focus its search for anti-Soviet elements across the USSR. At its peak, three-man teams (usually comprising a local party secretary, an NKVD chief and a procurator) carried out the policy, with arbitrary powers of sentencing, including execution. According to Getty, the population of the *Gulag* had doubled to over 2 million by 1939.[45]

To understand such extremity, we have to return to the problems of the first five-year plan. First, to implement such a policy, the party and state apparatus expanded hugely, with Communist Party membership increasing from 1.25 million in 1928 to 3.3 million in 1933.[46] Second, the 'scientific' basis of communist policy meant that any problems encountered stemmed necessarily from its implementation. This raised two interrelated questions: how reliable were the new recruits, and were the problems of the plan due to mistakes or deliberate sabotage? In Stalin's words, speaking to the party congress in 1934:

[From] now on nine-tenths of the responsibility for the failures and defects in our work rests, not on objective conditions, but on ourselves alone ... Bureaucracy and red-tape in our administrative apparatus; idle chatter about 'leadership in general' instead of real and concrete leadership; the functional structure of our organizations and lack of individual responsibility; lack of personal responsibility in work and wage equalization; the absence of a systematic check upon the fulfillment of decisions; fear of self-criticism – these are the sources of our difficulties.[47]

The solution was to initiate in 1933 a purge of the party membership. Careerists, incompetents and fraudsters were obviously targeted, as were those with an insufficient ideological understanding of Marxism–Leninism; but so too were those who undermined party policy or failed to carry it out in a sufficiently rigorous manner. As a result, approximately 18 per cent of party members were expelled.[48] Increasingly, the party began to uncover evidence of mismanagement and abuse of position within its ranks. By 1934, Stalin was talking of regional party bosses acting like 'feudal princes', bringing to the surface tensions within the party's centralized structure exacerbated by the pressures of the five-year plans.

The problems and disruptions of the 'great turn' sparked fear of discontent within and outside the party. In 1932, a group based around the former Moscow District Secretary M. N. Riutin was discovered to have drawn up a 'platform' criticising Stalin's dictatorship; former oppositionists came under renewed suspicion; and Stalin spoke of capitalist encirclement and 'unhealthy moods' penetrating the party. Then, following the seventeenth party congress in 1934, rumour spread of comrades proposing Sergi Kirov as a potential alternative to Stalin. On 1 December, Kirov was assassinated, providing the pretext for emergency legislation against 'terrorist' activity and the beginning of a full-scale assault on Stalin's enemies. Thus Zinoviev and Kamenev were found guilty of 'moral complicity' in Kirov's murder, while the uncovering of a 'Zinoviev counter-revolutionary group' turned the NKVD's attention towards what can be termed political crimes. By 1936, therefore, discontent as a result of the party purge, mounting international tensions, the 'uncovering' of opposition groups within the Soviet Union and the continued problems of implementing the five-year plan combined to convince Stalin of the need to unleash the Great Terror.

Once up and running, the terror took on its own momentum. The NKVD, now in the charge of Nikolai Yezhov, worked hard to confirm Stalin's worst fears, uncovering supposed terrorist groups of Trotskyists and Zinovievists working in league with German, British or Japanese counterintelligence services. Meanwhile, party officials sought to protect their own backs via displays of loyalty and vigilance to the leadership. Given that guilt was proven by association, a single arrest or suspicion could set in motion a domino effect by which groups of people were enveloped in the terror's net. But while the terror fed upon itself, responsibility for its initiation, continuation, direction and, ultimately, its termination lay with Stalin. As always, his attempt to exert ultimate control over the interpretation, dissemination and implementation of Soviet policy led to a process of coercion and repression.

Not surprisingly, the terror also affected the Comintern. Suspicion of foreign sponsored espionage led the NKVD directly to the International, particularly those members of its national sections exiled or working in Moscow. Thus extensive screening processes were introduced to assess the loyalty and reliability of Comintern comrades and émigrés seeking safe harbour in the Soviet Union, while vigilance campaigns were instigated to root out the 'enemy within'.[49] From this, lists of potential suspects were drawn up, the Comintern apparatus was purged, and thousands of non-Russian communists were arrested and many executed. In particular, the German, Yugoslav, Polish, Latvian and Hungarian parties were hard-hit. More generally, the Comintern apparatus virtually ceased to function under such circumstances: from 1937 through to its dissolution in 1943, the Comintern really can be described as a mere appendage of the Soviet regime.

External communist policy in the mid-to-late 1930s centred on the United and Popular (People's) Front, launched officially at the seventh Comintern congress in July–August 1935. The united front of the working class against fascism envisaged that 'unity of action be established between all sections of the working class, irrespective of what organization they belong to.' Fascism, not social democracy, was now recognized as the 'bitterest enemy' of the workers. The popular front, meanwhile, allowed communist parties to align with 'progressive intellectuals' and the urban petty bourgeoisie, up to and including the formation of an anti-fascist people's government.[50] Such an approach was based on the Comintern's understanding of fascism as an 'open terrorist dictatorship of the most reactionary, most chauvinistic and most imperialist elements of finance capital', a relatively narrow definition that facilitated a cross-class response by distinguishing a 'fascist dictatorship' from a 'bourgeois democracy'. In the immediate situation, the struggle against fascism and in defence of the workers' interests was prioritized over the pursuit of proletarian revolution.[51] Concurrently, the Soviet Union was by this time seeking to ally with Britain and France against the fascist threat.

The more collaborative approach of the popular front certainly brought dividends for certain national parties, particularly those parties working openly in countries such as Britain, the USA and France. Membership and influence increased, with the French party contributing to the election of a popular front government in 1936. Not surprisingly, however, given the three-way antipathy that existed between communists, social democrats and liberals, unity was always tenuous at best. The French Communist Party (*Parti communiste français*, PCF) gained significant numerical and industrial strength as a result of its unity policy, but its relationship with the ensuing government was tempered by the strike wave that accompanied its election and the party's pro-Moscow foreign policy initiatives.[52] In Spain, the PCE found itself embroiled in a civil war against nationalist forces led by General Franco. Here, with Soviet support and an associated growth in communist influence, the republican cause was hampered by intraparty disputes over the objectives and approach to the civil war. In the event, Franco proved victorious, defeating the republic with aid from Germany and Italy.

The 'popular front' period encapsulated the two sides of communism. On the one hand, communists were to the fore in the struggle against fascism throughout much of Europe. Party members fought fascists on the streets – as in the famous 'battle' of Cable Street in London in 1936, where CPGB members helped mobilize against Sir Oswald Mosley's British Union of Fascists – and on the battlefields of Spain, where international brigades of volunteers endeavoured to defend the Spanish republic. On the other hand, the 1930s saw terror in the Soviet Union and unsavoury defences of Stalin's policy from each of the Comintern's national sections. Where communists claimed to defend democracy in one sentence, they would advocate ruthless repression in another: an incongruity that did much to undermine the popular front. Thus contradictions cut through the Comintern's approach to a popular front. Yet it was the political 'turn' of 1939 that most blatantly exposed the extent to which the international communist movement had become subordinate to the interests of the USSR.

Communism and World War Two

Our final 'period' of communist history pre-1945 relates directly to the outbreak and development of World War Two. In this, communist policy reflected the Soviet Union's relationship with Nazi Germany, beginning with the signing of the Nazi–Soviet non-aggression pact in August 1939, through to the Nazi invasion of the USSR in June 1941, and onto the dissolution of the Comintern in May 1943, initiated by Stalin as a sop to his wartime allies. In each instance, the international communist movement responded to specifically Soviet determinants, with Comintern theory and policy realigning itself to comply with the political-diplomatic manoeuvring of Stalin.

Having led the struggle against fascism for much of the 1930s, the Soviet Union made a U-turn when it concluded its pact with Nazi Germany. Without delving too deeply into the miasma of Soviet foreign policy, its 'logic' lay in Stalin's wish to avoid becoming embroiled in a wider European war, and the refusal of Britain and France to ally with the Soviet Union in opposition to fascism. It was following the Munich Agreement of 1938, whereby Anglo–French appeasement of Germany all but granted Hitler access to Czechoslovakia, that Stalin began to develop once again the idea of a second 'imperialist war'. Thus agreement with Hitler allowed the Soviet Union to proceed with its industrialization and secure its borders via the pact's 'secret' protocols, which redistributed Polish and Baltic territory between Germany and Russia. At the same time, Stalin presumed the Nazi regime would become entangled in a protracted war on the Western Front, so providing him with the freedom to proceed with the construction of socialism in the USSR.

Ideological justification for Stalin's policy was certainly possible from a (crude) Marxist point of view, although the secret terms of the pact were kept secret for good reason, and the new line rode roughshod over the Comintern's previous six years of struggle. More importantly, the line was imposed directly from the Kremlin, imparted to the Comintern and dispatched to the national sections without even the pretence of wider discussion. No concern was paid to the different sets of circumstances faced by the various Comintern sections, and no world congress was held to ratify the change of line. As such, the war was interpreted as a conflict between rival imperialist powers analogous to World War One, meaning that communists were to campaign against the war and against the imperialist motives of their own national governments. The destruction of Poland, meanwhile, was simply dismissed by Stalin as the loss of another 'bourgeois fascist state'.[53]

Comintern response to the Soviet Union's change of direction was initially ambiguous. Throughout late August and early September 1939, the Comintern executive had sought to balance Stalin's agreement with Germany with a continued struggle against fascist aggression elsewhere.[54] Parties such as the CPGB and PCF could thereby accept the non-aggression pact as a demonstration of the Soviet desire for peace, and campaign 'on two fronts' against fascism and bourgeois imperialism. Once the official line had been 'straightened' at Stalin's bequest, however, such a position became untenable, leading to the (temporary) resignation of Harry Pollitt as CPGB general secretary, and to serious divisions throughout the PCF. In both cases, the struggle against fascism was replaced by attacks on their respective governments' imperialist ambition and social democratic compliance: even support for a 'defensive war' against fascist aggression was proscribed. Yet it would be wrong to suggest that communists beyond the Soviet Union were uniformly aghast at such a shift in theory and practice. For many, the change of line was welcomed as conforming to a more Bolshevik – or revolutionary – precedent. Communists had no loyalty to bourgeois democracy, and although Lenin's notion of transforming a 'capitalist' war into a civil war was never raised by Stalin or the Comintern, it could be interpreted in such a way by those who wished to do so.

Of course, things changed immediately following the Nazi invasion of the Soviet Union on 22 June 1941. Indeed, the Comintern appeared to be softening its line before then, with the rapid collapse of France allowing the PCF in June 1940 to declare its willingness to fight 'foreign imperialism'. Twelve months later, the imperialist war became a struggle to save the USSR, with communists entering wholeheartedly into the allied war effort, forging underground resistance to occupation and, in the Yugoslav case, implementing a successful revolution. From a Soviet perspective, it became a great patriotic war, with Stalin making his peace with Britain and the USA, and the Red Army mobilizing to defeat Nazism. In the process, the Soviet Union suffered greatly. The industrial bias of the five-year plans ensured that the USSR was equipped for battle, but food shortages remained a problem even in the nation's capital. As the Nazis left devastation in their wake, so living conditions deteriorated throughout the Soviet Union. Even on the most modest recent estimates, the total death toll of Soviet citizens imposed by the war amounts to some 25 millions.

It was in such a context of war and desperation that Stalin initiated the dissolution of the Comintern in 1943. Already, from the outbreak of war, lines of communication throughout the international movement were broken and disrupted; the Comintern's headquarters were even moved out of Moscow in late 1941 as the Nazi advance continued. The Great Terror had, in any case, severely compromised Comintern organization; as the events of 1939 demonstrated, all pretence of the Comintern world congress representing the highest authority of the international communist movement had gone. By 1943, therefore, with Stalin pushing the allies to open a Western Front, the Comintern was effectively used as a bargaining chip. Due mention was given to Marx's winding up the First International, and differences in national circumstances were belatedly recognized, but such reasoning simply obscured the fact that the Comintern was deemed a hindrance to Soviet security and thereby dismissed accordingly. From here on, the revolution would be exported on the back of the Red Army, paving the way for the formation of an Eastern bloc at the war's end.

Conclusion

When assessing the international communist movement between 1917 and 1945, it is important to remember the objectives and ideals of those who passed through its ranks. Unlike fascism, to which Soviet communism is now often compared, communists envisaged an inclusive, classless society in which all worked for the common good. The roots of division – inequitable wealth, property ownerships, nationalism and the various forms of social inequality – were to be expunged; communists eulogized education, science and modernity. At a grassroots level, communists worked to improve the lives of workers and subjugated peoples throughout the world. They saw themselves as a bulwark against tyranny and oppression, and strove to overcome the inequities of capitalism in order to construct a modern, just and resourceful social order. That the Soviet Union encompassed much that was the antithesis of its stated objective is therefore a bitter historical irony.

Certainly, the Bolsheviks have a lot of blood on their hands. The October Revolution was peaceful enough, but the road to socialism was thereafter strewn with victims of terror, civil war and repression. The society constructed within the USSR was a closed one; by the 1930s, the state – with its sprawling apparatus – was an integral part of people's day-to-day life. At the same time, such bureaucratization gave rise to widespread abuse, waste and incompetence. Moreover, this tension between the assumption of central authority and the shortfall of achievement became a source of weakness within the USSR and throughout the international communist movement. There were achievements. The communist party undoubtedly succeeded in modernizing the Soviet Union. But, as with capitalism, this was realized at great human (and environmental) cost. A literate, educated society was also forged; the threat of terror was 'complemented' by the security of a welfare state; the defeat of fascism was largely dependent on the Red Army. Yet the USSR would consistently fall short of its aspiration. Economic development was uneven, shortages remained a constant of Soviet life, and the democracy supposedly encompassed in the Soviet system was a chimera.

Beyond the USSR, the communist movement found expression across the world. In some countries, national communist parties became – and remain – an important political presence. In others, including Britain, communists existed largely on the margins of political and social life. More generally, the failure of the revolution to spread into Europe after World War One ensured that communism was forever associated with its Russian advocates. Indeed, the 'Bolshevization' and 'Stalinization' of the Comintern are often described as amounting to the 'Russification' of the communist movement. By the late 1920s, the Comintern can be regarded as an extension of the Soviet state apparatus. This, in turn, meant that Soviet security concerns sometimes appeared to conflict with the objectives of European revolution. At other times, however, as in Germany in the early 1920s and in Spain in the late 1930s, Soviet and international concerns appeared to coalesce. Similarly, the notion of communists in Italy, Britain, New Zealand, Argentina or wherever being simple 'slaves' of Moscow is too simplistic. While communist parties submitted to Soviet ideological and political leads, their members endeavoured to act within an array of circumstances and contexts: indigenous influences and traditions continued to impinge on communist parties, particularly at the rank-and-file level. What is certain is that communism – and the very existence of the Soviet Union – proved integral to the wider history of the twentieth century, providing hope for some while encapsulating the worst fears of others. The tragedy is that something conceived as a force for good provoked some of the worst excesses of the modern age.

Further reading

Historical accounts of the Russian Revolution and the Soviet Union can be listed in their thousands, so the following recommendations should be regarded as but the tip of an enormous historiographical iceberg. In terms of a general introduction to the subject, R. Service, *A History of Twentieth Century Russia* (London: Allen Lane, 1997) is excellent, and should be read alongside S. Smith, *The Russian Revolution: A Very Short History* (Oxford: Oxford University Press, 2002); C. Read, *The Making and Breaking of the Soviet System* (Basingstoke: Macmillan, 2002); and S. Fitzpatrick, *The Russian Revolution* (Oxford: Oxford University Press, 2001 edn). For an insight into the 'nuts and bolts' of Soviet communism, see M. Sandle, *A Short History of Soviet Socialism* (London: UCL Press, 1999). For the more adventurous, E. H. Carr's exhaustive (14-volume) study of the revolution through to 1929 remains unsurpassed in terms of detail and breadth. Similarly, O. Figes,

A People's Tragedy: The Russian Revolution, 1891–1924 (London: Pimlico, 1996) is brilliant in its depiction of Russian society and politics either side of the 1917 revolutions. With regard to the leading Bolshevik politicians, the best English-language biographies are currently R. Service, *Lenin* (London: Belknap Press, 2002); R. Service, *Stalin* (London: Macmillan, 2005); S. Cohen, *Bukharin and the Bolshevik Revolution, 1888–1938* (New York; Knopf, 1975); and G. Swain, *Trotsky* (London: Pearson-Longman, 2006), but see also Isaac Deutscher's classic three-volume biography of Trotsky (London: Verso, 2003 edn); K. McDermott, *Stalin: Revolutionary in the Era of War* (Basingstoke: Macmillan, 2006); and D. Watson, *Molotov: A History* (Basingstoke: Macmillan, 2005). For digging deeper, Yale University's 'Annals of Communism' series is indispensable. In particular, see J. A. Getty, and O. Naumov (eds), *The Road to Terror: Stalin and the Self-Destruction of the Bolsheviks, 1932–39* (New Haven: Yale University Press, 1999). Equally, there are countless studies of key aspects of Soviet history and development. Among the best are S. Fitzpatrick, *Everyday Stalinism: Ordinary Life in Extraordinary Times: Soviet Russia in the 1930s* (Oxford: Oxford University Press, 1999); J. A. Getty, *Origins of the Great Purges: The Soviet Communist Party Reconsidered, 1933–38* (Cambridge; Cambridge University Press, 1985); G. Gill, *The Origins of the Stalinist Political System* (Cambridge: Cambridge University Press, 1990); M. Lewin, *The Making of the Soviet System* (London: Methuen, 1985); E. Mawdsley, *The Russian Civil War* (London: Allen and Unwin, 1987); L. H. Siegelbaum, *Soviet State and Society between Revolutions, 1918–29* (Cambridge: Cambridge University Press, 1992); and G. Swain, *Russia's Civil War* (Stroud: Tempus, 2000).

The essential introduction to the Communist International is K. McDermott and J. Agnew, *The Comintern: A History of International Communism from Lenin to Stalin* (Basingstoke: Macmillan, 1996). Then see also W. J. Chase and F. Firsov, *Enemies Within the Gates? The Comintern and the Stalinist Repression, 1936–39* (New Haven: Yale University Press, 2001); N. Laporte, K. Morgan and M. Worley (eds), *Bolshevism, Stalinism and the Comintern: Perspectives on Stalinization, 1917–53* (Basingstoke: Palgrave, 2008); T. Rees and A. Thorpe (eds), *International Communism and the Communist International, 1919–43* (Manchester: Manchester University Press, 1998); and M. Worley (ed.), *In Search of Revolution: International Communist Parties in the Third Period* (London: I. B. Tauris, 2004).

Finally, national histories of communist parties beyond the USSR vary in quality and quantity depending on the country under consideration. For some English-language texts relating to the German,

French and British parties, see B. Fowkes, *Communism in Germany under the Weimar Republic* (London: Macmillan, 1984); N. LaPorte, *The German Communist Party in Saxony, 1924–33: Factionalism, Fratricide and Political Failure* (Bern: Peter Lang, 2003); E. Rosenhaft, *Beating the Fascists? The German Communists and Political Violence, 1929–1933* (Cambridge: Cambridge University Press, 1983); E. D. Weitz, *Creating German Communism, 1890–1990: From Popular Protests to Socialist State* (Princeton: Princeton University Press, 1997); N. Fishman, *The British Communist Party and the Trade Unions, 1933–45* (Aldershot: Ashgate, 1995); K. Morgan, *Against Fascism and War: Ruptures and Continuities in British Communist Politics, 1935–41* (Manchester: Manchester University Press, 1989); K. Morgan, *Bolshevism and the British Left, Vols I–III* (London: Lawrence and Wishart, 2006); A. Thorpe, *The British Communist Party and Moscow, 1920–43* (Manchester: Manchester University Press, 2000); M. Worley, *Class against Class: The Communist Party in Britain between the Wars* (London: I. B. Tauris, 2002); M. Adereth, *The French Communist Party: A Critical History (1920–84) from Comintern to 'the Colours of France'* (Manchester: Manchester University Press, 1984); J. Jackson, *The Popular Front in France: Defending Democracy, 1934–38* (Cambridge: Cambridge University Press, 1988); and E. Mortimer, *The Rise of the French Communist Party, 1920–47* (London: Faber, 1984).

Notes

1 V. I. Lenin, *What is to be Done?* (London: Penguin, 1989 edn), p. 188.
2 K. Marx and F. Engels, 'Preface to the Russian Edition of 1882', in *The Manifesto of the Communist Part* (London: Lawrence and Wishart, 1975 edn), p. 6.
3 H. Pollitt, *Serving My Time: An Apprenticeship to Politics* (London: Lawrence and Wishart, 1941), pp. 91–2.
4 For reasons of space, and given the geographical focus of this book, I have concentrated on communism in Europe.
5 'Theses and Report on Bourgeois Democracy and the Dictatorship of the Proletariat', in A. Adler (ed.), *Theses, Resolutions and Manifestos of the First Four Congresses of the Third International* (London: Pluto Press, 1983 edn), p. 12.
6 'Letter of Invitation to the Congress', in A. Adler (ed.), *Theses, op. cit.*, pp. 1–6.
7 The phrases come from Trotsky's 'Manifesto of the Communist International to the Workers of the World', delivered to the first Comintern congress and dated 6 March 1919. See Adler (ed.), *Theses, op. cit.*, pp. 27–36.
8 S. A. Smith, *The Russian Revolution: A Very Short History* (Oxford: Oxford University Press, 2002), p. 44.
9 'Theses and Report on Bourgeois Democracy and the Dictatorship of the Proletariat', in A. Adler (ed.), *Theses, op. cit.*, p. 12.

10 S. Fitzpatrick, *The Russian Revolution* (Oxford: Oxford University Press, 1994), pp. 91–2; S. A. Smith, *The Russian Revolution, op. cit.*, p. 47.
11 For an excellent history of the civil war see G. Swain, *Russia's Civil War* (Stroud: Tempus, 2000).
12 C. Wrigley (ed.), *Challenges of Labour: Central and Western Europe, 1917–20* (London: Routledge, 1993).
13 'Theses of the Third World Congress on the International Situation and the Tasks of the Comintern', in A. Adler (ed.), *Theses, op. cit.*, p. 184.
14 *Ibid.*, pp. 184–203.
15 'On Tactics', delivered to the Third Comintern congress in summer 1921, in A. Adler (ed.), *Theses, op. cit.*, pp. 274–99.
16 *Inprecorr* [*International Press Correspondence*], 20 December 1926.
17 'Theses on the Economic Situation in Soviet Russia from the Standpoint of the Socialist Revolution', in A. Adler (ed.), *Theses, op. cit.*, pp. 336–45.
18 Quoted by M. Sandle, *A Short History of Soviet Socialism* (London: Routledge, 1999), p. 161.
19 M. Worley, *Class Against Class: The Communist Party of Great Britain between the Wars* (London: I. B. Tauris, 2002).
20 China was seen as the other 'success' of the united front policy, where the Chinese Communist Party (CCP) formed an alliance with the Nationalist Kuomintang. This, however, ended with Chiang Kai-Shek's bloody repression of the CCP.
21 See K. McDermott and J. Agnew, *The Comintern: A History of International Communism from Lenin to Stalin* (Basingstoke: Macmillan, 1996), p. 32.
22 'Theses on the Current Questions of the International Communist Movement', in J. Degras (ed.), *The Communist International, 1919–43: Documents, Volume II* (London: Frank Cass, 1971), p. 257.
23 'Theses on the Bolshevization of the Communist Parties', in J. Degras (ed.), *The Communist International, op. cit.*, pp. 188–200.
24 K. McDermott and J. Agnew, *The Comintern, op. cit.*, p. 79.
25 *Ibid.*, p. 58.
26 *Ibid.*, pp. 58–68.
27 For one example see K. McDermott, *The Czech Red Trade Unions, 1918–29: A Study of their Relationship with the Communist Party and the Moscow Internationals* (New York: Columbia University Press, 1988).
28 *Inprecorr*, 20 December 1926.
29 N. N. Kozlov and E. D. Weitz, 'Reflection on the Origins of the "Third Period": Bukharin, the Comintern, and the Political Economy of Weimar Germany', *Journal of Contemporary History* 24 (3): 387–410 (1989).
30 E. D. Weitz, *Creating German Communism, 1890–1990: From Popular Protests to Socialist State* (Princeton: Princeton University Press, 1997), p. 187.
31 *Inprecorr*, 4 November 1926; 3 December 1926.
32 'Resolution of the Seventh ECCI Plenum on the Chinese Situation', in J. Degras (ed.), *The Communist International, op. cit.*, p. 336.
33 S. A. Smith, *The Russian Revolution, op. cit.*, p. 124.
34 Quoted by S. Fitzpatrick, *The Russian Revolution, op. cit.*, p. 130.
35 Quoted by M. Sandle, *A Short History of Soviet Socialism, op. cit.*, p. 235.
36 N. N. Kozlov and E. D. Weitz, 'Reflections', *op. cit.*, p. 403.

37 Executive Committee of the Communist International, *The World Situation and the Economic Struggle: Theses of the World Plenum ECCI*, London, 1929, pp. 1–15.
38 K. McDermott and J. Agnew, *The Comintern, op. cit.*, p. 122.
39 See for example F. Borkenau, *World Communism: A History of the Communist International* (Ann Arbor: University of Michigan Press, 1971), pp. 351–2.
40 J. Degras (ed.), *The Communist International, op. cit.*, pp. 252–54; E. H. Carr, *Twilight of the Comintern, 1930–35* (Basingstoke: Macmillan, 1982), p. 85.
41 K. McDermott and J. Agnew, *The Comintern, op. cit.*, pp. 120–30; J. Jackson, *The Popular Front in France: Defending Democracy, 1934–38* (Cambridge: Cambridge University Press, 1988).
42 A. Dallin and F. I. Firsov (eds), *Dimitrov and Stalin, 1934–43: Letters from the Soviet Archives* (New Haven: Yale University Press, 2000), pp. 7–43.
43 R. Service, *A History of Twentieth Century Russia* (London: Penguin, 1997), p. 192.
44 Quoted by S. Fitzpatrick, *Everyday Stalinism: Ordinary Life in Extraordinary Times: Soviet Russia in the 1930* (Oxford: Oxford University Press, 1999), p. 6.
45 J. Arch Getty and O. V. Naumov, *The Road to Terror: Stalin and the Self-destruction of the Bolsheviks, 1932–3* (New Haven: Yale University Press, 1999), p. 590.
46 T. H. Rigby, *Communist Party Membership in the USSR* (Princeton: Princeton University Press, 1968), p. 52.
47 Stalin's Speech to the Seventeenth Party Congress, 28 January 1934, in J. Arch Getty and O. V. Naumov, *The Road to Terror, op. cit.*, pp. 129–34.
48 'On Purging the Party', Supplement to the Protocol of the CC of the [CPSU], 28 April 1933, in J. Arch Getty and O. V. Naumov, *The Road to Terror, op. cit.*, pp. 124–5.
49 W. J. Chase, *Enemies Within the Gate: The Comintern and the Stalinist Repression, 1934–39* (New Haven: Yale University Press, 2001).
50 'Resolution on Fascism, Working Class Unity, and the Tasks of the Comintern', 20 August 1935, in J. Degras (ed.), *The Communist International Volume 3, op. cit.*, pp. 350–70.
51 See G. Dimitrov, *The Working Class against Fascism* (London: Martin Lawrence, 1935).
52 J. Jackson, *The Popular Front in France, op. cit.*
53 K. McDermott and J. Agnew, *The Comintern, op. cit.*, p. 193.
54 *Ibid.*, pp. 192–3.

7 Fascism: a 'revolutionary right' in interwar Europe

António Costa Pinto

When, on 23 March 1919 in Milan, around 100 people attended a meeting at which Benito Mussolini officially launched fascism, those present could not have imagined that they were coining what would become one of the twentieth century's most used concepts.[1] Yet it is here that we must begin, as part of the ideological and political character of the founding group gave identifying traits to a 'generic fascism' that appeared throughout Europe during the first half of the twentieth century. The 'revolutionary', 'anti-capitalist' and radical nationalist discourse; the 'militarized party', the anti-communism and the radical critique of liberal democracy; the electoral tactics and the political violence – all of these became regular features of fascism, irrespective of its national variations.[2]

At the beginning of the 1930s, when Mussolini was creating his New State from his position of authority, and National Socialism was being transformed into a movement with large electoral support, almost all European countries had parties of their own broadly similar to these. Although the factors that conditioned their emergence and the degree of their success varied from case to case, they were all easily identified by the common citizen as 'fascist'. The speed with which at least some of them obtained power had an appropriate symbol: Mussolini had become head of government only three years after the foundation of his party.

In 1932, Oswald Mosley founded the British Union of Fascists in the UK and Rolão Preto created the National Syndicalist Movement (*Movimento Nacional-Sindicalista*, MNS) in Portugal.[3] The following year, José Antonio Primo de Rivera established the Falange (*Falange Española*) in Spain, and Vidkun Quisling set up National Unity (*Nasjonal Samling*) in Norway.[4] Despite failing to achieve significant electoral success within the democracies, the diversity of their destinies typifies much of the history of fascist parties between the wars. While Mosley never seriously troubled Britain's democracy (see Chapter 8), the MNS was banned in 1934 by Portugal's new Catholic dictator, António de Oliveira Salazar. In neighbouring Spain, following the execution of its leader and despite its weak electoral support, the Falange lent some of its programme and political activism to General Franco, where it was transformed into the founding nucleus of his single party after his victory over the Spanish Second Republic. In Norway it was thought that, following defeat after defeat within the parliamentary system, there was no room for local fascism; however, the German occupation in 1940 changed Quisling's luck and raised him to a position of prominence even if the Nazis never allowed him real power. The 'new order' in Nazi-occupied Europe was incoherent, and many fascist groups died at the hands of their right-wing competitors. This was to be the fate of what had been perhaps the most successful fascist movement in eastern Europe, the Iron Guard (*Garda de Fier*), which, after briefly holding power in Romania, was eliminated by General Antonescu.[5]

The enemies of fascism readily bracketed it with many other movements of the extreme right. Yet its relations with rival conservative and right-wing parties and groups were not always easy. The consolidation of dictatorships involved various combinations. In the cases of Italy and Germany, the fascists dominated. In some instances, such as Franco's Spain and Dollfuss's Austria, they became junior parties in right-wing anti-democratic coalitions. There was also the kind of relationship which, in the further case of Salazar's Portugal (or indeed, overseas, in Getúlio Vargas's Brazil), led to fascism's eventual elimination.

Such tactical ambiguities, together with the Nazis' radical contribution to bringing about World War Two and the Holocaust, have made fascism and its legacy a fiercely debated topic. Since the 1930s, many observers and researchers have regularly returned to the classic questions: who were the fascists? how did they grow? who supported them? and what were the conditions most conducive to their rise? The structure of this chapter chiefly follows the three-stage cycle of fascism: (1) the creation of the movements and their role in the interwar political spectrum; (2) the seizure of power; and (3) the exercise of power. However, we need first to make a small detour into the world of definitions, which are particularly extensive in this subject.

Defining fascism

The sociologist Michael Mann has presented a particularly useful definition of fascism, in which he identifies three fundamentals: 'key values, actions and power organizations'. He sees it as 'the pursuit of a transcendent and cleansing nation-statism through paramilitarism.'[6] This suggests five essential aspects, some of which have internal tensions:

1 Nationalism: the 'deep and populist commitment to an "organic" or "integral" nation'.
2 Statism: the goals and organizational forms that are involved when the organic conception imposes an authoritarian state 'embodying a singular, cohesive will [as] expressed by a party elite adhering to the "leadership principle"'.
3 Transcendence: the typical neither/nor of fascism as a 'third way' – that is, as something transcending the conventional structures of 'left' and 'right'. Mann stresses that the core constituency of fascist support can be understood only by taking their aspirations to transcendence seriously. 'Nation and state comprised their centre of gravity: not class.'
4 Cleansing: 'Most fascisms entwined both ethnic and political cleansing, though to differing degrees.'
5 Paramilitarism: as a key element both in values and in organizational form. Like previous analysts, Mann stresses 'what essentially distinguishes fascists from many military and monarchical dictatorships of the world is [the] "bottom-up" and violent quality of its paramilitarism. It could bring popularity, both electorally and among elites.'

All this is not too far removed from other definitions of fascism, notably that suggested by Stanley Payne in his wide-ranging study.[7] For Robert Paxton, 'Fascism may be defined as a form of political behaviour marked by obsessive preoccupation with community decline, humiliation or victim-hood, and by compensatory cults of unity, energy and purity, in which a mass-based party of committed nationalist militants, working in uneasy but effective collaboration with traditional elite groups, abandons democratic liberties and pursues with redemptive violence and without ethical or legal restraints goals of internal cleansing and external expansion.'[8]

Some points are common to the definitions offered by Mann and Paxton. Perhaps the most important is the emphasis on ideology, collective action and organization. This allows Paxton to stress that 'what fascists did tells us at least as much as what they said.'[9] Or, as Mann puts it, 'without power organizations, ideas cannot actually do anything' – which means that we must add programmes, actions and organizations to the analysis.[10] Such approaches illustrate the more general point that, in recent years, the comparative study of fascism has become increasingly concerned with ideological and cultural dimensions – at times becoming ideology-centred. We could even say that the analysis of so-called generic fascism has moved from a sociological to a more political perspective, giving both ideology and culture much more importance than previously.

The fascists: where, when, who, how and why?

While acknowledging that the culture of fascism extended to other continents (most notably Latin America), most historians would agree with Roger Eatwell's description of it as being 'European-epochal'.[11] This reflects a consensus about its main placement in terms not simply of geography but also of periodization, with particular reference to the years between 1918 and 1945.

From the beginning of the twentieth century, several movements and ideological currents were already coming to embody some of the cultural and political principles from which the magma of fascism was to emerge. Historians such as Zeev Sternhell attempted to prove that the ideological synthesis of fascism was born in France on the eve of World War One.[12] Without doubt, it is possible to identify doctrinal precursors of fascism within that country: the radical 'socialist nationalism' of Maurice Barrès; the integral nationalism of Charles Maurras's neoroyalist *Action Française*; and the revolutionary syndicalism of Georges Valois. A large part of what was to become the fascist programme – with its radical nationalism, its antidemocratic stance, its communitarian and corporatist alternative and its antisocialist 'third way' – were all present in the European cultural milieu from the beginning of the century. However, it is equally important to recognize that fascism cannot be separated from a new type of political formation that appeared in the wake of the 1914–18 conflict: the 'revolutionary' militia party. Adopting the rhetoric of 'neither left nor right', the fascists relied here on an innovative brand of organization that was characteristic of the era of mass movements and of postwar European democratization.

Where do the fascists fit into the political scene of interwar Europe? Michael Mann frames the growth of fascism around four crises: 'war between mass citizen armies; severe class conflict exacerbated by the Great Depression; the political crises arising from the attempts of many countries at a rapid transition toward a democratic nation-state; and a cultural sense of civilisational contradiction and decay.'[13] Although these crises weakened the ability of elites to perpetuate their natural role as leaders within society, fascism offered solutions in every case. With further reference to these challenges, Mann suggests that this type of movement 'was strongest where we find distinct combinations of all four'. The problem remains, however, that many of the cleavages analysed previously are really those of authoritarianism in general.

Italian Fascism presented itself as an anti-party that was particularly hostile to communism. It had its own progressive social programme, with nationalism as the driving force of its political action. The initial anticapitalist features were very quickly removed from the movement's agenda following its failure in the 1919 elections. However, the most important change took place in 1920, with the emergence of *squadrismo* in the agricultural areas of the Po Valley and Tuscany. Having begun as a largely urban Jacobin and revolutionary movement, fascism now acquired the profile of an armed militia financed by the rural landowners and in violent conflict with the socialists and agricultural unions. In a very short space of time, it won over many supporters through a more authoritarian nationalist programme. At the end of 1920, the movement had more than 20,000 members. In May 1921 it possessed 35 parliamentary deputies, and by July its membership was approaching 200,000.[14]

The confirmation of Mussolini as the undisputed leader of the party was no easy task, as part of his success rested with the *ras* (powerful local party chiefs) who did not always accept the pacts he attempted to negotiate with the conservatives when they imposed limitations on *squadrista* violence. It was only with some difficulty that Mussolini was able to transform the Fasci into the National Fascist Party (*Partito Nazionale Fascista*, PNF), which consecrated the position of *Il Duce*. Although it was a minority element at the parliamentary level, the PNF very rapidly developed into a mass party of the new militia kind – not only because of its armed units, but also 'because its organisation, its political culture, its ideology and its way of life were derived from *squadrismo*.'[15]

The seizure of power in Italy was the product of a series of crises, in which the fascists became active participants. Despite the choreography of the March on Rome, they were called to power by the King under the terms of the constitution. However, a role was also played by the fascist activities that were taking place under the cover of a semi-peaceful insurrection – one that resulted in the occupation of dozens of public buildings, train stations and other locations without any repressive response from the government. Military intervention might have resolved the situation, but, as this did not occur, Mussolini was able to negotiate his takeover of power with the liberal politicians. While Italy had to wait one more year for fascist dictatorship to assert itself fully, the truth remains that 'for the first time in the history of the European liberal democracies, parliamentary government had been entrusted to the leader of a militia party who repudiated the values of liberal democracy and proclaimed the revolutionary intention of transforming the State in an anti-democratic direction'.[16]

Compared with the Italian fascist movement, Nazism in Germany consolidated itself much more slowly, but then arrived in power with a greater political and electoral strength. When, in 1921, Adolf Hitler imposed himself as the leader of the small extremist racist grouping that Anton Drexler had founded two years before, the programme of the new National Socialist German Workers' Party (*Nationalsozialistische Deutsche Arbeiterpartei*, NSDAP) underwent some conservative alterations. The most fundamental changes took place in the party's discourse and in its organization. Hitler's targets were the humiliation caused by the Versailles Treaty, together with the Jewish and Marxist conspiracies that had served to bring this about. As for the structural shifts, these included a concentration of leadership in one person who was renowned for his oratorical skills, increased discipline within the party's paramilitary formation, and the creation of the Protective Squadron (*Schutzstaffel*, SS) as a squad of personal bodyguards for the Führer.

In November 1923, Hitler became increasingly visible in the press, having led, with General Ludendorff, the attempted Munich Putsch, following which the Nazi party was banned and Hitler sentenced to five years' imprisonment. However, the Nazi leader was only to serve nine months, during which time he wrote the first part of *Mein Kampf*, a confused mixture of political ideas. In 1926, the party was restored to legality, and Hitler succeeded in controlling its local bosses and in returning to its leadership after outmanoeuvring his rival Gregor Strasser.

The economic crisis and its impact on the young Weimar democracy was reflected in the electoral polarization that favoured Hitler much more clearly than fascists in any other democracy. Between 1928 and 1930, the Nazi party's support increased from 2.6 to 18.3 per cent. Under conditions of mass unemployment, increasingly authoritarian measures and some political violence, the NSDAP won the biggest share of the vote (37.3 per cent) in the elections of June 1932. Although this decreased to 33.1 per cent in a further poll five months later, Nazism had more popular backing than its Italian counterpart ten years earlier, maintaining the characteristics of a fascist party with an extremist programme and a paramilitary praxis. Like Mussolini, Hitler arrived in power by broadly constitutional means, occupying the Reich Chancellery at the invitation of President Hindenburg. Although several conservative politicians pressed for this choice in January 1933,

Hitler then proceeded swiftly to marginalize them. Furthermore, the pace at which he dismantled the democratic system and dealt with dissident elements among his own *Sturmabteilung* stormtroopers was similarly impressive.

What did fascism offer the conservatives in Italy and Germany that led them to choose the fascist option instead of other possible alternatives? As Paxton puts it, 'the fascists offered a new recipe for governing with popular support, but without any sharing of power with the left, and without any threat to conservative social and economic privileges and political dominance.'The conservatives, for their part, held the keys to the door of power.'[17] At the beginning of the 1930s, with the rise of German National Socialism and Italian Fascism, the effect of contagion began to be very significant, and in almost every European country, broadly similar parties emerged. However, the successes of Hitler and Mussolini were not easily replicated. Not all the crises of democracy provoked a distinctively fascist response. This is particularly true where the authoritarian elite held power without fascist help. As we will see below, conservative regimes often provided unfavourable terrain for fascism to reach power. In some other cases, it was the decision of the conservatives that was at the root of fascist success. In Italy and Germany, the crises favoured the fascists and they were co-opted into power.

The role of the masses in the crisis of interwar democracies also needs some clarification. Most cases of authoritarian takeover in Europe during the 1920s and 1930s involved a problem that can be usefully analysed through the model of 'polarized pluralism' developed by Giovanni Sartori. He states that 'party systems (and the party elite) must restrain the forces of polarity inherent in political democracies. If party systems fail to constrain both the ideological range and the number of parties ... centrifugal forces will tear democracy apart.'[18] However, as Nancy Bermeo suggests, ordinary people are the 'stonemasons of polarization' in only a very small number of cases.[19] Thus it can be argued that elite polarization was much more important in the breakdown of democracy during the epoch in question.

In the case of France, historians have devised an abundance of classificatory polemics concerning extreme right-wing movements during the interwar period, and it has often been asserted by French writers that the country possessed an allergy to fascism.[20] Although these organizations came close to subverting the democratic order in 1934, their success had to await the coming of World War Two. During the 1930s, the many French extraparliamentary leagues developed more or less obvious links with employers' groups, the royalist elite, and traditionalist Catholics.[21] They also joined together in 1934 in a number of violent antigovernment demonstrations with conspiratorial undertones. Of the numerous extreme-right bodies, the most important was Colonel de La Rocque's *Croix de Feu* (Cross of Fire). However, the victory of the left in the 1936 elections and the formation of a Popular Front government led to bans on most of the leagues. In this same year, Jacques Doriot, a dissident communist, created the French Popular Party (*Parti Populaire Français*, PPF), which was the most 'working-class' of the fascist groupings. However, the most serious challenge once again stemmed from the *Croix de Feu*, which translated itself into a political party, the French Social Party (*Parti Social Français*, PSF). According to Paxton, the PSF was the only far-right movement 'that achieved mass catch-all party status between 1936 and 1940', with a radical nationalist and antiparliamentary programme that was nevertheless not antisemitic.[22] When La Rocque turned to the electoral struggle, he moderated his programme and abandoned his paramilitary style; however, he was never to compete directly for votes, as the 1940 elections did not take place because of the advent of war.

The Rexist movement founded by Léon Degrelle in Belgium sprang from Catholic traditionalism. Degrelle was a young militant, whose journal *Christus Rex* (*Christ the King*) challenged the Catholic Party's moderation. Rexism was largely inspired by Italian Fascist corporatism and by the traditional Catholic values of order and family. It erupted onto the political scene in 1936 when, even while still being organizationally weak, it obtained 11.5 per cent of the overall vote and showed some particular appeal to the Walloon community. In the same elections, its counterpart in the Dutch-speaking areas, the Flemish National League (*Vlaams Nationaal Verbond*, VNV), won 7.1 per cent. Waving the banner of authoritarian independence from francophone domination, the VNV was in contact with the Nazi movement from an early stage, and was chosen in 1940 by the German occupiers as their main point of positive contact with Belgian sympathizers. Isolated by the Catholic church, Rex was electorally and politically finished in 1939, when the VNV took 15 per cent of the vote in Flanders. The two movements were to converge in their collaboration with Nazism after the occupation, when both became active within the SS.[23]

Several other democracies survived until 1939. This was notably true of the Netherlands, Denmark and Norway, where small fascist parties, strongly influenced by Nazism, attempted to destabilize democracy. In the Netherlands, this influence was flagrant in the National Socialist Movement (*Nationaal-Socialistische Beweging*, NSB), which was founded in 1931 by Anton Mussert, and which had a programme that was practically copied from that of the Nazis. The NSB enjoyed some success in the 1935 regional elections, when it managed to elect four deputies, yet Mussert was isolated by both left and right until the German occupation.[24] In neighbouring Denmark, the Danish National Socialist Workers' Party (*Danmarks Nationalsocialistiske Arbejderparti*), founded in 1930, never managed to attract more than 1.8 per cent of the electorate, and was largely ignored during the German occupation. The same happened in prewar Norway and Sweden, where the coalitions of conservatives and socialists were powerful obstacles to fascism's antisystem dynamic.

The fascist movements were important actors in the democratic crises of the interwar period, even though in most countries they failed to achieve power at that stage. Some of the transitions to authoritarianism that occurred during the 1920s and 1930s involved ruptures with democracy that were simply violent, while others (such as the German and Italian cases) featured a more 'legal' assumption of power. There was, however, no strict correlation between either of these initial modes and the particular form taken by the radicalization that then occurred during the process of consolidating such dictatorships. Salazar in Portugal and Smetona in Lithuania, who arrived in power after a *coup d'état*, or Franco, whose rise was the result of a civil war, had much greater room for manoeuvre than either Mussolini or Hitler, who both achieved their positions through 'legal' routes and with the support of a radical right that was less inclined towards charismatic and totalitarian adventures.[25] The differences between these cases lay, above all, in the type of party and of leader that dominated the transitional process.

Exercising power

It is much easier to identify a fascist movement than a fascist regime. For many historians, only the dictatorships of Mussolini and Hitler can be truly classified as fascist, although it is obvious that their 'political engineering' once in government partially inspired some other European regimes during the 1930s. What was it, then, that distinguished fascism in power from the other right-wing dictatorships of the twentieth century?

Fascism in power was a powerful amalgam of different but broadly compatible conservative, fascist and radical-right ingredients 'bound together by common enemies'.[26] The question as to who dominates seems to be the vital issue. Paxton distinguishes between the regimes according to those tensions between certain poles of power that he describes as 'the four-way struggle for dominance':

> The fascist leader; his party (whose militants clamoured for jobs, perquisites, expansionist adventures, and the fulfilment of some elements of their early radical programme); the state apparatus (functionaries such as police and military commanders, magistrates, and local governors); and finally civil society (holders of social, economic, political, and cultural power such as professional associations, leaders of big business and big agriculture, churches, and conservative political leaders). These four-way tensions gave these regimes their characteristic blend of febrile activism and shapelessness.[27]

While the taking of power was possible only with the support of other conservative and authoritarian groups, the nature of the leadership and its relationship with the party appears to be the fundamental variable. As several historians have observed, the crucial element is 'to what extent the fascist component emancipated itself from the initial predominance of its traditional conservative sponsors and to what degree it departed – once in power – from conventional forms/objectives of policy-making towards a more radical direction.'[28]

Italian Fascism and German National Socialism were each attempts to create a charismatic leadership and a 'totalitarian tension' that was, in one form or another, also present in other dictatorships of the period.[29] After taking power, both these movements became powerful instruments of a 'new order', agents of a 'parallel administration', and promoters of innumerable tensions within dictatorial political systems. Transformed into single parties, they flourished as the breeding ground for a new political elite and as agents for a new mediation between the state and civil society. The ensuing tensions between their own monolithic structure and the apparatus of the state produced new patterns of political decision-making that concentrated power in the hands of Mussolini and Hitler, but which also removed it from the government and the ministerial elite, who were often increasingly subordinated to the single party and its 'parallel administration'.

Even so, the party and its ancillary organizations were not simply parallel institutions. They attempted to gain control of the bureaucracy and select the governing elite, thereby not only forcing some dictatorships towards an unstable equilibrium, but also becoming the central agents for the creation and maintenance of the leader's charismatic authority. The gradation of these tensions, which may be illustrated by the eventual emergence of a weaker or stronger 'dualism of power', appears to be the best determining factor when trying to classify the kinds of dictatorship that historically have been associated with fascism. These have been most typically categorized either as 'authoritarian' and 'totalitarian', or as 'authoritarian' and 'fascist'.[30]

Mussolini and Italian fascism

While Mussolini obtained power with the assistance of the PNF, the subsequent dismantling of the democratic regime was slow, and the reduced social and political influence of the party obliged Mussolini to accept compromises with the monarchy and the armed forces, as well as with other institutions such as the Catholic Church. The consolidation of the dictatorship had to involve the imposition of a greater degree of discipline within the party, whose actions during the initial phase of Mussolini's regime had not simply undermined the compromises essential for its institutionalization, but also threatened to increase the tensions within the tripartite system of party, dictator and state. Viewed overall, this Italian case was illustrative of takeover by a 'united political elite', whose base was a fascist party that was transformed into the primary motor for the institutionalization of the dictatorship and, from the 1930s, into the main instrument for the 'totalization' of power.

At times, Mussolini did use the party to abandon his concessions to bureaucratic–legal legitimacy, although he lacked the courage and the opportunity to abolish the monarchy and thus to eliminate the diarchy he had inherited.[31] When what remained of the liberal legacy was crushed during the latter half of the 1930s and when, under Starace, the PNF proposed the conquest of civil society, Mussolini's attempts to enhance his personal and charismatic authority through the party, state and cultural machines culminated in the creation of the 'cult of *Il Duce*'.[32] Several historians have suggested that it was this which signalled the completion of a shift from 'authoritarian' to 'totalitarian' fascism, both of which tendencies had coexisted during the earlier phases of the dictatorial consolidation.

Mussolini progressively abolished the formal limits to his power. In 1926, the PNF became *de facto* Italy's sole party. Two years later the Fascist Grand Council, the PNF's supreme body since 1923, was transformed into a state institution under Mussolini's leadership. This marked, at the very peak of the fascist political system, a fusion of party and state effected in a manner that did not subordinate the former to the latter. If the government had ceased to be a collegiate body when confronted by the Duce's all-powerful secretariat, the

Grand Council was transformed into the main focus of state–party union from above, even while remaining subordinate to the dictator. The secretary of the PNF, who was also secretary of the Grand Council, became the second most important figure of Italian fascism. The abolition of the Chamber of Deputies, the last vestige of liberal representation, led to the creation of the Fascist and Corporate Chamber (*Camara degli Fasci e delle Corporazione*), of which the PNF's leaders became automatic members.

Once Mussolini's regime had been consolidated, its ministerial elite was overwhelmingly dominated by men who had been fascists from the very earliest days. With the exception of military officers, nearly all of them were also members of the Fascist Grand Council. Ministers, undersecretaries and presidents of both Parliament and Senate came, almost without exception, from this inner circle. Before they entered government, the main emblematic figures of Italian fascism – men such as Dino Grandi, Italo Balbo and Giuseppe Bottai (PNF *ras* in Bologna, Ferrara and Rome respectively) – had all participated in the *squadristi*-led violence of the early 1920s. The few mainly conservative and monarchist officers of the armed forces who also rose to ministerial rank generally followed a path similar to that of Emilio de Bono, who joined the PNF in 1922 and then served in the fascist militia before achieving this political promotion.

As the sole arbitrator of an often unstable equilibrium between the party, the government and the administration, Mussolini reserved to himself the final say on all disputed political issues. From this perspective, the Duce matches the classic model of the 'strong dictator'. Yet his powers should not be overstated. Even though his cabinet was undoubtedly devalued in relation to the Grand Council, the relationship between Mussolini (who himself at times took direct responsibility for up to six departments) and his ministers remained a significant element in the policy-making process.

Despite having been transformed into a heavy – and sometimes clientelistic – machine, the PNF elite always included a large number of fascists who had joined the movement before the March on Rome.[33] The militia was the first institution to be taken out of the party's control and placed under Mussolini's direct command. The political police were never independent of the state, although several of the mass organizations (and particularly those involving youth, women or the working classes) were subjected to many different transfers. In this way, the PNF gathered to itself increasing control over the popular mass bodies. The National Workers' Recreational Organisation (*Opera Nazionale Dopolavoro*), a cultural grouping within the economics ministry, was the object of some rivalry between the ministry of corporations and the PNF before responsibility for it was finally placed with the latter in 1927, by which stage it was the largest mass organization within the regime.[34] A similar process was to take place in relation to the youth groups, which were initially voluntary bodies within the PNF. In 1929, however, responsibility for them was transferred to the ministry of education. A few years later, with Starace as its Secretary, the party regained control over them, and in 1937 they were amalgamated into a single youth movement, the *Gioventù Italiana del Littorio*. The monopoly over the political socialization of youth was not only a source of tension between the PNF and the state, but also involved the Catholic Church, which saw its independent Catholic Action youth organizations alternately tolerated and dissolved.[35] The PNF was also involved in the trade unions (syndicates). During the initial period, it had its own syndicates over which it maintained indirect control, as the interference of party organizations was recognized by the corporatist apparatus. The complementary nature of the relationship between the state and the party was also significant within the women's organizations, from the *Fasci Femminile* to the *Massaie Rurali*, in which the PNF invested heavily throughout the 1930s after earlier hesitations.[36]

By the eve of World War Two, Italian fascism had clearly evolved from one phase, which many historians describe as 'authoritarian', to another that was more 'totalitarian'. This was evident in the alliance with Nazi Germany, in the introduction of antisemitic legislation (1938), in the attempts to permeate Italian society with fascist values, and in the regime's expansionist imperialism. The decision to enter the war on the side of Germany was taken against the opinion of the most conservative sections of the Catholic Church, and was pursued partly through an imperialist desire to secure Italy as the hegemonic power in the Mediterranean and the southern Balkans. The military disasters experienced by the Axis after 1942 led, on the night of 25 July 1943, to the Fascist Grand Council dismissing Mussolini and restoring power to King Victor Emmanuel: a move that provoked the collapse of the Fascist regime. Having escaped detention with the assistance of Nazi forces, Mussolini established the Republic of Salò in German-occupied northern Italy. This new regime was riven by conflict between anti-fascist partisans and 'fascist republicans', and never amounted to anything more than a puppet of the Nazi Reich.

Hitler and German National Socialism

Hitler's dictatorship was much closer than Mussolini's to the model of charismatic leadership associated with fascist rule, and the Nazi party and its militias exercised a greater influence over both the political system and civil society.[37] Although in the immediate aftermath of Hitler's rise to power he had to overcome some opposition from elements within the NSDAP's own *Sturmabteilung* militia, it was his own firm control over Europe's most powerful fascist party that contributed towards the weakening of authoritarian decision-making within strictly state structures. Thus the Führer came to operate personally at the top of a system in which the 'coexistence [of] and conflict [between] uncoordinated authorities very often undermin[ed] solidarity and uniformity in the exercise of power.'[38] Whether as part of a deliberate strategy, or merely as a consequence of Hitler's leadership personality, this also provoked a multiplication of *ad hoc* decisions and ensured there would be no real or formal limits to his authority. Despite this concentration of power, his political and ideological beliefs led him to immerse himself excessively in such matters as the military and strategic defence and expansion of the Third Reich, at the expense of the 'command and control' dimension of the administration and of day-to-day domestic politics.

The Nazi cabinet was quickly transformed into a bureaucratic body totally subservient to Hitler. Even in this condition, it ceased to exist as a collegiate body because political power within the state was simultaneously concentrated in Hitler and dispersed throughout the various Nazi institutions, thus severely undermining ordinary governmental processes. In 1937, with Hans Heinrich Lammers as head of the Reich chancellery, ministerial access to Hitler became more difficult as he deliberately reduced the cabinet's status.[39] At the same time, the party-based secretariat of the Deputy Führer, headed by Rudolf Hess and later by Martin Bormann, moved closer to Hitler.

The tensions created by the legality of the Nazi takeover and the rapid development of Hitler's charismatic leadership were resolved by the publication of a series of decrees that conveyed total power to him, obliging the ministers to answer only to the dictator.[40] The NSDAP, even while experiencing internal crises, set about assuming control of the existing state apparatus and creating a parallel structure, in the process of which it multiplied and confused the spheres of decision-making in several areas of national and regional authority.[41] The existence of a large administration of NSDAP functionaries was symbolic of a revolutionary strategy. This aimed at undermining much of the previous pattern of bureaucratic control (although 'the Nazi leadership always relied on the old elite to maintain the essential functions of government', particularly within German territory as distinct from the eastern occupied territories, where party officials were more important).[42] The increasing legislative confusion that surrounded attempts to interpret the leader's will represents the most extreme subversion of the traditional methods of political decision-making employed by dictatorships. Not only did the bureau of the Deputy Führer as administered by Bormann become the most important channel to Hitler, but it also obtained some control over the government. Simultaneously, the party achieved political and financial autonomy, and developed as a parallel state apparatus.

According to Martin Broszat, three distinct centres of power began to emerge within a structure that was in a tense and unstable balance: 'the single party monopoly, the centralised governmental dictatorship and the absolutism of the Führer … undermin[ed] the unity of the government and the monopoly of government by the Reich cabinet.'[43] Special authorities, which were under Hitler's direct control, soon developed alongside the ministries at the same time as several political and police organizations, some of which were controlled by the NSDAP and others by the SS, began to act independently of the government. Among the former were organizations such as the German Road System and the German Labour Front (*Deutsche Arbeitsfront, DAF*), together with others that were more overtly political and repressive. Within the second category, we must include the Hitler Youth (*Hitler Jugend*). While still under the party's control, this was transformed into a Reich authority completely independent of the Ministry of Education. Thus it became a counterweight both to that ministry and to the armed forces in matters of political and ideological training. Heinrich Himmler's SS is a further example of this pattern. Its gradual assumption of the policing functions previously assigned to the interior ministry operated in a complex manner that generated innumerable tensions. Although the SS remained at least formally reliant on the party and on the state, it 'had detached itself from both and had become independent'.[44] Wilhelm Frick's interior ministry was thus emasculated of any practical authority over the police, just as the position of the minister of labour was partially weakened by the DAF's independence. It has to be admitted that the 'Nazification' of government bureaucracy was at times more superficial than real. Even so, those organizations that developed under Hitler into parallel party-based administrations represent the most extreme examples of the ways in which a fascist dictatorship might subvert the autonomy of the state.

By 1938, Hitler was the most powerful of Europe's dictators. The conservative constraints on his authority had been removed and the territorial enlargement of Germany had commenced through the annexation (*Anschluss*) of Austria. It was soon plain, however, that the Führer's ambitions were not limited merely to revision of the Versailles Treaty. The still bolder expansionism that led to the outbreak of World War Two continued even after 1939 as a form of new imperialism, whose ideological and ethnic violence was particularly obvious in the east. Some of the characteristics of the Nazi dictatorship help explain the increase in its ideological radicalization.[45] Although antisemitism and racial nationalism had been central elements in the NSDAP's political programme from the outset, it was in the context of the war, and especially the invasion of the Soviet Union, that the *ad hoc* means of annihilation became superseded by the systematically organized Holocaust. This decisive shift was possible only as a result of the independent development of institutions such as the SS and the Nazi party's 'parallel administration'. In the 1930s the euthanasia campaigns, the extermination of asylum patients, the enforced sterilizations were already extremely important examples of brutalization.

Fascism and other right-wing dictatorships

The regimes operated by Hitler and Mussolini affected even those other right-wing European dictatorships that opposed their own home-grown fascist movements and represented more traditionalist forms of authoritarianism. These further cases demonstrate the adaptability of fascist institutions, models and ideological components within the wider context of right-wing politics during this era. The most paradigmatic example was undoubtedly General Francisco Franco's dictatorship in Spain, although neighbouring Portugal was also significant for its emulation of some aspects of Italian fascism.

Iberian cousins

The main characteristic of Franco's regime, which eventually lasted until the mid-1970s, was its radical break with the Second Republic. His rule was the product of a protracted and bloody civil war, waged from 1936 to 1939, in which there were a greater number of political purges and executions than during the overthrow of any other democratic regime in the era after World War One. Francoism as a political system rejected the fundamentals of the liberal legacy and was inspired by fascism to a much greater degree than the Salazar regime in Portugal.

It was within those areas that had been occupied by his military forces that Franco created the embryo of his future political system – one marked by a reactionary and militaristic coalition of Catholics, monarchists and fascists. He formed a single party, based on the small, pre-existing fascist movement known as the Phalanx or *Falange Española*. The latter had been formed in 1933 by José Antonio Primo de Rivera, who was soon to be executed by the Republicans at the beginning of the Civil War.[46] Franco developed this into a broader organization under the amended title of *Falange Española Tradicionalista* (FET).[47] He did so by forcing the original Falangists to integrate with the Catholics and the monarchists, thus setting in motion his ambition to build a regime that was close to fascism from the very beginning. During the civil war, the old-style Falange lent Franco its ideological backing as well as the support of its political activists and its modest militia, in the hope that, after its enforced 'unification' with other right-wing elements, it would still be allowed to play 'a genuinely fascist role in the implementation of a mobilised society'.[48] However, the fascists saw their position weaken as a result of their inclusion within a single party that also incorporated several other 'political families'. This Francoist union was a heterogeneous one that maintained several identities, particularly at the intermediate levels.[49] Nevertheless, Franco and the victors of the civil war initially outlined the creation of a Spanish New State, even though the tentative outlines of its proposed totalitarianism were to be rapidly eliminated as the defeat of Nazi ambitions became more predictable.

In terms of legitimacy, Franco's regime resembled the charismatic model of fascism, even though his regime included a strong religious aspect that was practically absent in the Italian example and completely non-existent in the German one. His concessions to Spain's liberal past were very few and far between. Here the dictator did not have to deal with either a president or a king, subordinate or otherwise; nor, unlike Mussolini and Salazar, did he need to pervert a parliament. As Stanley Payne noted, in 1939 the Spanish dictator 'was the European ruler who, both formally and theoretically, retained the most absolute and uncontrolled power.'[50]

Some of Franco's personal characteristics, and his relationship with the institutions that were the basis of his victory, would influence the nature of the new political system. He was a general of very average ability with very few political ideas beyond the values of order, anticommunism, traditionalist Catholicism and an obsession with the 'liberal–Masonic conspiracy'.[51] His relationship with the FET was also more utilitarian than ideological. He was not the leader of the original Falangist movement; nor had its organization been a determining factor in his taking power, sensitive as he was to both the armed forces and the Catholic Church, which were the other significant institutions involved in founding the new regime. His educational background and professional career made it difficult for him to position himself as an outright fascist once he was in power; despite his pro-Axis sympathies, he maintained Spanish neutrality during World War Two.[52]

Franco placed the FET under the strict control of himself and his government. Nevertheless, the movement managed not only to provide itself with a party apparatus, but also to improve its access to both national and local administration. However, it is possible to detect the existence of some 'political families' (including Catholics and monarchists, as well as the original Falangists) within the single party. Until 1944, with 66 per cent of the leadership positions under its control, the last of these groupings dominated the party, while the Catholics were the second largest 'family' followed by the military. Despite being subordinated to Franco's firm control, the FET was initially integrated into certain administrative bodies within the state apparatus: for example, by uniting the position of civil governors with those of the party's regional secretaries. One important struggle that was immediately lost was the attempt to prevent its independent militia from falling under military authority. However, the party did maintain a considerable collection of ancillary organizations, such as the Youth Front, the Spanish University Union, the Women's Section, the Trade Union Organization, and the Education and Recreation Union Organization (equivalent to Mussolini's *Dopolavoro*). More importantly, the party retained responsibility for propaganda within the regime.

While never promoting the conquest of the state, 'the existence of a single party that was quite clearly subordinate was a notable counterweight'[53] to other means of access to the government during this period. Despite the FET's origins in the enforced unification of several heterogeneous movements, the Falangists managed to exert their supremacy, and ensured their position as the principal force within the new Francoist political elite. Tensions between the party and the state were infrequent and largely episodic in a situation where the government's domination was almost total, and where indeed the position of the party and of its Falangist core was rapidly diminished after 1945.

In the case of Portugal, a so-called New State was consolidated in the 1930s out of a military dictatorship that had been implanted in 1926.[54] Its leader was Oliveira Salazar, a university professor with links to the Catholic Party, who had become minister of finance in 1928 and who then went on to hold the premiership from 1932 until 1968. Salazar could not be considered a charismatic figure. Moreover, the military origins of his regime ensured that his position was linked to that of the president of the republic, General Carmona, who had been formally legitimated in direct elections and who retained the authority to dismiss him. The regime's single party, the National Union (*União Nacional*), was weak and elitist, created from above by the interior ministry and initially controlled by an administration over which the premier's rule was complete.[55] Salazar also benefited from a new constitution – the product of a compromise between corporatism and liberalism that had been approved by popular plebiscite in 1933. Within this structure, the *União Nacional* exerted no real control over either the government or the administration. It was merely a political tool, used to select members for the chamber of deputies and the local administration, and to provide some veneer of legitimacy in the regular 'non-competitive elections'.

In several of the dictatorial regimes associated with fascism, both the government and its administration were to some extent subjected to interference from a single party that had become an influential organization. This did not happen in Portugal, where a centrally controlled public administration was instead the main instrument of dictatorial political power. When the New State created such organizations as the paramilitary Portuguese Youth movement (*Mocidade Portuguesa*) and the anti-communist Portuguese Legion militia (*Legião Portuguesa*), these were controlled by the Ministry of Education and the Ministry of the Interior, respectively, upon whom they remained dependent for the duration of the regime. The same was true of Salazar's political police (*Polícia de Vigilância e de Defesa do Estado*, PVDE), which was similarly responsible to the Minister of the Interior.

The main characteristic of the New State's governing elite was that its members belonged to a small and exclusive political and bureaucratic class that almost completely dominated the senior ranks of the armed forces, the senior administration and the universities – within which the legal profession was strongly represented. Portugal's single party, being kept organizationally weak and dependent, was never an important element either in the political decision-making process or in the selection of the ministerial elite. Several organizations, such as the *Legião Portuguesa*, the *Mocidade Portuguesa* and the PVDE, were kept entirely dependent on the ministers. National propaganda was administered by a directorate-general within the state apparatus, equipped with its own autonomous leadership that was responsible to Salazar personally rather than to the party. Similarly, the National Federation for Happiness at Work (a modest Portuguese version of Mussolini's *Dopolavoro* and Hitler's DAF), was dependent on the Under-Secretary of State for Corporations. The party's main function was to select the local and the parliamentary elites, and it remained small and devoid of organizations capable of mobilizing political influence.

In sum, despite early Francoism's proximity to fascism, both Iberian regimes represented a dictatorial model that was closer to that of Catholic and corporatist traditionalism, complete with a strong military elite and a controlled fascist minority.

Central and eastern Europe

Compared with their contemporaries in southern Europe, the right-wing dictatorships that developed in central and eastern Europe were generally of much shorter duration and less institutionalized. They also tended to become more deeply conditioned by World War Two, and some were, to a greater or lesser degree, forced into agreements with home-grown fascist movements.[56]

The Dollfuss–Schuschnigg regime that was formed in Austria in 1934, and that ended with the country's annexation by Nazi Germany in 1938, has often been described as 'clerico-fascist' and compared with the Iberian dictatorships of Salazar and Franco.[57] It was a regime established from above and rooted in social Catholicism, with a corporatist constitution anchored in traditionalist Catholic values and in the establishment of a one-party state under the Fatherland Front (*Vaterländische Front*, VF). It suffered from the impact of an Austrian Nazi party that had strong links with Hitler's movement, and of a home-grown fascist movement, the *Heimwehr*. The course of the dictatorship was marked dramatically by the assassination of Chancellor Dollfuss in June 1934, undertaken by a group of conspirators from the banned Austrian Nazi party.[58] His policies were continued by his successor, Kurt von Schuschnigg. The latter strengthened Austria's links with Italy, despite his room for manoeuvre being increasingly restricted by the clandestine Nazi party and the growing alliance between Hitler and Mussolini from 1936 onward. Internal conflicts with the Heimwehr led it to leave the government and forced its integration into the VF, a symbol of the classic tension between the authoritarian elite and native fascism. Hitler's pursuit of *Anschluss* approached its climax in February 1938, when he forced Schuschnigg to legalize the Austrian Nazi party and include it in his government. Presented early the following month with an ultimatum from Hitler to nominate the Nazi Seyss-Inquart as Chancellor, Schuschnigg resigned, leading Hitler to announce an annexation that was generally welcomed by the Austrians themselves.

Poland was similarly fertile territory for the development of fascist movements, in a situation where national minorities comprised 35 per cent of the population, where significant levels of antisemitism existed, and where the consolidation of parliamentary democracy within the post-1918 republic had proved problematic. However, as in some other countries of the European periphery, a preventative *coup d'état* had limited the development of native fascism. After this was carried out in 1926 by General Pilsudski, he was able to establish a form of single-party rule. Yet his dictatorship did not establish authoritarian institutions on a scale comparable with its southern European counterparts. Nor did the German occupation (let alone the Soviet one) in 1939 help the local fascists, some of whom, particularly those involved with Boleslaw Piasecki's National-Radical Camp (*Obóz Narodowo Radykalny*), participated in the resistance.

The origins of Hungarian fascism are much stronger and clearer, with an important national socialist mark. Rooted in the collapse of the Austro-Hungarian Empire and in the counter-revolutionary movements that followed in 1918, the emergence of extreme right-wing paramilitary movements deeply affected Hungarian political life. Admiral Horthy, who was from 1920 theoretically the regent of a Hungary awaiting some form of restored monarchy, presided over the country's destiny until 1944. At that point, the leader's futile attempts to break his alliance with Germany and strike a deal with the advancing Red Army led to a phase of Nazi occupation.[59] The Hungarian fascist groups were highly antisemitic, blending their racism with a Christian fundamentalist mysticism. Several right-wing governments entered into conflict with the oft-banned fascists. In 1938, Ferenc Szálasi established a Hungarian national socialist party. Although swiftly proscribed, it equally quickly reappeared as the Arrow Cross Party. This was the banner under which the Hungarian fascists gained parliamentary representation with 48 deputies. The country's participation in World War Two on the side of Germany did not provide the fascists with access to power, however. It was only in 1944, following the Nazi occupation, and particularly after the Germans had provided support for an Arrow Cross coup against Horthy, that Hungary (now as a mere puppet state) came under fascist control for a few short months. Although antisemitic activities preceded Szálasi's arrival in power, a significant number of Magyar civil and military officials now became important actors in the deportation of Hungarian Jews to Auschwitz.

In Romania, the parliamentary regime endured several crises until 1938. As noted previously, this country was the birthplace of eastern Europe's most successful fascist movement, the Iron Guard. Founded in 1927 as the Legion of the Archangel Michael, and named after the famous Orthodox icon, this organization had a strong religious and mystical component.[60] It was strongly antisemitic and pro-rural, and attracted a significant number of young intellectuals. The movement was always at crossed swords with the liberal governments; its leader, Corneliu Codreanu, was often arrested and its activities were banned. In 1932, the party won five seats in Parliament – although the following year it was once again outlawed. Political violence was one constant of its existence, but the life of its legionnaires was to become much harder in 1938, with the establishment by Carol II of a royal dictatorship, which swiftly ordered Codreanu's own execution. In September 1940, Carol nominated General Antonescu as his prime minister. At a stage when concessions (such as the transfer of Transylvania to German control) were being made to Hitler, Antonescu himself speedily took over dictatorial powers and forced the king to abdicate in favour of his son Michael. Preparing to enter the war on the side of the Nazis, Antonescu called the Iron Guard's legionnaires into his government. Early in 1941, however, fearing a fracture in the authoritarian state's bureaucratic structure and acting with Hitler's approval, he dissolved the Iron Guard in response to a fascist rebellion and exiled many of its leaders to Germany. Antonescu's own brand of conservative military dictatorship then survived until 1944, when he was arrested on the authority of King Michael.

War and occupation

It is clear that the development of a number of existing dictatorships was strongly conditioned by the outbreak of World War Two. Yet certain other dictatorial regimes, including some that were rooted in local elites and that possessed various degrees of autonomy, came about only as the direct products of German occupation. The Vichy government led by Marshal Pétain is perhaps the best known of these, but they include Quisling's administration in Norway and Mussolini's Republic of Salò, among others. There were also cases, such as Tiso's regime in Slovakia and that of Ante Pavelić's Ustaše in Croatia, where dictatorships emerged in new countries with a view to fulfilling demands for autonomy or independence.

When in June 1940, following the German invasion, what remained of the French government led by Pétain installed itself in the town of Vichy, the old Marshal had complete power to write a new constitution and to govern by decree. He was to rule the part of France that was not under German direct control between 1940 and 1944, in an attempt to promote a 'National Revolution' that would make France 'authoritarian, hierarchical, corporatist, antisemitic, and Catholic'.[61] In its early incarnation, Vichy was strongly influenced by the ideology of *Action Française* and of conservative Catholicism. Under the slogan 'work, family and homeland', and beneath the gaze of bronze busts of Pétain, the regime undertook projects of corporatist organization, supported Catholic schools and abolished divorce. There was no single party in the dictatorship, which governed through an administration not so dissimilar in structure from the Third Republic. This pursued the antisemitic policies that, since 1940, had characterized the regime's active collaboration with the German occupiers. The majority of French fascist groups (for example, Doriot's PPF) remained in Paris with the Germans, where they criticised Vichy. In 1944, faced with conservative hesitation, Vichy increasingly became a police state in which the fascist influences increased – particularly those of Marcel Déat and Joseph Darnand.

The first Slovak republic was established in 1939 as a mere puppet regime after the Germans had partitioned former Czechoslovakia and directly occupied its western regions of Bohemia and Moravia. Under those circumstances, Hitler offered Slovakia its formal independence, which was immediately proclaimed by the Catholic priest Monsignor Tiso. The Slovak People's Party (*Slovenská l'Udová Strana*) renamed Hlinka's Slovak People's Party – Party of Slovak National Unity (*Hlinkova Slovenská l'Udová Strana – Strana Slovenskej Národnej Jednoty*) following the death of its founder, Father Andrej Hlinka, in 1938 – very quickly transformed itself into a single party with a youth section and a militia, the Hlinka Guard (*Hlinkova Garda*).[62] Dominated by Nazi Germany until the collapse of 1945, the movement that ran this Slovak satellite state was constantly marked by tension between its authoritarian Catholic section and the radical faction led by Vojtech Tuka, which was much closer to German National Socialism.

Extremist nationalism was also present in the short-lived independent state of Croatia between 1941 and 1945, which was led, under the protective wing of Germany and Italy, by Ante Pavelić's Ustaše movement.[63] This regime was characterized by its severe ethnic violence against Jews, gypsies, and particularly Serbs. The Ustaše's authority was quickly contested and, from 1942, it was only able to continue by means of the German military support that protected it from increasing antifascist guerrilla attack until 1945.

In the north of Nazi-dominated Europe, the most complete institutionalization of a local fascist regime with German support took place in Norway where, following the German occupation that began in April 1940, Vidkun Quisling's minuscule National Unity was installed in power. Inspired directly by Nazi Germany, with a Führer and a monopolistic party, tensions soon emerged between Quisling and the

German administration which, according to internal reports, did not give his government the respect it had expected.[64]

Conclusion

When, in 1945, Europe celebrated victory over fascism, and when what became generally known as 'the quislings' faced trial and even execution, the major political actors had no doubts about the end of fascism. While the extreme right had not disappeared in the rubble of World War Two, and while the Iberian dictatorships had survived the conflict, the 'fascist era' was over. During the interwar period, the two main challengers to liberal democracy had been fascism and communism. While the former had been limited both geographically and culturally, the latter now emerged not only partially victorious, but also with the capacity greatly to expand its influence during the later 1940s.

Even though fascist movements were a decisive feature of the interwar period, it was their arrival in power in Italy and Germany that provided a template for elsewhere. Certain characteristics of fascism in power were the common patrimony of the modern right-wing dictatorships of the twentieth century, with some even prospering after the 'end of fascism' in 1945: the ultranationalism, the communitarian and/or corporatist relationship between the state and civil society, the single party and the anticommunism. But could it be that the stage of radicalization shows us fascism at its most distinctive? Some historians perhaps exaggerate when they claim that the 'fascist regimes tried to redraw so radically the boundaries between private and public that the private sphere almost disappeared.'[65] However, it seems obvious that the 'totalitarian tension' is an area in which the fascists differed from the other right-wing dictatorships of the period. It is only recently that, regarding Mussolini's regime, certain aspects of this tension have been 'grouped' to underline the eventual radicalization of Italian fascism in power: the Ethiopian war, the 'totalitarian leap' (*svolta totalitaria*) of the 1930s, and the racist legislation against Jews (albeit more limited in scope than Hitler's decrees).[66] In the Nazi case, however, no doubt at all surrounds the completeness of extremism. There, as Paxton concludes concerning the issue of a total radicalization, 'comparison is hardly possible: only one fascist regime really reached it'.[67]

Further reading

The bibliography on fascism is so large that the main task is to pluck only the most important works from the shelves. As indicated by many of the detailed citations given in the Notes, fascism continues to attract a considerable degree of attention and many works have been published over the past few years. However, it is an area that has become more restricted in disciplinary terms, with historians clearly predominating, while sociology and political science seem to be paying less heed to the subject.

For many years, analysts of this topic paid little attention to what was written and said by fascists themselves. Yet that may well be the best place to begin here. Among the anthologies containing primary sources, Roger Griffin's *Fascism* (Oxford: Oxford University Press, 1995) is the best introduction. This should be supplemented with *The Fascist Reader* (London: Routledge, 2002), edited by Aristotle Kallis, which is an excellent secondary source. If the aim is to know almost everything on the subject, then the most up-to-date encyclopaedia is Cyprian P. Blamires's *World Fascism: A Historical Overview* (Santa Barbara: ABC-CLIO, 2006, two volumes). At the opposite end of the scale, the best short history is Kevin Passmore's, *Fascism: A Very Brief Introduction* (Oxford: Oxford University Press, 2002).

The most informed and complete history of fascism remains Stanley G. Payne's *A History of Fascism* (London: UCL, 1996). As well as its excellent introduction to theories and interpretations, Payne discusses all the national variants with great analytical rigour. More recently, Robert O. Paxton's *The Anatomy of Fascism* (London: Penguin, 2005) has managed to achieve a synthesis where the analysis is particularly perceptive concerning the relationship between movements and regimes.

In his very thorough work, *Fascists* (Cambridge: Cambridge University Press, 2004), Michael Mann offers us the most interesting account of European fascist movements and the conditions that led to their political success during the interwar years. Mann's work should be complemented with Nancy Bermeo's excellent *The Citizenry and the Breakdown of Democracy* (Princeton: Princeton University Press, 2004), which is a study of the mass support for extremist right-wing groups that also compares interwar Europe with Latin America.

The most complete comparative study of the crisis of democratic politics during the 'fascist era' is *Conditions of Democracy in Europe, 1919–39: Systemic Case Studies* (London: Macmillan, 2000), edited by Dirk Berg-Schlosser and Jeremy Mitchell; note also their *Authoritarianism and Democracy in Europe, 1919–39: Comparative Analyses* (Basingstoke: Palgrave, 2003). The fullest work on fascism and the extreme right-wing movements that it inspired overseas is *Fascism Outside Europe* (New York: SSM-Columbia University Press, 2001), edited by Stein U. Larsen.

There is an abundance of histories of German National Socialism, and an ample literature on Italian fascism too. Most of these works repeat – to a greater or lesser extent – what the others say, but there are few comparative studies of the two most emblematic dictatorships. One recent exception in the field of cultural history is Roger Griffin's *Fascism and Modernity: The Sense of a New Beginning under Mussolini and Hitler* (Basingstoke: Palgrave, 2007), while another is the excellent comparative picture provided by MacGregor Knox in *To the Threshold of Power, 1922–33: Origins and Dynamics of the Fascist and National Socialist Dictatorships*, Vol. 1 (Cambridge: Cambridge University Press, 2008).

Notes

1 See Adrian Lyttelton, *Seizure of Power: Fascism in Italy, 1919–1929*, (London: Routledge, 2004, 2nd edn). The concept itself derives from the Latin *fascis* (plural *fasces*): a bundle of rods lashed together around a protruding axe blade so as to symbolize the unity, strength and discipline of the magistracy in ancient Rome. This image would feature strongly in the visual propaganda developed by Mussolini's movement.

2 See Roger Griffin, *The Nature of Fascism* (London: Routledge, 1993, 2nd edn), pp. 26–52.

3 See R. Thurlow, *Fascism in Britain: A History, 1918–1985* (Oxford: Oxford University Press, 1987); A. C. Pinto, *The Blue Shirts: Portuguese Fascism in Interwar Europe* (New York: SSM-Columbia University Press, 2000).

4 See Stanley G. Payne, *Fascism in Spain, 1923–1977* (Madison: University of Wisconsin Press, 1999); Hans F. Dahl, *Quisling: A Study in Treachery*, (Cambridge: Cambridge University Press, 1995).

5 See R. Ioanid, *The Sword of the Archangel: Fascist Ideology in Romania* (New York: EEM-Columbia University Press, 1990).

6 M. Mann, *Fascists* (Cambridge: Cambridge University Press, 2004), p. 13. Further elements quoted from Mann's definition come from the pages immediately following.

7 Based on the Table 'Typological Description of Fascism' in S. G. Payne, *A History of Fascism, 1914–1945* (Madison: University of Wisconsin Press, 1995), p. 7.

8 R. O. Paxton, *The Anatomy of Fascism* (London: Penguin, 2005), p. 218.

9 *Ibid.*

10 M. Mann, *Fascists, op. cit.*, p. 12.

11 See R. Eatwell, 'Towards a New Model of Generic Fascism', *Journal of Theoretical Politics*, 4 (2): 161–94 (1992).

12 See Zeev Sternhell, *The Birth of Fascist Ideology* (Princeton: Princeton University Press, 1995); Sternhell, *Neither Right nor Left: Fascist Ideology in France* (Princeton: Princeton University Press, 1995).

13 M. Mann, *Fascists, op. cit.*, p. 23.

14 E. Gentile, 'The Fascist Party', in C. P. Blamires (ed.), *World Fascism: A Historical Overview, Vol. 1* (Santa Barbara: ABC-CLIO, 2006), p. 226.

15 *Ibid.*, p. 227.
16 *Ibid.*, p. 228.
17 R. O. Paxton, *The Anatomy of Fascism, op. cit.*, p. 102.
18 Giovanni Sartori, *Parties and Party Systems. A Framework for Analysis* (New York: Cambridge University Press, 1976), pp. 132–34.
19 This is the term used by N. Bermeo, *Ordinary People in Extraordinary Times: The Citizenry and the Breakdown of Democracy* (Princeton: Princeton University Press, 2003).
20 Michel Winock, *Nationalism, Anti-semitism and Fascism in France* (Stanford: Stanford University Press, 1998).
21 See Chapter 9 in this volume, and Brian Jenkins (ed.), *France in the Era of Fascism. Essays on the French Authoritarian Right* (Oxford: Berghahan, 2004).
22 Robert O. Paxton, 'France', in C. P. Blamires (ed.), *World Fascism, op. cit.*, p. 246.
23 Martin Conway, *Collaboration in Belgium: Léon Degrelle and the Rexist Movement, 1940–44* (New Haven: Yale University Press, 1993).
24 Gerhard Hirschfeld, *Nazi Rule and Dutch Collaboration: The Netherlands under German Occupation* (Oxford: Berg, 1988).
25 See J. J. Linz and A. Stepan (eds), *The Breakdown of Democratic Regimes* (Baltimore: Johns Hopkins University Press, 1978); D. Berg-Schlosser and J. Mitchell (eds), *The Conditions of Democracy in Europe, 1919–1939* (London: Macmillan, 2000).
26 R. O. Paxton, *The Anatomy of Fascism, op. cit.*, p. 206.
27 *Ibid.*, pp. 123–24.
28 A. Kallis, 'The "Regime-Model" of Fascism: A Typology', *European History Quarterly* 30: 96–97 (2000).
29 See A. C. Pinto, R. Eatwell and S. U. Larsen (eds), *Charisma and Fascism in Inter-War Europe* (London: Routledge, 2007).
30 See J. J. Linz, *Authoritarian and Totalitarian Regimes* (Boulder, CO: Lynne Rienner, 2000).
31 See Pierre Milza, *Mussolini* (Paris: Fayard, 1999).
32 See E. Gentile, *The Sacralization of Politics in Fascist Italy* (Cambridge, MA: Harvard University Press, 1996).
33 See E. Gentile, *La Via Italiana al Totalitarismo* (Madrid: Siglo XXI Ediciones, 2005), p. 183.
34 See V. de Grazia, *The Culture of Consent: Mass Organisation of Leisure in Fascist Italy* (Cambridge: Cambridge University Press, 1981), pp. 33–59.
35 See T. H. Koon, *Believe, Obey, Fight: Political Socialization of Youth in Fascist Italy, 1922–1943* (Chapel Hill: University of North Carolina Press, 1985), pp. 11–142.
36 V. de Grazia, *How Fascism Ruled Women: Italy, 1922–1945* (Berkeley: University of California Press, 1993), pp. 234–71.
37 See I. Kershaw, *Hitler, Vol. 1, 1889–1936: Hubris* (London: Allen Lane, 1998); I. Kershaw, *Hitler, Vol. 2, 1936–1945: Nemesis* (London: Allen Lane, 2000).
38 M. Broszat, *The Hitler State* (London: Longman, 1981), p. 351.
39 E. N. Peterson, *The Limits of Hitler's Power* (Princeton, NJ: Princeton University Press, 1969), pp. 26–33.
40 M. Broszat, *The Hitler State, op. cit.*, pp. 57–95.
41 See J. Caplan, *Government without Administration: State and Civil Service in Weimar and Nazi Germany* (Oxford: Oxford University Press, 1988), chapter 5.

42 M. H. Kater, *The Nazi Party: A Social Profile of Member and Leaders, 1919–1945* (Cambridge, MA: Harvard University Press, 1983), p. 238.

43 M. Broszat, *The Hitler State, op. cit.*, pp. 262 and 264.

44 *Ibid.*, p. 272.

45 See Ian Kershaw, *The Nazi Dictatorship. Problems of Interpretation* (London: Arnold, 2000, 4th edn), pp. 82–106.

46 Its even fuller title was the *Falange Española Tradicionalista y de las Juntas de Ofensiva Nacional-Sindicalista*, sometimes referred to as FET-JONS.

47 See S. G. Payne, *Fascism in Spain, op. cit.*, p. 487.

48 Ricardo Chueca, *El Fascismo en los Comienzos del Regime de Franco* (Madrid: CIS, 1983), p. 401.

49 See J. J. Linz, 'From Falange to Movimiento-Organización: The Spanish Single Party and the Franco Regime, 1936–68', in Samuel Huntington and Clement Moore (eds), *Authoritarian Politics in Modern Society; The Dynamics of Established One-Party Systems* (New York: Basic Books, 1970), pp. 128–203.

50 S. G. Payne, *Fascism in Spain, op. cit.*, p. 487.

51 See Paul Preston, *Franco: A Biography* (London: Harper Collins, 1993).

52 See Stanley G. Payne, *Franco and Hitler. Spain, Germany and World War II* (New Haven: Yale University Press, 2008).

53 C. Viver Pi-Sunyer, *El Personal Politico de Franco* (Barcelona: Editorial Vicens-Vives, 1978), p. 202.

54 See A. C. Pinto, *Salazar's Dictatorship and European Fascism: Problems of Interpretation* (New York: SSM-Columbia University Press, 1995).

55 See P. T. de Almeida, A. C. Pinto and N. Bermeo (eds), *Who Governs Southern Europe?* (London: Routledge, 2003), pp. 33–34.

56 See I. T. Berend, *Decades of Crisis: Central and Eastern Europe Before World War Two* (Berkeley: University of California Press, 2001), pp. 301–45.

57 See G. Bishof, A. Pelinka and A. Lassner, *The Dollfuss–Schuschnigg Era in Austria: A Reassessment* (New Brunswick: Transaction, 2003).

58 See B. Pauley, *Hitler and the Forgotten Nazis: A History of Austrian National Socialism* (Chapel Hill: University of North Carolina Press, 1981), pp. 28–133.

59 See M. Ormos, *Hungary Between the Two World Wars, 1914–1945* (New York: SSM-Columbia University Press, 2007).

60 See Constatin Iordachi, *Charisma, Politics and Violence: The Legion of the 'Archangel Michael' in Inter-War Romania* (Trondheim: Trondheim Studies on East European Cultures and Societies, 2004).

61 R. O. Paxton, *Vichy France: Old Guard and New Order* (New York: Columbia University Press, 2001).

62 See J. R. Felak, *'At the Price of the Republic': Slovak People's Party, 1929–1938* (Pittsburg: University of Pittsburg Press, 1995).

63 See Ivo Goldstein, 'Ante Pavelić: Charisma and National Mission in Wartime Croatia', in A. C. Pinto, R. Eatwell and S. U. Larsen (eds), *Charisma and Fascism in Inter-War Europe, op. cit.*, pp. 87–96.

64 See H. F. Dahl, *Quisling, op. cit.*

65 R. O. Paxton, *The Anatomy of Fascism, op. cit.*, p. 144.

66 See F. H. Adler, 'Why Mussolini Turned on the Jews', *Patterns of Prejudice* 39 (3): 285–300 (2005).

67 R. O. Paxton, *The Anatomy of Fascism, op. cit.*, p. 169.

8 Withstanding extremes: Britain and France, 1918–40

Nicholas Atkin

In summer 1918, with the war in deadlock, both sides increasingly presented it as a clash of values. For his part, Kaiser Wilhelm II pronounced that the fight was between 'two approaches to the world': 'Either the Prussian-German-Germanic approach, right, freedom, honour, morality, or the Anglo–Saxon, which would mean enthroning the worship of gold.' US President Wilson countered, 'The object of this war is to deliver the free peoples of the world from the menace and the actual power of a vast military establishment, controlled by an irresponsible government.'[1]

In presenting the struggle thus, Wilson was assisted by the earlier defeat of autocratic Russia, an alliance that had always posed headaches for Western propagandists, yet he was painfully aware that the liberal-democratic credentials of his remaining partners were not without blemish. In Britain, Italy and France, especially, wartime demands for greater political, social, economic and gender freedoms had been either parried or denied, while state power had grown stronger thanks to the 'total' nature of the conflict. Most uncomfortably, as Gary Sheffield reflects, Wilson was conscious that these nations had mobilized their vast colonial empires in support of the struggle, and viewed any resulting peace settlement as an opportunity to extend these territories, not scale them down and bestow independence.[2]

It was Wilson's hope that the 'moral compass' of his Fourteen Points, championing the values of self-determination, rule of law, liberal democracy and open diplomacy, would inform the peacemaking process, and in large measure they did.[3] Out of the old Austro-Hungarian, German, Ottoman and Russian empires emerged a series of independent states, supposedly guided by enlightened principles: Finland, Estonia, Latvia, Lithuania, Poland, Yugoslavia and Czechoslovakia. Similar values were also injected into the newly configured states of Austria and Germany. It was a truly seismic shift. As Martin

Blinkhorn writes, 'Ideological and cultural pluralism, religious and ethnic toleration, national self-determination, free-market economics, representative and responsible government, free trade unionism, and the peaceful settlement of international disputes' appeared to be the overwhelming precepts of the day.[4]

The mood of 1919, however, was not sanguine. As Martin Kitchen reflects, 'The self-confident certainties of nineteenth-century bourgeois liberalism had begun to crumble' well before 1914, and the war further undermined notions of progress.[5] In the words of the contemporary French writer Paul Valéry, the conflict had exposed 'the mortality of civilisations'.[6] The 1920s and 1930s appeared to bear out his pessimism, especially in respect of liberal ideals, as state after state fell prey to dictatorship. Here is not the place to recount that sorry roll-call, but to stress that, by the mid-1930s, only in Britain, France, the Irish Free State, Belgium, Luxembourg, Holland, Switzerland, Czechoslovakia and the Nordic countries did liberal democracy subsist, and even in these nations there were challenges from the extremes.

Little of this could have been foretold in 1919, but with the benefit of hindsight it can be asserted that the interwar years were hardly propitious ones for liberal democracy. World War One had produced a highly unstable climate that favoured extremism over moderation. The confidence of the ruling elites and state bureaucracies had been severely ruffled by the conflict, while soldiers returning home discovered an unwelcoming social environment that dented their confidence in the present and future. The 1919 Peace Settlement compounded matters by redrawing the map of central and eastern Europe in such a way that several new states, most obviously Hungary, Yugoslavia, Czechoslovakia and Romania, contained within their borders sizeable ethnic minorities who felt discriminated against. Frequently governments seemed incapable of resolving these nationalist tensions which were exacerbated by the economic dislocation that afflicted much of Europe in the immediate postwar period, and later during the Great Depression of the 1930s. In this context, the alternative solutions of Bolshevism and fascism became increasingly attractive. It was an unforgiving environment that encouraged previously good liberals to question their own value systems. As the Spanish intellectual and essayist Ortega y Gasset had forewarned in his 1929 *Revolt of the Masses*, liberal democracies carried within them the seeds of their own downfall: while the modern world was 'civilized', he wrote, the individual, open to manipulation, was not.[7] The rise of fascist regimes seemed only to bear out his gloom-laden analysis.

Such doubting was to be found in the two most eminent liberal democracies, Britain and France, yet both withstood the challenge of extremes. France succumbed only in 1940, when defeated militarily. What provided this resilience? It has been speculated that national context played a significant part. Britain was on the periphery of Europe and was thus relatively unaffected by 'continental developments'. In the words of one historian, it suffered 'less devastation due to the Great War', was less affected by immigration, and enjoyed 'a continuity of frontiers and hence of political institutions'.[8] It has been further suggested that the long-standing British values of fair play (at least for some), forbearance, reflection and toleration made the UK an unwelcoming world for extremists. France possessed a different set of ideals which, it is believed, were equally uninviting. As the birth place of the Declaration of the Rights of Man and the Citizen, the nation embodied longstanding 'ideological traditions', most obviously republicanism, which 'rendered the country largely immune to the appeal of fascism', if not to Marxism.[9]

These arguments may contain an element of truth, yet they also betray a complacency, and ignore the very real sense of crisis felt by contemporaries. In 1919, at a moment of industrial unrest in both countries and of uprisings abroad, there was a tangible fear of revolution. This anxiety persisted throughout the decade, exacerbated in 1924 by the election victory of Edouard Herriot's *cartel des gauches* and by Ramsay McDonald's minority Labour government. Middle-class anxieties were not assuaged by the 1926 General Strike in Britain, and the prospect of another Labour government in 1929. How would the right react? That became the overriding issue in the 1930s. The temptations to stray to extremist movements were great, notably to La Rocque's *Croix de Feu* and Oswald Mosley's British Union of Fascists. Within France, the fascist threat prompted left-wing parties to suspend their sectarianism and form a Popular Front, an idea that was also canvassed in Britain.[10] Ultimately the unconstitutional path was avoided in the two nations, and for similar reasons: a strong sense of national self-worth, stemming from the 1918 victory; resilient state structures; the willingness of mainstream political parties to defend parliamentary democracy, even though this was acknowledged to possess shortcomings; the failure of extremist movements to seize their moment; and an underlying social stability, although this is not to deny that many people were troubled by a nagging insecurity.

The 1920s: the threat from the left

As victorious powers in World War One, Britain and France escaped the sense of frustrated and bellicose nationalism that afflicted Weimar

Germany, yet it should not be believed that the mood in either country was necessarily confident. The public had to confront appalling casualty rates. 723,000 British soldiers had been killed, while an additional 500,000 had been severely disabled. France suffered 1,398,000 fatalities, and a similar figure endured some form of disability. Such losses were especially felt in a country that had long fretted about its low birth rate in comparison with Germany's. It has been speculatively calculated that 1,500,000 babies were never conceived because of mobilization (the figure is 700,000 for Britain).[11] New forms of commemoration became commonplace in both nations as families, relatives and friends attempted to come to terms with unprecedented death tolls.[12] In the social domain, those troops returning to the home fronts discovered that much had changed, especially within the world of work – the introduction of mass production techniques, the entry of women into the labour force and a flurry of new rules and restrictions on the shop floor (see Chapter 2). At least that was the experience for those able to find work. Although Britain experienced a shortlived postwar boom, demobilization brought with it high unemployment. Within the economic domain, the two countries were crippled by enormous debts incurred during the war. Not truly understanding how the international economy functioned, their governments became obsessed with a return to the gold standard, believing this was the only way to restore wider economic stability. And, on the international stage, neither country felt truly secure. While liberal opinion in Britain concurred with the economist John Maynard Keynes in his belief that the economic terms of the peace had been too harsh on Germany, a French public deemed them too lenient. This anxiety was best expressed by Marshal Foch, who famously likened the Versailles Treaty to a 20-years truce. British opinion might not have been so agitated by Germany, yet it was troubled by the ways in which the war had chipped away at empire. In recognition of their contribution to victory, the British Dominions were granted greater autonomy, and it was with some difficulty that London managed to resist similar concessions to India and Egypt. Irish Home Rule, however, could not be deferred forever and, after the Anglo–Irish war of 1919–21, the Irish Free State was established. In retrospect, this partial 'resolution' of the Irish question marginalized an issue that could easily have undermined political stability on the mainland.

The greatest fear in 1918–19, however, was that of communism. After the October 1917 Revolution, Marxism was no longer an abstract creed, but a working ideology that informed the decisions of one of Europe's foremost states. While intellectuals looked on with admiration as the Bolsheviks set about a radical overhaul of Russian society, governments were deeply unsettled by Moscow's avowed aim to promote worldwide revolution. As Michael Biddiss argues in Chapter 3, the Bolsheviks' appeal was further heightened by the fact that they bore no blame for the horrors of World War One, although it would not be long before they had other blood on their hands. For the most part, however, the horrors perpetrated in the name of the Revolution were kept from common view, at least until the 1930s, and even then Stalin maintained an allure. Whereas the capitalist system was stuck in the rut of the Depression, the USSR, through its ambitious five-year plans and collectivization programmes, appeared to be pressing ahead with an agenda of economic modernization. The British historian Raphael Samuel recalls how, in the 1940s, he and others gathered in a small London flat to listen to *The Russian Tractor Song*, a paean to collectivization and the transformation of Russian agriculture.[13]

Because of the revolutionary tradition of 1789, fear of communism (as well as enthusiasm for it) was always greater in France than it was in Britain. In 1918, there were still those who could remember the Paris Commune of 1871, a patriotic rebellion on the part of the capital against defeat in the Franco–Prussian war, and one that had become a radical experiment in social and economic engineering. When French forces faltered in early September 1914, senior army officers feared a repetition of the Commune, just as they would in May–June 1940. Anxieties about the militancy of the working classes grew in the course of World War One. Whereas in August 1914 socialist and trade union leaders sloughed off their earlier internationalism to evoke the patriotism of 1792, such resolve was faltering by 1917. Among calls for an international peace conference, the conflict was increasingly described on the left as 'a capitalist struggle'. The resolve of the workforce itself also appeared to be wavering. As Jean-Jacques Becker maintains, in 1914–15 labour protest was modest, yet as material shortages kicked in the number of stoppages mounted,[14] and were mirrored by the 1917 army mutinies. In the words of Guy Pedroncini, these were effectively 'strikes' on the part of soldiers disillusioned at the appalling conditions in which they had to fight.[15] On the part of the bourgeoisie, protests of all kinds were interpreted as support for a wider revolutionary movement. Further alarm sprang from the surge of support for trade unions. Although the General Confederation of Labour (*Confédération Générale du Travail*, CGT) could not match the membership of its British equivalent, the Trades Union Congress (TUC), which boasted 6,500,000 affiliates in 1920, it underwent an impressive period of growth: 100,000 in 1916; 600,000 in 1918; and 1,610,000 in 1920.[16]

As revolution swept through central and eastern Europe in 1918–19, it seemed France might follow suit. In early 1919, a miners' strike erupted in Lorraine; on May Day 500,000 protesters took to the streets of Paris; and in June there was a mass walkout of metal workers (*métallos*) in the north-eastern suburbs of the capital, an action copied by employees in the chemical industry and the staff of the Métro. In May the following year, the railways were brought to a halt – the beginnings of a general strike, although it is agreed that it was never very 'general'. Moreover, out of the December conference of the Socialist Party, the *Section Française de l'Internationale Ouvrière* (SFIO), there emerged the *Parti Communiste Français* (PCF). In between these episodes, there were innumerable unofficial walkouts, often led by young radical shop-floor stewards. It was partly to regain the initiative of the labour movement that, in May 1920, the CGT hesitantly came out in favour of a general strike to support the railwaymen.

Across the Channel, the situation superficially resembled that in France. Support for trade unions, which had increased markedly in the 1890s and 1900s, grew further in the course of the war: from 4,145,000 in 1914 to 6,533,000 in 1918. As in France, strikes were rare in 1914–15 but, remarks John Stevenson, over the next two years became ever more frequent: 'over five and a half million working days were lost in 1917, more than the total for 1915 and 1916 put together.'[17] In some industries, continues Stephenson, transport, mining and engineering especially, there existed a fragile truce between labour and capital which always threatened to erupt into something much more. In 1917, that moment seemed to have arrived. On Clydeside, there were attempts to create a Workers' Soviet, though this initiative was squashed by local magistrates. A year later, Glasgow was again the setting for left-wing protests when militants undertook a 48-hour walkout and hung the red flag from the town hall. In 1919 the miners, railwaymen and transport workers revived their Triple Alliance, which was quickly followed by protest on the railways. In 1920 it was the turn of the miners, and a general strike loomed, although Britain would not experience this phenomenon until 1926. Militancy was especially evident among demobilized soldiers whose discontents were expressed by the Sailors' Soldiers' and Airmen's Union, the National Federation of Discharged and Demobilised Sailors and Soldiers, and the Comrades of the Great War. And, in summer 1920, the Communist Party of Great Britain was founded.

Against this background, it was difficult for the middle classes to sleep soundly in their beds, their anxieties sharpened by conservative propaganda. In France the *bloc national*, the right-wing coalition that fought the 1919 elections, revelled in scaremongering tactics. One poster, in support of the *bloc*, famously depicted a Bolshevik brigand with a knife clutched between his teeth, apparently ready to slit the throat of France. In Britain, Lloyd George's coalition was more responsible in its sloganeering, although the same could not be said of the populist right-wing press, notably Lord Rothermere's *Daily Mail*. In truth, the situation in both countries was far from revolutionary. As the historian James McMillan observes, 'Clemenceau's France was not Kerensky's Russia.'[18] The same could be said of Lloyd George's Britain.

To begin with, state structures and institutions had not melted away in the course of 1914–18. If anything, they had been strengthened as governments mobilized the home fronts so as to endure a war of attrition. Governments were also prepared to defend themselves against civil disorder, with force if necessary. In France, police roughly dispersed the 1919 May Day demonstrators, leaving one protestor dead; the following month some 17,000 troops, many of whom were heavily armed, confronted the Paris *métallos*; and in 1920 soldiers were again deployed to break up the railwaymen's strike, the so-called 'civic battle of the Marne', when young middle-class men volunteered to help run the trains. In 1919, the British state had drawn up its own plans to create 'citizens' guards'; and in October 1920 the Emergency Powers Act authorized government to draft in troops to disrupt the miners' dispute. At the time of the General Strike in 1926, 130,000 enrolled into the Special Constabulary created by William Joynson Hicks, the Home Secretary, who had an unhealthy obsession with anything he deemed 'unBritish', including jazz, foreigners, homosexuality and nightclubs. When the crisis was over, government passed the Trades Dispute Act (1927). This outlawed sympathetic strikes, a clause never enforced, and stipulated that trade unions' contributions to political parties could come only from individual members who had signed a form agreeing to pay such a levy.

Tough measures were made more palatable by government moves to reinstate those democratic procedures disrupted as a result of the war. In Britain, a general election was 'well overdue'.[19] The previous one had been in 1910, the House of Commons deciding to extend its life so as to prosecute the war. With the conflict ended, the wartime prime minister Lloyd George restored the peacetime processes. On 14 November 1918, he announced the dissolution of Parliament for the 25th of that month, and fresh elections were arranged for December. The franchise included all men over 21, not just householders, and women over 30, an age limit that effectively perpetuated a male-dominated electorate. In France, there was less urgency about a new parliament given that elections had taken place in 1914. Clemenceau preferred to get on with the job of securing the Versailles settlement without having to trouble himself about the home front. As soon as those negotiations were concluded, elections went ahead in 1919.

In fighting their campaigns, both Lloyd George and Clemenceau promised a better future for those returning from the trenches, although progressive legislation was more extensive in Britain than it was in France, where government had been traditionally timid in its approach to the 'social question', as Pamela Pilbeam reveals in Chapter 2. By contrast, in Britain both Tories and Liberals had long recognized the need for reform, a tradition that was extended in 1919: the establishment of a Ministry of Health; a Housing and Town Planning Act, which assisted local authorities in the building of affordable homes for demobilized troops; and the Unemployment Insurance Act (1920), extending benefits to all groups of workers other than those in domestic service, the civil service and agricultural labour. Nor did government attempt to reverse the gains made by trade unions during the course of 1914–18, for instance their representation on wage boards and arbitration councils. Within France, Clemenceau might have pursued a similar path if he had remained in power. He was known to favour a progressive income tax and a system of worker representation. Such plans, however, troubled the right-wing chamber elected in 1919, which also feared that Clemenceau aspired to dictatorship. Moves were taken to block any such ambition, and progressive measures were limited to a law on collective agreements, and another introducing an eight-hour day. Even this was too much for the representatives of industry, better mobilized than their British counterparts. In addition to existing employers' organizations, the *Comités des Forges*, the *Union des Industries Metallurgiques et Minières* and the *Comité des Houillères*, there emerged in July 1919 the *Confédération Générale de la Production Française*, which reflected on the best ways to withstand trade union militancy, as well as on the problems of reconstruction.

Apart from the resilience of state structures and the willingness of the British and French establishments to defend themselves through a mixture of stick and carrot, it has to be questioned whether the general mood of the people in 1918–19 was revolutionary. Not if we are to judge the results of the general elections. Immediately after the war, electorates in both countries voted for those governments with which they felt most comfortable. In Britain, the election of 14 December 1918 was a victory for the wartime coalition of Lloyd George (338 conservative seats, 136 Liberal and 10 Labour/others). The opposition was fragmented: 48 non-coalition Conservatives, 59 Labour, 26

Liberals, 9 independents, 7 Irish Nationalists and 73 Sinn Feiners, the latter group refusing to take up their seats.[20] Within France, the 1919 elections were also a victory for the wartime coalition, known as the *Union Sacrée*, which by the end of the conflict had come to be dominated by the two principal right-wing parties, the traditionalist *Fédération Républicaine* and the more progressive-looking *Alliance Démocratique*. It was the most right-wing chamber since 1877.

Moreover, political power largely rested with the right for the remainder of the decade. In 1922, Conservative backbenchers ditched Lloyd George, with whom they had always felt uncomfortable, paving the way for a sizeable victory in the November 1922 elections. When the new Conservative prime minister Andrew Bonar Law died shortly afterwards, the premiership passed to Stanley Baldwin, who honoured his predecessor's promise to go to the country should new protectionist tariffs be deemed necessary, which he believed they were. The electorate was not pleased at being returned to the polling booths so soon. Although the Tories emerged with most MPs, they lost seats thanks to the excise issue, while Labour emerged as the second largest party pushing the Liberals, already in decline, into third place. In this situation, a case for a minority Labour government presented itself. This alarmed certain Conservatives, who looked to Italy, where two years earlier Mussolini had taken power with the avowed aim of keeping the socialists out.[21] Should the Conservatives do the same, aligning with the Liberals, suspending democratic procedures, and forming 'a government of national trustees' for a fixed two-year term of office?[22] The more general reasons why the Conservative party remained loyal to liberal democracy are discussed below; here it should be stressed that the leadership avoided any unconstitutional path, as it understood that a Labour government was likely to be shortlived and incapable of pushing through radical reform. So it proved. In February 1924, Ramsay MacDonald formed his cabinet. Reliant on Liberal support, it survived for ten months before admitting defeat and calling fresh elections, which were a landslide victory for Baldwin's Tories.

Across the Channel, the political narrative was not as straightforward. Executive power was weaker than in Britain, as was party discipline, engendering a constant turnover of cabinets. This, though, should not disguise an underlying stability. It has been calculated that nearly four-fifths of one ministry survived into the next, and it is frequently pointed out that the fall of a government did not entail a new election. Nor should this instability disguise the ascendancy of the right in the shape of the *Fédération Républicaine* and the *Alliance Démocratique*. This dominance was briefly shaken in 1924 when the electorate, tired of the austerity measures of the *bloc national*, voted in the left-wing *cartel des gauches* of Edouard Herriot, which won 139 seats for the Radical party and 100 for the Socialists. As with the MacDonald government in Britain, the propertied classes feared the worst, especially a capital tax on the super rich. Such anxiety was misplaced. Although committed to the ideals of 1789, the Radicals were a centrist grouping, and one that shied away from anything truly 'radical' lest this should disturb their core support among the peasantry and lower-middle class. It was also appreciated that the *cartel des gauches* was a weak coalition. The Socialists refused seats in the cabinet, and sniped at Herriot from the backbenches. Much of the premier's time was consumed by foreign policy, extricating France from the disastrous Ruhr occupation. The one contentious measure proposed, although never implemented, was to extend pre-1914 anticlerical legislation to the newly recovered provinces of Alsace and Lorraine. This prompted Catholics to rally in the *Fédération Nationale Catholique*. As we shall see, other right-wing leagues were also beginning to mobilize at the same time, yet at that point they did not pose a serious threat to the Republic, and their strength waned after 1926 when Herriot bestowed the premiership on the former president Raymond Poincaré, the only person seemingly capable of stopping a run on the *franc*. The 1928 elections proved an unambiguous victory for the right, this time headed by André Tardieu, a conservative modernizer whose ministry proved one of the most progressive under the Third Republic.

If the mood of the wider electorate was not revolutionary, what of the workers themselves? Without question, their disposition was more militant in France, where Marxism developed a genuine appeal, something it never achieved in Britain.[23] There were several reasons why this was so. The working classes in France, which had begun to ease out the older artisanal trades towards the close of the nineteenth century, possessed a strong class solidarity. Concentrated in specific geographical areas (the Nord-Pas de Calais, the Alpes Maritimes, Alsace and Lorraine, and the northern outreaches of Paris), subject to a brutal factory regimen and seemingly forgotten by government, they shared a similar outlook. Within Britain, argues Ross McKibbin, the labour force was more fragmented, 'scattered' by occupation, geography, varied employment practices, and the relatively small size of industrial plants, factors which militated against the emergence of a collective identity.[24] Among the British working classes, he continues, there also existed a strong 'associational culture' expressed through sports, religion, hobbies and leisure activities, which weakened the appeal of extremism. This was in marked contrast to France, where leisure amenities were often out of reach and too expensive for proletarians, who were frequently housed in bleak, purpose-built blocks of flats far away from town centres. McKibbin additionally argues that the British working class – through participation in local and parliamentary elections, and highly conditioned by and accepting of existing institutions, for instance monarchy and empire – did not feel separate from civil society. In this respect, a well established sense of national identity might have been important. Britain never had to promote a sense of 'Britishness' in the way in which the Third Republic had to engineer 'Frenchness' through a clumsy political and social process that heightened cultural, religious and political opposition to the centre.

The above factors go some way to explaining the willingness of French workers to elect militants as their representatives. Yet such behaviour and the growth of trade union membership should not necessarily be interpreted as support for revolutionary action. The majority of workers joined *syndicats* for obvious reasons: above all, to safeguard their material interests which seemed threatened in the postwar environment. If it took strike action to overcome these pressures, then workers were prepared to join such initiatives, yet they were reluctant to go further. When, in 1920, firebrands attempted to turn the French railwaymen's strike into a political dispute, they failed to win the backing of the smaller unions.

Within Britain, too, there was reluctance on the part of the trade union leadership to 'politicize' strike action, not surprising given what has been said about the lack of extremism among the workforce. Such disinclination was evidenced in the general strike of 1926, which erupted on 3 May after the breakdown of negotiations between coal-owners and miners, and the failure of government and the TUC to broker a compromise.[25] In the alarmist language of the *Daily Mail*, revolution again beckoned as the Triple Alliance came out in support of the miners, along with printers, dockers, gas and electricity workers, among others. Appearances were deceptive. The miners themselves had made no provision for revolutionary action, and were preoccupied with practical matters: rates of pay, hours of work and the nationalization of the pits. Although sympathetic to their grievances, the TUC leadership was desperate for a settlement, fearful that government might retaliate with punitive wage settlements, and worried that public opinion would irrevocably turn against the unions. To this end, it called off the strike after nine days, although the miners stayed out until the end of the year, when they returned to the pits out of financial necessity.

Even if the workforce had desired revolution, it is questionable whether their representatives could have delivered. Within France, this was because of the longstanding dispute between those who favoured a reformist path to power, partaking in 'bourgeois politics', and those favouring revolutionary action. Events in Russia brought matters to a head. In 1920, Lenin decided to jettison the Second Socialist International in favour of a Third, known as the Comintern (see Chapter 6). At the SFIO's seventeenth conference, held at Strasbourg in February 1920, there remained a wariness at joining this communist-led initiative, but over the next few months any remaining doubts evaporated thanks to a series of factors: dissatisfaction with the *bloc national*; continuing economic problems; the collapse of the May 1920 strikes, which had seen a fall in union membership; the mobilization of the employers (mentioned above); the influx of new party members into the SFIO, who craved the excitement of the trenches; allied intervention in the Russian Civil War; and favourable reporting on the USSR by SFIO emissaries.[26] So it was that, at the SFIO Congress of Tours in December 1920, a majority of delegates voted to create a separate communist party, the PCF. In September 1921, schism also afflicted the CGT, when militants seceded to establish the *Confédération Générale du Travail Unitaire* (CGTU).

Although the PCF was one of the largest communist parties outside the USSR, the revolution it craved seemed a long way off. As has been observed, Moscow remained preoccupied with internal affairs, the revolutionary movements within central Europe withered away, and the Third Republic stayed firm.[27] In this situation, the PCF heeded Moscow's advice: to concentrate on building up its internal discipline; to establish cells within factories, something it did with particular success in the northern outreaches of Paris; to conserve its energies in national elections (it won a mere 26 seats in 1924 and 12 in 1928), although it fought Socialist candidates with excessive zeal; and to await the golden day when a revolutionary moment might arise. Historians generally agree that the impact of events in Russia had thus not been to create a revolutionary moment, but to have sown bitter divisions among the French left, disagreements that would only be temporarily healed in the Popular Front of 1936.

If in France there was at least a will on the part of the Communists to prepare for revolution, across the Channel the left had no interest whatsoever in such a scenario. As Andrew Thorpe has demonstrated, in terms of leadership, ideology and membership, the Labour party was committed to constitutionality. Analysis of the 'big five' who dominated the Labour leadership in the 1920s – Ramsay MacDonald, Philip Snowden, Arthur Henderson, J. H. Thomas and J. R. Clynes – has revealed moderate men.[28] While 'diverse' in their social backgrounds, only Snowden and Henderson could be said to originate from the industrial working classes. They thus lacked any real sense of 'alienation or exclusively proletarian class consciousness', and remained committed to parliamentary processes.[29] A good many of Labour's leaders, at all levels, were also influenced by their religious backgrounds. There is much truth in the cliché that the party was driven by Methodism, not Marxism. Religion undoubtedly influenced the broader ideology of the party, which was committed to a fairer and more humane society. The aim was not to bring down capitalism, but to tame it from within, facilitating social reform and a wider distribution of the spoils. This was evidenced in the first Labour government of 1924, which was determined to prove its competence and moderation, thus overtaking the Liberals as the main opposition party. The decision of ministers to wear formal dress, top hat and tails, for court ceremonies was an early indication of the path to be pursued. Although there was a minority of socialists, congregated in the associated Independent Labour Party, which advocated a more militant approach, gradualism was generally shared by the mass membership. As Thorpe again writes, 'The leaders understood pretty well the hopes and fears of their constituents, the majority of whom were never faring so badly under capitalism as to want to rush headlong into a violent revolution the result of which no-one could have predicted.'[30]

Revolution was, of course, desired by the extreme left. When in late 1924 the *Daily Mail* published the infamous Zinoviev letter berating the MacDonald government and urging British communists to seize power, its sentiments were shared by many in the Communist Party of Great Britain (CPGB), even though the document itself was a forgery and was designed to make mischief. How to proceed? Membership of the party was tiny: 4000 at its founding; 10,000 at the time of the General Strike; and just below 3000 at the start of the Depression. None the less, the CPGB believed it could advance its cause by exploiting the great issue of the day, that of unemployment. To this end it helped create, in April 1921, the National Unemployed Workers' Committee Movement (NUWCM). With several hundred local branches and a membership of 50,000 in 1926, which it marshalled in a series of impressive demonstrations, the NUWCM promised much. Once again, success was limited. Government dole, although miserly, took some of the sting out of unemployment; after the General Strike, the Labour Party and TUC guarded themselves against NUWCM entryism; members of the NUWCM turned out not to be genuine revolutionaries, but workers merely seeking a betterment in their conditions, namely a job; and the NUWCM leadership was afflicted by sectarianism.

Divisions on the left, on both sides of the Channel, were one of the many reasons why revolution in the 1920s remained a long way off. Yet even if these disputes could have been overcome, the workforce was not in the mood for revolutionary change, and governments were prepared to defend themselves through a mixture of force and conciliation. War had not weakened state structures, but strengthened them. All might have been different if Britain and France had lost the war and had been victims of the geopolitical restructuring of the 1919 peace settlement. Around the corner, however, lay real dangers. The arrival of the Great Depression, the spread of fascism throughout much of central and eastern Europe and the rise of international tension created a series of conditions in which liberal democracy again seemed in peril, this time not so much from the left but from the right.

The 1930s: the threat from the right

The mood of 1918–19 had been a mixture of apprehension and anxiety, intermingled with relief that the war was over. A fragile optimism had even managed to get a hold by the late 1920s, reinforced by international developments epitomized in the Locarno Treaties of 1925, which had recognized the permanence of the geopolitical boundaries of the 1919 Peace Conference and the Kellogg–Briand Pact of 1928, which renounced war 'as an instrument of national policy'. By contrast, the atmosphere of the 1930s was dark, pessimistic and full of foreboding, once again a mood reinforced by events further afield, most obviously the coming to power of Hitler.

The tone was set by the Depression, triggered by the Wall Street Crash of October 1929. Given its financial links with the USA, Britain was quick to feel the effects – a fall in production and a loss of overseas trade – whereas France remained relatively unaffected until 1931, for reasons that economists disagree upon. It may be that France was cocooned by its reliance on agriculture. It has been further suggested that French industries were small and self-reliant, and thereby largely immune to the withdrawal of foreign investments. Certainly Poincaré's stabilization of the franc in 1926 had turned France into 'a haven for gold', which cushioned the early removal of capital.[31] It was this policy that the British Treasury blamed for exacerbating the slump, believing that it had 'forced other countries to take deflationary measures'.[32]

Whatever the case, the effects of the slump were eventually more dramatic in France than in Britain, and proved longer-lived. This was partly because the interwar years were generally unimpressive for the UK economy. There had been a brief boom in 1919, and another in the later 1920s, yet unemployment was always high at over 1 million. This meant that the lay-offs of the Depression years, although severe, were not such a jolt to the system as they were elsewhere, notably in Germany and France. The official registers recorded 1.5 million unemployed in the UK at the start of 1930, and 2.5 million by the close of the year. For those in work, the accompanying fall in prices inevitably raised standards of living, and it should be remembered that, amid the hunger marches and NUWCM demonstrations, certain sectors of the economy flourished, notably so-called 'new industries': car manufacture, electrics and plastics. Unemployment in France came as a greater shock, as it had been relatively low throughout the 1920s, at under 100,000. By 1936, official statistics revealed it had reached 433,700, in reality probably even higher, although still nowhere near as bad as earlier in Germany.[33] As in Britain, the drop in prices benefited industrial workers who enjoyed a job, yet hit the agricultural sector badly, and rattled the confidence of the lower-middle classes. There quickly emerged the fear of falling into what E. M. Forster called 'the abyss of poverty'. Anxiety also permeated the political parties. Although both Britain and France witnessed the emergence of 'national governments', determined to see the crisis through regardless of ideological differences, elsewhere voters and politicians questioned whether liberal democracy was capable of coping with the downturn. And, in the early 1930s, there was no shortage of alternative solutions, especially those offered by the extreme right.

In Britain, the Depression effectively unseated MacDonald's Labour government, elected in 1929. Although his party had emerged with the most MPs, its majority was fragile, and by-elections quickly revealed 'the temporary nature of Labour's ascendancy over the Conservatives'.[34] Divided over the need to press for progressive reform, for instance whether to repeal the Trades Dispute Act, it discovered its energies were exhausted by a search for an unemployment cure. To this end, MacDonald created the Economic Advisory Council, a type of think-tank which assembled trade unionists, economists and representatives of industry. A public works programme was introduced, yet it was not enough. Unemployment rates soared, and Labour's policies came in for sharp criticism from the Liberals, who sought greater commitment to public spending, and from the Tories, who favoured deflation and protection. All parties were troubled by the rising cost of unemployment relief, which ultimately did for the government. In August 1931, amid a run on the pound and bitter political infighting, MacDonald agreed to the idea of a 'National Government', comprising Liberals and Tories, which quickly eased the crisis by taking Britain off the gold standard. In

October, MacDonald went to the country, which returned a huge Conservative majority, Labour losing heavily thanks to its poor record in government. In what was known as 'the great betrayal', MacDonald agreed to stay on as the prime minister of a new 'National Government', though this was essentially Conservative except in name. In 1935 he eventually moved aside for Baldwin, whose Tories won the elections of that year, although the pretence of a national government persisted until the latter's resignation two years later, when the premiership passed to Neville Chamberlain.[35]

Within France, the eventual arrival of the Depression ended the progressive reforms of Tardieu, the conservative modernizer who had sought a five-year plan for 'national retooling', a scheme which alienated the right and angered the Socialists for stealing several of their clothes. In 1932, a left-wing Socialist/Radical coalition won the elections, yet as Julian Jackson remarks, the two parties could not agree on how to address the slump. 'The Radicals', he writes, 'wanted to cut government expenditure and eliminate the budget deficit; the Socialists believed this would deepen the Depression.'[36] The Radicals might have carried the day if they had been able to draw on conservative support, yet the right was wary of associating itself with a left-wing coalition that still talked of reform, so the Radicals were forced to rely on their unreliable Socialist allies. Paralysis of the political system followed, what is known as *immobilisme*: over 18 months there were seven cabinets. Troublingly, the gridlock was broken by the intervention of the right-wing leagues which, on 6 February 1934, demonstrated in the streets of Paris following the exposure of government corruption in the so-called Stavisky Affair, a scandal surrounding the activities of a small-time crook who had enjoyed the alleged patronage and protection of high-ranking Radical ministers. Whether the leagues sought to seize power at that moment is a question to which we must return, yet their intervention forced the creation of 'a government of national union' led initially by Gaston Doumergue, then by the centre-right politician, Pierre-Etienne Flandin, who was succeed by another conservative, Pierre Laval.

Against a backdrop of depression and political *immobilisme*, the extra-parliamentary leagues flourished. The most venerable of these was the neoroyalist and deeply xenophobic *Action Française*, founded by Charles Maurras in the 1890s. This had enjoyed considerable influence before 1914, but suffered a series of setbacks in the interwar years, notably in 1926 when it was condemned by Pius XI, who was fearful that the movement's message was increasingly paganistic. Thereafter it lost much of its Catholic support, and in the 1930s could muster a membership of only 60,000. By then, it was regarded as stale and lethargic – '*inaction française*' was the label applied to it by the fascist writer Lucien Rebatet.[37] It was also overtaken by those veterans' organizations that had evolved in the 1920s: the *Jeunesses Patriotes* of Pierre Taittinger, the champagne mogul, and the *Faisceau* of Georges Valois, a one-time syndicalist who had moved to the far right and who finished his political odyssey on the far left. Both these movements drew inspiration from Mussolini, and temporarily lost influence when Poincaré returned to power in 1926. In 1933, their star was again on the ascendant, but they were challenged by François Coty's *Solidarité Française*, another imitation of the Italian fascism, and the *Croix de Feu*. Originally a veterans' society, founded in 1927 by Maurice d'Hartoy, and open to those who had been awarded the *Croix de Feu* medal, this became the largest of the leagues. This transformation was effected by Colonel François de La Rocque, a nationalist army officer with an eye for organization, who widened membership to anyone. By 1935 it was some 300,000 strong. When, in 1936, the Popular Front outlawed the leagues, de la Rocque transformed the *Croix de Feu* into a political party, the *Parti Social Français* (PSF). Had not the 1940 elections been postponed because of the war, it is likely that it would have won several seats,[38] as would the *Parti Populaire Français* (PPF) established in 1936. Led by Jacques Doriot, a renegade communist who was thrown out of the PCF for advocating a Popular Front before Moscow had given its approval, the PPF enjoyed sizeable support among the working classes, amassing an estimated membership of 100,000 in 1937.

Britain never possessed the same variety of far-right organizations as France, and in the 1920s these were very much on the fringes, frequently inviting ridicule. Shortly after Mussolini's March on Rome, and in response to the growing power of the Labour Party, Rotha Lintorn Orman, a young woman who had driven an ambulance in World War One and who could not readjust to her earlier profession as a Somerset dairy farmer, founded the British Fascisti.[39] Although this never attracted more than a few hundred recruits, it soon had to compete with the Imperial Fascist League, established in 1929 by Arthur Reese, a former camel vet, whose love of animals was matched only by his hatred of Jews; and the Nordic League of 1935, originally the White Knights of Britain, whose membership was confined to the upper-middle class. As David Powell reminds us, there were also a series of purportedly apolitical bodies devoted to specific causes, which were undeniably far right in their orientation, among them the British Empire Union, the Middle Class Union and the National Citizens' Union, though none mustered mass membership.[40]

That was only achieved, if fleetingly, by the British Union of Fascists (BUF), inaugurated by Oswald Mosley, an aristocrat and Conservative MP who switched to Labour in 1924. Minister without portfolio in the 1929 MacDonald government, he became frustrated at Labour's failure to back his solutions to unemployment (a Keynsian package of reflationary measures known as the 'Mosley Memorandum'), and at the party's unwillingness to challenge the parliamentary system. To this end, in 1931 he founded the 'New Party', an embryonic fascist movement, which championed strong government and a corporatist economy. Attracting the support of a small number of maverick Conservative and Labour MPs, it performed disastrously in the 1931 elections. Convinced of the rightness of his cause and believing himself to possess messianic powers – thus providing the satirist P. G. Wodehouse with material for his character Roderick Spode in his Jeeves and Wooster novels – Mosley launched the BUF in October 1932. Membership was around 17,000 in February 1934, rising to 50,000 by June, when the movement paraded its supporters, and love of violence, at the Olympia rally. Thereafter the BUF lost members, and possibly counted a mere 10,000 nationwide when, in October 1936, Mosley's Blackshirts clashed with opponents in the 'Battle of Cable Street' in London's East End. Analysis of the social membership of the BUF is thus fraught with difficulties. All that can be safely said is that it was extremely eclectic, drawing on dissident members of the establishment, disgruntled lower-middle class Tory voters, disaffected working-class urbanites in the Midlands, London and Leeds, and a fair number of the criminal classes. Interestingly, about a fifth of its membership were women, partly because the movement offered them a role denied in traditional political parties, but largely because it supported progressive measures such as paid maternity leave and employment protection.[41]

Why did the extreme right, on both sides of the Channel, fail to emulate the success of its German and Italian counterparts? In the case of Britain, it should be stressed that this discussion pertains largely to the BUF, as this was the only truly sizeable movement, and it is a debate that has been heavily influenced by the writing of Richard Thurlow.[42] He has identified several explanations behind BUF failure. To begin with, the economic environment was not as bad in the UK as elsewhere, a point already stressed. Although the 1930s was a bleak decade, government policies – the departure from gold, low interest rates, tariff protection, imperial preference, modest government investment and, eventually, rearmament – staved off the worst. As with the NUWCM, Mosley's fascists discovered that the unemployed rallied only if something tangible was on offer, such as assistance with benefits, and even then those out of work were more likely to turn to the Labour party or the TUC.

British fascism, continues Thurlow, also had internal, structural problems. Mosley might have been a charismatic figure, but he was an extremely difficult man to work with, and unlike La Rocque, he had little talent for organization. Matters might have been different if the BUF had enjoyed the backing of influential patrons. Instead, it crucially lost the support of Rothermere's *Daily Mail* after the Olympia violence and the 'Night of the Long Knives' in Germany, together with the backing of several other business donors, leaving the movement dependent on Mosley's own cheque book and laundered funds from Mussolini's Italy. Although this association with the Duce was not widely known at the time, in the public mind the BUF was too closely associated with the violence perpetrated by fascists abroad, and seemed intent on importing this into the UK. Mosley himself did nothing to counter this impression, refusing to criticise Mussolini's invasion of Abyssinia in 1935 and Hitler's remilitarization of the Rhineland a year later. Convinced of the rightness of his cause, the BUF leader pressed home his message, yet this found little resonance among the public. Corporatism was recognized by the working classes to be largely a sham, a front for capitalist interests, as was indeed the case in Mussolini's Italy. Antisemitism did find an audience, but only at regional level, most obviously London's East End, where the left made a determined stand against fascism. This response was important, but equally so was a wider appreciation that Britain did not face a communist revolution. A fear of the left was a key driving force in the appeal of fascism elsewhere, yet, as has been seen, Britain was never seriously on the verge of revolution, something understood by a majority of the political elites.

Mosley also had to fight the appeal of the Conservative party which, by 1914, had established itself 'as the broad church of the political right'.[43] The Tories were no longer narrowly associated with aristocratic interests, but were acknowledged to represent a broad constituency: better-off elements of the working classes; country labourers, as well as farmers; professional and suburban middle classes; and the business community.[44] In this situation, it was difficult for the BUF to present itself as a credible alternative. Although it did manage to win over some fringe elements, Tory activists understood that to work outside the party, in the way that the maverick Henry Page Croft attempted in 1917–18, was to invite failure. Had the party endured a longer period of opposition in the interwar years, as in the period 1905–15, when it was tempted down the unconstitutional path over Irish Home Rule and reform of the House of Lords, its unity might have fractured.

However, in the postwar world its ascendancy was ensured, thanks to a series of factors: the victory of 1918, which enabled the party to wrap itself up in patriotism and the enduring symbols of British power, notably monarchy and empire; the 'first-past-the-post system' which, both then and now, normally gives a disproportionate advantage to the party that garners the most votes at a general election; the Irish settlement, which removed some 60 or so various 'progressives' and replaced them with 12 MPs, 10 of whom were nearly always Ulster Unionists; the decline of the Liberals, whose vote more often than not went to the Tories; and the weaknesses of Labour. The Conservatives thus seemed the 'natural party of government', an impression reinforced by the 'national governments' of the 1930s, which generally held their discipline despite having to tackle some sensitive issues, for instance the granting of greater autonomy to India, which so-called 'diehard' Tories saw as a betrayal of empire, and the abdication crisis.

The British state also played its part in containing the threat of fascism, on the domestic front at least. After the Olympia rally and Rothermere's dropping of Mosley, the press was urged to disregard the BUF, while the BBC was warned not to give the movement any undue publicity. Although the left carped that government was not doing enough to discourage the fascists, the Public Order Act, introduced after the Battle of Cable Street, did much to contain BUF violence, outlawing the wearing of paramilitary uniforms and insisting on a protocol for demonstrations, something that Mosley's men frequently heeded and the communists did not. And behind the scenes the security services kept a close watch on BUF activity, even if the far left continued to be viewed as the principal enemy. Analysis of 'the phoney war', the period between September 1939 and May 1940, has shown that the government was in several minds about how to deal with potential fifth columnists, yet when the crunch came, with the German victory in north-west Europe, measures were quickly taken to disband the BUF and intern some 1500 people for fascist or pro-Nazi sympathies.

It is sometimes argued that Britain's democratic culture also played a part in neutralizing the threat of fascism, although this argument is far more readily applied to France. Here was the cradle of the Enlightenment and the home of the Declaration of the Rights of Man and the Citizen, and a country where the principles of liberal democracy found a sophisticated expression in the Third Republic. Summarizing this argument, although not necessarily subscribing to it, Brian Jenkins writes, 'in the interwar period the French people already had fifty years continuous experience of adult male suffrage, elective and accountable government at both local and national level, open access to public office, freedom of the press and association – in contrast with neighbouring Italy and Germany, where such practices were arguably far less developed.'[45] Admittedly, there emerged in France several right-wing leagues, yet it is claimed that these were pale imitations of their counterparts elsewhere in Europe, and were by implication no real threat to the Republic. In the words of René Rémond, the *Croix de Feu* was little more than 'boy-scouting for grown ups',[46] and was a precursor of Gaullism in its respect for state legality. La Rocque himself, continues Rémond, was a military man, and as such was especially aware of constitutional boundaries and had no wish to overstep the mark. France succumbed to extremism, it is maintained, only when it was defeated militarily, and even then Vichy never truly transformed itself into a fascist state, except perhaps in the last months of its existence when firmly under the German heel.

The complexity of the Vichy moment has been studied exhaustively by historians, and it has been shown that this drew on a number of existing traditions, most troublingly an ideological and biological anti-semitism not so dissimilar from Nazism. No longer an aberration, it is widely agreed that the Pétain regime marked continuity in French political life.[47] These findings have inevitably led researchers to look more closely at the interwar years, and among non-French authors there is growing consensus that France did indeed produce its own fascists, not just shallow copyists of Mussolini's Blackshirts. To take again the example of the *Croix de Feu*, studied exhaustively by Robert Soucy and Kevin Passmore, this exemplified many of the overriding characteristics associated with fascism: a hatred of Marxism; a trenchant antiparliamentarianism; a distaste for liberalism; a love of violence and paramilitarism; a personality cult; and a vogue for radical rhetoric. On the other hand, it is questionable to what extent La Rocque and his supporters were prepared to overhaul society, an issue that troubles equally historians of Hitler's Germany and Mussolini's Italy.[48]

If France did produce its own distinct band of fascists, what held them back? Some historians have found the answer in the make-up of French society, what Stanley Hoffmann famously termed '*la société bloquée*'.[49] This phrase was used to describe the sleepy, parochial world of the 1930s, famously depicted in the novels of Marcel Pagnol and André Chamson, in which the interests of the peasantry, artisans and lower-middle classes were cushioned from the forces of economic change by government policies, for instance high tariffs, low taxes and the protection of property. Such an argument has much to recommend it, and further explains the alienation of the working classes and their attraction to Marxism. It was also a world that did not appear to have been seriously disrupted by either World War One or the Depression of the 1930s, at least not to the extent witnessed in Weimar Germany. A truly large shake-out of the economy did not arise until the so-called *trente glorieuses*, the economic miracle of the three decades that followed the Liberation in 1945. In this situation, writes Maurice Larkin, 'it is easy to forget that a large section of French society was reasonably content with things as they were', although the drawn-out sense of insecurity felt by many during the Depression should not be forgotten.[50] It was partially this unease which, in the 1930s, led to the rise of a peasant fascist movement in the shape of the Green Shirts of Henri Dorgères.

If French society put a brake on the rise of fascism, so too did the republican tradition. This was undeniably important, and made several French intellectuals, even those on the far right such as the novelist Robert Brassilach, wary of supporting movements which they viewed as essentially 'un-French'. Yet the republican tradition in itself was not enough to have saved France. Notions that La Rocque was a stickler for constitutional niceties, and unwilling to contemplate a *putsch*, should be rapidly dismissed. In 1937, reflecting on the victory achieved by the Popular Front in the preceding year, he told a rally, 'Do you understand today that if in the month of June I had ordered you to descend into the streets you would have been crushed?' Four years later, he tackled the same theme: 'We would have had to overcome the double shock of masses of people drunk with Popular Front demagoguery and of public authorities obedient to the orders of the government: the victory of the reds would have been certain.' As Soucy reflects, these were hardly the words 'of a man committed to republican legality.'[51] Rather, La Rocque understood the limited nature of street violence and its inherent inability to produce a takeover, something amply demonstrated on 6 February 1934, when the demonstrators lacked any real sense of purpose or discipline.

That was not how the left viewed matters. After 6 February 1934, it saw coups everywhere. While fears of a right-wing plot to topple the Republic were exaggerated (although the terrorist organization, the *Cagoule*, might have been planning this in 1937), the left had little confidence in the parties of the right to defend liberal democracy. To the chagrin of conservatives such as Tardieu and Mandel, France had no equivalent to the British Conservative party, but instead a highly fissiparous right which, as we have seen, was dominated by the *Fédération Républicaine* and *Alliance Démocratique*. Created at the time of the Dreyfus Affair, the *Alliance* had rallied conservatives under the republican banner, yet doubts remained whether supporters of the *Fédération* had made the same leap of faith. They were described by Poincaré as 'the men of the 16 May 1877', an allusion to the monarchist followers of Marshal MacMahon.[52] Significantly, in 1937 members of the *Fédération* would join with Doriot's PPF in a *Front de la Liberté*, supposedly an anti-communist alliance, yet one also directed at the PSF.

By that point, the left had its own coalition in the shape of the Popular Front, an emulation of the *Frente Popular* that had been created in Republican Spain. Interestingly, this initiative had sprung from the most sectarian of parties, the PCF, which was troubled by the rise of fascism both at home and abroad. Once Moscow had given its nod, the PCF entered into a pact with the SFIO in July 1934. This was not enough for the communists, who believed they had to win over those members of the lower-middle class, the group most attracted to the appeal of fascism. The Radicals were naturally cautious of such advances, but soon had a change of heart. This was due to their disappointments at the Flandin and Laval governments, neither of which seemed capable of turning round the Depression, and to their fear of being trounced at the polls by communists and socialists, who were doing well in municipal and by-elections. So it was they entered into a broad coalition of the left to fight the 1936 elections.

Although the Popular Front sent shock waves through the bourgeoisie, which feared the revolution they had always dreaded was now close at hand, its election augured a strengthening of liberal democracy in France. As Douglas Johnson remarked, this was reflected in the figure of the Socialist leader and prime minister Léon Blum.[53] In Johnson's words, he was 'a new man' who had not spent all his life playing the parliamentary 'game of politics'. Moreover, the Popular Front differed from previous coalitions in that it was designed to govern, not just win the election, even if the communists resorted to their sectarian ways, refusing seats in cabinet, as soon as the Front was elected. The social and economic programme was also far-reaching: widespread nationalizations; the removal of corruption in parliamentary life; the extension of civil liberties to trade unions; and the outlawing of the extra-parliamentary leagues, something quickly effected, though at the cost of boosting the membership of reconfigured PSF. Excited by the programme on offer, thousands of workers went on spontaneous strikes to celebrate Blum's election, ensuring that one of his first jobs in office was to get France back to work. In the event, much of his programme would not be realized and, in mid-1937, the Blum government collapsed thanks to a financial crisis and a belated decision to devalue. None the less, despite its brief lifetime, the Popular Front had not been a failure. While its accomplishments never matched its supporters' aspirations, it proved that French democracy was mature enough to accommodate a genuinely left-wing government.

With the collapse of the Popular Front, the Radicals under Edouard Daladier discarded their former left-wing allies and secured a parliamentary coalition with the right. This entailed the repeal of several of the social and economic gains agreed by Blum in the so-called Matignon Agreements. In their stead, Daladier pushed through a series of right-wing policies: the rounding up of Spanish Republican refugees into holding camps; a *rapprochement* with the Catholic Church; and the *Code de la Famille*, a pronatalist measure which provided for mortgage relief for those with large families. For some historians, these measures presage those of the Vichy regime. Yet, as other writers have countered, such parallels should not lead us to believe that democracy was terminally ill. By taking the Radicals in a rightwards direction, Daladier lent a stability to the Republic, even if this meant reneging on some of the more progressive measures of the Popular Front. In this situation, France was far better equipped to deal with the real menace, one that came not from within, but from without – Nazi Germany.

Conclusion

With the military collapse of the Third Republic and the institution of the Vichy regime, all the pent-up frustrations about French parliamentary democracy came tumbling out into the open. The Republic was blasted as a fraudulent, enfeebled, self-serving and selfish regime. No-one had a good word to say about it, including its former supporters. As Blum himself admitted in 1941, 'I won't hesitate to agree that the French governmental system suffered excessively from internal ills, that it bore within itself inherent elements of instability, discontinuity, inefficiency.'[54] Across the Channel, British commentators reached similar conclusions. As Henry Channon, private secretary to R. A. Butler, confided to his diary on 10 July 1940: 'The Third French Republic has ceased to exist and I don't care; it was graft-ridden, incompetent, Communistic and corrupt and had outlived its day.'[55]

Any assessment of liberal democracy in either Britain or France should be attempted outside the prism of 1940. Had France been defeated militarily in 1918, it is not hard to believe that the same sort of self-introspection would have engulfed the country, and that regime change would have followed. It is commonly remarked that no post-1789 French regime has survived defeat in war. Instead, victory in World War One was an endorsement of the Republic and reinforced state structures, just as it did in Britain. Both countries felt a strong sense of self-worth as victorious powers, even if the popular mood was not necessarily confident of the future; both countries were unaffected by geopolitical rearrangements or a sense of irredentism, although France welcomed back the lost provinces of Alsace and Lorraine, which were not unhappy to slough off their German masters; and both countries enjoyed a permanence in their political institutions, unlike many of the central and eastern European states carved out of the old Austro-Hungarian empire.

Moreover, the processes of parliamentary democracy, some of which had been suspended in the course of the war, were quickly restored. This is not to say that everyone was happy with those procedures, yet the mainstream political parties were largely content with things as they were, and did not countenance radical change. Things might have been different if the right had not been so dominant, yet power in the interwar years rested largely with conservatism. In Britain, the Tories were effectively in control, with the exception of two brief periods, and consolidated themselves as a broad coalition of the right. Across the Channel, there was no real equivalent of the Conservative party – perhaps the Radicals came closest in representing a broad range of social interests – yet the right still predominated. The left-wing experiments of 1924 and 1936 were short-lived. Admittedly, French politics drifted into *immobilisme*, especially in the Depression years, when it was unclear exactly who was in charge, but it could be argued that this was a strength as well as a weakness. It provided a consensus of sorts, and the parliamentarians remained alive to the dangers from without. The Republic had a fine tradition of defending itself when in danger, for instance at the time of the Boulanger and Dreyfus Affairs before 1914, and in the 1930s its defensive instincts stayed intact when confronted with the Stavisky riots and the extraparliamentary leagues. Among republicans, there was recognition that the republican tradition in itself was not enough to preserve liberal democracy.

Without doubt, the attractiveness of extremes was greater in France than it was in Britain. The nature of French society had given rise to a greater sense of frustration and alienation on the part of the working classes, which helped nourish a more vibrant communist party than was to be found in the UK. Yet it must be questioned whether the mood of the workforce was necessarily revolutionary. In any case, the left was far too splintered in France to deliver revolution, and the PCF was heavily guided by Moscow, which was preoccupied by affairs in the Soviet Union rather than fulfilling the revolutionary remit of the Comintern. In the case of Britain, the far left was a marginal force, unable to exploit effectively the very real grievances of the working classes, whereas the Labour party and TUC were fully committed to gradualism. The greater threat, in both countries, came from the extreme right. That challenge in the UK was undermined by the strength of the Conservative party, the many internal failures of the BUF, and the willingness of the state to defend itself. As already noted, that readiness was much in evidence in France, and found particular expression in the Popular Front, even if this led to a boost in membership of the PSF.

Fortunately, in both countries the economic trough of the 1930s was not great enough to produce the same number of *déclassés* as in Germany and elsewhere in central Europe. Things were undeniably bad, especially in France where the Depression became seemingly a permanent part of the scenery, yet unemployment levels were not as huge as in the Weimar Republic, and in certain parts of Britain they were a familiar experience, removing any element of surprise. Overall, the economic policies of the 'national governments' probably did just enough to contain the situation.

Ultimately, Britain had one defence against extremism which was denied to France – a relative security from invasion. Increasingly during the 1930s, the governments in London and Paris were troubled by the threat coming both from Bolshevism and from fascism, particularly in its Nazi form. In order to withstand the extreme, symbolized by Moscow, they were tempted into making a series of eventually futile endeavours aimed at appeasing the even more imminently dangerous one represented by Berlin. On balance, it was the French who fretted more and who became the greater champions of appeasement, only abandoning that policy almost at the last moment – and even then, in some cases, resuming its pursuit by throwing in their lot with Vichy. Here is not the place to rehearse the many reasons why France and its western European partners were defeated in 1940. However, it should be stressed that the causes of this disaster were overwhelmingly located in the field of battle, not in the National Assembly.[56] It was at this moment that the extremists had their chance. In June 1940, London naturally feared that it was next on Hitler's list of conquests, and it is likely that the UK would have responded to foreign occupation much in the same way as its former ally.[57] In the event, invasion and occupation were avoided. As is frequently said, France would go on to endure its 'dark years', and Britain its 'finest hour'.

Further reading

A robust political narrative of Britain during this period is to be found in Peter F. Clarke, *Hope and Glory. Britain, 1900–1990* (London: Allen

Lane, 1996); G. Peele and Chris Cook, *The Politics of Reappraisal, 1918–1940* (Basingstoke: Macmillan, 1976); and David Powell, *British Politics, 1910–35. The Crisis of the Party System* (London: Routledge, 2004). Although showing signs of age, Charles Loch Mowat, *Britain Between the Wars, 1918–1940* (London: Methuen, 1968) is still worth consulting. James F. McMillan, *Twentieth Century France* (London: Arnold, 1992) provides the French context, and may be usefully supplemented by Maurice Larkin, *France Since the Popular Front* (Oxford: Clarendon, 1988); and Richard Vinen, *France, 1934–70* (London: Macmillan, 1996). See also Paul Bernard and Henri Dubief, *The Decline of the Third Republic, 1914–1938* (Cambridge: Cambridge University Press, 1988). Robert and Isabelle Tombs, *That Sweet Enemy. The French and the British from the Sun King to the Present* (London: Heinemann, 2006) compare the two nations and draw some fascinating parallels.

An introduction to the wider social background is provided by John Stevenson, *British Society, 1914–45* (Harmondsworth: Pelican, 1984); Martin Pugh, *We Danced All Night. A Social History of Britain in the 1930s* (London: The Bodley Head, 2008); Eugen Weber, *The Hollow Years. France in the 1930s* (New York: Norton, 1992); and Stanley Hoffman, *Decline or Renewal. France Since the 1930s* (New York: Viking, 1974). Robert Graves and Alan Hodge, *The Long Weekend. A Social History of Great Britain, 1918–1930* (London: Faber and Faber, 1940) is a fascinating commentary. Martin Kitchen, *Europe Between the Wars* (London: Pearson, 2006 edn) compares European societies and contains useful individual chapters on Britain and France. Also see Piers Brendon, *The Dark Valley. A Panorama of the 1930s* (London: Jonathan Cape, 2000).

The wider impact of World War One is discussed in the many essays in Gordon Martel (ed.), *A Companion to Europe, 1900–1945* (Oxford: Blackwell, 2006). The failure of the extreme left (and right) to mount a challenge to liberal democracy in 1920s Britain is discussed in Andrew Thorpe (ed.), *The Failure of Political Extremism in Interwar Britain* (Exeter: Exeter University Press, 1989). Among a vast literature, see also Matthew Worley, *Class against Class. The Communist Party in Britain between the Wars* (London: Tauris, 2002). The essays in Ross McKibbin, *The Ideologies of Class. Social Relations in Britain, 1880–1950* (Oxford: Oxford University Press, 1990) do much to explain the limited appeal of Marxism to the British working classes, as well as the enduring popularity of the Tories. The French left is introduced in Roger Magraw, *A History of the French Working Class, Vol. 2* (Oxford: Blackwell, 1992).

The threat posed by the extreme right in France, and the vexed question as to whether there was ever such a thing as a French fascism, may be best approached through the edited volume by Brian Jenkins, *France in the Era of Fascism. Essays on the French Authoritarian Right* (Oxford: Berghahn, 2004), which contains an extensive bibliography and suggestions for further reading. Although primarily concerned with the Vichy period, Julian Jackson, *The Dark Years, 1940–1944* (Oxford: Oxford University Press, 2001) has much to say about the crisis decade of the 1930s. See, too, his *The Politics of Depression in France, 1932–1936* (Cambridge: Cambridge University Press, 1985) and his *The Popular Front in France. Defending Democracy, 1934–38* (Cambridge: Cambridge University Press, 1988). The British right in the same period is tackled by Roger Thurlow, *Fascism in Britain. A History, 1918–1985* (Oxford: Oxford University Press, 1987); and Martin Pugh, *Hurrah for the Blackshirts. Fascists and Fascism in Britain Between the Wars* (London: Cape, 2005). The most up-to-date biography of Mosley is that by Stephen Dorrill, *Blackshirt. Sir Oswald Mosley and British Fascism* (London: Viking, 2006).

Among reference works, see Andrew Thorpe, *The Longman Companion to Britain in the Era of the Two World Wars, 1914–1945* (London: Longman, 1993); and P. H. Hutton, *Historical Dictionary of the French Third Republic* (London: Aldwych Press, 1986).

Notes

1 Quoted by Michael Balfour, *The Kaiser and his Times* (Harmondsorth: Pelican, 1975 edn), p. 390.

2 Gary Sheffield, *Forgotten Victory. The First World War. Myths and Realities* (London: Headline, 2002).

3 The term 'moral compass' belongs to the British diplomat Maurice Hankey. See Margaret Macmillan, *Peacemakers. The Paris Peace Conference of 1919 and its Attempt to End War* (London: John Murray, 2001), p. 23.

4 Martin Blinkhorn, 'The Fascist Challenge', in Gordon Martel (ed.), *A Companion to Europe, 1900–1945* (Oxford: Blackwell, 2006), p. 311.

5 Martin Kitchen, *Europe Between the Wars* (Harlow: Longman, 2nd edn, 2006), p. 2.

6 Quoted by Julian Jackson, '1940 and the Crisis of Interwar Democracy in France', in M. S. Alexander (ed.), *French History since Napoleon* (London: Arnold, 1999), p. 224.

7 See J. Ortega y Gasset, *The Revolt of the Masses* (New York: Norton, 1932).

8 Andrew Thorpe, 'Introduction', in A. Thorpe (ed.), *The Failure of Political Extremism in Interwar Britain* (Exeter: University of Exeter Press, 1989), p. 9.

9 Brian Jenkins, 'Introduction: Contesting the Immunity Thesis', in Brian Jenkins (ed.), *France in the Era of Fascism. Essays on the French*

Authoritarian Right (Oxford: Berghahn, 2005), p. 2, although the author himself does not necessarily agree with this argument.

10 See Martin Pugh, 'The Liberal Party and the Popular Front', *English Historical Review* CXX1 (494), 1327–50 (2006).

11 Figures from David Stevenson, *1914–1918. The History of the First World War* (London: Penguin, 2004), pp. 544 and 551.

12 See Jay M. Winter, *Sites of Memory, Sites of Mourning. The Great War in European Cultural History* (Cambridge: Cambridge University Press, 1995).

13 See R. Samuel, *The Lost World of British Communism* (London: Verso, 2006).

14 J. J. Becker, *The Great War and the French People* (Leamington Spa: Berg, 1985).

15 G. Pedroncini, *Les Mutineries de 1917* (Paris: Presses Universitaires de France, 1967), pp. 53–100.

16 Roger Magraw, *A History of the French Working Class, Vol. 2* (Oxford: Blackwell, 1992), p. 159.

17 For much of the material here, see John Stevenson, *British Society, 1914–45* (Harmondsworth: Pelican, 1984), pp. 85–89.

18 See James F. McMillan, *Twentieth-Century France. Politics and Society* (London: Arnold, 1992), pp. 86–88, for much of what follows here.

19 C. L. Mowat, *Britain Between the Wars, 1918–1940* (London: Methuen, 1955), p. 2.

20 *Ibid.*, pp. 2–9.

21 Richard Griffiths, *Fellow Travellers of the Right* (Oxford: Oxford University Press, 1983 edn).

22 T. O. Lloyd, *Empire to Welfare State. English History, 1906–1967* (Oxford: Oxford University Press, 1970), p. 128.

23 Ross McKibbin, 'Why was there no Marxism in Britain', in Ross McKibbin (ed.), *The Ideologies of Class. Social Relations in Britain, 1880–1950* (Oxford: Oxford University Press, 1991), pp. 1–41.

24 *Ibid.*

25 See Julian Symons, *The General Strike. A Historical Portrait* (London: Stratus, 2001).

26 M. Kelly (ed.), *French Culture and Society* (London: Arnold, 2001), pp. 263–64.

27 P. Bernard and H. Dubief, *The Decline of the Third Republic, 1914–1938* (Cambridge: Cambridge University Press, 1988), pp. 154–55.

28 Andrew Thorpe, 'The Only Effective Bulwark against Reaction and Revolution. Labour and the Frustration of the Extreme Left', in A. Thorpe (ed.), *The Failure of Political Extremism in Interwar Britain, op. cit.*, pp. 11–27.

29 *Ibid.*, p. 16.

30 *Ibid.*, p. 27.

31 Julian Jackson, *The Politics of Depression in France, 1932–1936* (Cambridge: Cambridge University Press, 1986), pp. 22–23.

32 R. Tombs and I. Tombs, *That Sweet Enemy. The French and the British from the Sun King to the Present* (London: Heinemann, 2006), p. 525.

33 Alfred Sauvy, *Histoire économique de la France entre les deux guerres, 1931–1939, Vol. 2* (Paris: Fayard, 1967), p. 554.

34 D. Powell, *British Politics 1910–35. The Crisis of the Party System* (London: Routledge, 2004), p. 160.

35 See G. R. Searle, *Country before Party. Coalitions and the Idea of 'National Government' in Modern Britain, 1885–1987* (London: Longman, 1995) and Philip Williamson, *National Crisis and National Government. British*

Politics, Economy and the Empire, 1926–1932 (Cambridge: Cambridge University Press, 1992).

36 Julian Jackson, *France, The Dark Years, 1940–1944* (Oxford: Oxford University Press, 2001), p. 71.

37 Lucien Rebatet, *Les Décombres* (Paris: Denoël, 1942).

38 H. R. Kedward, *Occupied France. Occupation and Resistance, 1940–1944* (Oxford: Blackwell, 1985), p. 23.

39 Much of the material in this paragraph comes from Roger Eatwell, *Fascism. A History* (London: Chatto & Windus, 1995), pp. 175–91.

40 D. Powell, *British Politics 1910–35, op. cit.*, p. 180.

41 J. Gottlieb, *Feminine Fascism. Women in Britain's Fascist Movement, 1923–1945* (London: Tauris, 2000).

42 Roger Thurlow, *Fascism in Britain. A History, 1918–1985* (Oxford: Oxford University Press, 1987).

43 B. Coleman, 'The Conservative Party and the Frustration of the Extreme Right', in A. Thorpe (ed.), *The Failure of Political Extremism in Interwar Britain, op. cit.*, p. 50.

44 Ross McKibbin, 'Class and Conventional Wisdom. The Conservative Party and the Public in Interwar Britain', in R. McKibbin (ed.), *The Ideologies of Class, op. cit.*, pp. 260–62.

45 Brian Jenkins, 'Introduction: Contesting the Immunity Thesis', *op. cit.*, p. 11.

46 René Rémond, *La droite en France de 1815 à nos jours* (Paris: Aubier-Montaigne, 1954).

47 The historiography of the Vichy regime may be usefully followed in S. Fishman, L. Lee Downs, I. Sinanoglu *et al.* (eds), *France at War. Vichy and the Historians* (Oxford: Berg, 2000).

48 Robert Soucy, 'French Fascism and the *Croix de Feu*. A Dissenting Interpretation', *Journal of Contemporary History* 26 (1), 159–88 (1991), and K. Passmore, 'Boy Scoutism for Grown-ups? Paramilitarism in the *Croix de Feu* and the *Parti Social Français*', *French Historical Studies* 19: 527–57 (1996).

49 Stanley Hoffmann (ed.), *In Search of France* (Harvard: Harvard University Press, 1963).

50 Maurice Larkin, *France since the Popular Front* (Oxford: Clarendon, 1988), p. 1.

51 Robert Soucy, 'Fascism in France. Problematising the Immunity Thesis', in Brian Jenkins (ed.), *France in the Era of Fascism, op. cit.*, p. 76.

52 J. Jackson, *France, The Dark Years, op. cit.*, p. 67.

53 Douglas Johnson, 'Léon Blum and the Popular Front', *History* 55 (184): 201 (1970).

54 Quoted by R. O. Paxton, *Vichy France. Old Guard and New Order, 1940–1944* (New York: Alfred Knopf, 1972), p. 185.

55 Robert Rhodes James (ed.), *Chips. The Diaries of Sir Henry Channon* (London: Phoenix, 1999 edn), p. 261.

56 See Julian Jackson, *The Fall of France. The Nazi Invasion of 1940* (Oxford: Oxford University Press, 2003).

57 See Andrew Roberts, 'Hitler's England. What if Germany had invaded Britain in May 1940?', in Niall Ferguson (ed.), *Virtual History. Alternatives and Counterfactuals* (London: Papermac, 1997), pp. 281–320.

9 The origins of World War Two in Europe

Steve Morewood

World War Two was a catalyst in the twentieth century. It accelerated the demise of Europe's global influence, bringing to centre stage two great powers, the Soviet Union and the USA, which afterwards helped to hasten the collapse of European colonial empires. It finally brought an end to Germany's bid to dominate the Continent, dating back to 1870–71, paving the way for reconciliation with France and the formation of the Common Market. And, through the arrival of nuclear weapons, it ushered in a new era, when the protagonists for global hegemony confronted each other via proxies, arms races, economic warfare, culture and propaganda, because a hot war between them risked mutual annihilation.

But while the outcomes of the conflict are clear-cut, its origins remain controversial. 'Responsibility for this terrible catastrophe', insisted Neville Chamberlain on the day Germany invaded Poland, 'lies on the shoulders of one man, the German Chancellor, who has not hesitated to plunge the world into misery in order to serve his own senseless ambitions.'[1] Although German aggression lies at the heart of any answer as to which power provided the main impetus for the outbreak of general hostilities, it is too simplistic to speak merely of 'Hitler's war'. German 'white books' issued during the conflict to justify Nazi foreign policy were insistent that Britain and France forced the hostilities on Germany. In that perspective, it was more Chamberlain's war than Hitler's. The Third Reich's expansionism had proceeded unchecked until September 1939. There is also evidence to suggest that when Poland was invaded, Hitler gambled again that Britain and France would merely protest in the same ineffectual way as they had done over Germany's transgression of the Munich Agreement. Equally, it is clear that Hitler was determined to implement his ideologically driven foreign policy, which was bound to lead to a wider war.

It can be argued that the power vacuum in central-eastern Europe arising from World War One and the peace settlement, in combination with Germany's reluctance to accept its post-1918 eastern frontiers, rendered conflict inevitable. But the timing and manner of its outbreak was down to Hitler, whose racial ideology, fanaticism and persistent chance-taking added new dimensions to German foreign policy. Any examination of the causes of World War Two needs to ask why the counter-challenge to Hitler was so long delayed, and whether an earlier abandonment of appeasement might have postponed or limited the ensuing conflict. Why the Western powers, especially Britain, eventually moved towards confrontation is another key question. A diagnosis should take into account how and why the post-1918 settlement unravelled. Recent work demonstrates that the 1920s are worthy of greater consideration in pinpointing where mistakes were made, even if the most critical decisions belong to the succeeding decade. The unsettling effect of Benito Mussolini's Mediterranean ambitions, and especially of the Abyssinian Crisis, which destroyed the credibility of the League of Nations and got Germany out of isolation, also helps us to understand how the drift to war accelerated towards September 1939. Again, assumptions and miscalculations made in the post-Munich period demand investigation. Nor should we forget the three further stages in the expansion of the European conflict down to June 1941: Mussolini's declaration of war on the Western powers, the subsequent spread of hostilities to the Balkans, and Hitler's invasion of the USSR.

Faultlines of the postwar peace settlement

The Allied decision to allow an armistice in November 1918, rather than fight on until Germany was invaded and occupied, ensured that extreme nationalists, like Hitler, could argue that defeat arose from a 'stab in the back' by treacherous Jews and communists at home rather than from military collapse. As one authority sees it, 'the war ended through what proved to be an unstable accommodation.'[2] Marshal Ferdinand Foch famously predicted in 1919 nothing more than a 20-year truce. The French insistence on a victor's peace, British support for reparations, and American idealism produced a convoluted and contradictory settlement. Thus the Rhineland was demilitarized rather than annexed, as France would have preferred; self-determination was applied selectively and denied where Germany would be strengthened; its overseas empire, with the potential for U-boat bases, was eradicated; conversely, Britain and France expanded their imperial holdings at German and Turkish expense. The German army was reduced to an internal police force bereft of offensive capabilities, the air force was abolished, and the navy became a shell of its former self. The terms, arising from the infamous 'War Guilt clause' of the Treaty of Versailles, shocked the German population, even though they might have been far worse. The Weimar Republic was forever tainted with having signed the 'treaty of victors', but had little alternative unless it wanted to face a continued Allied blockade and even the prospect of renewed hostilities. Germany also became a pariah state in the new international order, being denied membership of the newly formed League of Nations. None of these handicaps proved permanent, however, and the reasons for that continue to provoke debate.

The French wished to maintain the *status quo*. Between 1920 and 1935, France concluded treaties with Belgium, Czechoslovakia, Poland, Romania, the USSR and Yugoslavia. These reflected its defensive posture and sought to contain Germany by threatening a multifronted war. A key factor is that the French interpretation of Versailles – as a mechanism to keep Germany down in perpetuity – soon clashed with the British preference for gradual revision. After the mass slaughter on the Western Front, Britain was reluctant to resume military engagement on the continent and sought to reduce tensions via diplomacy. British lack of support for France and Belgium, when they occupied the Ruhr to punish Germany for lapses in fulfilling its reparations schedule, instilled in those countries a pessimism that would influence their positions in the 1930s. American idealism remained inherent in the peace settlement notwithstanding the USA's ignominious retreat into political isolation. The League became predominantly a forum to resolve quarrels peacefully rather than to enforce settlements on disputants. It depended on their willingness to come to the negotiating table, or otherwise on the readiness of its most powerful members to use coercive force. During 1923, Italy's occupation of Corfu ended when the Royal Navy backed League arbitration with the threat of intervention. In 1925, France led an attempt to introduce the Geneva Protocol,[3] incorporating swingeing economic and military sanctions against aggressors, but the British, mustering Dominion support, resisted successfully. The British Foreign Secretary, Austen Chamberlain, denounced sanctions as futile and rejected the notion that 'the vital business of the League is not so much to promote friendly co-operation ... as to preserve peace by organising war'.[4] Afraid of overstretching its forces by turning them into world policemen, Britain refused to ratify the protocol.

The alternative British approach was epitomized by the Treaty of Locarno, concluded later the same year, which pursued a regional solution. Bringing Germany back into the international fold after the reduction of reparations through the Dawes Plan (1924), the treaty guaranteed the existing frontiers of Germany, France and Belgium. Moreover, Germany voluntarily accepted a demilitarized Rhineland. Here, as Jon Jacobson recognizes,[5] it was not so much Germany but France that was being appeased, with Britain promoting Franco–German reconciliation to keep Soviet Russia isolated. Chamberlain, alongside his German and French counterparts, Gustav Stresemann and Aristide Briand, received the Nobel Peace Prize for concluding what appeared to be a landmark peace settlement, which, in some ways, supplanted Versailles. In 1926 Germany was belatedly admitted into the League. Later regarded as a 'failed' peace treaty, Locarno has more recently been judged as successful at the time, giving Germany the chance to negotiate over terms and improving its relations with Britain and France for several years.

None the less, serious flaws were eventually exposed. First, there was no automatic obligation on the other signatories to resist a German remilitarization of the Rhineland. Indeed, despite the Chiefs of Staff's annual insistence that Britain was in no position to fulfil the Locarno obligations, successive Cabinets refused to countenance funding a rapid reaction force. This was despite the fact that bombers could now reach England from the Rhineland and that, privately, Chamberlain considered that Germany could never be a suitable ally.[6] Second, the Germans proposed and got a Western security pact, but deliberately left the door open to future revision of their eastern frontiers. Indeed, in spring 1925 Germany protested when Chamberlain declared that it was ready to renounce war to reconstitute those borders. Although Germany concluded simultaneous arbitration treaties with Czechoslovakia and Poland, territorial disputes were excluded. Nor were the latter Powers any more reassured by the French revision of their treaties of mutual guarantee, which were adjusted to cover only direct German aggression. Moreover, Locarno was not a general domestic success either in France or indeed in Germany, where the extremist parties especially refused to accept Stresemann's bargain. In both countries a sustained period of stability and rising living standards might have made the difference, but the timing of Locarno – just four years before the Great Depression swept in and created the conditions for Nazi success – was unfortunate and doomed it to failure.[7]

What is often underemphasized is the extent to which Versailles, as a repressive treaty, had already received some heavy blows before Hitler assumed power. Stresemann's initiative leading to Locarno was prompted by the Allies' refusal, in January 1925, to evacuate their forces from Cologne. The changed international atmosphere produced withdrawal one year later, when Britain and France rewarded Weimar

Germany for its policy of so-called 'fulfilment'. In February 1929, Berlin accepted the Kellogg–Briand Pact renouncing war. The 'spirit of Locarno' and the economic whirlwind of the Depression, which most affected Germany and gave impetus to political extremism there, greatly accelerated the revisionism favoured by the British. They came to perceive the peace settlement as too harsh towards Germany, now seen as a potentially valuable economic partner and as a bulwark against the spread of Bolshevism. Thus in 1928 the Allied Control Commission was withdrawn (rendering rearmament easier), and in 1930, five years ahead of schedule, Allied forces left the Rhineland. Two years later, in the depths of the Depression, reparations were suspended altogether. Nor was there retribution for the illicit German rearmament that the Anglo–French intelligence agencies reported, as Britain tended to blame this on France's intransigence over disarmament – a trend that continued when Hitler came to power. Furthermore, through enlisting the assistance of another pariah state, Soviet Russia, the German military were able to conduct experiments, especially with tanks and aircraft, which provided a platform for later *Blitzkrieg* tactics. The emphasis on armour acted as a force multiplier, substituting for the lack of troops and promising the offensive capability to overturn the peace settlement.

The peace settlement challenged

The Kellogg–Briand Pact for the renunciation of war, signed in August 1928, marked the high point of the idealism that characterized the 1920s. It was soon shattered by Japan's invasion of Manchuria in 1931. For the first time, the League was made to look feeble. It lacked coercive military power and, when it sheepishly criticised the aggressor, the Japanese responded defiantly by annexing their conquest and leaving the League. There was a sense that the next crisis would test decisively whatever credibility the League still retained. Crucial here was Article 16 of the Covenant, designed to bring aggressors into line through punitive sanctions. However, this provision had been undermined by amendments introduced (although not formally adopted) by the Geneva Assembly in 1921. Where the original Article had anticipated a state of war between the Covenant-breaker and other members (thus involving the immediate severance of trade and financial relations and mutual support, and the deployment of armed forces), the revisions left more wriggle-room for reluctant enforcers. The impact of the Depression in creating the conditions for Hitler to assume power was also critical. As Zara Steiner says of 1929–33, these were the '"hinge years" ... in which many of the experiments in internationalism came to be tested and their weaknesses revealed'.[8]

Before Mussolini started to challenge the *status quo*, his fellow-dictator in Berlin began making serious noises. Hitler took Germany out of the Geneva Disarmament Conference and the League in October 1933. The following July, he orchestrated the murder of the Austrian Chancellor, Engelbert Dollfuss, and only Italian military posturing at the Brenner Pass prevented *Anschluss* with Austria. Most significant of all, in March 1935 the disarmament provisions of Versailles were openly denounced as Nazi Germany admitted to the Luftwaffe's existence and reintroduced army conscription. The message was clear: if Berlin could not get what it wanted by diplomacy, then it would countenance use of force. The shock waves produced the Stresa Conference, orchestrated by Mussolini, the following month – aimed at containing Germany through a loose front comprising Italy, Britain and France.[9]

In recent years, the Rhineland remilitarization has tended to receive more emphasis than the Abyssinian Crisis as a key turning point towards another world war. But the importance of the latter should not be underrated. The Abyssinian case, like the Manchurian one, involved clear-cut aggression. Disregarding the efforts of the League and the Western powers to reach a peaceful resolution of its territorial dispute with Abyssinia, Italy invaded on 3 October 1935. Against British wishes, Abyssinia (the only independent African state apart from Liberia) had been admitted to the League in 1923. Stalwarts of the organization now saw a golden opportunity for Geneva to reassert its authority by imposing pulverizing economic and military sanctions on an Italian regime that needed to import virtually all its raw materials and mineral requirements, and whose forces were reliant on the British-dominated Suez Canal for reinforcements and supplies.

The world held its breath as the League declared Italy an aggressor, bringing Article 16 into force. In the event, it was not until mid-November that 50 out of 54 members imposed sanctions. Symbolic rather than punitive, they proved of more benefit than hindrance to Mussolini. At the time, his forces were struggling to overcome Abyssinian resistance. To buttress domestic support, he cannily presented Italy as the 'victim' of sanctions. In truth, Britain and France, the leading members at Geneva, were not anxious to bring Italy to heel. Indeed, the unscrupulous French leader, Pierre Laval, used ambiguity to encourage Mussolini to invade. Laval cherished the secret Italo–French military agreements – concluded earlier that year to respond to any renewed German attempt at *Anschluss* – far more than the salvation of a barbaric nation, which still practised slavery. The British browbeat the French into supporting sanctions, but the latter complied only on condition that these did not assume a military character, such as an oil embargo and the closure of the Suez Canal to Italian troop and supply vessels. Either measure would have severed the Duce's lifeline to Abyssinia. To puncture Italian propaganda at home, a naval blockade of Italy promised a crippling effect. Again, had Abyssinia been supplied with modern weapons, Italy might have faced a defeat similar to that of Adowa, where in 1896 its earlier empire-building in East Africa had been brought to a humiliating halt. If Mussolini's credibility had been thus shattered, his regime might well have fallen.

The British were best placed to plunge the dagger into fascist Italy's heart. They had previously been alarmed by propaganda suggesting that their Mediterranean Fleet could be sunk by Italian bombers operating from Sicily. As a precaution, the ships had been moved from their normal base at Malta to Alexandria. Lest Mussolini should turn 'mad dog' in reaction to sanctions, Britain mustered all available forces to defend its imperial interests in the eastern Mediterranean, radiating from Egypt, and to act as a deterrent. The arrival of reinforcements had coincided with a speech made at Geneva on 11 September by the Foreign Secretary, Sir Samuel Hoare, which was widely misinterpreted as signalling that Britain meant business. This impression was strengthened by the ensuing campaign for the general election, held in November 1935, when Baldwin's Conservative-dominated National Government adopted the slogan 'all sanctions short of war', and represented the League as the cornerstone of its foreign policy. In fact, this was a cynical and successful manoeuvre to spike the guns of Labour, which advocated military sanctions, and to win over the electorate whose fervent support for Genevan diplomacy had manifested itself in the recent League of Nations Union Peace Ballot. At the same time, the Canadian delegate at Geneva rocked the boat by tabling an oil sanction. Why, then, did the Western powers prefer the ignominy of appeasement?

Britain refused to see the League as a coercive instrument, and within Whitehall there was even talk of eliminating Article 16. Rearmament had only just begun against Germany and Japan, which were considered the real dangers, and the resentment at the disruption to defence programmes occasioned by the crisis was epitomized by an air force officer's reference to 'this silly African business'.[10] The Chiefs of Staff, and especially the Admiralty, were anti-League, seeing it as a threat to existing contingency plans. Nor was there a desire to make an enemy out of Italy, the blithe assumption being that Mussolini would maintain the Stresa front and revert to a more friendly posture once the crisis had passed. Although the Chiefs of Staff always stressed that, if it came to war, ultimate victory over Italy was assured, they presented a worst-case scenario predicting catastrophic losses. The Royal Navy could lose precious capital ships (only 15 existed by this time), which would affect plans to send a main fleet to Singapore via Suez if Japan became hostile. Any Royal Air Force (RAF) losses would threaten to disrupt the scheme to attain parity with the *Luftwaffe* by 1937, while depletion of armoured vehicles would hinder the proper mechanization of the army Field Force earmarked for deployment against Germany.

But there was an alternative voice. The 'men on the spot', the commanders in the eastern Mediterranean, insisted that Italy could be dealt with swiftly and at minimal loss. Admiral Sir William Fisher, heading the Mediterranean Fleet, was angered by the pessimism of the Chiefs of Staff who insisted that French support must be secured. Convinced his forces could act unaided, he devised plans to bombard the Italian coastline and to use fleet aircraft against the Italian navy anchored at Taranto. He was also confident that Suez could be closed to enemy shipping and an oil sanction successfully enforced. It is now known that, on the eve of invasion, the Italian high command was petrified of facing the Royal Navy and believed defeat to be unavoidable in any such wider conflict.[11]

Instead of instigating decisive action, the British hid behind excuses. French unwillingness to promise military support was a constant, as London refused to join Paris in guaranteeing Austria against *Anschluss*. Nor, because of fears of retaliation, was France keen to yield to British pressure that it should launch a bombing campaign against the Duce's aircraft factories in northern Italy. An oil sanction was represented as ineffectual because of increased American supplies to Italy. Suez, it was maintained, could not be closed because of the 1888 Constantinople Convention guaranteeing access – even though there was expert counter-advice that closure to Italian shipping was justified because of Mussolini's clear violation of international law. The Mediterranean Fleet was portrayed as being more severely short of anti-aircraft ammunition than was truly the case. After the general election, Baldwin accelerated secret efforts to find a negotiated solution that was also acceptable to the French. This led to the infamous Hoare–Laval Pact, which proposed to reward the aggressor. The public outcry that its premature leak aroused in Britain and France forced the resignations of those two negotiators. But a reversal of policy did not follow, despite the elevation of the most pro-League member of the British government, Anthony Eden, to Foreign Secretary, or indeed the news of Mussolini's employment of mustard gas to break the military stalemate. In April 1936, with Italian forces near to taking Addis Ababa, an angry House of Commons demanded Suez's closure – to which the Home Secretary retorted that this could not be achieved with paper boats. The Chiefs of Staff even began withdrawing units from the eastern Mediterranean before the crisis was officially over. Only in the lifting of sanctions, in July 1936, did the National Government, anxious to restore normal relations with Italy, finally take the lead.

Was such failure over Abyssinia the key turning point towards another world war? Certainly the potential was there to deal an aggressor a telling blow – although it does not follow that the League would have always prevailed thereafter. British naval power, however vital here, was of no use in landlocked central and eastern Europe. At the start of the crisis, Germany hedged its bets by offering Britain stocks of anti-aircraft ammunition while also increasing coal and arms exports to Italy. While Hitler might have used the opportunity given by Mussolini's embroilment in Abyssinia to try again for *Anschluss*, he refrained from doing so, exhibiting sympathy for his fellow-dictator's predicament. On 7 November 1935 the German government officially declared its neutrality. This reflected its belief that Britain would soon deal decisively with the Duce's recklessness. News of the Hoare–Laval Pact came as a shock to Berlin and diminished Hitler's respect for the British – a point to which he would return on the eve of his invasion of Poland. At the same time, his admiration for Mussolini rose exponentially. Having considered the Duce reckless to the point of folly, the Führer now spoke of him as a genius. Thus the Abyssinian affair accelerated the drift to war, brought Italy and Germany together in the Rome–Berlin Axis, and sealed the fate of Austria.

The immediate result was Hitler's biggest gamble thus far: the remilitarization of the Rhineland, a move brought forward by a year. The French military attaché in Berlin predicted on 10 December 1935 that Anglo–French disarray would lead Hitler to march into the Rhineland using the forthcoming ratification of the Franco–Soviet Pact as a pretext. From early 1935, French intelligence reviews adopted a worst-case scenario with the result that 'at key stages civilian policy makers were presented with flawed assessments of the military balance.'[12] The Deuxième Bureau accurately predicted *when* remilitarization would occur, but General Louis Maurin, the Minister of War, and General Maurice Gamelin, army chief of staff, conspired to blacken the intelligence still further to avert what the latter described as a 'madcap solution'.[13] They then removed from the Cabinet memorandum the German weaknesses identified by the Deuxième Bureau, such as the likelihood that the *Wehrmacht* possessed only one operational tank and lacked sufficient trained officers – doing this in order to browbeat civilian ministers into accepting a *fait accompli*. Indeed, Gamelin advised that Germany, enjoying superior war potential and a fully mobilized armaments industry, might mobilize 120 divisions. Maurin increased these distortions by conflating military police, *Schutzstaffel* (SS), and members of the National Labour Service with the regular army, making it appear that a more formidable invasion force, amounting to 15 divisions, had entered the Rhineland than was actually the case. In fact only three brigades were involved, with orders to retreat at the first sign of resistance. Civilian ministers inclined towards a military response were presented with a bleak picture. Although Gamelin was fully alive to the strategic implications of a remilitarized Rhineland – rendering France unable to aid the Little Entente powers – this accorded with the defensive mentality of the General Staff. His real purpose was to frighten politicians into endorsing massive rearmament and to secure a definite continental commitment from London.[14] For a scapegoat to explain their passive stance, the French pointed towards Britain, which had likewise virtually written off the Rhineland as a lost cause. In the weeks before remilitarization, Baldwin sought to use the Rhineland as a carrot to persuade Hitler to endorse arms limitation, especially for bomber forces. However, the intended gambit was pre-empted when German troops fronted by a military band marched into the zone on a weekend. Hitler dealt his cards well, offering to renew League membership and to conclude non-aggression pacts with Belgium and France. He spoke of 25 years of peace, playing the reasonable diplomat until the storm passed and 'concessions' could be quietly dropped. The British Chiefs of Staff exploited the crisis to emphasize that they were in no position to make a military response because of the resented diversion of forces to the Mediterranean.[15]

Only in retrospect did the Rhineland crisis appear to be a decisive turning point. At the time, the main British complaint was the manner in which remilitarization was achieved. Faced with Hitler's *fait accompli*, London was even less willing to contemplate a military riposte. For the French, the remilitarization effectively relieved them of the capacity to aid their allies in eastern Europe. The General Staff saw this as a blessing in disguise, which reinforced their defensive reliance on the Maginot Line. There was a sour aftermath, though. Alarmed by the Rhineland episode, on 14 October 1936 Belgium renounced its military alliance with France and declared its neutrality. In the longer term, this was of vital strategic importance because it meant that the Maginot defences could not be extended to the Belgian coast and might be outflanked. What the effective casting adrift of France's Eastern allies did was to project Britain, through appeasement, into the lead role in trying to prevent war as Hitler oriented German foreign policy eastwards in pursuit of *Lebensraum*.

Diplomatic drift

Italo-German military involvement in the Spanish Civil War (July 1936–March 1939) merely confirmed the seeming effeteness of the Western powers. In France, the Popular Front government of Léon Blum was at first inclined towards action, but the British soon persuaded it to prevent a general conflagration by settling for 'non-intervention'. After his Rhineland triumph, Hitler's penchant for ever-bigger gambles encouraged him to go far beyond General Franco's request for fighter aircraft and anti-aircraft guns. The Führer ordered 20 *Junkers 52* transport aircraft to Morocco in July 1936, allowing the stranded Army of Africa to be returned to Spain in support of the rebel Nationalists. Mussolini's contribution, which included 60,000 'volunteers' as well as bombers and tanks, was more impressive for quantity than for effectiveness. In contrast, Germany crucially provided the Condor Legion, which guaranteed the Nationalists aerial supremacy as the *Luftwaffe* honed its combat skills.

Foreign intervention (the Axis for the Nationalists, the Soviet Union for the Popular Front Republican government elected in February 1936) undoubtedly sustained the conflict, even if the fighting on the ground was predominantly between Spaniards. It also produced diplomatic complications, which dominate the British and French files for 1936–37. The Non-Intervention Agreement, signed in August 1936 by 27 countries, including Germany, Italy and the Soviet Union, proved singularly ineffective. Eden informed the British Cabinet in January 1937: 'the struggle in Spain was becoming less an internal struggle than an international one between the fascist and Bolshevik states.'[16] On 18 November 1936, shortly after Madrid came under siege and the proclamation of the Rome–Berlin Axis, Germany and Italy recognized Franco's Nationalist regime as the government of Spain. The Comintern raised the International Brigades to counter fascist 'volunteers'. Stalin could not but respond to the Republican government's pleas for assistance, although he confined it to fighter aircraft (without spares), limited armaments, military experts and advice. His foreign minister, Maxim Litvinov, sought, in vain, to forge an anti-Axis front with the Western democracies, a failure that deepened Stalin's doubts about working with Britain and France, and after the spring of 1937 Soviet aid dwindled further. Significantly, Vyacheslav Molotov, his future foreign minister, told a French journalist in late 1936 that he believed 'an improvement in Soviet–German relations possible', a feeler not taken up by Berlin at this point.[17] Mussolini's constant infringement of undertakings to limit Italian involvement confirmed Eden's impression that he exhibited a gangster mentality. As symbolic punishment, Britain and France withheld *de jure* recognition of the Italian conquest of Abyssinia. Ultimately, their caution favoured a Franco victory (achieved in March 1939 after the fall of Madrid), not least because a communist one was anathema to both countries and because Stalin became distracted by imagined threats to his position from senior military staff. A month before the end, the Soviet leader scrawled on a desperate message seeking more arms: 'This question is no longer important.'[18]

The Civil War continued even as the international scene darkened elsewhere. In July 1937, Japan invaded China – identified by some historians, most recently Niall Ferguson,[19] as the starting point for World War Two. The challenge posed by Japan to British and French interests in the Far East accentuated the fear that Tokyo would take advantage of a European conflict to seize the rich possessions of the Western empires. At the same time, Mussolini substantially reinforced the Italian garrison in Libya, creating a threat to Egypt. He also intensified anti-British propaganda in the eastern Mediterranean. The Chiefs of Staff were not unduly concerned, however, because of their awareness of the logistical problems inherent in an invasion through the Western Desert, their contempt for Italian fighting capabilities, and their utter determination that the priority accorded to the defence of Britain would not, as in 1935–36, be disrupted by Mediterranean deployments. However, they could not ignore the piracy manifested by Italian submarines off Spanish waters. The resulting Nyon Agreement of September 1937 produced Anglo–French antisubmarine destroyer patrols, which, ironically, the Italians joined in. A. J. P. Taylor interpreted this as an indication that collective resolve could stop Mussolini in his tracks.[20] At the time, Eden saw it as evidence that a firm line worked with the dictators.[21] His prime minister, however, took a very different view.

Neville Chamberlain's accession to the premiership in May 1937 marks a significant milestone on the road to war. Controversy still rages as to whether he encouraged aggression through appeasement, or was a resolute realist who recognized British weaknesses and tried to avert another war while also putting Hitler clearly in the wrong. Chamberlain described himself as a 'go-getter for peace', anxious to soothe Axis grievances after the drift in foreign policy under Baldwin.

Regarding Mussolini, this meant instigating a personal correspondence. In the case of Germany, Lord Halifax was sent there in November 1937, ostensibly for hunting but in reality as Chamberlain's envoy, to indicate that Britain would not block peaceful rectification of defects in the 1919 settlement. In effect, Chamberlain became his own foreign secretary, often sidelining officials viewed as opposing closer relations with the Axis dictators. Such initiatives, critics argue, convinced Mussolini that the British Empire, now led by umbrella-carrying gentlemen lacking the bulldog spirit of old, was on its last legs, and persuaded Hitler that his opponents were 'small fry'.[22] 'The British', sneered Count Ciano, 'do not want to fight.'[23]

When the Chamberlain government records were opened in the late 1960s, a revisionist school emerged. This sought to understand rather than condemn, and identified the constraints that allegedly made appeasement the only realistic option. The Chiefs of Staff spoke of 'the three-cornered bogey': the prospect of simultaneous conflict with Germany, Italy and Japan. The chiefs advised the government that there was no likelihood of winning, not least because of the lack of effective allies, and urged that the triple threat must be reduced, with Italy the favoured candidate for conciliation. France was seen as politically unstable, split between left and right, and as suffering from weak air defences. The USA, with its isolationist Congress, was viewed as unreliable, preaching pious words from afar but offering only impractical schemes for peace. The Soviet Union was weakened by purges of the High Command, and in Conservative circles its communist ideology was often perceived as being more threatening than the fascist challenge. The Dominions, which backed appeasement at the 1937 London Imperial Conference, stressed that they could not be expected to fight against the principle of self-determination. Fears that the empire would not survive another world war provided another dimension to appeasement. Financial strength represented a fourth arm of defence, and needed to be conserved if Britain was to become engaged in a long war. It was argued that, devoid of strong allies, such resource would need to sustain a protracted struggle – linked to naval blockade and bombing aimed at demoralizing German civilians – in order to achieve victory. This meant that all-out rearmament was regarded as potentially self-defeating, not least by Chamberlain, the former Chancellor, with his intimate knowledge of the financial position and his conservative economics. Moreover, the exact point when a world war might break out could not be predicted.[24]

Until mid-1939, rearmament was seriously in arrears. A proper programme had started only in 1935–36, when priority was accorded to deterrent bomber forces. The air industry, long starved of government orders, feared that the policy might be merely transient, and was thus inclined to prioritize export markets. Matters were not assisted by the Air Ministry's constant alterations to aircraft specifications. The Midlands motor industry was enlisted to shadow airframe and aero-engine production, but found the transition difficult. The upshot was that bomber production did not match Germany's. Faulty intelligence also enhanced the plausibility of the worst-case scenario as perceived by the myopic Chiefs of Staff. It encouraged an erroneous assumption that Hitler would be intimidated by a bomber force capable of hitting major German cities and production centres; a failure to appreciate that the *Luftwaffe* was intended primarily as a support arm for the army rather than as a strategic bomber force; and an inflation of German aircraft figures that accentuated the British shortcomings.

Chamberlain's position was therefore not easy. However, as a counter-revisionist school has argued,[25] there were choices to be made, and in many ways the prevailing constraints proved convenient in reinforcing his insistence that four great powers – Britain, France, Italy and Germany – held the key to peace. Chamberlain made no effort, for example, to get on closer terms with the USA. In July 1937 he declined as inopportune Roosevelt's invitation to come to Washington for a 'frank exchange of views'.[26] Subsequently, Eden was vexed by Chamberlain's contemptuous dismissal of Roosevelt's secret offer of January 1938 about mediation in Europe. Washington was equally sceptical about British foreign policy. As Joe Kennedy, the American Ambassador in London, wrote in March 1938 following the *Anschluss*:

> My early talks with British and other diplomats convince me more than ever that there is no war in the immediate offing. Nobody is prepared to talk turkey to Messrs. Hitler and Mussolini, and nobody is prepared to face the risk of war by calling their bluffs. At this writing, it seems to be fundamental that the British will not do anything to check either one of them unless they actually fire guns. If that guess is correct, I am sure I am right that none of these various moves has any significance for the United States outside of general interest.[27]

What made matters worse was the Foreign Office's failure to recognize that Kennedy and Roosevelt were at odds politically, which nullified efforts to influence the President through his ambassador.[28] Roosevelt's exasperation with British foreign policy was vented to Sir Arthur Willert in March 1939:

Why did we not have conscription? Why did we let the Germans have a monopoly of intimidation? Why did we not build more bombers or anyhow say that we were building more? Why did we not let stories leak out about the tremendous preparations afoot to bomb Germany? [...] Things are moving here ... But if only you British would give me the lead.[29]

To be fair to Chamberlain, it is by no means certain that even had he cultivated the Americans, they would have come around. As the premier himself rued, all they offered regarding the Axis threat were sanctimonious words rather than tangible support. The dictators knew this, and when on 15 April 1939 Roosevelt sought Axis assurances regarding 31 named countries, Hitler responded with withering mockery.

Having written off the League as irrelevant, Chamberlain was indifferent towards Soviet efforts to revive collective security. His acute distrust of communism prejudiced him against any schemes associated with the Kremlin. The mistrust was mutual, as Stalin also viewed British foreign policy ideologically. Chamberlain perceived a new collective front against Germany as being too reminiscent of the encirclement that had contributed to causing World War One. Nor did his government seek to educate the public on the dangers of Nazism. Rather, much of the press was manipulated into presenting appeasement as a viable policy. Just before his resignation, Eden wrote to Chamberlain condemning the Chiefs of Staff for portraying potential allies as broken reeds and exaggerating the coherence of the powers constituting the triple threat.[30] The constraints then served to convince Chamberlain, whose overconfidence in his own judgement smacked of arrogance, that the course he was pursuing was the only feasible one.

The fundamental problem for the appeasers was in coming to terms with the phenomenon of Nazism. The German dictator, as Halifax ruefully remarked, shunned the normal rules of diplomacy. It proved difficult to pin him down on specifics or to procure his signature on any agreement.[31] When Halifax met Hitler, his probing only elicited generalities about colonies, with no specific territories being mentioned.[32] None the less, Chamberlain invested enormous effort to determine which former German colonies (other than those in British possession) might be restored to the Reich, in the forlorn hope that its expansionism could be satiated outside Europe. It was also wrongly assumed that Germany would wish to return to a reformed League and, when the *Luftwaffe* was operating mercilessly in Spain, the ludicrous hope was held out that Berlin would endorse a ban on heavy bombers. The *démarche* was effectively killed off when Sir Nevile Henderson, the British

Ambassador to Berlin, was received by the Führer in March 1938. By then, the turn of events had put appeasement in the frontline of efforts to prevent the onset of another European conflict.[33]

Appeasement did not set Hitler's agenda: the quest for *Lebensraum* in the east was at the heart of his foreign policy. Until March 1939, however, he succeeded in camouflaging his real objectives by presenting Nazi expansionism as something that corrected the injustices of 1919 through incorporating German-speaking peoples into a Greater Reich. Hitler's exact intentions remain controversial. He came nearest to defining them at a meeting held on 5 November 1937, written up in the Hossbach protocol, and attended by the ministers of war and foreign affairs together with the heads of the armed forces. 'Intentionalist' historians argue that Colonel Hossbach's minutes (even though never formally endorsed by Hitler) clearly demonstrate a determination to set off a European war, while 'functionalist' ones suggest that this is to overinterpret the document. The problem is compounded by the fact that the original document did not survive and the typed copy may be shorter.[34] Although, as Taylor argued,[35] most of the scenarios envisaged by the Führer, such as a civil war in France or an Anglo–Italian conflict in the Mediterranean, did not come to pass, the critical point is that Hitler was here disclosing his intention not simply to redress the grievances of Versailles, but also to acquire *Lebensraum*. He was recognizing that this could be achieved only by force, thereby indicating the centrality of ideology to his future foreign policy. Hitler went on to say that he was not aiming to gain territory at the expense of the British and French empires. Implausibly, given their recent propensity to negotiate rather than confront, he characterized the Western powers as 'hate-inspired antagonists', and drew comfort from the imperial overstretch afflicting Britain and the internal political difficulties of France. The absorption of Austria and Czechoslovakia, separately or simultaneously according to prevailing circumstances, was specifically mentioned. Such annexations offered the prospect of protecting Germany's southern and eastern flanks, enhancing its food resources, expanding the *Wehrmacht* by around 12 divisions, and adding to its armament production. In the case of the Czechs, Hitler sensed that only a local war was likely, as Britain – and probably France too – had already written them off as indefensible.[36]

The significance of this conference lies in what followed. Three of those attending objected to Hitler's programme as being much too risky, fearing it would bring conflict with Britain and France before rearmament was complete. These were the War Minister, Field Marshal Werner von Blomberg; the conservative Foreign Minister, Baron

Konstantin von Neurath; and the *Wehrmacht* commander, General Werner von Fritsch. By February 1938, all three had been removed: having abolished the post of War Minister, Hitler appointed himself supreme commander of the armed forces; General Wilhelm Keitel became chief of the high command; and Joachim von Ribbentrop took over the Foreign Ministry.

Staving off war: the Munich agreement

World war might well have come in 1938 but for Anglo–French determination to appease Hitler through compelling the Czechs to cede the Sudetenland to Germany. France was obligated by treaty to defend Czechoslovakia and content to let Britain lead in seeking a diplomatic solution after Hitler alleged mistreatment of the Sudeten Germans. Once the Führer had achieved his long-desired *Anschluss* between Germany and Austria in March 1938, the French and British military chiefs regarded the formidable Czech defences as fatally vulnerable to outflanking. As the Sudeten crisis reached its climax in September, it became clear that France was unwilling to make any military move against Germany – which made it easier for the Soviets to offer support to Paris in the expectation that nothing would come of this. Whether or not the USSR would have entered the fray remains an open question (units in Kiev and Byelorussia were brought to a state of readiness, but the purges had diminished the Red Army's offensive capacity). In any event, Soviet forces would need to come through Poland – which aligned itself with Germany and Hungary to share the spoils from this first stage of Czechoslovakia's dismemberment – the Baltic States or Romania. Nevertheless, there was sufficient uncertainty about the situation for Hitler to embrace the Munich settlement of 29 September. He was conscious of the ambivalent Soviet position, the mobilization of the British fleet, the unpreparedness of his own forces for *Blitzkrieg*, the inclination of German public opinion towards peace, and Mussolini's last-minute hesitations. However, the Führer soon came to regret his Munich decision. Part of the reason why world war came a year later lay in Hitler's keenness to avoid repeating what he regarded as a diplomatic defeat. The Führer was furious with Chamberlain for spoiling his march into Prague, and determined never again to be so humiliated.[37] This resolve rendered a wider European conflict inevitable, because henceforth only war and not appeasement could stop Hitler.

Although born of an emergency situation, the Munich Agreement represented Chamberlain's vision of a European peace shaped by four great powers. What came immediately afterwards was most important to him: a signature from Hitler, endorsing the Anglo–German Declaration that pledged both parties to peaceful settlement of any future differences. It enabled Chamberlain, returning in triumph and waving the document aloft at Heston aerodrome, to proclaim 'peace for our time'. Unfortunately it meant nothing to Hitler, who remarked privately that he had merely given an old man his autograph. Within days, Hitler was consulting Keitel on plans to occupy the remainder of Czechoslovakia, leading to two directives by the end of the year.[38] It was then only a matter of choosing the right moment to spring his surprise.

Chamberlain called the Munich Agreement 'the prelude to a larger settlement in which all Europe may find peace'.[39] Accordingly, he refused to bring the leading anti-appeasers (Winston Churchill and Eden) into his Cabinet, opposed suggestions about coalition with Labour, ruled out introducing peacetime conscription or firmly committing an Expeditionary Force to aid France, and merely sought to accelerate rearmament. By early 1939, however, this position had become untenable. British intelligence picked up some very unflattering remarks by Hitler on Chamberlain, shattering any illusions of a special bond. More important still, the events of *Kristallnacht* in November 1938 brought home to the British public that the racist Nazi regime was bent on ever more extreme measures against German Jews. That brutality undermined Chamberlain's desire to separate German domestic and foreign policies and to treat Hitler's government as normal. Lord Halifax, increasingly disaffected with Chamberlain, convened a special meeting of the Cabinet Foreign Policy Committee to review the situation following *Kristallnacht*.[40] The public became increasingly anti-Nazi, marking the failure of government efforts to portray Germany as eminently appeaseable. With a general election looming on the horizon, domestic opinion mattered all the more.

Chamberlain now sought to influence Berlin through Rome. In November 1938, the Anglo–Italian Agreement, concluded the previous April, was activated after Britain grasped the nettle of recognizing Italian sovereignty over Abyssinia. Ironically, the same month saw Mussolini promulgating new racial laws, bringing closer ideological alignment with Germany. Although Halifax visited Rome in January 1939, British efforts to detach Italy from Germany, or to persuade Mussolini to encourage Hitler to keep the peace, failed lamentably. In November 1938, Italy had laid claim to Nice, Corsica and Tunis, thereby antagonizing France. Similarly, Mussolini's expansionist agenda involved an even greater lust for Britain's holdings in the eastern Mediterranean. Meeting the umbrella-wielding British leaders face-to-face only served to convince Mussolini that their Empire was in terminal decline and ripe for the plucking when circumstances allowed.[41]

At the beginning of 1939, the dictatorships and democracies moved closer towards military confrontation. Hitler's *Reichstag* speech of 30 January, commemorating the Nazi assumption of power, pledged German backing for Italy in any eventuality. This prompted Chamberlain to declare a matching commitment to France, promising dispatch of an expeditionary force in the event of hostilities with Germany. When British intelligence was misled by Hitler's opponents into believing that an invasion of Holland was imminent, a further and secret undertaking to aid the Dutch was also given.[42] Chamberlain now had to take cognisance of a more unruly Cabinet, especially the younger element. Nevertheless, he remained convinced that Berlin would abide by the Munich Agreement, informing reporters on 10 March that 'Europe was settling down to a period of tranquillity'.[43] This was wishful thinking, abetted by Henderson's overoptimistic dispatches from Germany.[44]

From Prague to European war

Hitler's invasion of Czechoslovakia on 15 March 1939 came as a rude awakening. German intelligence predicted meek acceptance by the Western powers.[45] The initial British reaction was indeed muted: the postponement of a Berlin visit by the President of the Board of Trade, and Chamberlain's lame excuse that, because the Czech state no longer existed, neither did the guarantee of its post-Munich frontiers. Such a position was unsustainable in the face of public outcry. One MP recorded: 'the feeling in the lobbies is that Chamberlain will either have to go or completely reverse his policy.'[46] Previously, pro-appeasers had argued that Germany was pursuing revisionist policies based acceptably on self-determination and righting the wrongs of Versailles. Now, however, non-Germans were being incorporated into the Third Reich, suggesting much greater ambitions. Chamberlain acknowledged this to his Cabinet, and then on 17 March in a scheduled public speech which was hastily revised to reflect the new reality.

How could Hitler now be prevented from running amok in central and south-eastern Europe? When Romania seemed endangered, the British Chiefs of Staff emphasized that any Anglo–French action must have Polish and Soviet support so as to deter Germany through a threat of two-front war, which Hitler said he would never fight. The idea of a Four-Power Declaration quickly emerged.[47] While France readily agreed, Poland objected to Soviet inclusion. The policy was therefore abandoned in favour of Anglo–French guarantees to the

Poles against aggression. Chamberlain and Halifax concurred that Poland's inclusion in a 'peace front' was more important than the USSR's. This was an extraordinary decision, springing from anti-communist prejudice, which robbed the 'peace front' of a credible deterrent. Neither Britain nor France was in any position to aid Poland or Romania, whereas the Soviet Union was on their doorstep. A false claim by the Romanian Minister in London that his country had received an ultimatum from Germany set in train the guarantees.[48] They were the product of the charged political atmosphere following the fall of Czechoslovakia, when panic was generated over where the Axis would strike next. This was exacerbated when Germany seized the port of Memel from Lithuania and Italy invaded Albania, generating other promises (to Greece and Romania) of doubtful viability.

The guarantee to Poland is often seen as marking a revolution in Britain's diplomatic policy as, for the first time, it promised to defend an East European state. There was a mixture of reasons. Fundamental was the psychological blow administered by Hitler's decision to incorporate non-Germans into his Reich. The shift in Anglo–French public opinion raised expectations that a stand would be made. Chamberlain faced an election in the near future, and to ignore the changed mood risked losing it. Hitherto, Hitler had been careful not to threaten Britain's vital interests, so long as the UK, like France, remained willing to avoid war over German expansion in central Europe. By guaranteeing Poland, however, Britain and France threw down the gauntlet, doing so in the hope that Nazi policy would revert to peaceful revisionism, including negotiations about the former German port-city of Danzig. Crucially, the Polish guarantee covered independence and not frontiers, a distinction recognized by *The Times* whose editor, Geoffrey Dawson, remained sympathetic towards the government. In April, at French insistence, Britain introduced its first peacetime conscription. Hitler was not deterred. The takeover of rump Czechoslovakia had bagged an invaluable haul of extra modern tanks and increased armaments production capacity. War might well have been averted in the immediate future had Poland accepted Nazi demands, joined the Anti-Comintern Pact and become a German satellite. Hitler could then have attacked the USSR before the West. By April 1939, Hitler had concluded that a military solution to the Polish question was necessary after the Warsaw government rebuffed his demands for access to East Prussia through the so-called 'Danzig corridor'. The Anglo–French backing now guaranteed to Warsaw made the Poles even more obstinate, deluding them into believing that salvation was at hand. On 3 April, an enraged Hitler ordered preparations for Case White, the invasion of Poland. At the end of the month, in a speech broadcast live across Europe and the USA, the Führer renounced the 1935 Anglo–German Naval Agreement, and also the 1934 German–Polish Non-Aggression Pact on the basis that Poland had violated its conditions through accepting the guarantee and mobilizing troops. On 22 May, Hitler at last concluded a formal alliance with Italy through the Pact of Steel. The following day he informed senior generals of his intentions towards Poland.[49] Richard Overy contends that Hitler was encouraged by his London embassy to believe that hysteria over the Prague coup had died down and that the British were seeking a way out of their guarantee to Poland. Such intelligence, Overy argues, 'strengthened Hitler's determination to press the Danzig crisis to a conclusion'.[50]

The Soviet Union became the key player in the situation. After dismembering Czechoslovakia, Germany was now capable of outflanking Polish defences. A familiar war of nerves was repeating itself, but the outcome was now less certain to be a bloodless victory for Hitler. On 3 April, British military chiefs, who had not been consulted over the Polish guarantee, advised that only the Soviets were in a position to aid the Poles.[51] In mid-April, Moscow proposed to revive collective security through alliance with Britain and France. However, Soviet adhesion was made conditional on the Polish guarantee applying only to German aggression and on an Anglo–French pledge not to conclude a separate peace after hostilities commenced. Although the French were keen to grasp this nettle, Chamberlain's government believed that there could never be a German–Soviet rapprochement, and thus that there was no urgency about such a deal with Stalin. It maintained this inertia about embracing Moscow, notwithstanding the dismissal of the pro-Western Litvinov, a Jew, as Soviet Foreign Minister. His replacement by Molotov elicited bewilderment rather than alarm in Whitehall. During May and June, however, Chamberlain came under increasing pressure to secure an alliance with the USSR. His military chiefs began to see the Red Army as an asset rather than a liability, and the Soviet navy as capable of distracting Germany's Baltic fleet. Anglo–French staff talks also revealed General Gamelin's determination to maintain a defensive posture. These factors persuaded the Cabinet to enter negotiations with Moscow, a decision France backed because of its alliances with Poland and Romania. Discussions were not helped by the British insistence on including Switzerland, Luxembourg and Holland on the list of guaranteed states, nor by the Soviet desire to extend such protection to Finland and the Baltic states notwithstanding their aversion to Moscow's 'assistance'. After several sessions wrangling over the definition of indirect aggression, Molotov demanded that political and military agreements must be concluded together. By this point, 23 July 1939, the Western powers had dropped their proposal about guaranteeing the three neutrals, while the Soviet side was now treating the indirect aggression question as a minor issue. Although exasperated, Molotov was not yet ready to welcome political overtures from Germany.[52]

Early in August, a British Military Mission went to Moscow headed by the obscure Admiral Sir Reginald Plunket-Ernle-Erle-Drax, travelling on an antiquated ship that took all of five days to reach Leningrad. Peter Neville has challenged the traditional view that, instead, Lord Halifax and the Chiefs of Staff should have been sent, and by the fastest means. The key point is, however, that the British and French governments could not deliver on the Soviet demands for the Red Army to have free passage through Poland and Romania. Despite frantic French efforts, neither Warsaw nor Bucharest would play ball, fearing, not without reason, that once Soviet forces were allowed into their territory they would never leave. By 17 August, six days after the military talks commenced, there was stalemate. On 21 August the French delegation was ordered to settle any deal it could extract from the Soviets. Ominously, the same day, a German–Soviet economic agreement was struck in Berlin. Two days later, the world learned the shocking news of the Nazi–Soviet Non-Aggression Pact. Stalin, frustrated at the lack of progress made with Britain and France, accepted the territorial bait offered by Hitler: the division of Poland, a free hand in Finland, Estonia, Latvia and Lithuania, as well as recognition of a Soviet interest in Bessarabia, then part of Romania. 'The Soviet government', notes G. Bruce Strang, 'made this choice fully aware that it would ensure the failure of any deterrent and that it made war a virtual certainty.'[53]

The Nazi–Soviet Pact stunned the Western democracies. It did not quite render war inevitable. Ever since the Abyssinian crisis, Hitler had recognized that threats to the sensitive spots of the British Empire gave London pause for thought. He was now relying on Japan and Italy to apply pressure, and for a time they obliged: Tokyo through the Tientsin crisis, and Rome through its familiar trick of massing extra forces in Libya. However, both pressures fell away following the Nazi–Soviet agreement. Border clashes in Manchuria between Japanese and Soviet forces made the Pact very unpalatable news in Tokyo, where the fall of the pro-Axis government removed any immediate prospect of Anglo–Japanese conflict over Tientsin. In June 1939, Chamberlain had already foreseen that the 'Italians would be on the lookout for any excuse to keep out of the war.'[54] Now Mussolini took fright at the chief implication of the Pact – that Poland would soon be attacked – which Hitler confirmed in a letter to the Duce. In response, an enormous list of immediate war requirements was remitted to Berlin. As intended, it proved impossible to fulfil, thus temporarily freeing Rome from its obligation to give military support to Germany. A further blow to Hitler came when Britain turned its guarantee to Poland into a full-blown alliance. This was preceded by a letter from Chamberlain which underlined that there should be no misunderstanding as in 1914: London would stand by its commitment.[55] These developments shattered the picture of weak-willed British leadership that Joachim von Ribbentrop, the Anglophobe Foreign Minister, had presented to his Führer.[56] Momentarily rattled, Hitler postponed the Polish invasion, scheduled for 26 August, until the end of the month.[57]

Hitler used the interlude to make an extraordinary proposal: in return for a free hand over Poland, he would guarantee the British Empire and seek agreement on disarmament.[58] Rightly, given his record, neither offer was taken seriously. Nor did Britain or France exert against the Poles the kind of pressure they had put on the Czechs in 1938. Accommodation with Berlin over Danzig was certainly mentioned, but never under the threat of abandonment. In any event, Warsaw was in no mood for compromise. Notwithstanding its outdated armed forces, the Polish government deluded itself that, just as the Red Army had been repulsed in 1920, so a Nazi invasion could be defeated by sheer bravery and élan. Its obstinate Foreign Minister, Colonel Josef Beck, refused to treat with either Hitler or Stalin, while erring 'in his naive belief in the sincerity of Allied guarantees and assurances'.[59] When Berlin demanded, on 29 August, that a Polish plenipotentiary be sent to accept the German terms over Danzig and the Corridor within 24 hours, none appeared. Two days later, Mussolini's proposal of a conference was completely undermined by false claims that German wireless stations near the Polish border had been attacked. Using that pretext, invasion commenced at 4.45 am on 1 September. In the end, influenced by misleading intelligence reports about the slowness of British and French rearmament, Hitler had not backed down. A week earlier, Germany had successfully tested an aircraft jet engine. Meanwhile, Nazi intelligence was seriously underestimating the progress that Britain had made regarding plane production and air defences: for example, its crucial chain of radar stations (mistaken for radio towers) was now virtually complete.[60] The development of the *Blitzkrieg* doctrine was also vital to Hitler's calculations for averting a repeat of the attritional warfare of 1914–18.[61] A major benefit of the Nazi–Soviet Pact was the promise of raw materials and minerals to help in frustrating any renewed British attempt at economic strangulation. On 19 August 1939, the Russians had agreed to provide Germany with raw materials valued at 180 million Reichsmarks. This was supplemented by two further economic accords in February 1940 and January 1941. Between January 1940 and June 1941 the flow increased, including 2 million tons of petroleum products, 1.5 million tons of grain and 100,000 tons of cotton, which greatly reduced the impact of the British naval blockade.[62]

There remained the possibility that, as Hitler ideally wanted, the conflict could be localized and that, after Poland's defeat and its partition between Germany and the Soviet Union, an uneasy peace could be restored. That this did not happen owed much to the resolute attitude of British public and parliamentary opinion. At the end of August, a Gallup poll found 89 per cent favouring a fight against 'Hitlerism'. The position taken by Chamberlain on 2 September – that provided Germany withdrew its forces from Poland, all would be forgiven – quickly proved unsustainable. Assailed by friend and foe alike, and faced with ministerial revolt, that evening he bowed to the inevitable. After an emergency Cabinet meeting he agreed to send an ultimatum with a short time limit. When Hitler received it, he was aghast, turning on his Foreign Minister to ask: 'What now?' For once Ribbentrop showed some insight, rightly predicting that a French ultimatum would follow. Notwithstanding its misgivings, the Daladier government recognized that it must sink or swim with its British allies. Berlin failed to reply to either ultimatum. So, on 3 September, the British, at 11 am, and the French, at 5 pm, declared war. Thus the German–Polish conflict became transformed into a European conflagration.[63] Hitler anticipated 'theatrical gestures' and a *Sitzkrieg* (phoney war).

The eastward expansion of the conflict

It is arguable that in September 1939 Hitler did not get the war he wanted. Following the defeat and partition of Poland, the rebuff that Britain and France gave to Nazi peace feelers meant that Germany had to set about knocking out the Western powers. Thus Hitler's next objective became the defeat of France, which would isolate Britain and, it was believed, force London to come to terms. The Führer was conscious that the longer the conflict lasted, the more likely US intervention would become, with Britain offering a military base. At this point, further expansion eastwards was not on Hitler's immediate agenda, although it remained constantly in his mind. In October he expressed satisfaction with the Soviet alliance, while also remarking that no treaties were eternal and the situation could well change in the near future.[64]

Hitler recognized that swift conquest of France was absolutely vital. Any repeat of stalemate on the Western Front (which Stalin expected and hoped for) would be calamitous. Finding the military planning (Case Yellow) against France too predictable, and worried by weather and transport problems, the Führer postponed his offensive until the spring. In February 1940, he seized on General von Manstein's bold plan to sweep through the Ardennes, whose forests the French commanders regarded as impenetrable and therefore covered only with light forces. In the event, the offensive was delayed by a week because of the invasion of Denmark and Norway on 9 April, which Hitler ordered to thwart Allied efforts to deny German access to vital Swedish iron ore and other raw materials, as well as to secure submarine bases for the Battle of the Atlantic. When Allied counter-action in Norway quickly collapsed, Chamberlain was swept from power and replaced by Churchill, whose fighting spirit would prove crucial to the conflict's enlargement into a pan-European war.

Churchill became Prime Minister on 9 May, the day before Germany invaded the Low Countries and France. Hitler was convinced this campaign would be over within six weeks, and that Britain would then sue for peace.[65] Holland fell within five days, followed by Belgium on 18 May, with German armour swiftly sweeping forward to reach the Channel by 20–21 May. The opportunity to destroy the British Expeditionary Force at Dunkirk was lost through over-caution, but at the time this did not seem a mistake by Hitler, as it no longer posed a threat, and he did not anticipate that Churchill's government would present its miraculous evacuation almost as a national victory. Field Marshal Goering's hollow promise that his *Luftwaffe* alone could destroy the Allied troops beleaguered at Dunkirk was compounded by his airmen's subsequent failure to win the Battle of Britain, which raged from July to September. Fighter Command's narrowly achieved success vindicated Churchill's resistance to the Cabinet faction led by Halifax, which saw continued belligerence as pointless. Crucially, Churchill had been supported by the ailing Chamberlain, who still remained as leader of the Conservative Party. Hitler was perplexed by the British decision to fight on. He increasingly saw the USSR as the reason for Churchill's obstinacy. Hitler remarked that 'our attention must be turned to tackling the Russian problem and prepare planning.' He was convinced that, compared with the fighting in the west, 'a campaign against Russia would be child's play.'[66] As the war continued, such thinking intensified, linking foreign policy with the ideology of *Lebensraum* and of Slavic racial inferiority. Stalin, mortified by Nazi successes in the West, moved forces into the Baltic States in mid-June to provide greater depth to Soviet defences. His military build-up in southern Russia, providing backbone to Soviet diplomacy in the Balkans, persuaded German commanders to reinforce the divisions already scheduled for transfer to the east.[67]

The Balkans was a sensitive area for Germany, offering vital raw materials and minerals. Romania's Ploesti refineries, in particular, were regarded as essential to the oil needs of the Nazi war economy. Germany was the leading trading partner in the region, a position built on barter arrangements supported by increasing intimidation.[68] The fall of France exercised a traumatizing effect through demonstrating the power of *Blitzkrieg* and the military weakness of Britain. Now standing virtually alone (except for support from its Dominions), Britain found it impossible to persuade Balkan states openly to take its side.[69] When Mussolini joined the war in June 1940, Turkey failed to act against him – thus reneging on an agreement made with Britain in October 1939. Surrounded by Germany and its allies, Yugoslavia's regent, Prince Paul, although an Anglophile, felt fearful about provoking a German invasion.[70] Hitler's aura of invincibility was such that in spring 1941, when the Turks appeared tempted by British efforts to draw them in, the German Embassy in Ankara arranged the showing of a film depicting the triumphant *Blitzkrieg* against France. Berlin also sought to add eastern European states to the Tripartite Pact, concluded with Italy and Japan on 27 September 1940, in order to put further pressure on the British and deter American belligerency. This effort succeeded with Romania, Hungary and Slovakia in November 1940, and then in March 1941 with Bulgaria and (temporarily) Yugoslavia.

Hitler's keenness to prevent the conflict spreading to the Balkans meant resolving territorial disputes and restraining Italian ambitions. On the first point, Berlin succeeded. After the USSR forced Romania to concede Bessarabia and Northern Bukovina in June 1940, Bulgaria and Hungary renewed their own claims on former territories. Under German pressure, Romania restored South Dobrudja to Bulgaria and the three 'Szekler' territories and North Transylvania to Hungary, in return for guarantees concerning the truncated state that remained. On the second point, in August 1940 Berlin managed to dampen Italian ardour for an invasion of Greece. Mussolini's urges to pursue his 'parallel war' against Yugoslavia were also emasculated by Hitler. In early October 1940, however, German forces entered Romania via Hungary, ostensibly at the invitation of its pro-Axis dictator, Ion Antonescu. This move irked Mussolini, who was not consulted. He decided to pay Hitler back in kind, and on 28 October 1940 launched an ill-considered invasion of

Greece just as winter was setting in. The Greek leader, General Ioannis Metaxas, faced by a three-hour ultimatum requiring surrender of unspecified 'strategic points', responded with '*ochi*', the most famous 'no' in his country's history.[71] Hitler hurried to Florence to try to head off Mussolini, only to be greeted with the words, 'Führer, we are on the march.' The Italian leadership expected only token resistance and envisaged a ten-day campaign at worst. To the surprise of most military commentators, the Greeks not only repelled the incursion, but threw the invader back into Albania, where protracted but inconclusive fighting ensued in mountainous terrain. These Greek successes marked the first land victories against the Axis. However, the looming threat of German intervention persuaded Turkey and Yugoslavia, Greece's allies in the 1934 Balkan Pact,[72] to remain neutral. By pouring reinforcements into Albania, Italy managed to frustrate Greek ambitions to drive its forces into the sea. Although Britain stood by its guarantee to Greece, it could not provide more than token support. The fact that the Churchill government anticipated another German attempt to invade the British mainland in 1941 meant that any military resources for Greece must derive from the Middle East Command, which itself had already had to confront an Italian invasion of Egypt in September 1940.

The build-up of Nazi forces in Romania and the infiltration of Bulgaria by German technicians were noted by British intelligence sources. It was feared that Hitler was preparing to rescue his stricken Italian ally and intending to seize the Middle East oilfields through Anatolia. In fact, his primary concerns were the protection of Ploesti and the southern flank of the planned invasion of the Soviet Union (Operation Barbarossa). Greek determination to continue the Albanian campaign and the associated presence of RAF bombers caused alarm in Berlin, despite the refusal of Metaxas to allow their deployment near Salonika, within range of the Ploesti refineries. By December 1940 Hitler had decided to crush Greece, essentially to deprive the British of army and air force bases. Ribbentrop informed the Japanese Ambassador to Berlin: 'Germany would not tolerate England's establishing a foothold anywhere on the Continent. Wherever the English should make such an attempt, in the Mediterranean, in Greece … they would be driven out at once.'[73]

In January 1941, Metaxas rejected the offer of a British expeditionary force for Salonika, fearing it would provoke the Germans and yet be too small to repel them. The Greek dictator's sudden death at the end of the month effectively made the pro-British monarch, George II, the national leader. When asked again what military assistance

Britain could provide, Churchill sent Eden on a mission to encourage the formation of a Balkan front between Greece, Turkey and Yugoslavia, aimed at deterring or frustrating a German invasion.[74] Although Eden persuaded the Greeks to accept an Allied expeditionary force, it was too lacking in armour and air support to give the Germans pause for thought. Nor did it persuade the Turks or Yugoslavs to come off the fence. In any event, even had a Balkan front been formed constituting around 70 divisions, the lack of modern forces and tactics would have proved a decisive impediment. However, Bulgaria's mountainous terrain was not an ideal launch pad for another *Blitzkrieg* campaign, therefore the *Wehrmacht* needed to be able to move other divisions through Yugoslavia. When the hapless Belgrade government yielded to German pressure to join the Tripartite Pact, it was overthrown in a pro-British coup. An enraged Hitler now added Yugoslavia to Greece as Germany's next intended victim. Both were attacked on 6 April 1941, and fell within a matter of weeks.

Whether the Balkan campaign caused a decisive five-week delay in launching Operation Barbarossa remains debated,[75] but Hitler was certainly determined to wage a war against the USSR to fulfil his quest for *Lebensraum*. Inconclusive negotiations with Molotov in Berlin during November 1940 provided the catalyst for the fatal decision taken the following month about preparing 'to crush Soviet Russia in a rapid campaign'.[76] Molotov's refusal to entertain suggestions of taking India and his resolute upholding of Moscow's interest in the Balkans convinced Hitler that a German–Soviet war was inevitable. The Führer also worried about Russian designs on the Romanian oilfields. Stalin's efforts to buy further time were reflected in the continued trainloads of supplies to Germany in fulfilment of Soviet obligations, despite mounting evidence of a Nazi military build-up. Stalin chose to believe that this was intended to ensure favourable oil prices and that Hitler would not launch an invasion while the British remained in the contest. The German drive through the Balkans provided a further plausible rationale for the massing of Nazi forces (although most were concentrated in Poland), and helped discredit Soviet intelligence agents who were correctly pinpointing 15 May 1941 as the invasion date originally set.[77] When this passed, Stalin inclined towards appeasement, not least because of the rapid collapse of Yugoslavia and Greece.[78] On their side, Hitler and the German military leadership seriously miscalculated, believing it was possible to defeat Soviet Russia in a single campaign. The Red Army's ineptitude in Finland during the Winter War (1939–40) encouraged this view, as did perceptions of Slavic racial inferiority. The human, material and ideological resources of the

USSR were completely underestimated. Hitler launched Barbarossa on 22 June 1941, but was later recorded as saying that he would have acted otherwise had he known what lay ahead.[79] In the end, the USSR's superiority in manpower and armaments production, allied to American lend–lease supplies, and Stalin's willingness to sustain huge losses, proved fatal to the Nazi cause.[80]

An overview

There is the view that another war was inevitable after 1919, granted that Germany was not fatally weakened by the peace settlement and that, once the nation recovered militarily, the new states in the east would be insufficiently strong to defend their borders. Again, had appeasement run deeper in the 1920s and early 1930s, there would have been fewer grievances for Hitler to exploit. As it was, Weimar Germany had begun revisionism by stealth, not accepting its eastern frontiers as permanent. But it remains far from certain whether its leaders would have gone beyond obtaining certain revisions that might well have been achieved without a general conflagration. Indeed, the Nazis' own territorial successes from 1933–38 indicated the room for such manoeuvre.

Where Hitler's foreign policy proved different was in its concern for race and *Lebensraum*, and for the development of a fanatical nationalism that seemed impervious to reason. British governments struggled to understand the Nazi phenomenon. Chamberlain treated the fascist dictators as sharing his aversion to conflict, rather than coveting war. He believed that limited concessions would satisfy them, instead of whetting their appetites for further expansion. Much later, General Douglas MacArthur, defending his desire to confront the Chinese during the Korean War, would declare to Congress: 'history teaches with unmistakable emphasis that appeasement but begets new and bloodier war.'[81] Halifax encapsulated the chasm between the two sides in a letter written shortly after the outbreak of war:

> The last fortnight before the decision was very heartbreaking. Being always a natural optimist, I thought that we had a good chance of getting through and inflicting on Hitler a moral defeat. But either we were wrong in these hopes all the time or else something happened to defeat them. War must, I suppose, generally be reckoned as the failure of the Foreign Secretary, but I don't honestly know what more we could have done, and the unanimity and feeling is remarkable.[82]

The pursuit of appeasement did at least put Nazi Germany firmly in the wrong, which was critical in mustering support from the Dominions and, by increments, from the USA. Thereafter it was the coming to power of the arch anti-appeaser, Churchill, in mid-1940 that kept Britain in the fight, encouraged the Empire to remain loyal, and helped convince Roosevelt to provide critical financial and material support while also waging an undeclared Atlantic war against German submarines.

Several key points serve towards explaining why war erupted in September 1939, rather than sooner or later. First, after March 1939 appeasement was no longer a credible policy to pursue openly (although it remained a live issue behind the scenes well into 1940, with Churchill's succession far from inevitable). It needed to be bolstered by deterrence, through Britain and France drawing a clear line beyond which the dictators could not venture without conflict becoming certain. Second, deterrence failed to work. The 'peace front', hastily constructed for political reasons, lacked military credibility without the USSR. There is no evidence that Hitler was concerned at the prospect of the bombing of German cities, and the failure of the British Air Ministry to achieve parity with the Luftwaffe ruptured any deterrent effect that Bomber Command might have exerted by the eve of war. The much weaker French Air Force reduced it still further. On the ground, neither Britain nor France possessed any offensive capability or intention, as the small British Expeditionary Force could only play a defensive role, and the French General Staff remained determined to shelter behind the Maginot Line. Poland could be saved from collapse only through Soviet intervention, an eventuality that was unwelcome to a nation that remembered vividly the invasion attempt of 1920. Given the USSR's military weaknesses at this point, Stalin's primary concern was to buy time, which he anticipated coming in sufficient measure through repeat of the Great War's western stalemate. Third, Hitler could have halted German expansionism after Munich and been hailed as one of the greatest German leaders in history. It was his refusal to stop that created recurring crises and the impetus towards another European conflict. He was a risk-taker who, once he stepped beyond the revision of Versailles to reveal a wider policy of aggression, greatly reduced his chances of further bloodless victories and eventually indulged in a brinkmanship that took Germany over the precipice. His assassination might have made all the difference, but, when in April 1939 the British Military Attaché in Berlin advocated this, the proposal made no headway because Hitler was regarded as a legitimate head of state.[83]

All this is not to say that the Führer failed to see that eventual conflict with Britain and France was likely. Much of his reasoning derived from Germany's experience in World War One, and especially his analysis of its defeat. Thus he was determined to avert the crippling effects of a British naval blockade, and to prevent the establishment of another Salonika front, which was seen as having begun Germany's collapse in autumn 1918. He also anticipated eventual American participation.[84] Hitler's consciousness of his own ageing is another factor: at 50 he remained vigorous, but also worried about the time left for fulfilling his grand vision. In the end, he did not step back even when it became clear that a wider conflict could not be averted except through immediate withdrawal from Poland. The fact was that its partition was an essential stepping stone towards Hitler's ultimate objective, the conquest of Soviet Russia and the achievement of *Lebensraum*. In October 1939 Hitler ordered the *Wehrmacht* to treat Poland as an assembly area for future operations. The next month he informed his generals: 'We can oppose Russia only when we are free in the West.'[85]

Adam Tooze has recently argued, after examining neglected German economic documents, that Hitler deliberately unleashed a war with Poland in the expectation of a wider conflict. As he told the Italian Ambassador in March 1939, 'as regards its armed forces, Germany is now in a position to face all eventualities.'[86] This challenges the generally accepted interpretation, put forward by Richard Overy and Ian Kershaw, that Hitler miscalculated and was not intending a larger war until the mid-1940s.[87] The new view suggests that Britain's reaction to the Prague coup – the introduction of peacetime conscription and greater RAF spending – alarmed the Führer, whose fears lest a strategic window of opportunity was closing prompted him to act quickly. Moreover, after Roosevelt's State of the Union address of 4 January 1939, warning of the Nazi German threat to national security, Hitler recognized the increasing likelihood of American support for the Western democracies. The US President went further on 18 March 1939, following the takeover of Czechoslovakia, when stinging tariffs were imposed on German imports. Hitler's intelligence staff also reported French procurement officials viewing Boeing bombers. In May 1939 the *Wehrmacht*'s economic expert warned that already the Axis was being outspent by Britain, France and the USA. Therefore Hitler chose to act before he faced an overwhelming coalition. Tooze also emphasizes the ideological dimension inherent in Hitler seeing 1939 as a critical year. He began it by threatening publicly to eliminate the Jews if they instigated another world war. By this time the Führer perceived an international conspiracy against Germany, which was pervaded by Jewish influence and formed a variant on the encirclement obsession which had helped drive the Kaiser's government into

European conflict. The depth of Hitler's antisemitism certainly helps to contextualize his decision-making in the prelude to war.[88]

This fresh interpretation does not nullify the fact that Hitler was so contemptuous of the British and French leaders that he still anticipated a localized war with Poland, which in effect is what he got, as neither of its allies could intervene directly. The Führer's peace overtures in October also suggest a hope that, once Poland (the ostensible cause of war) had been removed, Germany would be allowed to recover before proceeding to the next phase of its quest for eastern *Lebensraum*. These proposals involved, however, acceptance of his Polish partition, which for the Western powers was politically out of the question. Sensing this, Hitler was already preparing to attack in the west before Chamberlain's formal rejection of Germany's peace proposal in the House of Commons.[89] What Anglo–French intervention did was to interrupt Hitler's progress towards showdown with the USSR. When this finally came, in June 1941, the 208-division invasion force, the largest ever assembled, was actually little stronger than a year before – with insufficient tanks, artillery and anti-tank guns, and employing even more horses per soldier than Napoleon had done in 1812. The gamble taken in invading France had paid off handsomely, and the scale of Hitler's triumph in the West had deceived him into believing that the hardest campaign had already been won. In 1941, however, Germany faced a bigger opponent operating in a vast arena, which afforded strategic depth. The elusiveness of Red Army units, the Soviet High Command's continuing ability to summon reserves despite heavy losses, the prospect of deserters being shot by the secret police, the recuperative powers of the USSR's war economy, and Stalin's refusal to yield coalesced to frustrate Hitler's grand design. Once *Blitzkrieg* failed to deliver early victory, Germany became saddled with an unwinnable campaign of attrition. Hitler's dream conflict had turned into the nightmare of a multifront war, for which he would pay the ultimate penalty.

Finally, the obsession of British and French military planners with an attritional war as the key to victory meant that opportunities were missed to partake in shorter engagements or to demonstrate real resolve far earlier than eventually occurred under Churchill's leadership. This might have arrested the drift towards a general conflict, thereby providing more time for rearmament programmes. The Abyssinian Crisis has been presented as providing probably the best opportunity to humiliate the aggressor. The chance to challenge Mussolini did not recur because the German and Japanese threats grew exponentially, meaning that thereafter Britain never concentrated its forces so strongly in the Mediterranean. Again, the French by themselves could have reversed the remilitarization of the Rhineland but lacked the resolve to do so. Several historians, including Williamson Murray, Niall Ferguson and Zara Steiner, regard the Munich Crisis of 1938 as another missed chance.[90] As it was, Hitler abandoned his immediate plans to smash Czechoslovakia militarily, and at one point asked Chamberlain's close adviser, Horace Wilson, whether 'England wants world war?'[91] Indeed, Hitler conceded to General Jodl that, if he attacked Czechoslovakia at that stage, he 'would have to wage war against England, against France, which I could not wage.'[92] German military chiefs were acutely aware that their western defences were incomplete. Indeed, Hitler's new Chief of Staff, General Franz Halder, was planning a *coup d'état* if it came to conflict.[93] The Soviet Union and its ally, Czechoslovakia, a much more formidable military proposition than Poland a year later, ought to have been brought into the negotiations, but the Western powers rebuffed Soviet efforts to stage a conference. Too often, as here, senior British and French military figures could not see beyond the weaknesses of their own forces to illuminate the deficiencies of their potential enemies. As the counter-revisionist R. A. C. Parker argued, a grand alliance of Britain, France and Soviet Russia was conceivable in 1938, whereas it proved impossible to constitute in 1939 when Stalin considered the pass had already been sold at Munich.[94] Instead, Hitler was allowed to run rampant with a string of unbroken successes, which encouraged him to play for ever-higher stakes, until eventually overreaching himself.

Further reading

The best overview is now provided by Zara Steiner, *The Lights that Failed. European International History 1919–1933* (Oxford: Oxford University Press, 2005) and for the later 1930s *The Triumph of the Dark: European International History, 1933–1939* (Oxford: Oxford University Press, 2009).

On the debates see P. M. H. Bell, *The Origins of the Second World War in Europe* (London: Longman, 2007, new edn); P. Finney (ed.) *The Origins of the Second World War* (London: Arnold, 1997); and Gordon Martel (ed.), *The Origins of the Second World War Reconsidered. A. J. P. Taylor and the Historians* (London: Routledge, 1999).

For a multidimensional view of the peace settlement see M. F. Boemeke, G. D. Feldman and E. Glaser (eds), *The Treaty of Versailles. A Reassessment after 75 Years* (Cambridge: Cambridge University Press, 1998). For the Paris deliberations see M. Macmillan, *Peacemakers: The Paris Conference of 1919 and its Attempts to End War* (London:

John Murray, 2001). For Franco–British differences over the management of the peace see W. Laird Kleine-Ahlbrandt, *The Burden of Victory: France, Britain and the Enforcement of the Versailles Peace* (Lanham, MD: University Press of America, 1995). For the British perspective see A. Lentin, *Lloyd George and the Lost Peace: From Versailles to Hitler, 1919–1940* (Basingstoke: Palgrave Macmillan, 2001). For the American perspective see T. J. Knock, *To End All Wars: Woodrow Wilson and the Quest for a New World Order* (Princeton, NJ: Princeton University Press, 1995). For the treaty and its aftermath see R. Henig, *Versailles and After, 1919–1933* (London: Routledge, 1995). For the economic dimension see D. H. Aldcroft, *From Versailles to Wall Street, 1919–1929* (London: Allen Lane, 1977).

For the League of Nations see Lord Cecil, *The Great Experiment* (London: Hodder and Stoughton, 1941); Ruth Henig, *The League of Nations* (Edinburgh: Oliver and Boyd, 1973); A. H. M. van Ginneken, *Historical Dictionary of the League of Nations* (Lanham, MD: Scarecrow Press, 2005); F. S. Northedge, *A History of the League of Nations* (Leicester: Leicester University Press, 1989); and F. P. Walters, *A History of the League of Nations*, two volumes (Oxford: Oxford University Press, 1969).

On the military dimensions see R. M. Citino, *The Path to Blitzkrieg: Doctrine and Training in the German Army, 1920–1939* (Boulder, CO: Lynne Rienner, 1999); R. M. Citono, *Quest for Decisive Victory: From Stalemate to Blitzkrieg in Europe, 1899–1940* (Lawrence, KS: University Press of Kansas, 2002); B. J. C. McKercher and R. Legault (eds), *Military Planning and the Origins of the Second World War in Europe* (Westport, CT: Praeger, 2001); A. R. Millett and W. Murray (eds), *Military Effectiveness: The Interwar Period* (London: Routledge, 1990); W. Murray and A. R. Millett (eds), *Military Innovation in the Interwar Period* (Cambridge: Cambridge University Press, 1996); and D. C. Watt, *Too Serious a Business: European Armed Forces and the Approach of the Second World War* (Berkeley, CA: University of California Press, 1975).

On intelligence, see W. Murray and A. R. Millett (eds), *Calculations. Net Assessment and the Coming of World War II* (New York: Free Press, 1992); and W. K. Wark, *The Ultimate Enemy: British Intelligence and Nazi Germany, 1933–39* (London: I. B. Tauris, 1985).

On individual countries and their policies see the following. Balkans: D. Deletent, *Hitler's Forgotten Ally: Ion Antonescu and His Regime, Romania 1940–1944* (Basingstoke: Palgrave Macmillan, 2006); J. S. Koliopoulos, *Greece and the British Connection 1935–1941* (Oxford: Oxford University Press, 1977); S. Lawlor, *Churchill and the Politics of War, 1940–1941* (Cambridge: Cambridge University Press, 1994); B. Millman, *The Ill-Made Alliance. Anglo–Turkish Relations 1934–1940*

(Montreal: McGill–Queens University Press, 1998); R. M. Salerno, *Vital Crossroads: Mediterranean Origins of the Second World War, 1935–1940* (Cornell: Cornell University Press, 2002); G. Schrieber, D. Vogel and D. S. McMurry, *Germany and the Second World War, Vol. III: The Mediterranean, South-east Europe and North Africa, 1939–1941* (Oxford: Clarendon Press, 1995). France: M. S. Alexander, *The Republic in Danger. General Maurice Gamelin and the Politics of French Defence, 1933–1940* (Cambridge: Cambridge University Press, 1992); P. M. H. Bell, *France and Britain, 1900–40: Entente and Estrangement* (London: Longman, 2001); R. Boyce (ed.), *French Foreign and Defence Policy 1918–1940. The Decline and Fall of a Great Power* (London: Routledge, 1998); R. Davis, *Anglo–French Relations before the Second World War. Appeasement and Crisis* (Basingstoke: Palgrave, 2001); P. Jackson, *France and the Nazi Menace. Intelligence and Policy Making 1933–1939* (Oxford: Oxford University Press, 2000); A. Sharp and G. Stone (eds), *Anglo–French Relations in the Twentieth Century: Rivalry and Co-operation* (London: Routledge, 2000); E. Weber, *The Hollow Years. France in the 1930s* (New York: Norton, 1994); and R. Young, *In Command of France: French Foreign Policy and Military Planning, 1933–40* (Harvard: Harvard University Press, 1979). Germany: A. Hillgruber, *Germany and the Two World Wars* (Harvard: Harvard University Press, 1981); D. Irving, *The War Path. Hitler's Germany 1933–1939* (London: Michael Joseph, 1978); C. Leitz, *Nazi Foreign Policy* (London: Routledge, 2003); I. Kershaw, *Hitler 1889–1936: Hubris* (London: Allen Lane, 1998); I. Kershaw, *Hitler 1936–1945: Nemesis* (London: Allen Lane, 2000); B. Wegner (ed.), *From Peace to War: Germany, Soviet Russia and the World, 1939–1941* (Oxford: Berghahn Books, 1997); G. L. Weinberg, *The Foreign Policy of Hitler's Germany: Diplomatic Revolution in Europe, 1933–36* (New York: Humanities Press, 1994); and G. L. Weinberg, *Hitler's Foreign Policy 1933–1939: The Road to World War II* (New York: Enigma Books, 2004). Great Britain: J. Charmley, *Chamberlain and the Lost Peace* (London: Hodder and Stoughton, 1989); A. Crozier, *Neville Chamberlain* (London: Hodder Arnold, 2008); D. Dutton, *Neville Chamberlain* (London: Arnold, 2001); R. Self, *Neville Chamberlain. A Biography* (Aldershot: Ashgate, 2006); T. C. Imlay, *Facing the Second World War: Strategy, Politics and Economics in Britain and France 1938–1940* (Oxford: Oxford University Press, 2003); P. Neville, *Hitler and Appeasement. The British Attempt to Prevent the Second World War* (London: Hambledon, 2005); R. A. C. Parker, *Chamberlain and Appeasement: British Policy and the Coming of the Second World War* (Basingstoke: Macmillan, 1993); G. C. Peden, *Arms, Economics and British Strategy*

(Cambridge: Cambridge University Press, 2007); and R. Self, *Neville Chamberlain. A Biography* (Aldershot: Ashgate, 2006). Italy: M. Knox, *Mussolini Unleashed 1939–1941* (Cambridge: Cambridge University Press, 1982); D. Mack Smith, *Mussolini's Roman Empire* (London: Longman, 1976); R. Mallett, *Mussolini and the Origins of the Second World War* (Basingstoke: Palgrave Macmillan, 2003); and G. Bruce Strang, *On the Fiery March: Mussolini Prepares for War* (Westport, CT: Praeger, 2003). Soviet Union: G. Gorodetsky, *Grand Delusion: Stalin and the German Invasion of Russia* (New Haven: Yale University Press, 2001); J. Haslam, *The Soviet Union and the Struggle for Collective Security in Europe 1933–39* (Basingstoke: Macmillan, 1984); K. Neilson, *Britain, Soviet Russia and the Collapse of the Versailles Order, 1919–1939* (Cambridge: Cambridge University Press, 2006); G. Roberts, *The Soviet Union and the Origins of the Second World War* (Basingstoke: Macmillan, 1995); and S. Pons, *Stalin and the Inevitable War 1936–1941* (London: Frank Cass, 2002). Spain: M. Alpert, *A New International History of the Spanish Civil War* (Basingstoke: Macmillan, 1994); T. Buchanan, *Britain and the Spanish Civil War* (Cambridge: Cambridge University Press, 1997); J. F. Covendale, *Italian Intervention in the Spanish Civil War* (Princeton: Princeton University Press, 1975); S. Payne, *The Spanish Civil War, the Soviet Union and Communism* (New Haven: Yale University Press, 2004); W. Podmore, *Britain, Italy, Germany and the Spanish Civil War* (Lampeter: Edwin Mellen Press, 1998); G. A. Stone, *Spain, Portugal & the Great Powers, 1931–1941* (Basingstoke: Palgrave Macmillan, 2005); and R. Whealey, *Hitler and Spain: The Nazi Role in the Spanish Civil War, 1936–1939* (Lexington: University Press of Kentucky, 1989). USA: R. Dallek, *Franklin D. Roosevelt and American Foreign Policy, 1932–1945* (Oxford: Oxford University Press, 1979); R. F. De Bedts, *Ambassador Joseph Kennedy 1938–1940: An Anatomy of Appeasement* (New York: P. Lang, 1985); R. Ovendale, *'Appeasement' and the English Speaking World: Britain, the United States, the Dominions, and the Policy of 'Appeasement' 1937–1939* (Cardiff: University of Wales Press, 1975); C. A. MacDonald, *The United States, Britain and Appeasement, 1936–1939* (Basingstoke: Macmillan, 1981); and W. R. Rock, *Chamberlain & Roosevelt. British Foreign Policy and the United States, 1937–1940* (Columbus: Ohio State University Press, 1988).

Notes

The author wishes to acknowledge the invaluable comments of Derek Aldcroft, Steffen Prauser and Zara Steiner on earlier drafts.

1 Quoted by I. Kershaw, *Hitler 1936–1945: Nemesis* (London: Penguin, 2000), p. 224.
2 D. Stevenson, '1918 Revisited', *Journal of Strategic Studies* 28: 107–39 (2005), p. 109.
3 See P. Noel-Baker, *The Geneva Protocol: for the Pacific Settlement of International Disputes* (London: G. S. King & Son, 1925).
4 Quoted in L. S. Amery, 'The Abyssinian Crisis', *Daily Mail*, 3 October 1935.
5 J. Jacobson, 'Locarno, Britain and the Security of Europe', in G. Johnson (ed.), *Locarno Revisited. European Diplomacy 1920–1929* (London: Routledge, 2004), pp. 17–18.
6 J. Jacobson, 'Locarno, Britain and the Security of Europe', *op. cit.*, pp. 18–28.
7 See Z. Steiner, *The Lights that Failed. European International History 1919–1933* (Oxford: Oxford University Press, 2005), chapter 8.
8 *Ibid.*, p. vii.
9 See R. Mallett, *Mussolini and the Origins of the Second World War, 1933–1940* (Basingstoke: Palgrave Macmillan, 2003), chapter 3.
10 Quoted by S. Morewood, *The British Defence of Egypt 1935–1940* (London: Frank Cass, 2005), p. 46.
11 See R. Mallett, *The Italian Navy and Fascist Expansionism 1935–1940* (London: Frank Cass, 1998), Appendix 2: Meeting of the Supreme High Command, 13 August 1935, and *idem*, 'The Italian Naval Command and the Mediterranean Crisis, January–October 1935', *Journal of Strategic Studies* 22: 77–102 (1999).
12 Peter Jackson, *France and the Nazi Menace. Intelligence and Policy Making 1933–1939* (Oxford: Oxford University Press, 2000), p. 161.
13 *Ibid.*, p. 169.
14 M. S. Alexander, *The Republic in Danger. General Maurice Gamelin and the Politics of French Defence, 1933–1940* (Cambridge: Cambridge University Press, 1992), pp. 259–63.
15 L. R. Pratt, *East of Malta, West of Suez. Britain's Mediterranean Crisis 1936–1939* (Cambridge: Cambridge University Press, 1975), pp. 32–34.
16 Cabinet 1 (37), 13 January 1937, The National Archives, CAB23/87.
17 Quoted by V. Rothwell, *The Origins of the Second World War* (Manchester: Manchester University Press, 2001), p. 116.
18 Quoted by G. Howson, *Arms for Spain: The Untold Story of the Spanish Civil War* (London: John Murray, 1999), p. 122.
19 N. Ferguson, *The War of the World. History's Age of Hatred* (London: Allen Lane, 2006), p. 474.
20 A. J. P. Taylor, *The Origins of the Second World War* (London: Penguin, 1961), p. 163.
21 The Earl of Avon, *The Eden Memoirs. Facing the Dictators* (London: Cassell, 1962), p. 473. For a more nuanced reading of the Nyon effect, see G. Stone, 'Yvon Delbos and Anthony Eden: Anglo–French Cooperation, 1936–38', *Diplomacy and Statecraft* 17: 799–820 (2006), pp. 805–7.
22 Quoted by I. Kershaw, *Hitler 1936–1945*, *op. cit.*, p. 208.
23 Ciano diary, 12 January 1939, in M. Muggeridge (ed.), *Ciano's Diary, 1939–1943* (London: Heinemann, 1947).
24 See G. C. Peden, *British Rearmament and the Treasury: 1932–1939* (Edinburgh: Scottish Academic Press, 1979).

25 See P. Finney, 'The Romance of Decline: The Historiography of Appeasement and British National Identity', *Electronic Journal of International History*, June 2000: www.history.ac.uk/ejournal/art1.html

26 W. R. Rock, *Chamberlain and Roosevelt. British Foreign Policy and the United States, 1937–1940* (Columbus: Ohio State University Press, 1988), pp. 28–33.

27 Joe Kennedy to Arthur Krock, 21 March 1938, in A. Smith (ed.), *Hostage to Fortune. The Letters of Joseph P. Kennedy* (New York: Viking, 2001).

28 D. C. Watt, 'Personalities and Appeasement', in W. R. Louis (ed.), *Adventures with Britannia. Personalities, Politics and Culture in Britain* (Austin: University of Texas, 1995), p. 86.

29 Cabinet Foreign Policy Committee, Conversation between President Roosevelt and Sir Arthur Willert, 25 and 26 March 1939, The National Archives, CAB 27/627.

30 Eden to Chamberlain, 31 January 1938, The National Archives, PREM 1/276.

31 Ribbentrop, not Hitler, had signed the Anglo–German Naval Agreement of June 1935.

32 P. Neville, *Hitler and Appeasement. The British Attempt to Prevent the Second World War* (London: Hambledon Continuum, 2005), p. 75.

33 P. Neville, *Appeasing Hitler: The Diplomacy of Sir Nevile Henderson* (Basingstoke: Palgrave Macmillan, 1999), pp. 51–53.

34 See J. Wright and P. Stafford, 'A Blueprint for World War? Hitler and the Hossbach Memorandum', *History Today* 38: 11–17 (1988).

35 A. J. P. Taylor, *The Origins of the Second World War, op. cit.*, pp. 169–73.

36 *Documents on German Foreign Policy 1918–1945*, Series D, Volume 1 (Washington, DC: US Government Printing Office, 1949).

37 I. Kershaw, *Hitler 1936–1945, op. cit.*, pp. 163–66.

38 P. Shen, *The Age of Appeasement. The Evolution of British Foreign Policy in the 1930s* (Stroud: Sutton, 1999), pp. 218–19.

39 Quoted by F. Beckett, 'Who was the Best 20th Century Prime Minister?', *BBC History* 7 (9): 2006, p. 41.

40 P. Neville, *Hitler and Appeasement, op. cit.*, p. 157.

41 R. Lamb, *Mussolini and the British* (London: John Murray, 1997), p. 240.

42 See E. M. Robertson, 'Hitler's Planning for War and the Response of the Great Powers (1938–early 1939)', in H. W. Koch (ed.), *Aspects of the Third Reich* (London: Macmillan, 1985).

43 Quoted by P. Shen, *The Age of Appeasement, op. cit.*, p. 220.

44 P. Neville, *Appeasing Hitler, op. cit.*, pp. 137–39.

45 R. J. Overy, 'Strategic Intelligence and the Outbreak of the Second World War', *War in History* 5 (4): 451–80 (1998), p. 458.

46 N. Nicolson (ed.), *Harold Nicolson, Diaries and Letters, 1930–1939* (London: Collins, 1966), p. 393.

47 G. Roberts, *The Soviet Union and the Origins of the Second World War* (Basingstoke: Macmillan, 1995), p. 61.

48 The Polish guarantee was extended by Britain and France on 31 March; towards Greece and Romania on 13 April 1939.

49 E. Holt, *Hitler's War* (London: Robert Hale, 1988), pp. 101–2.

50 R. J. Overy, 'Strategic Intelligence and the Outbreak of the Second World War', *op. cit.*, p. 461.

51 P. Neville, *Hitler and Appeasement, op. cit.*, p. 172.

52 G. Roberts, *The Soviet Union and the Origins of the Second World War*, *op. cit.*, p. 82.

53 G. Bruce Strang, 'John Bull in Search of a Suitable Russia: British Foreign Policy and the Failure of the Anglo–French–Soviet Alliance Negotiations, 1939', *Canadian Journal of History* XLI: 47–84 (2006), p. 84.

54 Minutes of Committee of Imperial Defence, 22 June 1939, The National Archives, CAB 2/8.

55 Daladier sent a similar letter at the same time.

56 See Z. Shore, *What Hitler Knew. The Battle for Information in Nazi Foreign Policy* (Oxford: Oxford University Press, 2003), chapter 6.

57 I. Kershaw, *Hitler 1936–1945*, *op. cit.*, pp. 211–19.

58 *Ibid.*, p. 213.

59 N. Davies, *God's Playground. A History of Poland, Vol. II* (Oxford: Oxford University Press, 2005), p. 319.

60 R. J. Overy, 'Strategic Intelligence and the Outbreak of the Second World War', *op. cit.*, pp. 548–60. See also D. Zimmerman, *Britain's Shield: Radar and the Defeat of the Luftwaffe* (Stroud: Sutton Publishing, 2001).

61 See C. Messenger, *The Art of Blitzkrieg* (London: Ian Allan, 1991).

62 G. Roberts, *The Unholy Alliance. Stalin's Pact with Hitler* (London: I. B. Tauris, 1989), pp. 174–75.

63 See P. Neville, *Appeasing Hitler*, *op. cit.*, pp. 190–97; I. Kershaw, *Hitler 1936–1945*, *op. cit.*, pp. 222–23.

64 *Ibid.*, p. 285.

65 *Ibid.*, pp. 293–94.

66 *Ibid.*, p. 305.

67 *Ibid.*, pp. 305–6.

68 For the economic complexities see D. H. Aldcroft, *Europe's Third World. The European Periphery in the Interwar Years* (Aldershot: Ashgate, 2006).

69 See C. Catherwood, *The Balkans in World War Two: Britain's Balkan Dilemma 1939–41* (Basingstoke: Palgrave Macmillan, 2003).

70 See N. Balfour and S. Mackay, *Paul of Yugoslavia. Britain's Maligned Friend* (London: Hamish Hamilton, 1980), chapters IX–XI.

71 See M. Cervi, *The Hollow Legions. Mussolini's Blunder in Greece 1940–1941* (London: Chatto & Windus, 1972), chapter 6. 28 October is commemorated in Greece as *Ochi* Day.

72 Romania, the other original signatory, dropped out of the Balkan Entente and renounced the British guarantee in the summer of 1940.

73 Record of the conversation between the Foreign Minister and Ambassador Oshima, 23 February 1941, in *Documents on German Foreign Policy 1918–1945, Series D*, XII (78) (London: HMSO, 1951).

74 See J. S. Koliopoulos, *Greece and the British Connection 1935–1941* (Oxford: Clarendon Press, 1977), chapters VII–IX.

75 See, for example, M. van Crevald, *Hitler's Strategy 1940–1941. The Balkan Clue* (Cambridge: Cambridge University Press, 1973); H. Boog, J. Forster, J. Hoffman *et al.*, *Germany and the Second World War, Volume 4: The Attack on the Soviet Union* (Oxford: Oxford University Press, 1994).

76 I. Kershaw, *Hitler 1936–1945*, *op. cit.*, p. 335.

77 For Soviet intelligence failures see G. Goredtsky, *Grand Delusion: Stalin and the German Invasion of Russia* (New Haven: Yale University Press, 2001).

78 G. Roberts, *The Unholy Alliance*, *op. cit.*, p. 201.

79 The Finland tape, 4 June 1942, recorded without Hitler's knowledge, cited by I. Kershaw, *Hitler 1936–1945, op. cit.*, pp. 524–25.
80 See R. J. Overy, *Why the Allies Won* (London: Penguin, 1995).
81 Quoted by R. Bernstein, 'Good War gone Bad', *New York Review of Books*, 25 October 2007, LIV (16): p. 48.
82 Halifax to Lindsay, 12 September 1939, The National Archives, FO 794/17.
83 E. Butler, *Mason-Mac: The Life of Lieutenant-General Sir Noel Mason-MacFarlane: A Biography* (London: Macmillan, 1972), p. 75.
84 See A. Hitler, *Mein Kampf* (Munich: 1943); G. Weinberg (ed.), *Hitler's Second Book: The Unpublished Sequel to Mein Kampf* (London: Enigma Books, 2006).
85 C. Messenger, *The Art of Blitzkrieg, op. cit.*, p. 176.
86 Quoted by A Tooze, *Wages of Destruction: The Making and Breaking of the Nazi Economy* (London: Penguin, 2006), p. 315.
87 See R. J. Overy, *The Origins of the Second World War* (London: Longman, 1998, 2nd edn); I. Kershaw, *Hitler 1936–1945, op. cit.*, chapters 4–5.
88 A. Tooze, 'Hitler's Gamble?', *History Today* 56 (11): 22–28 (2006); A. Tooze, *Wages of Destruction, op. cit.*, chapter 9.
89 I. Kershaw, *Hitler 1936–1945, op. cit.*, pp. 265–66.
90 W. Murray, *The Change in the European Balance of Power, 1938–1939: The Path to Ruin* (Princeton, NJ: Princeton University Press, 1984); N. Ferguson, *The War of the World, op. cit.*, pp. 361–72; Z. Steiner, 'Of Men and Arms: 1919–39: Unfinished History?', lecture at King's College, London, 2 November 2006.
91 N. Ferguson, *The War of the World, op. cit.*, p. 361.
92 *Ibid.*, p. 362.
93 I. Kershaw, *Hitler 1936–1945, op. cit.*, p. 123.
94 R. A. C. Parker, *Chamberlain and Appeasement: British Policy and the Coming of the Second World War* (Basingstoke: Macmillan, 1993).

10 Experiences of Total War: 1939–45

Giacomo Lichtner

Throughout the summer of 1940, the dreaded planes of the Luftwaffe were routinely bombing New York City, the heart of the free world. With its ally France forced into submission by a lightning German campaign and Great Britain immobile in its island fortress neutrality, the East Coast of the United States was on its knees. Yet, with the resilience that comes from righteousness, they fought on. Even under the bombs, New York retained its pioneer spirit. Intrepid fire-fighters took on the blaze; street-wise immigrants found professions out of clearing rubble; defiant crowds continued to pour into baseball stadia and cinemas; young crew-cut college boys queued up to enlist, their girlfriends proudly looking on. In Harlem, jazz parlours reinvented themselves in the bunkers, the saxophone notes billowing higher than smoke and the bass beat resounding deeper than bombs.

Of course, none of this happened; but, in some respects, it might just as well have done. If the Hollywood blockbuster *U-571* (Jonathan Mostow, USA, 2000) has appropriated to a US commando the 1940 British capture of an Enigma encoding machine, then it is only a matter of time before ever-perceptive producers conspire to adapt the bravery and suffering of the Blitz, its immense patrimony of human stories, for the consumption of American audiences. *U-571* was certainly not the first example of popular cinema changing history for dramatic or commercial purposes, but it was highly unusual. American forces were never involved in that particular operation, and the USA had not as yet entered the war. The film thus illustrates the status of World War Two in contemporary culture: no longer a historical event to study and learn from, but a mythical battle between good and evil. The example of *U-571* also suggests that the 1939–45 conflict has obtained an air of familiarity that few historical events achieve: today we feel we know its history so well that we can even make it up.

If the historical liberties taken by popular culture will never cease to exasperate historians, the cultural pervasiveness of World War Two is not surprising. The conflict is widely considered as being the defining moment of the twentieth century. The causes, course and consequences of the war – together with its political and ethical significance – clearly changed not only the path of history, but also many aspects of human thought. Its roots went deep into the nationalist struggles of the nineteenth century, and its links to the struggle of 1914–18 were such as to encourage many to view it as the final phase of a new 'Thirty Years' War'. Similarly, the consequences for Europe after 1945 were dire and long-lasting.

Much of the continent was physically and economically ruined, and was soon to be divided by an Iron Curtain as the Cold War froze over. Additionally, World War Two virtually bankrupted the former imperial nations of Britain, France and the Netherlands, thus catalysing the process of decolonization. As nation-states emerged out of the former colonies in Africa and Asia, a small band of western European countries embarked on the unsteady and uneven path towards European integration. Hence the war is clearly central to the twentieth century for more than just its temporal setting.

Ethically, the conflict signalled the horrors of modernity by illustrating the extent to which industrialization had made possible the pursuit of genocide. If the killing fields and the chemical warfare of World War One – and subsequent horrors such as the Italian use of gas in Ethiopia and the German bombing of Guernica – had already anticipated this fact, the years between 1939 and 1945 made it frighteningly clear. Mass aerial bombings and the first use of nuclear weapons against Japan in August 1945 were additional proof, weakening the notion that technological progress was an inherently beneficial force. If any doubts remained, it was only necessary to reflect on the implementation of the Holocaust, which had been carried out with industrial precision in the death factories of Treblinka, Sobibor, Belzec and elsewhere.

Notwithstanding these developments, World War Two used to be considered almost exclusively as a matter for military and political historians. This is hardly surprising, given that it was a conflict that revolutionized the conduct of warfare. It was fought in the African summer and the Arctic winter, on mountains and in jungles over four continents; it involved unprecedented battlefield tactics, especially in the deployment of tanks, artillery, air and sea power, submarine and amphibious warfare; it also witnessed covert and non-conventional fighting techniques, including undercover military operations, espionage and guerrilla warfare by irregular forces. In these regards, it offered students of military operations a wealth of exciting questions to reflect upon. More recently, however, historians have deepened their concern to take in wider issues. They have focused on the experiences of ordinary women and men; on the many microhistories of this vast conflict; and on the way it has been remembered and represented in the postwar period.[1]

In its analysis of World War Two, this chapter reflects and privileges these recent approaches by attempting to explain what Total War meant, not just to the soldiers, but also to the civilians involved.[2] The approach owes much to Philip Bell's lucid and comprehensive treatment of the war in the previous edition of this work.[3] The present account broadly follows a similar chronological template, but adds to it a thematic structure that zooms in from the universal to the particular, in order to show how Total War was played out at all levels, from the global to the domestic, from high politics to everyday life. It also highlights how the experiences of those hundreds of millions involved were different, yet eminently comparable.

Total War as global war

World War Two is rightly considered as the first truly global conflict. World War One had effectively been a European affair, in which extra-European powers, such as the USA and Japan, became involved. While non-European forces, such as those from Australia and New Zealand, were engaged, they fought principally on European battle-fields and because of their allegiance to a European 'mother country'. In the conflict that ended in 1945, however, the USA and Japan played a much larger role and the different fronts, spread across four continents, had serious reciprocal effects on one another: for instance, war in the Pacific interconnected with the South-East Asian front, while war in north and north-eastern Africa was crucial for the continued British control of the Middle East, whose oil resources and geopolitical significance were paramount for the UK's survival.

World War Two was also global because of the nature of the supply routes that made its conduct possible. The intervention of the USA following the Japanese attack on Pearl Harbor was decisive not simply in widening the military scope of the conflict, but in making available to the Allies the enormous economic and technical resources of the USA. Hence the war for control of the seas had an emphatically global ambit. In particular, the battle for the Atlantic, like that for control of the Mediterranean and Suez, was crucial: it safeguarded the supply routes to and from Britain, preventing starvation, and allowed for the massive transfer of men and equipment from North America, resources that were beginning to tell by December 1942.

The other markedly global aspect of the conflict was the war in the air, fought as much in laboratories and map rooms as in the skies. As well as playing a part in each campaign of World War Two, air power achieved several crucial objectives, such as cutting off supply lines to and from the front, and destroying industries vital to the war effort such as fuel and armament factories. For example, in 1944, shortly after D-Day, the British intercepted a message by the German commander of a parachute regiment stationed in France lamenting the dire lack of fuel: from that day on, and for the rest of the war, British and American bombers consistently targeted German refineries in order to ensure this kind of problem was never solved. Inevitably, civilians were caught up in such attacks, which demonstrated the possibilities of strategic bombing which affected morale as much as it did the enemy's economy.[4]

The conflict became a 'world war' on 7 December 1941 when, in a surprise attack, the Japanese air force destroyed much of the US Pacific fleet anchored in the Hawaiian port of Pearl Harbor. Yet it can also be argued that the conflict did not properly count as a world-wide engagement until four days later, when Hitler declared war on the USA. Japan had already engaged the European powers in the Indian Ocean and the South China Sea; now Germany was dragging the Americans into Europe. Did Berlin widen the war out of loyalty to its Japanese partner, or in the hope that this Axis ally might now attack the Soviet Union? Was Hitler driven by an ideological belief that all the liberal democracies would have to be defeated, or was he carried away by sheer enthusiasm? Whatever the case, the Führer's decision was his second major mistake of the war, following the one he had made in June 1941 when he launched his invasion of the Soviet Union. It could even be argued that it was his third, if we count his courtship of Mussolini's Italy. He must have known, however, that the German declaration of war against the USA would make it impossible for congressional isolationists in Washington to ignore Europe any longer. Thus the Nazi dictator had unwittingly ensured that, sooner or later, American military and economic resources would turn the course of the war in Europe and bring about Germany's eventual defeat. Had Hitler shown restraint, it is conceivable that the American government, conscious of public opinion, might have restricted its war to that with Japan in the Pacific. How then did the conflict initially evolve after its outbreak within the European domain?

Total War as regional war

World War Two started as a European war, and so it largely remained until December 1941. In the strictest of senses, it had been provoked by Hitler, dictator of Germany since 1933, whose desire to build a greater Reich led eventually to the invasion of Poland on 1 September 1939, an event that snapped Britain and France out of a policy of appeasement, which in any case was already wavering. In this opening phase, therefore, the conflict resembled World War One in being primarily a conflict between powers competing for influence on the European continent. After reclaiming the Rhineland in 1936, precipitating the *Anschluss* with Austria and annexing the Sudetenland in 1938, and then seizing the rest of Bohemia and Moravia in spring 1939, Germany now sought further 'living space' in eastern Europe. Nothing had prevented Hitler's earlier expansionism and, in the minds of some, Germany's ambitions in the Rhineland and Sudetenland were entirely reasonable. Then came the bombshell of the Nazi–Soviet Pact of August 1939, in which the Reich struck a partnership with the Soviet Union. This facilitated the dismemberment of Poland between two dictatorships, and caused dismay and confusion among left-wing sympathizers throughout Europe. Poland was quickly defeated: the last charge of the Polish cavalry against the German Panzers became mythologized as a symbolic act, which signalled the passing of an age and the advent of a kind of permanent revolution in the conduct of warfare. Over the next five-and-a-half years no one would doubt this, although it is questionable whether Britain and France had done enough to modernize their forces to fight the Germans in 1939–40. Until May 1940, there ensued in western Europe the so-called 'phoney war', in which the two Allies reflected on how best to combat the German threat, while public opinion became increasingly convinced that the war it had always dreaded might never happen.[5]

When the time came, the Germans were anything but indecisive: within six weeks the campaign against France was over. By early to mid-June 1940, the British Expeditionary Force had been hastily evacuated across the Channel; Hitler was sightseeing in Paris; Alsace-Lorraine and part of the French border with Belgium had been annexed by Germany; the Atlantic coast and the North of France, including the capital, were under German military occupation; and the pro-German government of Marshal Pétain was soon to establish itself at Vichy, from where it would administer what remained of France. Even Mussolini got in on the act, declaring war when the fighting was clearly over, and occupying a small south-east corner of French territory, including Nice.

Why the French, or rather the Allies, lost so easily is a difficult question to answer. It has traditionally been argued that French collapse was due to an internal decadence that overwhelmed both the political system and its elites, yet it is virtually impossible to provide empirical evidence by which to measure such alleged decay. Today, there is growing certainty that the causes of the collapse are to be located in the military domain. It is generally acknowledged that the Allies were as well equipped as the Germans, and that they possessed more tanks, although they had fewer aircraft. In the event, the Allies misjudged the German tactics of Blitzkrieg and, crucially, misjudged the Nazi invasion route which came through the heavily wooded Ardennes, previously deemed 'untankable'. Left with no proper strategic reserve, the Allies were unable to prevent encirclement by the Nazis.

The defeat of France was the first potentially decisive turning point of the war because of its far-reaching effects not only on France itself, but also on Britain as its former ally, and on Germany as its new master. First, Hitler's easy victory proved wrong all those on the Allied side who thought the war would be one of attrition, along the lines of the previous conflict. Second, it gave the Germans an air of invincibility which, despite their inability to subdue Britain, they would retain for over two years – until the debacle of Stalingrad. This added weight to Hitler's domestic propaganda, which stressed the racial superiority of the German people and the inherent weakness of the liberal democracies, while instilling awe and dread in Germany's opponents, allies and subordinates alike. Third, in the 1930s France had served as a refuge, albeit begrudgingly, for antifascists and refugees from Spain, Italy and Germany, whose individual and collective cause suffered from the host nation's collapse. Fourth, the fall of France alarmed the USA and emboldened Japan, which could now move to exploit Britain's predicament, replacing the UK as the dominant imperial force in Asia. Finally, and most crucially, the fall of France was not just a military debacle but a surrender, accompanied by the formation of a government friendly to the occupying forces.

Despite some excellent recent treatments of Vichy, such as Julian Jackson's *France: The Dark Years 1940–1944*, the seminal studies on France under the occupation were written during the 1970s.[6] Chief among them is Robert Paxton's *Vichy France: Old Guard and New Order*, published in 1972.[7] He and others show that, in many ways, Vichy made all the difference. First, by controlling a vast territory, both in metropolitan France and overseas, it allowed the Germans to spare valuable troops from patrolling a potentially hostile population – the subsequent trouble the Resistance gave the occupying forces provides a clear sense of how useful Pétain was to the Nazis. Second, his government had come to power essentially through legal means, by dint of a vote in the National Assembly. Pétain's regime thus embodied institutional continuity, despite what de Gaulle's London-based Free French argued. In 1940, the latter figure was still an unknown, while Pétain was a Marshal of France and the famous hero of Verdun. Although a number of colonies would eventually go over to the Free French, those that remained loyal to Vichy, notably Syria, Algeria and Morocco, made the Allies' task that much more difficult. Vichy's stance also forced the Royal Navy to destroy the French fleet at Mers-el-Kébir so as to prevent it falling into German hands. Above all, the Franco–German armistice of June 1940 left Britain to fight alone, except for the support supplied by its Dominions. The nation's survival was crucially assisted by its island position. This made a land invasion virtually impossible unless the Germans achieved dominance of the Channel and in the air over Britain, neither of which was accomplished. Historians are divided as to which one of the armed forces contributed most to Britain's survival: the Royal Navy or the Royal Air Force. Pivotal, too, was the inspired leadership of Churchill, the newly appointed premier, whose speeches rallied the nation. Much has been made of the British traditions of respect and tolerance, which brought people together in a time of need, although the extent of this unity has been questioned. Also controversial was the preparedness of government to intervene in running the economy in pursuit of production targets, a move that, in the longer term, possibly enshrined outdated management and work practices.[8]

In the course of 1941, Britain broke out of its island fortress to take the war to the Germans and Italians in Africa and the Mediterranean. By aiding Greece in its resistance to the Italian invasion, the UK forced Hitler to divert south and dangerously to delay his attack on the USSR. This was eventually launched in June 1941, and proved another turning point in the war, eventually leading to Germany's defeat.[9]

Why the German High Command decided to venture into the vast expanses of Russia remains debatable. While Germany wrought havoc in Europe, the Soviet Union had not been idle: it had occupied eastern Poland, invaded Finland, and extended its influence over Romania and Bulgaria. Conflict was thus inevitable in the longer term. This undoubtedly troubled Hitler, who was also tempted by the immense energy, mineral and food supplies of the Caucasus, the Urals and the Ukrainian plains. These territories would also provide additional living space for the German peoples. In this respect, ideology was crucial. Not only would Hitler dislodge and destroy millions of Jews who had settled in these regions, he would also overturn communism, a creed he despised even more than liberal democracy.

With the German invasion of the USSR, the first phase of World War Two ended. Until this point, the conflict had been essentially regional rather than global, fought chiefly on several fronts within Europe. Of these, the vast Russian one was the largest. By early 1942, this front extended 2000 miles from the Arctic Circle to the Caucasus, with the easternmost flank stretching German supply lines to a perilous degree. The early German advance was fierce, and remained unchecked until late November 1941, when it was stopped just outside Moscow. The freezing conditions of the Russian winter, which had decimated Napoleon's troops in 1812, have often been credited with preventing the German capture of Moscow. The weather unquestionably made warfare harder, notably in the delivery of supplies, and certainly made conditions for troops almost unbearable. For instance, the cold took the lives of thousands of ill-equipped Italians, from Alpine divisions, who Mussolini begrudgingly offered to Hitler.

However, it was not just the weather that stopped the German advance. The reasons for the successful defence of Moscow at the end of 1941, and the Soviet Union more generally, are chiefly located elsewhere.[10] Thanks to its geography, the USSR was able to stretch the German advance. Credit is also due to the massive mobilization of the Russian economy, a truly gargantuan feat, which enabled the Soviets to outmatch German war production. And, strikingly, among the peoples of Russia, there emerged a belief that national soil had to be defended at any cost, a conviction that was not simply the product of Bolshevik propaganda, but a genuine and deeply felt impulse.

In Hitler's eyes, 1942 should have been the decisive year in the Soviet campaign and, consequently, in the war overall. That summer witnessed yet more German triumphs: although Moscow held firm, Nazi forces poured into the oil-rich Caucasus and laid siege to Stalingrad. In the meantime, the British suffered further setbacks in North Africa and Singapore. But, in the event, far from marking Hitler's victory, 1942 saw the turn of the tide. On 26 October British, Australian, New Zealand, South African and Indian forces won the decisive battle of El Alamein. In November, the Red Army began counter-attacks at Stalingrad and in the Caucasus. Stalingrad was the worst defeat as yet suffered by the Germans,[11] while stiff fighting in the Caucasus forced Hitler to relinquish ambitions of reaching Grozny and the Caspian Sea. By the end of 1942, the Axis was on the back foot across all the principal fronts involved in a global war.

Why did the fortunes of the war turn in favour of the Allies in 1942? It has been argued convincingly that this depended on the good management of superior military, industrial and economic resources. In

1942, the Allies produced 105,000 airplanes and over 50,000 tanks, as opposed to Germany's 15,400 and 9400, respectively. None the less, three other factors came into play.

First, there was the British mastery of code-breaking. In the last three years of war, the Allies were covertly intercepting Germany's most secret communications. At El Alamein, intelligence was crucial even before the battle itself started, by revealing the schedule of the German and Italian supply shipments, an impressive amount of which were swiftly destroyed; at Kursk, the largest tank battle of the war, the decoding of German messages, shared with the Soviet Union, denied Hitler's forces the benefit of surprise; and in the Atlantic, the ability to reveal the position and orders of German U-boats kept Anglo–American supply lines open. At Bletchley Park, by 1943 British code-breakers had deciphered not only the German 'Enigma' code, but also the Italian 'C38M' and the Japanese 'Purple'. There, 5000 women and men worked, deploying and adapting their skills as mathematicians, linguists and historians.

Second, Germany's ability to sustain the war was damaged by the economic and military collapse of its Axis partners, for instance Romania, but more importantly Italy. By 1943, Mussolini's regime was perhaps only marginally less unpopular than when it entered the war three years earlier. The lure of imperial grandeur, which earlier conquests in Africa and Albania had promised, had been unfulfilled as colony after colony was lost. Italy had additionally become a liability to Hitler, who now found himself ever more tightly encircled. Defence of the southern end of Fortress Europe could not be entrusted to Mussolini. Identifying Italy as 'the soft underbelly of Europe', Anglo–American troops landed an attack in Sicily in July 1943. The invasion of Italy was enough for the leaders of Rome's Grand Fascist Council to demand the resignation of Mussolini. With an irony befitting this Italian brand of totalitarianism, the dictator who gave the world fascism was deposed by a majority vote.

The remaining factor is Hitler's increasingly paranoid conduct of the war. Since the Soviet counter-attack at Stalingrad in November 1942, the German dictator had assumed an even closer personal command of military operations. From that point on, he would seldom accept the advice of generals on his staff or in the field. In October 1943, when General Von Kleist ordered his troops to retreat from the Crimea and regroup further west, Hitler personally reversed that order. This obduracy clearly had detrimental effects on the German war effort: it condemned to a dreadful fate General von Paulus's Sixth Army, which had had several opportunities to abandon the siege of Stalingrad and escape encirclement by the Red Army. Perhaps more critically, Hitler's leadership style exacerbated the lot of the German people, who were condemned to fight until the total capitulation of Nazism.

Despite this decisive shift in fortunes, it would take over two further years of war and the opening of two more European fronts to achieve the total defeat of Nazi Germany. The first, in 1943, was not the mass invasion of northern Europe that Stalin had long been demanding from his Western allies, but the aforementioned invasion of Italy, begun in Sicily, then extended to the Italian mainland at Salerno, south of Naples, and Anzio, south of Rome. This operation was both a natural extension of the war in the Mediterranean and a new development, signalling the fact that the initiative now rested with the Allies, not Hitler. The campaign was certainly instrumental in bringing about the fall of Mussolini's regime and the Italian armistice.

It was not a straightforward operation, however. Militarily, the campaign lasted much longer than the Allies had originally hoped, including two protracted and difficult winters. The capitulation of Italy in itself did not help much, given the heavy German presence on the territory. Also, the diplomacy of the affair was botched. On 25 July 1943, King Victor Emmanuel III sacked and arrested Mussolini, giving the reins of government to Marshal Pietro Badoglio and reassuring Hitler that Italy would continue to honour the alliance. The bluff was quickly spotted. German intelligence had discovered, from Italian and Allied sources, that negotiations for an Italian surrender were imminent Thus, when on 8 September the royal family and Badoglio escaped to Brindisi, in the southern Allied-occupied zone, Hitler was ready to take over the country and rescue Mussolini, while suppressing any opposition from Italian forces that had been left bereft of orders from their superiors. Across many war fronts, in Russia and Greece as well as in their own peninsula, hapless Italian troops saw their former ally turn on them with the ferocity reserved for traitors. Many thousands were taken prisoner and sent to concentration camps; in the Ionian island of Cephalonia, the entire Italian contingent was rounded up and murdered. This German massacre of soldiers, and the repression of civilians under the military occupation of northern Italy, laid bare the selfish and irresponsible actions of the Savoy dynasty and the Badoglio government: having hastily divested the black shirt, they continued to show for the Italian people the same fascist contempt.

The other new European front was finally opened on 6 June 1944 in northern France. The choice of Normandy was in some ways surprising, as most people, including the Germans, thought the Allies would attack closer to the German border, perhaps in the Pas de Calais or along the Belgian coast. For several days, Hitler did not commit his army reserves, believing the invasion to be a diversion. The question thus remains as to why the Allies waited so long. Did the invasion of Italy facilitate this second landing by tying up German forces, or would it have been preferable to have pressed ahead with an invasion of France as early as 1943, as Stalin had demanded? Like many of the military and strategic questions still surrounding World War Two, any answer can only be speculative. One factor is certain. Had the D-Day invaders been pushed back into the sea, the consequences for the Allies would have been catastrophic.

The Normandy landings are among the best known and most represented campaigns of the war. The codenames of the invasion beaches – Omaha, Utah, Juno, Gold and Sword – are well known to most in the English-speaking world, in part through films such as *The Longest Day* (1962) and Stephen Spielberg's *Saving Private Ryan* (1998). It is little wonder film-makers and others have dwelled on this key event. For the French population, the Allied invasion was a long-awaited liberation; to the British, it was a symbolic return to the land they had evacuated hastily in 1940; to millions of subjugated Europeans, to prisoners of war and to partisans, the Normandy campaign meant that Hitler would lose the conflict. The effect of the landings on wartime and postwar popular imagery was reinforced by the amphibious nature of the attack (also supported by air power), and by the fact that it was covered live by embedded radio and print journalists. The sheer scale of operations was also impressive: the Allies utilized thousands of warships and aircraft, together with 18,000 paratroopers; by the end of 6 June 155,000 Allied soldiers had landed in France, a figure that had become 355,000 four days later.[12]

Notwithstanding the political, military and psychological significance of D-Day, the extent to which it has dominated memory and study of World War Two reveals the extent to which the industries both of entertainment and of historiography have been western-centred. Soviet campaigns in the east are only just being discovered by film-makers and properly explored by scholars.

Within four days of the Normandy landings, several parallel regional wars were thus taking place: in Italy, northern France, on the Eastern Front from Finland to Romania, and in the far east (China, Burma, New Guinea and the Pacific Ocean). As already argued, these many fronts can be considered as separate conflicts, yet they were all interdependent. These regional conflicts were further interconnected by the fact that at least two of the belligerents, Britain and the USA, were fighting in several of them. It is similarly important to note that the powers involved, on each side of the struggle, frequently coordinated their strategic targets, although there was little cooperation in the particular case of Nazi Germany and Japan. Furthermore, all these wars were interconnected by the experiences of those who fought in them: although the terrain of battle varied, soldiers and civilians often underwent similar shared experiences.

Total war as domestic war

In any study of World War Two, a critical consideration must be the way in which the conflict impinged on both soldiers and civilians, and how their lives were inextricably linked. World War One had already changed the shape of wartime societies, notably through the widespread involvement of women in industry and the new roles played by mass media and propaganda. World War Two witnessed further developments, notably in the use of bombing against civilians, and those crimes against humanity perpetrated by the Nazis and by the Red Army.

The possibilities of strategic bombing had been explored before 1939. It was understood that strategic industrial and military bases were necessary targets. Yet it was additionally realized that civilians would be caught up in such attacks, thus affecting overall morale. Generally it was the urban working classes, who most typically lived in these industrial areas, who bore the brunt of such raids. Furthermore, technology and the need to act mostly at night to minimize the risk of anti-aircraft fire meant that precision was scarce. From 1942 onwards, the RAF explored the possibility of carrying out consecutive nighttime raids: the first would cause a large fire in the vicinity of the target, which would provide the later wave of bombers with a more accurate approach path.

The killing of civilians in the pursuit of military objectives always raises ethical problems, but these are at their most pressing with regard to the deliberate and indiscriminate destruction of cities. Widespread bombings of civilian areas were routine events in World War Two, becoming even more frequent and more ferocious during its later stages. From the London Blitz onwards, there were many attempts to use air superiority alone to overwhelm the enemy. In most cases, the strategy did not pay off, but morale was undoubtedly affected. This was evident in the so-called 'Baedeker' raids of late April 1942, when the RAF and the *Luftwaffe* traded heavy bombardments of historic town centres such as Lübeck, Rostock, Bath, York and Coventry. In Britain alone, these raids claimed almost 1000 civilian lives, but it was the destruction of celebrated landmarks, the assault on a country's collective memory, that most affected people's spirits. By the end of the war, the Allies came to accept civilian morale as a legitimate military target, razing to the ground Hamburg and then Dresden in July 1943 and February 1945, respectively. The casualties of the latter will never be known exactly, but probably range from 30,000 to 40,000. The majority of civilians were burnt alive, crushed by the rubble, or asphyxiated in underground bunkers. Even if we try to consider assaults against morale as a part of the war effort, and take into account what a formidable and heinous enemy Nazi Germany had been, the legitimacy of these targets remains doubtful. Only on one occasion were aerial bombardments directly sufficient to force the enemy's surrender: in the non-European context of the nuclear annihilation of Hiroshima on 6 August 1945, and Nagasaki three days later. A chilling irony of Total War is that in many territories occupied by Axis powers, Allied bombings brought not only destruction, but hope of relief. The contradiction is only apparent: each raid demonstrated to the inhabitants that the Allies were advancing, that Hitler was losing, and that liberation would come. This was the case in France, where pilots of the Free French forces had to face the unenviable moral dilemma of carrying out actions in their homeland, potentially causing the deaths of their own compatriots. It was also the case in Italy, where the population hailed the Allies as liberators despite the heavy bombardment of the peninsula. In the history of war, civilians have always been casualties. But World War Two changed the dynamics of their involvement. Civilians were no longer victims simply of war-related famines and disease, or of pillaging after battle. During this conflict, civilians on all sides became, like soldiers, physical victims of the fighting itself. Crimes against humanity, such as mass murders, rapes and deportations, were widely committed. Proper attention has recently been given to the crimes of the advancing Red Army, especially in Berlin and across eastern Germany.[13] Yet only the Nazis managed to transform war crimes into a systematic form of governance. In all cases, the most vulnerable sections of civilian society were the hardest hit. Women, in particular, were victimized in victory and in defeat, both by occupying and by liberating armies.

Throughout Axis-occupied Europe, World War Two was a domestic affair as civilians had to decide on their attitude towards the occupying forces. Most chose to wait on events; a minority collaborated, although it was difficult not to collude with the occupier in a wider sense; and a number chose to resist. The most spectacular manner of resistance was through guerrilla warfare, sabotage and other underground military operations. Resistance was active, especially in eastern Europe, but also in Greece, and in Italy from late 1943. In each territory, resistance groups adopted different characteristics and performed different roles, nowhere more so than within Russia. Here resistance was a part of the national war effort, and the Red Army supplied bands of partisans operating behind Nazi lines. Soviet resistance severely tested German forces in the Ukraine, the Baltic countries and Belarus, as well as in occupied Russia.

Elsewhere, the Resistance was less involved in direct warfare and was less coordinated. In Poland, for example, it started as early as October 1939, and was directed against both the German and the Soviet occupiers. Here, it tried its best to protect Jews and other persecuted individuals, to maintain social and cultural institutions, and to aid the Allied war effort through the ferrying of intelligence. The very existence of a Polish underground, in a country held under the strictest martial law by German authorities who – because of their racial convictions – needed no excuses to murder over 3,000,000 Poles, is remarkable. With the Warsaw rising of August 1944, these Polish warriors staged the largest open revolt against the German army, while the Red Army advance stalled nearby on the other side of the Vistula. As in most places where irregular or partisan forces defied the Germans in open warfare, the revolt was a failure.

In countries with openly pro-German governments, resistance often took on the characteristics of a civil war. This was the case in Yugoslavia, where the Communist guerrillas of Josif Broz – better known as Tito – and the separate nationalist militia of Colonel Draza Mihailović fought not only the German, Italian, Hungarian, Romanian and Bulgarian occupying forces, but also the Croatian Ustaša, a fascist organization led by Ante Pavelić. Although Yugoslavia had officially ceased to exist in 1941, Tito's fight for liberation, supported by the British, was also a political struggle for the future of the nation. Similarly, as a Croatian nationalist, Pavelić saw in Hitler's victory the future hegemony of the Croats over their hated Serbian neighbours, who he continued to persecute viciously.

If in Yugoslavia the assessment of the situation was complicated by the heterogeneous religious and ethnic composition of the fledgling state, in Italy resistance was more clearly defined. On the one hand, there were the fascist forces of Mussolini, reinstated by Hitler as head of the Italian Social Republic, or Republic of Salò, based in northern Italy; on the other hand, the alliance of all antifascist forces, from the communists to the nationalist monarchists loyal to Victor Emmanuel III, affecting a false control of Italy from his base in the Allied-occupied

South. Yet here too there were ambiguities: first, the Resistance was formed late, in 1943, after Italy had been a fascist power for two decades and had become a close ally of Hitler; second, the broad alliance of occasionally opposing ideological positions was not devoid of internal strife, and thus proved short-lived after the war; third, the role of the Italian Social Republic could easily be downplayed as that of a German puppet state. The latter point, in particular, has made it possible for postwar Italy to exploit the bravery of those involved in the Resistance to wipe out the memory of 20 years of fascism, and so present the nation as a victim, rather than as an accomplice, of Hitler. Only in the 1990s, thanks to the work of Claudio Pavone, has the Resistance been recognized as a civil war.[14]

As is the case throughout Europe, it has proved difficult to assess the scale of participation within the Italian Resistance. A rough estimate suggests that it probably never counted more than 100,000 active members. For the most part, these were regular Italian soldiers who had found themselves stranded after the armistice; others were young men who had taken to the hills when faced with the choice between fighting for the Social Republic and deportation to Germany; some were communist and left-wing militants who had sometimes been active antifascists well before 1943. Whatever the case, they operated throughout German-occupied Italy, in the hills and mountains of the Apennines and Alps, in the Po valley, and in urban environments. Despite what was suggested for a long time after the war, their military role was not particularly significant. In many cases they formed small groups, poorly armed and seldom properly trained. Nevertheless, they performed significant acts of sabotage, destroying supply routes and goods, randomly but routinely attacking German troops, and even achieving the highly symbolic feat of liberating some Italian cities before the arrival of Allied troops. But their main role was not military: they helped stranded Allied soldiers reach safety; they provided intelligence and logistic support; and they circulated propaganda. Perhaps the most crucial role the Resistance played in Italy was to return to the people a sense of dignity.

Within France, resisters took part in similar activities, although there is growing consensus that the country was not locked in a civil war.[15] The Vichy government certainly collaborated with the Nazi authorities, notably in the setting up of the Milice, which was designed to seek out partisans, and some individuals clearly joined the German-inspired movements such as the Charlemagne division of the Waffen SS. However, no regular French troops fought alongside the Germans. Moreover, by 1944 Vichy's authority was so dilapidated, and the Germans so unpopular, that the majority of the population sided with the Allies even if they did not become active resisters. It is the French Resistance that has most strongly captured the public imagination. Partly this is thanks to de Gaulle who, at the Liberation and after, established an orthodoxy according to which virtually all French people had in some way taken part in the Resistance.[16] In truth, resistance in France was slow to evolve and was often the work of isolated individuals, although organizations began to emerge in late 1940. After June 1941, and the German invasion of the Soviet Union, the communists became prominent in the *Front National*, though several had engaged in partisan activities on an individual basis before then. Under the skilful leadership of de Gaulle, metropolitan resistance groups achieved some measure of unity in 1943, their numbers swelled by young men fleeing compulsory work service to Germany, introduced at the start of that year. Such deserters took to the scrubland, the *maquis,* hence their name *maquisards*. With Liberation impending, the *maquis* began to take on the Germans in a series of open battles, although it was an unequal fight.

Two further points ought to be made about the resistance in Nazi-occupied Europe at large. First, in all its various incarnations, the partisan formations were extremely heterogeneous in their social and ideological make-up, and often had little more in common than a will to resist. The differentiation between communist and nationalist partisan movements was particularly marked in almost every country. Second, taking part in the resistance necessitated not only courage, but also a moral awareness, as partisans knew that each guerrilla incident or act of sabotage might provoke fierce German retaliation against civilians. It was common practice for the occupying forces to execute ten civilians for each German killed; in eastern Europe, the ratio was often much higher. The fact that the local population frequently continued to support partisans, despite these reprisals, is still awe-inspiring. It is in the relationship between partisans and civilians that the principal significance of resistance can be measured: it was a moral refutation of Nazism which gave hope to millions.

Throughout Europe, occupied or otherwise, civilians were drawn into the business of sustaining the war effort. One vital aspect of this was the maintenance of their morale. Governments of all persuasions were aware of the critical importance of propaganda, whether through the press and posters, or through radio and cinema. For example, in Britain, entertainment was the only commodity never to be rationed. There the film industry in particular was incorporated into the war effort from the very beginning. It sought to educate the public about the importance of the struggle against Nazism, and entertain them with newsreels and propaganda films shown together. Other belligerent nations were equally aware of the importance of entertainment, and especially of cinema as a new and vital mass medium. The Soviet Union, which had pioneered the use of film as political propaganda in the 1920s, now employed it to motivate troops and civilians alike for the Great Patriotic War. Before 1939, Nazi Germany had been equally sensitive to the needs of propaganda and, with films such as *Triumph Des Willens* (*Triumph of the Will*, Leni Riefenstahl, 1935), exploited in full the grand, persuasive spectacle of the moving image.

In France, the German authorities were far-sighted enough to preserve the cinema industry, the most developed and, arguably, the most accomplished in prewar Europe. Their approach was threefold: first, generally to tolerate French productions even while using censorship when necessary; second, to set up a German-owned production company, the Continental; third, to market films produced in the Reich by replacing the names of the German actors with those of their French dubbers. In Italy, too, the vibrant prewar film industry was reinforced with the creation of the Cinecittà film studios and the Centro Sperimentale della Cinematografia, the first film school in the country. During the war, Italian cinema alternated military propaganda with feel-good films, which have later been called *Telefoni Bianchi* (white-telephone films), a name coined because they invariably featured upper-middle-class characters.

In involving every aspect of the daily life of civilians, World War Two was domestic in the most intimate meaning of the word. A generation of children were raised as orphans. Those lucky ones whose parents survived the battlefront and the home front, the bullets, the hardships, and the bombs, were none the less affected. The number of those harmed by the war is unclear, but it runs into millions. Many children saw an unknown soldier return as their father: Martin Gilbert quotes Australian author Germaine Greer wondering at 'the stranger who slept with my mother'.[17] When soldiers returned, they were finally revealed as essentially civilians in uniform. They were often mutilated physically, and many more were affected psychologically. Social taboos of the time worsened the conditions of veterans and civilian survivors by making them unable to tell their stories. In Europe, the effects of the global trauma of the war were felt, in some way or another, within nearly every household.

'The war against the Jews'

In the pursuit of a long-lasting European supremacy, Nazi Germany attempted not only to conquer Europe, but also to redesign it according to its own racial template. Consequently, the German authorities extended different treatment to those occupied populations that they considered as Aryan, found for example in Norway, Denmark and Holland, and those they considered inferior, located in the Slavic countries of eastern Europe and the Balkans. In the latter areas, atrocities against civilians were a daily occurrence. German racial theory was so warped that persecution was not deemed inhuman, as the victims were considered barely human. Europe would forever be changed by the German concentration and extermination camp system, where the racial hierarchy postulated by the Nazis came close to realization by their 'willing executioners'. Members of allegedly inferior races such as Slavs, Gypsies and Jews; people considered socially or morally dangerous such as homosexuals and certain religious minorities; Soviet prisoners of war; victims of the Todt organization of compulsory labour in Germany; common criminals – all were there to be exploited, humiliated and murdered in the macabre realization of a parallel universe that inverted the values of the outside world.

Within that overall context, any attempt to erect a hierarchy of suffering is contentious. Yet it is the experience of those directly subjected to the horrors of the Holocaust that has come to dominate the memory of World War Two. Even when concentrating on the military aspects of World War Two, it is not possible to overlook the attempted annihilation of the Jews. Their persecution by the Nazis was the conflict's longest campaign, launched even earlier, soon after Hitler's accession to power. The Holocaust – or *Shoah* (Hebrew word meaning destruction) as it has more appropriately been termed – had all the characteristics of a military undertaking, albeit an unusual one. First, like any war objective, it was formulated in theory, planned in detail, and executed through a complex organization of tasks and allocation of resources. The genocide soon became a logistical nightmare: how to transport millions of people over thousands of miles? How to pay for the cost of transport and execution? In response, the Nazis treated the genocide of the Jews as any other industrial pursuit. They rationalized the random killing sprees that had characterized the first phase of the genocide up until the invasion of the Soviet Union; they cut costs and maximized returns. Jews would be concentrated in places where only death awaited them: first Chelmno; then Belzec, Treblinka and Sobibor, veritable death factories. Finally came Auschwitz, where the imperatives of labour and murder were most closely enmeshed. The Nazis experimented with killing methods, eventually opting for gas: first the carbon monoxide of Chelmno's poisoning vans; then the more cost-effective Zyklon B. In a chilling irony, the valuables they confiscated from Jews all over Europe financed their transport: the Jews had to pay for their own death. So as to minimize the number of troops required for this macabre work – which proved early on to exact a heavy psychological toll – the Nazis recruited their antisemitic allies. They even imposed and exploited a racial hierarchy among the victims themselves, forcing Jews to participate in the killing process through the so-called *Sonderkommandos*. Perhaps the worst crime of the Nazis was to attempt to drag their victims down to their own level.

Second, like any other strategic war operation, mass murder was covered in secrecy. In January 1942, at Wannsee, representatives of the *Schutzstaffel* (SS), the Nazi party, the foreign office and the bureaucracy – that is to say, the key representatives of the German state – met to iron out the procedural details of a genocide already effectively begun. The Wannsee Conference Protocol, a minute of proceedings compiled by Adolf Eichmann, is one of few documents to have survived that manages to present the overall plan of slaughter. In it, the estimated figure of Jews to be eliminated is 11,000,000, including those of countries as yet neutral or unoccupied. This demonstrates a degree of forethought that the Germans reserved to little else but the persecution of the Jews. The survival of the Protocol was a mistake: had the Nazis succeeded in their plan and in their attempts to keep it secret, the Jews of Europe would not only have been killed, but would also have been robbed of their name and of any trace of their existence.

Third, as in any other military campaign, Germany sought the support of its allies in implementing genocide. Some resisted. The example of the Danish crown, which organized the mass shipping of Jews across to Sweden on the eve of the occupation, stands to mind. The fascist government in Bulgaria also gave protection to its Jewish compatriots. In Vichy France, where the Pétain government had been quick to introduce discriminatory measures, the chief minister Laval brokered a squalid deal in which he handed over foreign and recently naturalized Jews.[18] Across in Italy, the Fascist regime had been openly and independently antisemitic since the issuing of the racial laws in 1938. Yet Mussolini's regime was less willing than its Axis partners to sanction the murder of its Jews, although this position would change dramatically after the formation of the Social Republic. Before the armistice, however, in Italian-occupied territories in southern France, Yugoslavia and Greece, the Italian army infuriated its German ally by refusing to hand over even foreign Jews – despite Mussolini himself having seemingly given instructions to this end. For a long time, this apparent contradiction has strengthened Italian claims that the Duce was not as bad as Hitler, that fascism was not as cruel as Nazism, and that Italy was not fundamentally antisemitic. However, recent research by

Davide Rodogno suggests that the actions of the Italian army in occupied territories were almost always motivated not so much by humanitarian instincts, as by the desire to assert independence from Germany.[19]

Genocide claimed the lives of about 6,000,000 European Jews, including the virtual annihilation of those living in eastern Europe, who had previously possessed a distinct and vibrant culture. Jews were deported and killed in every country that came, even briefly, under German occupation. In Poland – the principal location of the slaughter, where Nazi occupation lasted throughout the war – 4,000,000 Jews from within and beyond that country were murdered alongside as many non-Jewish Poles. In Hungary, where military occupation was brief, 300,000 Jews were murdered in a matter of months. When the outcome of the war looked dire, with Germany threatened on three fronts, Hitler continued to dedicate vital human, logistic and financial resources to the round-up, deportation and killing of Jews all over occupied Europe.

Right until the end of the war, the Germans continued this ghastly business. In its meticulous planning, in its systematic nature and in the manner of its implementation, the war against the Jews was different from any other war or atrocity against civilians. In its scale and long-term effects, it was probably Hitler's most successful campaign. By May 1945, Germany might not have been predominant in Europe and it might not have achieved the goal of living space in the east. Even so, Hitler took comfort in the fact that large areas of Europe were devoid of Jews.

Conclusion

The consequences of Total War for Europe are well known. The conflict left the continent physically and emotionally ravaged. Some countries lost almost an entire generation of young male citizens: in the USSR, Stalin decorated fertile and unmarried mothers as war heroes. It is estimated that the total death toll attributable to the war, across the globe, might be as high as 22,000,000 military personnel and 28,000,000 million civilians. Possibly 10,000,000 Soviet military lost their lives, alongside, 10,000,000 civilians. Germany suffered 4,500,000 military deaths and 2,500,000 civilian ones; Poland 123,000 military and 4,000,000 civilian; France 250,000 military and 350,000 French civilian; the UK 300,000 military and 50,000 civilian; and Italy 400,000 military and 100,000 civilian.[20] Even in countries that experienced only short periods of open war, such as Greece and Yugoslavia, the repression of partisan warfare and the persecution of ethnic minorities led to many deaths, about 500,000 in the former case and 1,500,000 in the latter.

Most European countries had been fought over or bombed, usually both. Eastern Europe and Germany were the worst hit. Agricultural production was decimated and industrial production was at a standstill. The situation was worsened by a vast movement of people: millions trod the roads of Europe or were placed in camps for displaced people, some for years after May 1945. There were also stranded armies and prisoners of war returning home, ethnic Germans fleeing from the Soviets, survivors of the concentration camps seeking a refuge elsewhere in Europe, or in the Americas or Palestine. In many countries, war had been followed by retribution and revolution, as popular perspectives and the geopolitical balance of power changed forever. The new Cold War spelt the end of many broad antifascist wartime alliances. In May 1947, in Italy and France, the coming of the Marshall Plan signalled the simultaneous expulsion of communist parties from governments of national unity. In the meantime, the USSR was well on course towards turning the nations of eastern Europe into one-party states. Those Poles who, on 3 September 1939, had laid flowers on the steps of the British and French embassies in Warsaw must have been wondering about the protection of their democracies. In Greece, the conflict was followed by a long civil war between communist and non-communist forces, during which the latter were supported by British who, with considerable American aid, made quite sure the country did not upset the postwar balance of power. Caught in the spiral of attack and retribution, Greek civilians once again paid the heaviest price.

The independence of eastern Europe was not the only thing sacrificed to the purposes of the wartime alliance. Throughout western Europe, former partisans had been hunting down Nazi and fascist elements, and collaborators in former occupied territories. In their thousands, these were summarily arraigned and executed, while many others were put on trial by the Allies. None the less, the need to ensure stable, competent and friendly ruling classes in former Axis countries under Western control meant that any systematic process of denazification was soon abandoned, as were any sustained efforts at mass re-education. Everywhere the temptation was to blame the conflict uniquely on the Germans. In France, Vichy apologists and de Gaulle's resistancialist orthodoxy quickly ignored the more sinister aspects of Pétain's regime. In Italy, popular culture aided the deliberate psychological removal of 20 years of fascism by consistently representing Italian fascists as foolish and cowardly servants of the Germans, who were invariably represented as beastly, sometimes as sexually deviant. So it was that many countries refused to confront head-on the true horrors of the war, especially the Holocaust. Out of this refusal also stemmed the belief that the Nazis were inhuman monsters. Of all the deliberate and unwitting inaccuracies that litter the popular and institutional memory of World War Two, this has been one of the most serious. By ascribing the conflict's many atrocities to 'monsters', we are in danger of overlooking what World War Two tells us about the limitations of humanity itself.

Further reading

The literature on World War Two is vast, and the student of this subject is more likely to suffer from excessive than insufficient choice. Among the many general histories of the war, it is worth mentioning Jeremy Black's *World War Two: A Military History* (London: Routledge, 2003); and the latest edition of Richard Overy's *Why the Allies Won* (London: Pimlico, 2006). Martin Gilbert's *Second World War* (London: Phoenix Press, 2000) is especially judicious. See too Peter Calvocoressi and Guy Wint, *Total War. Causes and Courses of the Second World War* (Harmondsworth: Allen Lane, 1972); Norman Davies, *Europe at War, 1939–1945. No Simple Victory* (London: Allen Lane, 2006); Gerhard Weinberg, *A World at Arms. A Global History of World War* (Cambridge: Cambridge University Press, 1994); Joanna Bourke, *The Second World War. A People's History* (Oxford: Oxford University Press, 2001); R. A. C. Parker's solid *Struggle for Survival. The History of the Second World War* (Oxford: Oxford University Press, 1989); and Roger Chickering, Stig Förster and Bernd Greiner (eds), *A World at Total War. Global Conflict and the Politics of Destruction, 1937–1945* (Cambridge: Cambridge University Press, 2005). On civilians, see Robert Gildea, Olivier Wieviorka and Anette Warring (eds), *Surviving Hitler and Mussolini. Daily Life in Occupied Europe* (Oxford: Berg, 2006); and Nicholas Atkin (ed.), *Daily Lives of Civilians in Wartime Twentieth-Century Europe* (Westport, CT: Greenwood, 2008). The issues of collaboration and resistance are tackled by Rab Bennett, *Under the Shadow of the Swastika: The Moral Dilemmas of Resistance and Collaboration in Hitler's Europe* (Basingstoke: Macmillan, 1999); Henri Michel, *Shadow War: Resistance in Europe* (London: Deutsch, 1972); and Werner Rings, *Life With the Enemy: Collaboration and Resistance in Hitler's Europe, 1939–1945* (London: Weidenfeld and Nicolson, 1982). Good reference works include I. C. B. Dear (ed.), *The Oxford Companion to World War Two* (Oxford: Oxford University Press, 2001 edn); and John Campbell (ed.), *The Experience of World War II* (London: Grange Books, 1989).

Notes

1 See for instance Nicholas Atkin (ed.), *Daily Lives of Civilians in Wartime Twentieth-Century Europe* (Westport, CT: Greenwood, 2008), especially chapters 1 and 5.

2 See Roger Chickering and Stig Förster, 'Are we there yet? World War Two and the Theory of Total War', in Roger Chickering, Stig Förster and Bernd Greiner (eds), *A World at Total War. Global Conflict and the Politics of Destruction, 1937–1945* (Cambridge: Cambridge University Press, 2005), pp. 1–18. See also Hugh Strachan, 'Total War in the Twentieth Century', in Arthur Marwick, Clive Emsley and W. Simpson (eds), *Total War and Historical Change. Europe 1914–1955* (Buckingham: Open University Press, 2001), pp. 255–83; his essay 'On Total War and Modern War', *International History Review* 22 (2): 341–70 (2000); and William J. Philpott, 'Total War', in Matthew Hughes and William Philpott (eds), *Modern Military History* (Basingstoke: Palgrave Macmillan, 2006).

3 Philip Bell, 'Europe in the Second World War', in Paul Hayes (ed.), *Themes in Modern European History, 1890–1945* (London: Routledge, 1992), pp. 249–73.

4 On the morality of strategic bombing see the criticisms levelled in Jorg Friedrich, *The Fire. The Bombing of Germany, 1940–1945* (New York: Columbia University Press, 2006) and A. C. Grayling, *Among the Dead Cities. Is the Targeting of Civilians in War ever Justified?* (London: Bloomsbury, 2007 edn). Also see Frederick Taylor, *Dresden, Tuesday 13 February 1945* (London: HarperCollins, 2004), as well as Paul Addison and Jeremy Crang (eds), *Firestorm. The Bombing of Dresden 1945* (London: Pimlico, 2006).

5 The most up-to-date account of the campaign in 1940 is to be found in Julian Jackson, *The Fall of France: The Nazi Invasion of 1940* (Oxford: Oxford University Press, 2003).

6 Julian Jackson, *France: The Dark Years 1940–1944* (Oxford: Oxford University Press, 2001).

7 Robert Paxton, *Vichy France: Old Guard and New Order, 1940–1944* (New York: Knopf, 1972).

8 See Corelli Barnett, *The Audit of War. The Illusion and Reality of Britain as a Great Nation* (London: Macmillan, 1986). See too Sonya Rose, *Which People's War? National Identity and Citizenship in Wartime Britain, 1939–1945* (Cambridge: Cambridge University Press, 2003); and Jose Harris, 'Britain and the Home Front during the Second World War', in Gordon Martel (ed.), *The World War Two Reader* (London: Routledge, 2004).

9 See especially Richard Overy, *Why the Allies Won* (London: Pimlico, 2006 2nd edn).

10 See Rodric Braithwaite, *Moscow 1941. A City and its People at War* (London: Profile Books, 2006).

11 Antony Beevor, *Stalingrad* (London: Penguin Books, 1999).

12 Martin Gilbert, *Second World War: A Complete History* (London: Phoenix Press, 2000), p. 425.

13 See, for example, Anthony Beevor, *The Fall of Berlin, 1945* (New York: Viking, 2002).

14 Claudio Pavone, *Una guerra civile. Saggio storico sulla moralità della Resistenza* (Turin: Bollati Borlinghieri, 1991).

15 See particularly Harry Roderick Kedward, *Resistance in Vichy France: A Study of Ideas and Motivation in the Southern Zone, 1940–1942* (Oxford: Oxford University Press, 1978). This proved to be a vital landmark within the whole field of research into this general topic.
16 See Henry Rousso, *The Vichy Syndrome: History and Memory in France since 1944* (Cambridge, MA: Harvard University Press, 1991).
17 M. Gilbert, *Second World War, op. cit.*, p. 746.
18 See Michael Marrus and Robert Paxton, *Vichy France and the Jews* (New York: Basic Books, 1981).
19 Davide Rodogno, *Fascism's European Empire: Italian Occupation during the Second World War* (Cambridge: Cambridge University Press, 2006).
20 Figures from I. C. B. Dear (ed.), *The Oxford Companion to World War Two* (Oxford: Oxford University Press, 2001 edn), pp. 224–27.

11 Europe and the wider world, 1890–1945

Michael Biddiss

Today we hear much talk of the 'globalization' of politics, economics, communications and culture. The developments encompassed by that term have certainly accelerated in the course of the past few decades, yet they also possess a much longer history, running back at least to the age of Columbus. By the time the nineteenth century drew to a close, their leading features were very strongly evident in the way that nearly every part of the world was being transformed by the overlapping processes of 'Europeanization' and 'Westernization'. However, there also existed a certain tension between these two phenomena, which was most strongly apparent in Europe's often ambiguous relations with the rising power of the USA.

The ascendancy of Europe

Between the 1880s and the outbreak of World War One in 1914, Europe appeared to be securing a control over global affairs on a scale hitherto unattained, either in its own history of colonizing activity or in that of any other continent. This ascendancy looked all the stronger as the massive changes experienced inside this region during the course of the nineteenth century had an ever greater impact on the rest of the world. By the years around 1900, the inhabitants of Europe – together with others of European stock who were now pursuing their fortunes in lands far beyond – enjoyed a superiority of wealth and force that encouraged many of them to view their civilization as the highest manifestation of the relentless march of 'progress'. Much of the globe had come under their direct rule, while very little of the remainder found itself exempt from the otherwise more informal exercise of their influence or interference. This process also served undoubtedly to increase Europe's own beneficial exposure to the wider world, in ways that enriched the range of available material products and that had a cultural impact on fields such as art, anthropology, the investigation of comparative religion, and the new academic study of the social sciences in general. However, the patterns of interaction between European and non-European societies remained essentially asymmetrical. In the broad domain of political and economic control, above all, the disparities of power were unquestionable.

The driving forces behind this enlargement of hegemony were complex, particularly where extensions of formal sovereignty were at issue. There has been much debate about the importance of economic factors such as the search for new markets, the development of improved opportunities for the investment of surplus capital, or the rising demand for raw materials. The explanations that Marxists and many others have based on those elements may sometimes seem plausible overall, yet they frequently look inadequate when specific areas of expansion are studied in detail. Desire for territorial annexation virtually as an end in itself was often equally or even more significant, and many relevant initiatives stemmed from soldiers and administrators on the spot, rather than from plans carefully laid in the chancelleries or entrepreneurial boardrooms of Europe. Nor can the wellsprings of imperialism be properly understood without reference to the realms of cultural and even spiritual development, where notions of 'civilizing mission' often held sway. In short, any sweeping generalization about the complex relationships between, for example, trade, flag and Bible is perilous.

It is indisputable, however, that this new wave of imperialism emerged from, and then itself intensified, a long-established sense of the pre-eminence of European civilization. By the end of the nineteenth century this was also being expressed, to a greater degree than ever before, in terms of an innate racial superiority. At best, this self-conferred status was interpreted as serving to increase the burden of moral responsibility that Europeans must carry in bringing their rule to bear upon less favoured peoples; at worst, it often acted as a justification for denying human dignity to those deemed inferior. In either case, the belief in racial destiny became associated not only with a supposed duty to enlarge the ambit of white rule, but also with assumptions about the permanence and immutability of Europe's global ascendancy.

Prominent among the sources of hegemony was the dynamism of demographic growth. Between 1800 and 1900, Europe's population, including that of the Russian empire, rose from some 190 million to around 420 million. This represented an advance from one-fifth to one-quarter of the worldwide total. Moreover, by 1914 there were also some 200 million people of European birth or (just as tellingly) of European descent now living outside a continent which, during the nineteenth century, had been a major source of far-flung emigration. Their growing numbers overseas were significant for the spreading of European ideas and culture, including the rival forms of Christianity preached through Catholic and Protestant missionary endeavour, and not least for shifts in the large-scale geography of language distribution (especially with regard to English and French, which increasingly contributed, alongside Spanish, to processes of linguistic globalization).

This growth and geographical spread of population also boosted demand for the products that Europe was now able to offer because of a vast enlargement of its manufacturing potential. From the early nineteenth century onward Britain, increasingly joined by other regions on the European mainland, had played a pioneering role in an economic transformation centred on the introduction of large-scale industrialization. There was also matching refinement in the techniques of capitalist funding, which enabled the City of London to consolidate its position as the world's principal centre for banking and finance. Through this increasingly globalized economic system Europe enjoyed, in return for its export of capital and of industrial manufactures, ready access to new sources of raw materials, and food from countries such as the USA, Argentina, Australia and New Zealand. During the course of the twentieth century, the habits and processes of industrialized production initiated by Europeans extended to many other areas of the globe in ways that broadened this whole fundamental revolution in patterns of life, labour, and material consumption. Even before 1900, one particularly notable feature of Europe's industrial achievement was the development of steam-shipping, which had now supplanted sail as the key to the trans-oceanic deployment of armed naval force and to the conduct of global maritime commerce. Similarly, Europeans secured an ever-growing pre-eminence in the sphere of mechanized weaponry. On land and at sea alike, this enabled them to use the threat (and not infrequently the reality) of an unprecedented firepower for the purposes of projecting their authority or influence far beyond Europe itself.

Some areas were already well established as territories intended for permanent settlement by European migrants and their descendants. There the incomers had largely succeeded in transplanting and sustaining much of what remained familiar to them by way of systems of law, property-holding, education and worship, doing so typically at the cost of marginalizing or even destroying indigenous cultures. Towards the close of the nineteenth century, the most important settler areas were to be found, first, in certain parts of the British Empire. These included chiefly South Africa, Australia and New Zealand, together with Canada. The latter is particularly notable for having won 'Dominion' status in 1867, and thus for being the first of this group to achieve the right of domestic self-governance that was eventually gained by the other three soon after the turn of the century. Moreover, due to its particular geographical position, the Canadian example serves to remind us of the fact that, second, nearly all the remaining regions of major European settlement that lay beyond British rule were also located on the vast continent of America. The various sovereign states developing across its southern regions had already proclaimed their liberation from Spain (or from Portugal, in the case of Brazilian independence) earlier in the century. However, the management of their political and economic affairs remained in the hands of those who were still strongly linked to the Iberian peninsula through ties of kinship, language and commerce. As for North America, there it was not Canada but the neighbouring USA that in the nineteenth century served as the main destination for a continuous emigration process unmatched in scale along any other route leading outward from Europe. As we shall see, not only the size but also the ethnic diversity of this trans-Atlantic resettlement would significantly influence the future pattern of relations between the Old World and the most dynamic society that was now emerging within the New.

Europe's ascendancy had also long been evident in the form of rule over colonial territories, where the objective of any major new settlement by whites remained largely absent from the agenda. By the mid-nineteenth century, much of the enlargement of British possessions, in particular, was principally attributable to a determination to secure the naval bases and the other aids to supply or communication upon which the maintenance of global maritime and commercial supremacy depended. In this context, the most striking case was that of the Indian subcontinent, where British residents never featured as more than a tiny minority alongside the teeming native population. There, over many years, the East India Company had increasingly become not simply an instrument of trade, but also one of rulership over peoples greatly diverse in language, culture, religion and social organization. This process reached the point where, following the Mutiny of 1857, there seemed little alternative other than to transfer the Company's responsibilities for government to the British crown. In 1876, Disraeli prompted Queen Victoria to assume the title of 'Empress of India'. Operating through a viceroy, and in many areas also through administration devolved to local princes, she was by 1890 sovereign over a subcontinental empire that now comprised more than 250 million subjects and extended east of the Bay of Bengal so as to embrace

Burma too. Viewed as a whole, these Indian territories, stretching from Karachi to Rangoon and from the Punjab to Madras, had become pivotal to the consolidation of an even broader network of British imperial holdings that included the precious tin and rubber resources of Malaya lying further south.

A new imperialism

During the final quarter of the nineteenth century it was, however, the 'scramble for Africa' that constituted the most striking manifestation of Europe's imperial ambitions. Except in some limited areas, this process was not driven by schemes involving substantial white resettlement. Although resembling the Indian case in that respect, the African developments were in other ways significantly different. Not least, European expansion here accelerated at an unprecedented rate and featured a wider range of states in active competition for new territory and other spoils of empire.

Until the late 1870s, Africa contained only two regions of significant European colonization. In 1830, the French had mounted an invasion of Algeria, which, although it soon destroyed formal Ottoman control, marked only a beginning to the protracted campaign that was needed before they could fully establish their own authority over the indigenous population. At the other end of the continent, control over the Cape and its hinterland had shifted during the course of the Napoleonic wars. Henceforth it was the British who held the upper hand over the earlier Dutch colonizers, to the point where in the mid-1830s many of the latter felt compelled to pursue resettlement by moving north-eastwards. The 'Great Trek' of these so-called Afrikaners enabled them to establish, by the early 1850s, their own 'Boer' republics in the form of the Orange Free State and Transvaal. Elsewhere, however, only the most intrepid of white explorers had managed to penetrate into the interior of 'the dark continent'. Although the ports and estuaries were often perilous locations, the vast and uncharted expanses of land beyond them clearly presented even greater dangers of tribal resistance and – especially in the tropical latitudes – of exposure to malaria and other deadly diseases. Eventually, the quinine that would save so many Europeans and the Maxim gun that would terrorize or kill so many Africans combined to transform the situation. Until the 1870s, however, the white man's impact remained largely confined to certain coastal areas. The British had gained control over Gambia, Sierra Leone, the Gold Coast and Lagos, while the French administered Senegal. Meanwhile, the Portuguese were still clinging rather insecurely to longer-established holdings along the Angolan and Mozambican seaboards in western and eastern Africa, respectively.

By 1914, the map looked utterly different. The African continent was now almost totally partitioned into a whole complex of colonial zones, apportioned very unequally between no fewer than seven European countries. During the 1870s, following its defeat by Prussia, France had sought to salve some of its wounded pride by enlarging its west African power base beyond Senegal. That effort led not only to confrontation with local indigenous rulers, but also to the risk of conflict with Britain's competing interests along the same coast. The latter rivalry worsened as the French, who had supervised the building of the Suez Canal (opened in 1869), found themselves losing control over the running of this strategically and economically vital waterway. Their plight became all the clearer in 1882, when the British, intent on protecting a key route to India, themselves occupied Egypt and thus supplanted an increasingly inefficient Turkish administration. By that stage, further along the Mediterranean seaboard, France had set about protecting its Algerian colony through military occupation of neighbouring Tunisia. Meanwhile, Belgium too was entering the African picture as an entirely new colonial aspirant. Its ruler, King Leopold II, pursued his ambitions by making skilful use of a remarkable, and indeed ruthless, British explorer. Between 1874 and 1877, Henry Morton Stanley (already famous for his 'discovery' of David Livingstone) had begun to open up the Congo basin, even while inflicting much brutality on its indigenous peoples. In 1879 he became Leopold's hired agent, and during the early 1880s pursued the project of establishing a central African empire under the king's control.

One effect of these developments was to encourage the summoning of an international conference for the discussion of imperial claims over Africa. This convened during the winter of 1884–85, in Berlin. The choice of venue acknowledged Bismarck's leading role in advocating the meeting. His desire for it reflected, in turn, the fact that the new German Reich, which had recently declared protectorates in south-west Africa (Namibia), Togoland and Cameroon, was yet another European power now in pursuit of territory overseas. Those who participated in the Berlin Conference committed themselves to working for the abolition of slavery and of the slave trade, and further agreed that effective occupation of a colonial region was an essential prerequisite for any recognition of its valid annexation. Their most immediately operative decision was to yield to Leopold's argument that, if they did indeed desire to designate the Congo as an area freely open to international trade, it would be best to invest him with the sovereign authority over this vast river basin rather than leave the region vulnerable to any conflicting claims generated as between the larger powers. In effect, this so-called Free State, which the Belgian king never visited, served for more than 20 years as his private fiefdom. There his royal agents, operating a reign of terror over the native population, crudely exploited the economic potential of a territory particularly rich in copper as well as in other mineral and agricultural resources. It was not until 1908, after the full horror of the labour conditions had become widely publicized, that the Brussels parliament intervened. At that point, its members stripped Leopold of his personal and autocratic role in the governance of the largest colony in equatorial Africa, and asserted instead their own more distinctively national authority over what was now renamed the Belgian Congo.

It became clear during the 1880s and 1890s that the African scramble was not the kind of competition in which hitherto the British had often preferred to engage – one where the exercise of informal influence might yield sufficient advantages without risking entanglement in the trammels of direct annexation. All around Africa, and even across its interior, European flags were being raised with far more concern for the assertion of formal sovereignty over annexed territories. Although such changing emphasis towards conquest did attract some criticism from within the colonizing nations, the new imperialism was strongly reinforced by growing mass support and especially by the 'jingoism' of the popular press. Generally contemptuous of indigenous sociopolitical structures such as those presented by the Zulu or Herrero peoples of southern Africa, the builders of empire increasingly advanced as if convinced that nature must surely abhor any vacuum not yet filled by white governance. Even areas that a European state might have been reluctant to grab in other circumstances (such as huge tracts of desert or swampland devoid of any real prospect of economic yield) became urgently desirable for loosely 'strategic' reasons when its colonial rivals began to cast acquisitive eyes in the same direction.

This was the heyday of Cecil Rhodes who, believing the British to be the finest race in the world, repeatedly proclaimed his determination to paint the map of Africa in the red of Victorian empire all the way from the Cape to Cairo. He and his compatriots came close indeed to achieving that goal, but were frustrated most crucially by further competition from the Second Reich, which consolidated a hold on German East Africa during the 1890s. Elsewhere along Rhodes's axis, however, the British held sway by the time of his death in 1902. Their hold on Kenya and Uganda had been secured with the help of the East Africa Company, while in 1890 Germany itself had yielded to Britain the offshore island of Zanzibar (peacefully exchanged for the far smaller one of Heligoland, lying much nearer home beyond the Wilhelmshaven coast). Further north on the African continent, victory against the followers of the Mahdi at the battle of Omdurman, and a peaceful resolution to the confrontation with French forces at Fashoda (both occurring in 1898), had opened the way for the establishment of an Anglo–Egyptian condominium over the Sudan. Meanwhile, in southern Africa, the British had enlarged their sphere of influence far beyond the Cape Colony. Control now stretched across Natal, and via Bechuanaland into what became the two Rhodesias and Nyasaland. By the end of the Boer War of 1899–1902, Britain had also formally annexed the Orange Free State and Transvaal. Thereby it sought to reverse its earlier misfortune in having pushed the Dutch–Afrikaner trekkers towards unanticipated treasures – into lands that had soon turned out to contain not simply the diamond riches of Kimberley, but also the vast gold-bearing reef known as the Witwatersrand. Not surprisingly, the resentment of the Boers against their fellow-European colonists would continue to ferment long after the British, in 1910, consolidated their position at this end of the continent by incorporating many of their holdings into a Union of South Africa. They accorded it 'Dominion' status, and therewith conferred upon it rights to internal self-governance. However, neither here nor elsewhere across the rest of white-controlled Africa was there, as yet, any real question of extending to the indigenous majority populations those modest concessions towards mass democratic participation that European colonial powers were now tending to yield to their own peoples back home.

During the first decade of the twentieth century the French, anxious not to be entirely outdone by the British, continued to push out from their bases in Algeria and Senegal. Thus they consolidated their leading position in the north-west of the continent, claiming sovereignty over most of the Saharan desert. However, France's further aim of establishing a protectorate over Morocco brought protests from Germany and provoked an international crisis in 1905–06. Although this was defused by a conference at Algeciras, the dispute re-erupted in 1911. The following year saw Berlin winning comparatively minor concessions elsewhere, in return for permitting France and Spain to partition the Moroccan spoils. This was also the stage at which Italy sought to reassert itself as a colonizing power. In the early 1890s, the recently unified kingdom had managed to establish a claim to part of Somaliland, the remainder being under British and French administration. However, the most ambitious aspect of Umberto I's quest to create an empire in north-east Africa had collapsed when the Italians, having colonized Eritrea in 1889, attempted to use it as the base for a deeper thrust into Ethiopia. When this was launched in 1896, it gave rise to the battle of Adowa, where the army of Emperor Menelik II succeeded in registering the first decisive victory for indigenous African forces confronting a major European advance. After such humiliation, it became all the more vital to the Italians that, once they turned their ambitions towards the north African seaboard, further failure should be avoided. In the event, the invasion of Tripolitania (Libya), conducted in 1911 with the aim of wresting control from the waning authority of Ottoman Turkey, proved successful enough to repair some of Italy's self-esteem. There it used the new invention of the aeroplane, soon deployed also by France in the Moroccan campaign of 1912, and so underlined yet again the role of superior technology in the advance of empire.

It remains to be observed that, even as this whole scramble for Africa progressed, European influence was also growing in Asia and in the Indian and Pacific oceanic regions. Britain's hold on the subcontinental Raj (as previously discussed), as well as on neighbouring Ceylon, helped it to protect long-distance maritime routes that were vital to Europe's global trading, such as those that ran via Suez and Aden to the Dutch East Indies (colonized from the seventeenth century onward) and to Australia, or via the Cape and Singapore to China. By the 1890s the Malay states, which were not only vital as sources of rubber, but also pivotal within the wider geography of seaborne commerce, had become federated under British rule. Meanwhile, France had created Indo-China out of another colonial union, embracing Cambodia, Annam and Laos. The final decade of the century also witnessed a race for the islands of the Pacific. Here, again, Britain and France played a notable role. Yet the competition also involved Germany (which asserted claims, for example, over the Marshall archipelago and parts of New Guinea), and, very sharply from 1898 onwards, the USA as well.

As for China, the most populous country in Asia, there the vast but failing Manchu empire of the Qing dynasty managed to avoid the worst of a European scramble for its territory. None the less, as the 'opium wars' of the 1840s and 1850s had shown, Western imperialism could still make its influence strongly felt without the need for extensive seizures of land. The central aim was, instead, to establish some satisfactory measure of secure control over the major trading ports. Towards the end of the nineteenth century, this was most fully pursued in the cases of Hong Kong and Macao, where Britain and Portugal, respectively, went so far as to consolidate formal rights of governance over limited but crucial areas. However, there were also increasing signs of Chinese resentment at foreign interference, which came together in the Boxer Rising of 1899–1900. This was directed against a whole range of European legations, and indeed against American and Japanese interests too. Although the intervention of a six-power expeditionary force eventually restored the *status quo*, the foreigners' decision to impose the humiliating Peking Protocol of 1901 served only to hasten the replacement of the Qing Emperor by a new republic with more vigorously nationalistic potentialities. This revolution of 1911 contributed towards the development of a process that, much later in the twentieth century, would convert China into a major source of challenge to Western ascendancy.

However, the global map, as it stood in 1914, still tended largely to conceal the future vulnerability of those whose dynamism had done so much to redraw it during the preceding quarter-century or so. If we leave out of account the polar regions (principally the huge but barely habitable continent of Antarctica, over parts of which the UK attempted in 1908 to make the first claims involving territorial possession), the chart now showed that some four-fifths of the world's land surface was covered by countries largely inhabited, or in some other way formally controlled, by peoples of European birth or European descent. Within that context, the British Empire alone accounted for no less than a quarter of the globe's territory and population alike. Moreover, even across the residual regions of the planet where such Western dominance did not directly prevail, there remained only a handful of states retaining some substantial measure of autonomy in the face of this alien ascendancy, whether the latter was being projected via land or sea, and whether through commerce or armed force. In Asia only Japan and Siam, and in Africa only Ethiopia and to a lesser extent Liberia, had survived as significant exceptions to the globalized hegemony of the West.

Challenges to ascendancy

With hindsight, we can readily appreciate that, while movements of direct anticolonial resistance were as yet limited in scope, there were other reasons why the permanence of Europe's ascendancy within this world system was in reality less secure than it seemed to be on the eve of World War One. First and foremost, there were the deep ambiguities embedded in transatlantic relations with the USA. Here was the sphere of interaction where 'Westernization' and 'Europeanization' might most readily part company. Viewed from one angle, the Western hegemony seemed centred on a substantial convergence between US and

British interests, and thus on a coupling of the two major countries within what was already often known as 'the English-speaking world' or 'the Anglo-Saxon world'. Yet the exclusivity implied by this particular linkage and labelling was also capable of generating resentments elsewhere across Europe, not least within France or Germany. Other difficulties were compounded by the fundamental fact that the USA owed its own origins to a revolution conducted against European – and, most specifically, British – colonial rule. Moreover, even while American society profited in population and talent from subsequent waves of migration from Europe, much of that flow towards the New World had been generated precisely by a desire to escape the poverty and inequality associated with the Old. Where positive ethnic ties did remain strong across this oceanic divide, by the early twentieth century they also related to a network far more complex than anything focused simply on 'Anglo-Saxon' ties – one that reflected, for example, the later currents of migration from Ireland, Germany, Scandinavia, Italy, Russia and Poland. The situation was further complicated by an increasing number of arrivals from Asia.

By the 1890s, the USA already contained a population of more than 80 million, and, as well as being rich in agricultural resources, it had overtaken the UK as the world's leading industrial producer. In essence, it was being tempted not only to play an ever-larger role on the global stage, but also to do so with policies naturally directed towards the service of its own interests rather than towards the maintenance of any form of European ascendancy. Furthermore, despite their aversion to the Old World's concepts of 'empire', nineteenth-century US administrations had not hesitated to practise their own brand of imperial domination and expansion, eventually couched in the language of 'manifest destiny'. Even after the Civil War had achieved the abolition of slavery, they had continued to deny to the African-Americans any substantial implementation of the principles of racial justice and equality. Meanwhile, the overland advance of the USA's domestic frontier had proceeded with much slaughter and expropriation of the indigenous 'Red Indian' tribes. After the earlier acquisitions of Louisiana and the Floridas, the Union's sovereignty had been extended further during the 1840s and 1850s to Oregon (where conflict with Britain over the northern boundary was averted through compromise), and to Texas and California (both fully secured only after war with Mexico). In 1867 the huge Alaskan wilderness, too, was purchased cheaply from Russia.

In the course of the nineteenth century, the USA had also increasingly projected a more informal version of hegemony across the southern half of the American continent. As early as 1823, the Monroe Doctrine had warned the European powers against any attempt at intervening there in the hope of reversing the region's liberation from Spanish or Portuguese colonial authority. Later in the century, successive administrations continued to insist that Central and South America must be regarded as falling primarily within the US sphere of influence and protection. The point was underlined when, in 1903, President Theodore Roosevelt won control of a Panama Canal project that had already bankrupted the French financiers initially involved in its sponsorship. Eventually completed in 1914, this 50-mile crossing of the isthmus between the Atlantic and the Pacific also helped the USA to consolidate, across the second of these oceans, the further projection of imperial authority recently achieved during the presidency of William McKinley. In April 1898, he had declared war on Spain, thus seeking to assist Cuban rebels now fighting against their colonial masters. By the end of that year, McKinley's naval and other forces had registered a victory that, in the Caribbean, yielded to the USA direct possession of Puerto Rico as well as a protectorate over Cuba. Even more striking, however, was the simultaneous demolition of Spain's remaining influence in the Pacific region. Here the Americans had exercised effective control over the Hawaiian islands since the 1840s, and from the 1850s onward they had played a crucial role in opening up Japan to Western trading and other influences while also enlarging their commercial interests in China. Now, as a result of the 1898 war against Spain, the USA assumed full sovereignty over the Philippines and Guam, each of which was located well towards the Asian side of the Pacific Ocean and thousands of miles distant from the California coast. These annexations clearly signalled an American primacy across this whole region, and reflected the rising status of a new competitor for the global ascendancy hitherto shared among the European colonial powers.

Russia formed a second source of potential challenge. Here too – as in the American case, although mainly for different reasons – there was much ambiguity surrounding the relationship with Europe. Since the eighteenth century, the Romanov empire had clearly developed into one of the continent's great powers. Even before the tally of Tsar Nicholas II's subjects passed the 150 million mark soon after 1900, it had long been by far the most populous of European states. Around the beginning of the twentieth century, Russia also featured some of Europe's most rapidly industrializing regions. Yet the country was continuing to suffer familiar internal tensions between those who accepted the need to modernize by adopting policies of Westernization, and those who preferred to rely on a more distinctively Russian (and often sharply anti-Western) path of political, social and cultural development. The situation was complicated further by the fact that, as the nineteenth century proceeded, the empire had been emerging not simply as a European force, but increasingly as a Eurasian one. Like the USA, Russia had engaged in major expansion overland. While in Europe the tsarist regime had been frustrated by the outcome of the Crimean War in 1856, and of the Berlin Congress in 1878, it had none the less managed to strengthen its position in Asia. By 1900, advances south-eastwards beyond the Caspian Sea had yielded gains that projected the Romanov sphere of control to the mountainous borders of Persia, Afghanistan, India and western China. East of the Urals, too, the colonizing effort of the Russians made a particularly notable contribution to that diffusion of European ethnicity which characterized so much of global history in the later nineteenth century. There, they not only consolidated their hold across the vast region of Siberia, but also extended their territories to the Amur river, to Vladivostok (founded in 1860), and to the island of Sakhalin. Construction of the Trans-Siberian railway began in 1891, and seven years later the Russians negotiated with China a lease on Port Arthur that gave them a permanently ice-free base for their Pacific fleet.

This was the stage, however, when Russia's ambitions in the Far East brought it into direct conflict with Japan. Here was another rising power that would soon be presenting across the Asian–Pacific hemisphere an even broader challenge to European or Western ascendancy. Crucial to this development was the so-called 'Meiji Restoration' of 1868. By reasserting the firm central authority of the imperial court, it enabled Japan to escape the forms of alien control exerted over India and China. In this exceptional instance, a virtually unavoidable exposure to Western influences from the 1850s onward did not bring about subordination, formal or otherwise. During the final three decades of the nineteenth century, Japanese leaders pursued a strategy that might be described, paradoxically, as preventive modernization. Although strongly inspired from abroad, this was devised essentially to promote their own national interests. It involved accepting change, but principally in order to serve deeper conservative purposes. The ensuing transformation was selective enough to preserve much of Japan's cultural distinctiveness while also being sufficiently far-ranging to generate the innovations needed for the protection of the country's political autonomy against undue foreign interference. A new generation was increasingly encouraged to travel and study overseas, with a view to bringing back from Europe and the USA ideas and techniques adaptable to the task of modernizing the nation's governmental, legal, bureaucratic, educational, banking, industrial and transport structures. There was also a programme of army reform, based largely on the Prusso–German experience, that ran in parallel with the creation of a navy whose construction and operation owed much to the British model.

Modern Japan's emergence as a significant military force towards the end of the nineteenth century was first evident in the victories registered against China in 1894–95. Pressure from the Western powers, which was widely resented, led to a reduction of the concessions initially promised by the defeated empire. Even so, the Japanese now gained the island of Formosa (Taiwan), and, on the Asian mainland, effective economic control over the Korean peninsula (which was eventually annexed in 1910). Around the turn of the century, the significance of Japan's transformation was already imposing enough to prompt Britain to depart from its general policy of avoiding, in peacetime, the making of formal military commitments to other countries. The Anglo–Japanese alliance of January 1902 bound each of the parties to remain at least neutral if the other found itself at war with a third power, while also promising active assistance in the event of either co-signatory finding itself in armed conflict with two or more powers.

Such growing globalization of international relations between major states became directly relevant when the interests of Japan and Russia directly collided over the future of Manchuria. The sudden attack launched on Port Arthur by the Japanese in February 1904 was followed by 18 months of warfare, during which the tsarist forces were increasingly discredited. After defeat on land at Mukden, and at sea in the Straits of Tsushima, Russia accepted peace terms that were brokered principally by President Theodore Roosevelt. The fact that the resulting treaty of September 1905 was signed at Portsmouth, New Hampshire, further reflected the USA's rising global stature. As for the settlement itself, this required the Russians to acknowledge Japan's supremacy in Korea and its control of the South Manchurian railway, and to cede to the victors the southern part of Sakhalin island as well as territory in the region of Port Arthur. For many Europeans, the earlier Italian humiliation at Adowa now paled in significance when compared with the shock delivered by this Japanese triumph, even if the victory of 1904–05 itself owed much to weaponry and techniques first developed in the West. The outcome of the conflict with Russia clearly fed the racist prejudices of those who, like Kaiser Wilhelm II, were already tending to view the Slav-dominated empire of the

Romanovs less as an effective bulwark against the rise of the 'yellow peril', than as a major conduit for that same threat. However, less impassioned observers, too, could hardly escape the need to consider the future implications of the plain fact that, on its Asiatic flank, even the largest of the European states had shown itself to be anything but invincible.

European civil war

The pace at which any or all of these potential challenges to global ascendancy might reach critical levels was also conditioned by one further factor, of a kind largely related to the internal dynamics of the European state-system. From time to time, as the Fashoda incident or the Moroccan crises suggested, imperialistic competition for colonies and influence overseas had put strain on relations between the major powers. Even so, for more than 40 years after the Franco–Prussian war of 1870–71, Europe's leading states had managed to avoid armed engagement against each other. Once such restraint had ended in 1914, the ensuing carnage increasingly called into question the permanence of their global ascendancy. While the principal causes of World War One (analysed in Chapter 4) lay within Europe itself, the conduct and, above all, the consequences of the conflict had a broader ambit. Viewed close up, the main European theatre of warfare appeared as a battle for power between a variety of distinct states. From a broader, indeed global, perspective, the same hostilities could also be viewed as constituting a civil war within one single continent. They were being conducted, moreover, with an internecine intensity that made a mockery of pretensions to 'civilising mission' and threatened to undermine the dominance that Europe had established over the wider world by the opening of the twentieth century.

The clearest confirmation of the new shifts now developing in the global balance of power came in April 1917. At that point the USA abandoned isolationism towards Europe and entered the fray in response to Gemany's resumption of submarine warfare – a mode of fighting that threatened not only American shipping but also trans-atlantic supplies of food and military material vital to Britain's survival. Thus, with US forces beginning to be deployed on the Western Front, the New World stepped in to hasten the end of the military stalemate that was decimating the Old. President Wilson authorized his country's involvement as an 'Associated Power' even while being aware that, at home, currents of opposition (flowing, for example, from the German or Irish ethnic 'lobbies') still ran strong. Notwithstanding the difficulties that his domestic critics would continue to make for him during the eventual peace settlement, that decision of 1917 clearly marked a watershed in the history of international relations between America and Europe.

Elsewhere in the English-speaking world, the Dominion governments of the British Empire had also linked themselves with the war effort, doing so from the very outset. The question of participation was substantially divisive only in the case of South Africa, where many Afrikaners were understandably resistant. Canada, Australia and New Zealand, on the other hand, rallied much more readily to the cause of Britain and its allies. Over the period 1914–18 they supplied, between them, more than a million troops, and suffered losses that were disproportionately heavy when gauged both against their size of population and against their own immediate interest in the principal issues at stake.

The campaigns of World War One, although less fully globalized than those that from 1941 onward would later characterize an even broader conflict, also extended beyond the European continent itself. If we leave aside for later consideration the issue of Japanese involvement on the Far Eastern flank, two other principal points remain. First, the Balkan unrest that provided the immediate trigger for hostilities in 1914 is comprehensible only within the broader setting of the long-term decline of the Ottoman regime, which chose to fight on Germany's side. Once war began, it was not merely Turkey's residual foothold on European territory that became imperilled, but also its surviving empire in Asia Minor and the Middle East. At various stages and in various combinations, Britain, France, Russia and Italy negotiated secret wartime agreements about how to distribute the spoils of eventual victory over the sultanate. By the end of the war, defeated Turkey was deeply vulnerable. The British and French, assisted by the Arab Revolt that had begun in June 1916, had destroyed Ottoman control over the Middle East, including Mesopotamia (Iraq); Russian forces had taken over part of Armenia; and even the Turkish heartland of Anatolia stood in danger of partition. Second, the extra-European dimension to the war also embraced Germany's newly formed colonial empire. There the territories were awkwardly dispersed and militarily undermanned. Those in the Pacific islands and New Guinea, together with Togoland, and in Asia the Qingdao holding on the Chinese mainland, had been lost even before the end of 1914. Once south-west Africa and Cameroon had similarly fallen in the course of 1915–16, the East African colony became the only remaining overseas possession of the Reich, whose surrender was delayed until November 1918. Beyond that point, the issue of future sovereignty over all these areas, like that of control over the Ottoman domain, became part of the agenda for the Peace Conference which began its work at Paris in January 1919.

A new world order?

The Paris proceedings (discussed more fully in Chapter 5) focused mainly on a European settlement. None the less, as the conference involved representatives drawn from most of the world's major states (Bolshevik Russia being the chief absentee), its outcome was bound to have substantial implications for Europe's future development as part of a broader global system. Particularly noteworthy is the fact that, although the dynastic empires of the Hohenzollerns, Habsburgs and Romanovs had crumbled by the end of the war, their collapse certainly did not mean that other manifestations of European imperial authority in the wider world would immediately suffer the same fate. Indeed, the Peace Conference allowed the British and the French to pursue yet another bid for additional colonial territory – even if, in due course, this would also turn out to have been nearly the last instance of such scrambling.

Despite the victors' frequent talk of national self-determination, this was not a concept urgently prioritized in those parts of the Paris settlement that dealt with areas outside Europe. Where the outcome of the war dictated a need for adjustments of imperial territory, these were generally made according to the progressive Wilsonian rhetoric of 'mandates'. The latter constituted forms of trusteeship operative under the auspices of the new League of Nations. In the case of 'A-mandates', the controlling powers were indeed expected to work on preparing a path for the eventual independence of the relevant territories. Allocation to category 'B' presupposed that the regions concerned would remain indefinitely under colonial rule, while those covered by 'C-mandates' were to be governed simply as an integral part of the administering state. Such was the broad framework within which the peacemakers attempted to resolve the principal extra-European territorial issues that confronted them, with respect to the fate of the former German colonies and of the previous Ottoman possessions.

The Versailles treaty that was imposed on Germany in June 1919 confirmed the complete loss of that country's overseas holdings. Through C-mandates, south-west Africa came under the aegis of South Africa, while Japan and Australia were the chief beneficiaries of the transfers authorized for the relevant Pacific islands and for part of New Guinea, respectively. Among the European victors, it was Britain and

France that carried off the rest of Germany's holdings. Within the 'B' category of colonies, Togoland and Cameroon each became the object of Anglo–French partition, while the whole of German East Africa (relabelled Tanganyika) now fell solely under British administration. As for the settlement with defeated Turkey, this was first attempted in the unratified Sèvres treaty of 1920. Terms were not properly finalized until 1923, when the less punitive Lausanne treaty was agreed with the new post-Ottoman republic headed by Kemal Atatürk. By then, the Turks had already frustrated the postwar attempts made by Greece to extend its authority and its 'Great Idea' into Asia Minor. It was, instead, Britain and France that seemed, on the face of things at least, to be the real beneficiaries from Ottoman collapse – especially in the Middle East. Here, where A-mandates were principally at issue, questions of control over the region's vast oil resources were beginning to move up the international political and economic agenda. The outcome differed from the treatment of the German colonial question in so far as the Middle Eastern arrangements did not involve a mere redistribution of territories that were already governed from Europe. Instead, there was an actual enlargement of the geographical scope of the authority being wielded by European powers.

The British now took control of Palestine, Transjordan and Iraq, while the French assumed responsibility for Syria and Lebanon. However, throughout the 1920s and 1930s, the resulting ascendancy would be constantly challenged by Arab nationalists who believed themselves to have been the victims of Anglo–French betrayal. By 1932, Britain had found it prudent to yield effective independence to Iraq, even while maintaining some military presence on its territory. Four years later a similar arrangement was settled with Egypt, which had been formally declared a protectorate in 1914, and where the security of the Suez Canal remained a vital strategic concern. Meanwhile, the British also faced particularly knotty problems in Palestine, the scene of increasingly acrimonious confrontation between the majority Arab community and new Jewish immigrants. The latter had been encouraged by the Balfour declaration of 1917 to anticipate the early creation of a Zionist homeland within this territory, and the increase in their numbers accelerated markedly once Hitler's antisemitic movement came to power in Germany.

As the 1920s and 1930s proceeded, it became clearer that, despite what the latest world map might indicate on the surface of things, the global influence of Britain and France was fraught with vulnerability. The former found itself having to cope, for example, with the nationalistic radicalization of Gandhi's Congress movement in India (much fuelled by the Amritsar massacre of 1919), even while the new Irish

Free State controlled by De Valera's Fianna Fáil was still challenging the remnants of British colonialism in Ulster. Meanwhile, France had to face in Indo-China the emergence of Vietnamese nationalist aspirations orchestrated by Ho Chi Minh, as well as rising tensions in North Africa between the generally intransigent *colons* and the indigenous peoples whom they dominated. Many of the difficulties troubling the Paris and London governments stemmed from the fact that, in addition to being increasingly burdened overseas (whether as colonial rulers or simply as foreign policemen), they were also still having to struggle with the challenge of securing lasting peace within Europe itself. The growth of fascism, first in Italy and then in Germany, presented the leading liberal democracies with new dilemmas. So, too, in the years after the Bolshevik Revolution of 1917, did the consolidation of communist power in Russia, as well as across the rest of the Eurasian empire formerly ruled by the Romanovs.

Even as the resulting ideological confrontations deepened, the weaknesses of the League of Nations as the supposed pivot of a new global order became ever more sharply exposed. Administered from Geneva, the organization came to look like a Eurocentric rather than fully international venture. Not least, it found itself operating without the benefit of US participation. Even while acting in Paris as the leading advocate for the League's creation, President Wilson had failed to win the support of Congress back home. Thus in March 1920 a majority of US senators, daunted by the prospect of further involvement in the bloodbaths of the Old World, and anxious to revive a predominantly isolationist policy towards European affairs, had voted against ratification of the Versailles treaty and thus also of American entry into the League itself. This new body therefore assumed a form that merely enlarged the burden which any defence of liberal democracy was liable to impose upon Britain and France instead.

The reassertion from Washington of a transatlantic isolationism was readily understandable. Yet it was also short-sighted. Under the circumstances prevailing in the post-1918 world, the isolationist option generated a severe mismatch between the USA's supposed political interests and a vitally important aspect of the country's economic concerns. In essence, and for better or worse, its people had now acquired a huge financial stake in the maintenance of the Old World's political stability – just as Europeans were also becoming deeply reliant on the continuance of American prosperity. Much of this hitherto unprecedented degree of transatlantic interdependence related to the loans that had flowed eastwards in order to sustain the Allied war effort between 1914 and 1918. It also derived from the fact that the

USA had then continued to make massive exports of capital to those European countries that were basing a large part of their postwar regeneration strategies on higher expenditures – that is, on early outlays due to be recouped as German reparations payments eventually replenished the coffers. Following the adjustments made by the Dawes Plan, such was the framework within which most of Europe (apart from the Soviet Union) generally prospered during the later 1920s, particularly in terms of improvements to its global trading position.

However, this system did not survive the unanticipated collapse that in October 1929 devastated the Wall Street stock market and triggered desperate bids to recall the huge loans invested in Europe. The repercussions of the 'Crash' underlined the point that New York was already supplanting London as the world's key financial centre. More generally, the ensuing Great Depression (analysed in Chapter 2) gave Europeans their first major experience of a globalization process that was now capable of operating to their disadvantage – one where, having long stamped their own influence on the world at large, they found themselves becoming instead the hapless, and even unintended, victims of external forces that seemed to lie largely beyond their control. As the volume of trade spiralled downwards, a massive rise in unemployment cut demand still further. So, too, did the response of most European governments, who were initially reluctant to abandon the economic orthodoxy of meeting crisis with retrenchment. By 1931–32, the slump was spreading and deepening across Europe to a degree that could only enhance the popularity of alternatives to liberal democracy. One of the chief beneficiaries was Hitler. The other was Stalin who, at the very epoch when capitalism seemed to be entering on a terminal crisis, headed a regime that remained largely insulated from the rest of the international economic system, and was now dynamically pursuing its own first Five-Year Plan according to the allegedly superior principles of communism. When faced with those growing threats during the 1930s, the European liberal democracies looked all the more vulnerable precisely because, back in the USA, the Depression had served essentially to reinforce the ascendancy of isolationist attitudes that continued to resist further embroilment in the political affairs of the Old World.

The global slump, although not instantly fatal to colonial power, undoubtedly complicated Europe's position in regard to dependencies where hitherto the experience of subjection to imperial authority had often been eased by the accompanying consolations of participation in economic growth. Henceforth any such convergence of interest could be all the more readily questioned, especially under circumstances where the profits available from exporting primary products to the metropolis were tumbling far more quickly than the prices still being demanded for the manufactured goods offered in return. The future for colonial deference looked increasingly bleak. In the case of the British Empire, where the 1931 Statute of Westminster had already been used to confirm the existing self-governing Dominions as 'autonomous communities' within a so-called Commonwealth of Nations, four years later the London government found itself having to concede a new Government of India Act that granted enlarged elements of self-rule within a far less stable context of nationalist and intercommunal discontents. By the time a new world war supervened in 1939, the French, too, were finding themselves increasingly confronted by pressures towards decolonization from Algerian, Tunisian and Vietnamese activists in particular. Viewed overall, the 1930s constituted a decade in which there was only one further instance of the direct expansion of European imperial authority. This was the act of fascist aggression that in October 1935 launched the last round of the scramble for Africa – a phase that effectively ended seven years later in the Egyptian desert around El Alamein. By then, Hitler as well as Mussolini would have become involved. For the moment, however, the initiative lay more specifically with the Duce, whose forces conducted a swift and brutal annexation of Ethiopia, which they completed in May 1936. It was a victory that provided Italy with its revenge for the national humiliation suffered at Adowa 40 years earlier.

From European to global war

Viewed in broad geopolitical perspective, World War Two contained two main strands. The first, whose origins are surveyed in Chapter 9, was the struggle that centred on Europe itself. There, after two decades of peace within the continent, general warfare resumed in September 1939. Towards the end of 1941, as noted in Chapter 10, this conflict became entwined with a second strand, relating principally to Asia and the Pacific. Even during the preceding phase, however, the hostilities being pursued between the European powers had already developed certain features with direct bearing on the links between their continent and the wider world.

In the case of France, the outbreak of war had led to a summoning of colonial troops to Europe. Some 80,000 were already serving there by June 1940, when the military and political system collapsed in the face of Nazi *Blitzkrieg*, and the Vichy administration took over. Led by Pétain, this collaborationist regime aimed to keep the overseas empire intact and to resist any colonial pact either with Britain or with the

Free French movement inspired by De Gaulle. Although the colonies in French Equatorial Africa swiftly backed the Gaullist line, most of the others gradually acquiesced in accepting Vichy's authority – at least, until the fortunes of war began to work against Hitler. One immediate response from Britain to the defeat of France came on 3 July 1940, at the Algerian port of Mers-el-Kébir, where the Royal Navy partially destroyed a French fleet that had followed orders not to yield itself to control from London. Similarly, a year later, British forces (assisted by a small Free French contingent) pre-empted a possible Axis advance by swiftly removing Syria and Lebanon from Pétain's sphere of governance.

Remaining undefeated at least within its own island territory, the UK had opted for continuing to defy Germany, even after the military rout that culminated in the evacuation from Dunkirk. When fighting on under the new leadership of Churchill, the British were not so entirely 'alone' as legend often has it. Most significantly, the survival of the imperial metropolis gave their Dominions, in particular, both the incentive and the time to muster a level of support that proved invaluable. From June 1940, when Mussolini decided to enter the war, British and Commonwealth forces were engaged in combating the Duce's efforts to expand his North African empire from Libya eastwards into Egypt. Although the initial Italian advance was soon repulsed, the arrival of Axis reinforcements early in 1941 in the form of Rommel's Afrika Korps enabled the fascist dictators to hold the upper hand during the next 18 months or so of a desert war. The threat to Alexandria, and to the Suez Canal beyond, remained very real until November 1942, when Allied victory in the third battle of El Alamein at last turned the tide and proved decisive to the eventual outcome of the North African campaign.

The opening phase of the war also saw the UK deeply engaged in another large but less well defined region of conflict, which stretched far beyond the shores of Europe itself. As in World War One, the question of long-term survival was inseparable from the issue of control over sea-lanes. Most vital here was the battle of the Atlantic, fought throughout the whole period from 1939–45. It involved air power as well as naval force on both sides, and became characterized especially by a scale of submarine warfare that far exceeded the deployments pioneered during the years 1914–18. One element in the UK's response to German aggression was to take, in May 1940, pre-emptive action to enforce upon Iceland the establishment of military bases that greatly enlarged the range over which British warships and warplanes could patrol in protection of essential maritime convoys.

Even more generally, the importance of transatlantic supply also accentuated the urgent need to secure a reversal of the USA's isolationist stance towards European affairs. It was fortunate that President F. D. Roosevelt was himself increasingly prepared to work, albeit cautiously, at the task of reshaping majority congressional opinion towards more active support for the antifascist cause. At the end of 1940, he used a radio broadcast to express to the American public his view that the USA now constituted the 'arsenal of democracy'. The passing of the Lend–Lease Act in March 1941 opened the way for the shipment of massive quantities of food and war supplies to Britain, and later to the USSR as well. Moreover, in July of the same year the Americans began to share with British and Canadian forces the task of protecting the vital Icelandic bases, and in August Roosevelt and Churchill promulgated their Atlantic Charter concerning protection of the freedoms imperilled by the Axis.

Although even then the USA was not a declared belligerent, June 1941 had marked the stage at which the scope of the European conflict became hugely enlarged by Hitler's attack on communist Russia. Only towards the end of the year was the full linkage between total and global warfare finally forged. While the air strikes that devastated the US Pacific fleet at Pearl Harbor in Hawaii on 7 December rendered inevitable an American mobilization against Japan, it was Hitler's decision to confront Washington with a German declaration of war four days later that saved Roosevelt from having to face any further debate as to whether direct engagement in the European sphere should still be avoided. Two further points assist an understanding of why these main strands of World War Two had now become entangled in this way. First, the rise of Japanese power, already noted during the period up to the victories registered against Russian forces in 1904–05, had been strongly sustained over the following 35 years; and second, it had increasingly challenged not simply the US variant of imperialism, but also the desire of certain European states to perpetuate their own hold over parts of the Asian and Pacific regions.

Japan had entered World War One in 1914, on the side pitted against the Austro–German alliance. While the major European states were preoccupied with fighting each other, the nation had taken the opportunity both to strengthen its competitive position in relation to their Asian markets and to expand its sphere of territorial control. During the course of this same war, the Allies had acquiesced in the demands that the Japanese government was making on the new Chinese republic for the relinquishment of southern Manchuria and Shantung. Elsewhere along the coast of mainland Asia, the colony of Qingdao had been seized from the Germans in 1914. At the peace settlement, the holdings of the former Wilhelmine empire among the north Pacific islands were similarly confirmed as now belonging to Japan. The 1920s proved to be a turbulent period in the country's domestic politics, and ended with the economy suffering badly from the first stages of the worldwide Depression. Increasingly anxious to ensure self-sufficiency, militaristic nationalist groupings began to outflank the official government in Tokyo. During the autumn of 1931, in an action sometimes viewed as opening the prelude to World War Two proper, Japan launched a rapidly successful assault on the rest of the vast Manchurian province. By the end of 1936, Tokyo's increasingly militarized regime had concluded with Germany an Anti-Comintern Pact (soon involving Italy too), which was clearly intended not simply to deter any challenge from the Eurasian USSR, but to serve as a warning to the liberal democracies as well. With its security enhanced to that degree, Japan then proceeded in mid-1937 to build on its Manchurian gains by mounting a full-scale invasion of the northern and central regions of China – a country progressively weakened by internecine rivalry between nationalist and communist movements, each of which had been grafting different elements of European political thinking into its own distinctive programme.

These developments in the eastern hemisphere plainly threatened the interests both of the USA and of Britain, France and the Netherlands as the most relevant European colonial powers. With Japan continuing to make gains at the expense of the Chinese, Roosevelt sought in July 1939 to limit the damage by threatening Tokyo with the imposition of trade sanctions six months hence. The defiant response was to try to improve the Japanese empire's economic self-sufficiency by projecting its power still more forcefully southwards. When France fell, the opportunity was taken to set up air bases in northern Indo-China; and soon the Dutch East Indies were yielding to the pressure that would make Japan the principal destination for their oil exports. Towards the end of 1941, the Tokyo government reached the conclusion that, particularly under circumstances where the USSR now needed to concentrate on stemming the advance of the Wehrmacht in Europe rather than on entering any Asian war, the national interest could best be served by registering a decisive pre-emptive blow against the USA.

Once this had been struck at Pearl Harbor, Japanese forces made (beneath the slogan 'Asia for the Asians') rapid advances in three broad directions. First, on the Asian mainland, they not only continued their war against China but also moved south-westwards in a drive that carried them beyond French Indo-China into Thailand (formerly Siam), whose anti-Western ruler cooperated in their occupation, and thence into British Burma. After the fall of Rangoon in March 1942 and of Mandalay two months later, the empire of Hirohito stretched even to the frontiers with India. Second, still broader southern advances produced capture of the Philippines, and a campaign through Malaya that culminated in February 1942 with the surrender of the British, Indian and Commonwealth troops guarding Singapore. This left the way open for further seizures across the whole arc of the Dutch East Indies, and for gains extending even to the Australian territories of Papua and New Guinea. Third, by driving eastwards and south-eastwards from its own offshore heartland, Japan had also swiftly asserted its dominance over the seas and islands that comprised nearly half of the vast Pacific Ocean. This whole explosive expansion, the speed and scale of which had been quite unanticipated by those now struggling to contain it, only began to falter in May–June 1942, when US forces severely damaged Japanese naval power at the battles of the Coral Sea and Midway.

From that stage onwards, the ability of the USA to deploy its massive military and economic resources in both of the principal theatres of global warfare made an increasingly vital contribution to the Grand Alliance, now centred on the figures of Roosevelt, Stalin and Churchill. Anglo–American cooperation made possible the landings of November 1942 that destroyed Vichy's control in Morocco and Algeria and thus hastened the capitulation of Axis forces in Libya six months later. North Africa was now free for Allied use as the base from which to launch the first invasions aimed at the eventual liberation of western Europe. These were directed towards Sicily in July 1943, and then towards mainland Italy in September. The Normandy landings of June 1944 resulted from an even larger scale of collaboration between US, British and Canadian forces, with smaller contingents of exiled Europeans also participating, especially in the naval support. Meanwhile, there had been a growing American contribution to the strategic bombing campaign waged from the skies above Germany. Not least, the revival of Soviet fortunes on the vast killing fields of the Eastern Front owed much to the Lend–Lease programme that increasingly underpinned Stalin's war effort, with resources coming overland via Persia and, after trans-shipment into convoys of British merchant vessels, via the Arctic sea route into Murmansk.

At the Yalta and Potsdam conferences of 1945, the UK continued to rank, formally, as one of 'the Big Three'. In reality, however, the victory that the Grand Alliance finally registered over Nazism in May of that year left most of the continent Hitler had sought to master divided simply into two new spheres of control. One was dominated by the USSR, the other by the USA. Each of what now became the 'super-powers' had long experienced, as previously noted, its own distinctive form of ambiguous relationship with Europe. While they would continue to pursue their separate versions of imperialistic assertion, neither had much sympathy for the brand hitherto practised by Britain, France, or any other colonial power in the classic tradition. Europe itself would certainly continue to be a major focal point for Cold War confrontation between the leading communist regime and its chief capitalist rival. Even so, particularly under the conditions of financial and infra-structural prostration that marked the start of the postwar epoch, no European state – nor any combination of European countries – was any longer capable of successfully asserting on its own account a position of global parity, let alone of ascendancy. The two atomic bombs that allowed the USA to speed the final collapse of Japan in August 1945, followed four years later by Stalin's acquisition of similar nuclear weaponry and by the emergence of a communist regime in China under Mao Zedong, confirmed that world history was entering a new era.

The aftermath

Although any proper consideration of Europe's postwar global position lies beyond the scope of the present book, it is essential to highlight two interrelated repercussions from the conflict of 1939–45, in so far as these would proceed to affect the increasingly prominent issue of decolonization. First, although most imperial authority was promptly reasserted at the end of the war, the course of the fighting destroyed much of the image of invincibility upon which the creation and survi-val of empire had been deeply reliant. The French, Dutch and Belgian versions of colonialism never regained the degree of authority they had enjoyed prior to the rapid defeats inflicted at home in 1940. Moreover, while the offshore islanders of the UK had fared better in their defi-ance of German power, much of the British holding in Asia and the Pacific had fallen with similar swiftness to the early advances of the Japanese. As for the Italian fascist brand of restored Roman empire overseas, it was already clear by 1943 that this had no future at all. Second, such demonstrable vulnerability accelerated a shift in the nature of anti-colonial movements. These had typically originated among educated elites, who often adapted to their own purposes many of the nationalist ideas originally generated within Europe itself. Now such organizations would attract an ever broader mass following that would prove all the more difficult for alien officials to control.

Early landmarks in the decolonization process included the British withdrawal from India (partitioned with a new Pakistan), Burma, Ceylon and Palestine during 1947–48; across the East Indies, the eventual Dutch acceptance of an independent Indonesia in 1949; and the defeat inflicted by the Vietnamese liberation movement on French forces at Dien Bien Phu in 1954. Two years after that, the ineptitude of the Anglo–French handling of the Suez Canal crisis further confirmed the waning international position of Europe's two leading colonial powers. Over the next two or three decades, the processes of decolonization, often operating at a pace which produced confused transitions of authority, affected all the European states that still laid claim to territory in Africa and Asia alike. By the time the Cold War ended around 1990, only a few remnants of colonial rule survived, such as those Britain and Portugal were preparing shortly to abandon in Hong Kong and Macao, respectively.

To the extent that, across much of the world, 'Western' values appeared to have prevailed over the Soviet alternative, they now sprang more from economic and cultural 'Americanization' (often overconfident in its triumphalism) than from the older forms of 'Europeanization'. At the turn of the millennium, it was none the less arguable that the countries of Europe still retained some capability of playing an actively influential role across the wider international stage, especially as in recent times so many of them – latterly from the eastern as well as the western regions – had accepted the need for greater pooling of their own political and economic strengths. Yet even those who favoured this interpretation generally recognized that, under changing conditions of intensified globalization (in such matters as terrorism, migration, corporate business operations, international competition for scarce energy resources, and major climatic shifts across the whole planet), Europeans were now increasingly vulnerable to the impact of external forces upon their national and continental destinies. In essence, both the scale and the nature of any influence that their own societies might continue to exert on the wider world were now radically different from what they had once been, particularly at the height of Europe's global dominance during the quarter-century preceding 1914.

Further reading

A highly readable and judicious general survey of global development is J. M. Roberts, *The Penguin History of the World* (3rd edn, London: Penguin, 1995). The same author also pursues relevant themes in *The Triumph of the West* (London: BBC, 1985). More controversial but unfailingly stimulating are two volumes by E. J. Hobsbawm. *The Age of Empire, 1875–1914* (London: Weidenfeld, 1987); and *Age of Extremes: The Short Twentieth Century, 1914–1991* (London: Joseph, 1994). Gloomy in emphasis but brilliant in its analysis of the 'longer' twentieth century is N. Ferguson, *The War of the World: History's Age of Hatred* (London: Penguin, 2007). Other useful surveys include M. Howard and W. M. Louis (eds), *The Oxford History of the Twentieth Century* (Oxford: Oxford University Press, 1998); W. Keylor, *The Twentieth-Century World: An International History* (Oxford: Oxford University Press, 2000, revised edn); and S. Marks, *The Ebbing of European Ascendancy: An International History of the World, 1914–1945* (London: Arnold, 2002). Ingeniously helpful mapping is available in *The Times Atlas of World History* (London: Times Books, 1993, 4th edn).

Important items within the vast historical literature on 'empire' include D. K. Fieldhouse, *The Colonial Empires: A Comparative Survey from the Eighteenth Century* (New York: Delacorte, 1967); V. G. Kiernan, *European Empires from Conquest to Collapse, 1815–1960* (London: Fontana, 1982) and the same author's *Lords of Human Kind: European Attitudes to the Outside World in the Imperial Age* (London: Weidenfeld, 1969); and W. Mommsen, *Theories of Imperialism* (Chicago: University of Chicago Press, 1982). E. W. Said's widely criticised *Orientalism* (London: Routledge, 1978) remains a particularly thought-provoking contribution. B. Porter, *The Lion's Share: A Short History of British Imperialism, 1850–1983* (London: Longman, 1984) also offers lively subversion of received wisdom concerning the most extensive venture into formal and informal empire witnessed during our period.

The course of transatlantic relations is analysed in: M. Silberschmidt, *The United States and Europe: Rivals and Partners* (London: Thames & Hudson, 1972); and W. LaFeber, *The American Age: US Foreign Policy at Home and Abroad, 1750 to the Present* (New York: Norton, 1994, 2nd edn). Broad surveys of other areas and countries include: D. Lieven, *Empire: The Russian Empire and its Rivals* (London: Murray, 2000); R. Storry, *Japan and the Decline of the West in Asia, 1894–1943* (London: Palgrave, 1979); W. G. Beasley, *Japanese Imperialism, 1894–1945* (Oxford: Oxford University Press, 1987); J. D. Spence, *The Search for Modern China* (London: Hutchinson, 1990); and J. Iliffe, *Africans: The History of a Continent* (Cambridge: Cambridge University Press, 1995).

M. MacMillan, *Peacemakers: The Paris Conference of 1919 and its Attempt to End War* (London: Murray, 2001) does justice to both the European and extra-European aspects of the attempt to establish a new world order; while D. Fromkin, *A Peace to End All Peace: The Fall of the Ottoman Empire and the Creation of the Modern Middle East* (New York: Holt, 1989) focuses more tightly on a crucial regional aspect. D. H. Aldcroft, *From Versailles to Wall Street, 1919–1929* (Harmondsworth: Penguin, 1987) and C. P. Kindleberger, *The World In Depression, 1929–1939* (Berkeley: University of California Press, 1986, revised edn) provide reliable analyses of the international economic scene during two crucial decades. Regarding the road towards renewed global warfare that was travelled in the 1930s, A. Iriye, *The Origins of the Second World War in Asia and the Pacific* (London: Longman, 1987) supplies a valuable complement to the generally more familiar literature on the European side of things. P. Calvocoressi, G. Wint and J. Pritchard, *Total War: The Causes and Courses of the Second World War* (London: Penguin, 1995, 2nd edn) offers comprehensive coverage of the conflict in both the western and the eastern hemispheres. The most perceptive analysis of linkages between its various geographical strands is, however, G. Weinberg, *A World at Arms: A Global History of World War II* (Cambridge: Cambridge University Press, 1994). For the years after 1945, M. E. Chamberlain, *Decolonization: The Fall of European Empires* (Oxford: Blackwell, 1999, 2nd edn) presents a particularly lucid introduction to the study of authority in decline.

Timeline

1890	March	Bismarck's dismissal and replacement by Caprivi as German Chancellor
1892	August	Military Convention between Russia and France
1894		Dreyfus Affair begins in France (and lasts until 1906)
	January	Franco–Russian Alliance
	August	Nicholas II succeeds the assassinated Alexander III as Tsar of Russia
	October	Hohenlohe replaces Caprivi as German Chancellor
1896	March	Italian forces defeated by Ethiopians in Battle of Adowa
1897	June	Tirpitz becomes German Secretary for the Navy
1898	April–August	Spanish–American War
	July	Fashoda Crisis
1899	October	Start of Boer War
1900		Boxer Rebellion in China against Western influence
	October	
		Bülow becomes German Chancellor
1901	January	Commonwealth of Australia accorded status of a British Dominion
1902	January	Anglo–Japanese Alliance
	May	End of Boer War
1903	August	Russian Social Democratic Workers' Party splits into Bolsheviks and Mensheviks
1904	February	Start of Russo–Japanese War
	April	Anglo–French Entente
1905	January	Revolution breaks out in Russsia
	March	Start of First Moroccan (Tangier) Crisis
	September	End of Russo–Japanese War
	October	Norway becomes independent of Sweden
		Russian constitution granted through October Manifesto
1906	January	Algeciras Conference over Morocco

1907	August	Anglo–Russian agreement enabling formation of Triple Entente, including France
	September	New Zealand accorded status of a British Dominion
1908	July	Young Turk rebellion leads to overthrow of Abdul Hamid II
	November	Belgian state annexes the Congo Free State, ending the personal control of King Leopold II
	October	Bulgaria declares its complete independence of the Ottoman Empire
		Austria-Hungary fully appropriates Bosnia-Herzegovina
1909	July	Bethmann Hollweg becomes German Chancellor
1910	May	Union of South Africa created and accorded the status of a British Dominion
1911	July–November	Second Moroccan (Agadir) Crisis
	September	Italy declares war on Turkey over Tripolitania (Libya)
1912	October	First Balkan War begins (ends May 1913)
1913	June–July	Second Balkan War
1914	June	Franz Ferdinand assassinated in Sarajevo
	July–August	Start of World War One
	August	Battle of Tannenberg
	September	Germans pushed back in First Battle of the Marne
		Battle of the Masurian Lakes
	September–October	'Race to the sea'
	November	Turkey enters war
		First Battle of Ypres
1915	January	Germans first use gas shells
	April	Allied landings at Gallipoli
	May	Sinking of the *Lusitania*
		Italy declares war on Austria-Hungary
	August	Italy declares war on Germany
	October	Bulgaria joins the Central Powers
1916	January	Allies evacuate Gallipoli
	February–December	Battle of Verdun
	April	Easter Rising in Dublin
	June–October	Brusilov Offensive
	July–November	Battle of the Somme
	August	Romania enters the war on the Allied side
	November	Francis Joseph I of Austria dies (succeeded by Charles I)
1917	February	Germany starts campaign of unrestricted submarine warfare
		Revolution in Russia
	March	Tsar Nicholas II abdicates (replaced by Provisional Government)
	April	USA enters the war
		Chemin des Dames offensive

	June	Start of Kerensky offensive
	July–November	Third Battle of Ypres (Passchendaele)
	October	Bolshevik Revolution
	October–November	Battle of Caporetto
	December	Bolsheviks sign Armistice
1918	January	President Wilson publishes the Fourteen Points
	February	Women over the age of 30 granted vote in the UK
	March	Brest–Litovsk Treaty between Germany and Russia
	March–July	German offensive in the west
	May	Start of Allied intervention in Russia
	June	Bolsheviks introduce War Communism
	July	Beginning of Allied counter-offensive
	November	Armistice between the Allies and Germany, and abdication of Kaiser William II
	December	Cheka established
		Khaki elections held in the UK
1919		Spanish flu epidemic
	January	Opening of Paris Peace Conference
		Spartacist Rising in Berlin
	March	Comintern meets in Moscow
	June	League of Nations comes into being
		Treaty of Versailles with Germany
	July	Constitution of Weimar Republic formally adopted
	September	Treaty of St-Germain confirms dissolution of Austro-Hungarian Empire
	November	Treaty of Neuilly with Bulgaria
1920	March	US Senate votes against ratification of Versailles Treaty and participation in the League of Nations
	June	Treaty of Trianon with Hungary
	October	Treaty of Sèvres with Turkey (left unratified, eventually superseded by Treaty of Lausanne with post-Ottoman regime in 1923)
1921	February	Suppression of the Kronstadt uprising
	March	War Communism replaced by the New Economic Policy
1922	April	Germany and Russia sign Rapallo Pact
	May	Creation of Irish Free State
	October	Mussolini takes power in Italy
	November	Turkish Republic formally proclaimed
	December	Creation of the USSR
1923	January	France and Belgium start occupation of the Ruhr
	August	*Putsch* of Miguel Primo de Rivera in Spain
	November	Hitler's failed Munich Beer Hall *Putsch*
1924	January	Death of Lenin (with Stalin eventually emerging as successor)
	August	Dawes Plan on reparations

1925	April	Hindenberg becomes President of Germany
	December	Locarno Treaties signed
1926	May	General strike in UK
1928		First Five-Year Plan and collectivization introduced in USSR
	August	Kellogg–Briand Pact on renunciation of war
1929	January	Banishment of Trotsky from USSR
	August	Young Plan on reparations agreed
	October	Wall Street Crash, soon followed by onset of Great Depression
1930	September	Nazis obtain 107 seats in the Reichstag
1931	April	Alfonso XIII exiled from Spain; Second Republic formally proclaimed (December)
	August	First National Government in the UK
	December	Statute of Westminster extends extensive freedoms to British Dominions
1932	June–July	Lausanne Conference suspending reparations
	July	Nazis obtain 230 seats in the Reichstag
		Salazar becomes Prime Minister of Portugal
1933	January	Hitler becomes Chancellor of Germany
	October	Founding of the Falange by José Antonio Primo de Rivera
1934	February	Right-wing demonstrations in Paris
	July	Assassination of Chancellor Dollfuss by Austrian Nazis
	August	Death of Hindenburg; Hitler becomes German Head of State
1935	March	Germany repudiates military clauses of Versailles Treaty
	April	Britain, France and Italy agree to the Stresa Front
	May	Franco–Soviet Mutual Assistance Pact
	June	Anglo–German Naval Agreement
	October	Italy invades Abyssinia
	December	Hoare–Laval Pact
1936	February	Election of the Popular Front in Spain
	March	German remilitarization of the Rhineland
	June	Election of Popular Front in France
	July	Start of the Civil War in mainland Spain
	October	Beginnings of the Great Purges in the USSR
1937	April	Bombing of Guernica
	November	Hitler's 'Hossbach' Conference
1938	March	*Anschluss* between Germany and Austria
	September	Munich Agreement
	October	Germany enters Czech Sudetenland
	November	*Kristallnacht*

1939	March	German dismemberment of Czechoslovakia
	April	Franco declares Nationalist victory in Spanish Civil War
		Germany, Italy, Spain and Japan sign anti-Comintern pact
	August	Signing of Nazi–Soviet Pact
	September	Germany invades Poland, and World War Two begins
		Britain and France declare war on Germany
		USSR invades Poland
	November	Start of the 'Winter War' between Finland and the USSR
1940	March	End of Winter War
	April	German invasion of Norway and Denmark
	May	German offensive in Belgium, Holland and Luxembourg
		Churchill replaces Chamberlain as British Prime Minister
		Surrender of Holland and Belgium
	June	Italy enters the war against France and Britain
		USSR occupies Lithuania, Latvia and Estonia
		Evacuation of Dunkirk by British forces
		Signing of Franco–German armistice
	July	Pétain becomes head of the Vichy regime
		Baltic states appropriated by the USSR
	August	Battle of Britain begins
	September	Start of the Blitz
		Germany, Italy and Japan sign Tripartite Pact
	November	Hungary, Romania and Slovakia join Tripartite Pact
1941	March	Bulgaria joins Axis
		President F. D. Roosevelt approves Lend–Lease
	April	Axis forces invade Greece and Yugoslavia
	June	Germany invades Soviet Union (Operation Barbarossa)
		Finland declares war on Soviet Union
	August	Atlantic Charter
	December	USA enters war following Japanese attack on Pearl Harbor
		Hitler declares war on USA
1942	January	Twenty-six nations sign UN Declaration
		Conference at Wannsee on the 'Final Solution'
	November	Battle of El Alamein
		Germany occupies all of France
1943	January	Casablanca Conference
	February	German armies surrender at Stalingrad
		Red Army victory at Kursk

	April	Uprising in the Warsaw ghetto
	June	Comintern disassembled
	July	Allies invade Sicily
		Enforced resignation of Mussolini
	August	Capitulation of Italy
	September	Allies land in mainland Italy
	October	Italy declares war on Germany
	November	Teheran Conference
1944	January	Anzio landings
		End of the 900-day siege of Leningrad
	March	Germany occupies Hungary
		Allied forces enter Rome
	June	D-Day landings
	July	Failed Stauffenberg plot to assassinate Hitler
	August	Warsaw Rising of the Polish Home Army
		Liberation of Paris
		Landing of Allied troops in southern France
		Dumbarton Oaks Conference on formation of the UN
	September	Surrender of Finland
	October	Moscow Conference of Allied Foreign Ministers
		Women granted the vote in France
1945	January	Soviet forces take Warsaw
		Hungary signs Armistice
		Liberation of Auschwitz
	February	Yalta Conference
		Bombing of Dresden
	March	Tito forms new government in Yugoslavia
		US forces cross the Rhine
		Soviet forces enter Austria
	April	Occupation of Vienna and Berlin
		Deaths of Mussolini and Hitler, and of Roosevelt (succeeded by Truman)
	May	'Victory in Europe' proclaimed
	July–August	Potsdam conference
		Attlee replaces Churchill as British Prime Minister
	August	Nuclear bombs dropped on Hiroshima and Nagasaki followed by Japanese surrender
	November	International Military Tribunal begins trial of leading Nazis at Nuremberg

Index

Themes in Modern European History since 1945
Edited by Rosemary Wakeman

This collection explores the most important transformations and upheavals of post-1945 Europe in the light of recent scholarship. Ten chapters consider key socio-political, cultural and economic changes of an era that needs re-evaluation and reconsideration from a historical perspective.

Themes in Modern European History since 1945 is structured around recent theoretical debates on the postwar. The era saw unprecedented economic growth in the "golden age" of prosperity up to 1973, and it witnessed a social flux that dramatically transformed the fabric of European society. After 1989, Europe grappled with the first Eastern European revolutions and faced the challenge of reintegrating the continent after 75 years of partition and conflict. At the beginning of the 21st century, the concept of "European civilization" remains ambiguous.

This authoritative survey provides an indispensable guide to the crucial subjects in postwar history for all students of History or European Studies.

ISBN10: 0-415-21987-7 (hbk)
ISBN10: 0-415-21988-4 (pbk)

ISBN13: 978-0-415-21987-7 (hbk)
ISBN13: 978-0-415-21988-4 (pbk)

The Routledge Companion to Modern European History since 1763

Chris Cook and John Stevenson

The Routledge Companion to Modern European History since 1763 is a compact and highly accessible work of reference. It covers a broad sweep of events since 1763, from the last days of the *ancien regime* to the ending of the Cold War, from the reshaping of Eastern Europe to the radical expansion of the European Union in 2004.

Within the broad coverage of this outstanding volume, particular attention is given to subjects such as:

- the era of the Enlightened Despots
- the Revolutionary and Napoleonic era in France, and the revolutions of 1848
- nationalism and imperialism and the retreat from Empire
- the First World War, the rise of the European dictators, the coming of the Second World War, the Holocaust, and the post-war development in Europe
- the Cold War, the Soviet Union and its break-up
- the proest and upheavals of the 1960s, was well as social issues such as the rise of the welfare state, and the changing place of women in society throughout the period

With a fully comprehensive glossary, a biographical section, a thorough bibliography and informative maps, this volume is the indispensable companion for all those who study modern European history.

ISBN10: 0-415-34582-0 (hbk)
ISBN10: 0-415-34583-9 (pbk)

ISBN13: 978-0-415-34582-8 (hbk)
ISBN13: 978-0-415-34583 -5 (pbk)

Related titles from Routledge

The Nazi Germany Sourcebook
An Anthology of Texts
Edited by David Davies

The Nazi Germany Sourcebook is an exciting collection of documents on the origins, rise, course and consequences of National Socialism, the Third Reich, the Second World War, and the Holocaust. Packed full of both official and private papers from the perspectives of perpetrators and victims, these sources offer a revealing insight into why Nazism came into being, its extraordinary popularity in the 1930s, how it affected the lives of people, and what it means to us today.

The Nazi Germany Sourcebook focuses on key areas of study, helping students to understand and critically evaluate this extraordinary historical episode:

- the ideological roots of Nazism, and World War I
- the Weimar Republic
- the consolidation of Nazi power
- Hitler's motives, aims and preparation for war
- World War II
- the Holocaust
- the Cold War and recent historical debates.

The Nazi Germany Sourcebook contains numerous documents that have never before been published in English, and some documents, such as Goebbels' 1941 diaries, that have only recently been discovered. This up-to-date and carefully edited collection of primary sources provides fascinating reading for anyone interested in this historical phenomenon.

ISBN10: 0-415-22213-3 (hbk)
ISBN10: 0-415-22214-3 (pbk)

ISBN13: 978-0-415-22213-6 (hbk)
ISBN13: 978-0-415-22214-3 (pbk)

Available at all good bookshops
For ordering and further information please visit:
www.routledge.com

European Dictatorships 1918–1945, 3rd Edition

Stephen J. Lee

European Dictatorships 1918–1945 surveys the extraordinary circumstances leading to, and arising from, the transformation of over half of Europe's states to dictatorships between the first and the second World Wars. From the notorious dictatorships of Mussolini, Hitler and Stalin to less well-known states and leaders, Stephen J. Lee scrutinizes the experiences of Russia, Germany, Italy, Spain and Portugal, and Central and Eastern European states.

This third edition has been revised throughout to include recent historical research, and has expanded sections on the setting for dictatorships and comparisons between them. There are more detailed discussions of Mussolini, Hitler and the Holocaust and an entirely new survey of Turkey. This edition also includes a completely new chapter on types of dictatorship which explores both the meaning and widely different forms it can take.

Extensively illustrated with photographs, maps and diagrams, *European Dictatorships 1918–1945* is a clear, detailed and highly accessible analysis of the tumultuous events of early twentieth-century Europe.

ISBN10: 0-415-45484-0 (hbk)
ISBN10: 0-415-45485-9 (pbk)

ISBN13: 978-0-415-45484-1 (hbk)
ISBN13: 978-0-415-45485-8 (pbk)